fushigi yûgi™

The Mysterious Play
VOL. 12: GIRLFRIEND

Story & Art By
YÛ WATASE

FUSHIGI YÛGI
THE MYSTERIOUS PLAY
VOL. 12: Girlfriend
SHÔJO EDITION

This volume contains the FUSHIGI YÛGI installments from Animerica Extra
Vol. 7, No. 5 through Vol. 7, No. 7 in their entirety.

STORY AND ART BY YÛ WATASE

English Adaptation/William Flanagan
Translation/Yuji Oniki
Touch-up & Lettering/Bill Spicer
Touch-up Assistance/Walden Wong
Design/Hidemi Sahara
Editors/Elizabeth Kawasaki and Frances E. Wall

Managing Editor/Annette Roman
Editor-in-Chief/Alvin Lu
Director of Production/Noboru Watanabe
Sr. Director of Licensing & Acquisitions/Rika Inouye
Vice President of Sales/Joe Morici
Vice President of Marketing/Liza Coppola
Executive Vice President/Hyoe Narita
Publisher/Seiji Horibuchi

© 1992 Yuu Watase/Shogakukan, Inc. First published by Shogakukan, Inc. in Japan as
"Fushigi Yugi." New and adapted artwork and text © 2004 VIZ, LLC. The FUSHIGI YÛGI logo
is a trademark of VIZ, LLC. All rights reserved.

Printed in Canada

Published by VIZ, LLC
P.O. Box 77010
San Francisco, CA 94107

Shôjo Edition
10 9 8 7 6 5 4 3 2 1
First printing, September 2004

  store.viz.com

www.viz.com

CONTENTS

STORY THUS FAR

Miaka is a cheerful junior high school girl who's physically drawn into the world of a strange book – THE UNIVERSE OF THE FOUR GODS – where she is offered the role of the lead character, the Priestess of the god Suzaku. Miaka is charged with saving the nation of Hong-Nan, and in the process will be granted three wishes. While Miaka makes a short trip back to the real world, her best friend Yui is sucked into the book only to suffer rape and manipulation, which drives her to attempt suicide. Now, Yui has become the Priestess of the god Seiryu, the bitter enemy of Suzaku and Miaka.

Yui blames Miaka for the torments that she has experienced, and the only way for Miaka to gain back the trust of her former friend is to summon the god Suzaku and wish to be reconciled, so she re-enters the world of the book. It doesn't hurt that going back into the book also grants Miaka the chance to see more of the dreamy Suzaku warrior Tamahome! Miaka's first attempt to summon Suzaku is foiled by the Seiryu warriors, but the oracle, Tai Yi-Jun, has a new quest for Miaka and her Celestial Warriors of Suzaku— to obtain Shentso-Pao, or treasures, from the countries of the two other gods, Genbu and Byakko, that will allow them to summon Suzaku.

The Seiryu warriors again thwart Miaka's plans, stealing the first treasure from Miaka's hands and subjecting her to various tortures through the tricks and traps of their devious spells. Yui, now closely allied with malicious Seiryu warrior Nakago, is still furious with Miaka and jealous of Miaka's budding relationship with Tamahome. Determined to summon the god beast Seiryu and get her revenge, Yui deceives Miaka into handing over another of the Shentso-Pao. Yui prepares for the ceremony to summon Seiryu while Miboshi, another Seiryu warrior, protects Yui from any interference by taking over Suzaku warrior Chiriko's body and conjuring up fearsome, vicious monsters to attack Miaka. Chiriko sacrifices himself in order to kill Miboshi and rescue Miaka, but now it's up to her to stop Yui from completing the summoning ritual. Will Miaka make it in time, or will Chiriko's sacrifice be in vain?

THE UNIVERSE OF THE FOUR GODS is based on ancient Chinese legend, but Japanese pronunciation of Chinese names differs slightly from their Chinese equivalents. Here is a short glossary of the Japanese pronunciation of the Chinese names in this graphic novel:

CHINESE	JAPANESE	PERSON OR PLACE	MEANING
Hong-Nan	Konan	Southern Kingdom	Crimson South
Qu-Dong	Kutô	Eastern Kingdom	Gathered East
Bei-Jia	Hokkan	Northern Kingdom	Armored North
Xi-Lang	Sairô	Western Kingdom	West Hall
Tai Yi-Jun	Tai Itsukun	An Oracle	Preeminent Person
Shentso-Pao	Shinzahô	A Treasure	God's Seat Jewel

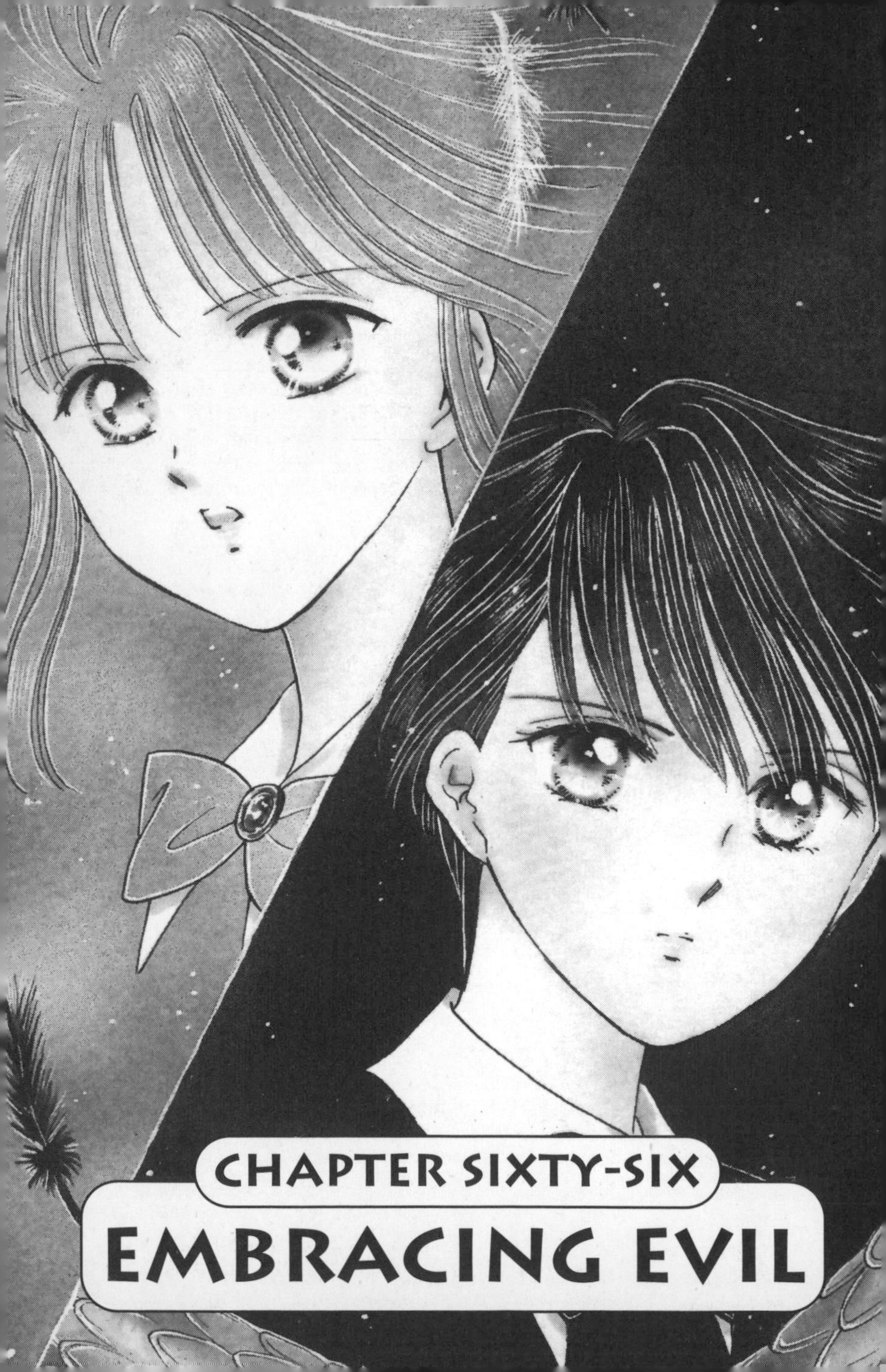
CHAPTER SIXTY-SIX
EMBRACING EVIL

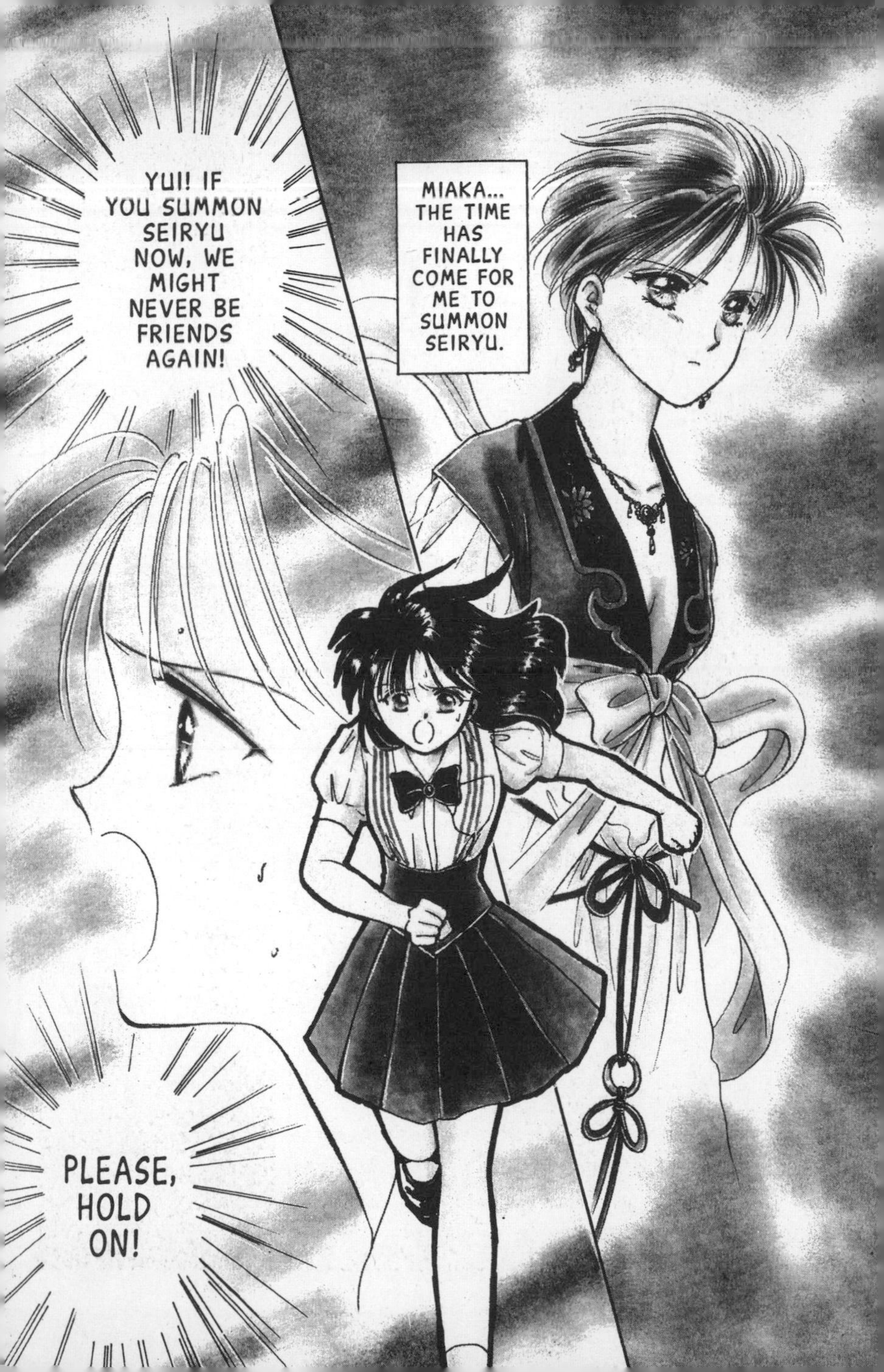
MIAKA... THE TIME HAS FINALLY COME FOR ME TO SUMMON SEIRYU.
YUI! IF YOU SUMMON SEIRYU NOW, WE MIGHT NEVER BE FRIENDS AGAIN!
PLEASE, HOLD ON!

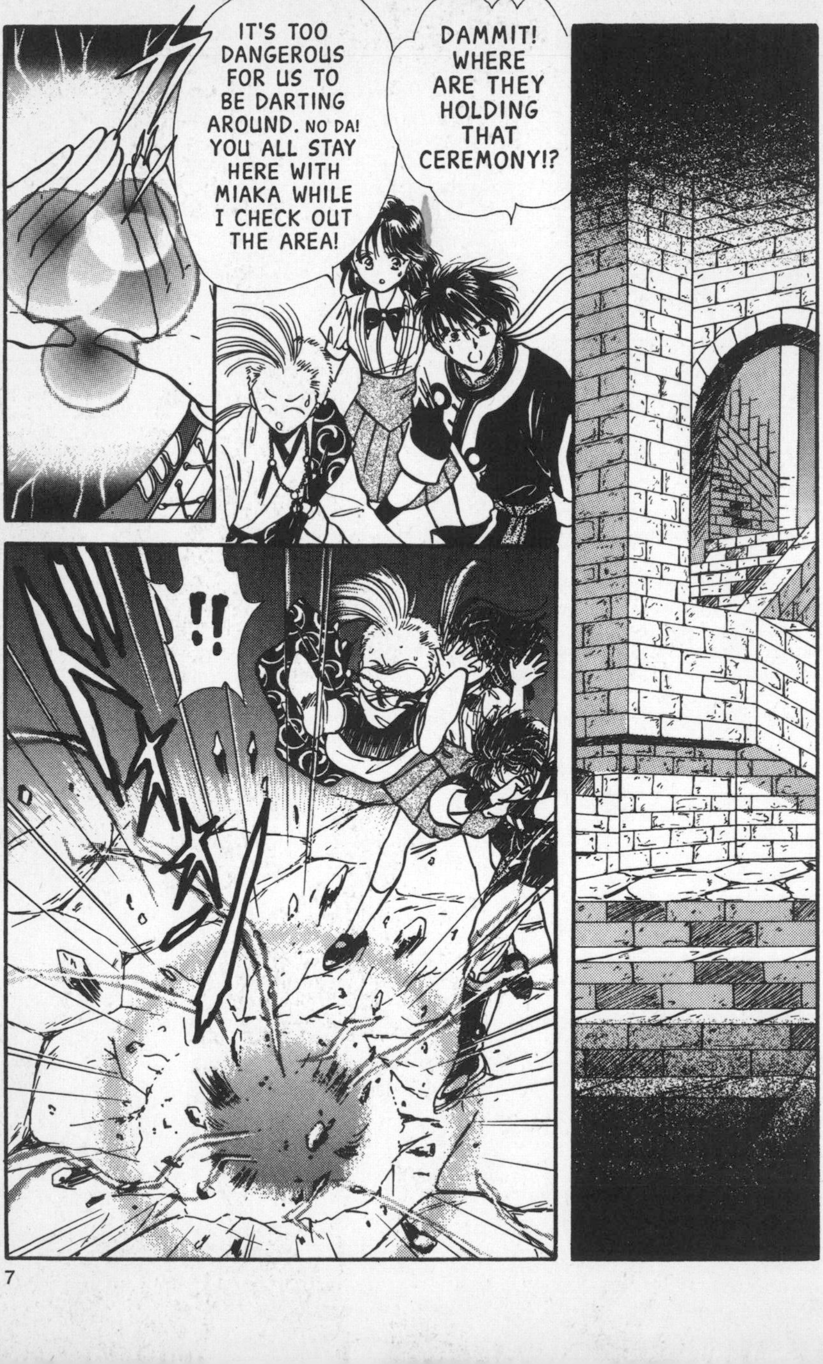
DAMMIT! WHERE ARE THEY HOLDING THAT CEREMONY!?
IT'S TOO DANGEROUS FOR US TO BE DARTING AROUND. NO DA! YOU ALL STAY HERE WITH MIAKA WHILE I CHECK OUT THE AREA!
!!

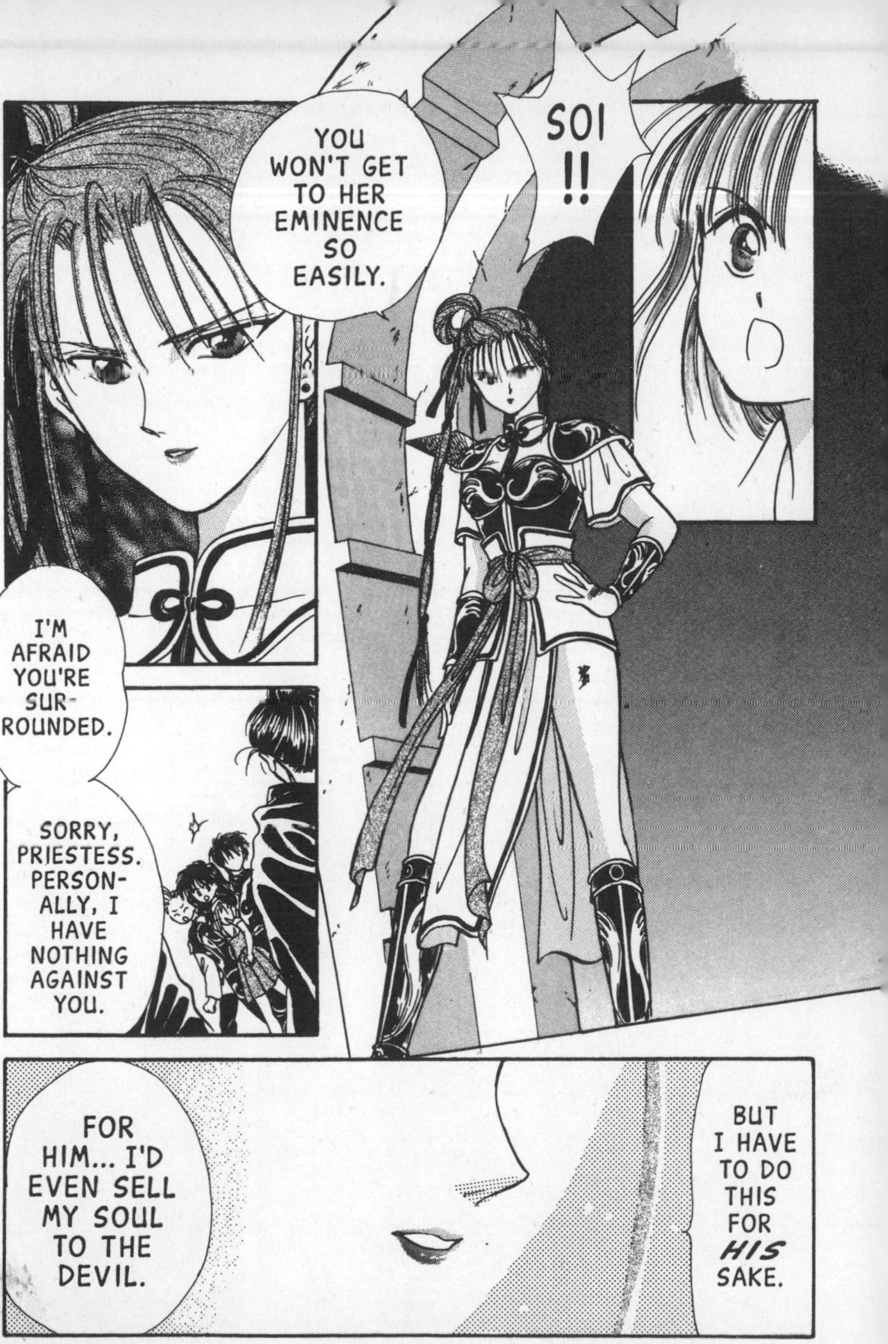
SOI !!
YOU WON'T GET TO HER EMINENCE SO EASILY.
I'M AFRAID YOU'RE SUR-ROUNDED.
SORRY, PRIESTESS. PERSON-ALLY, I HAVE NOTHING AGAINST YOU.
BUT I HAVE TO DO THIS FOR *HIS* SAKE.
FOR HIM... I'D EVEN SELL MY SOUL TO THE DEVIL.

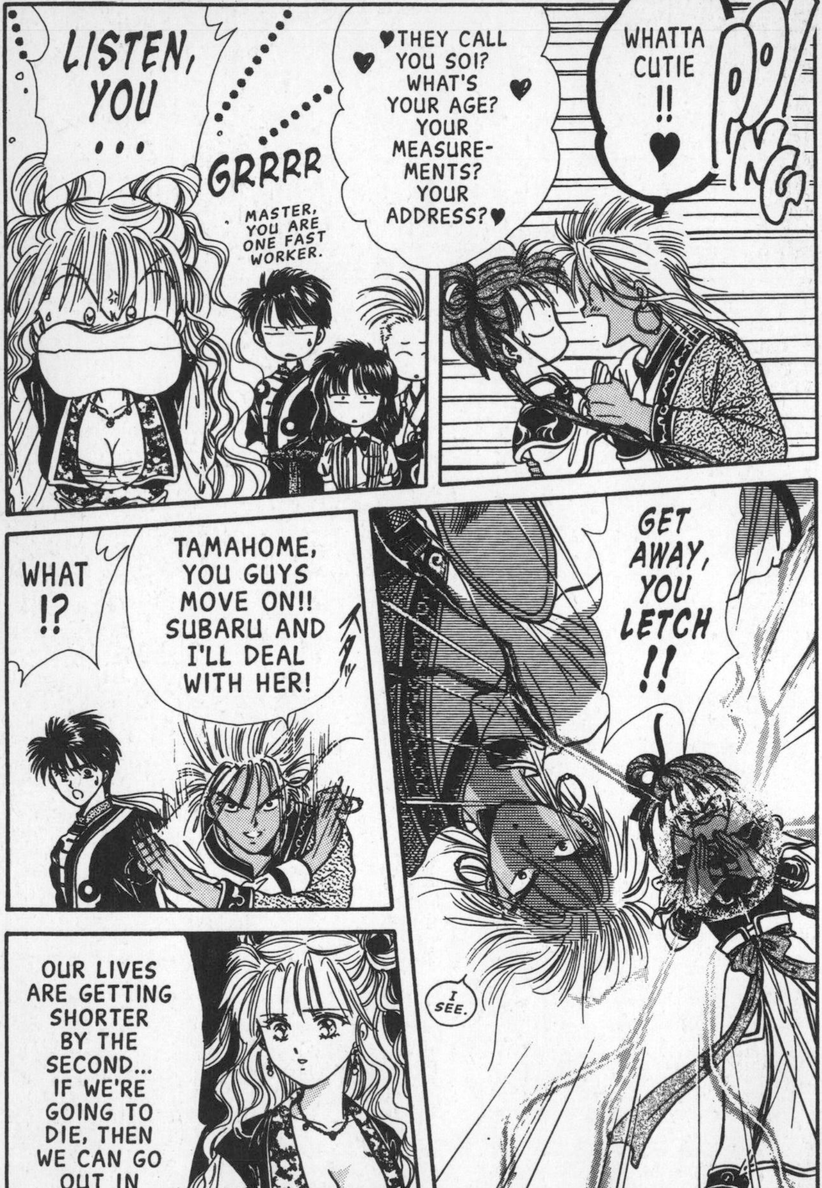
WHATTA CUTIE !! ♥
POING
♥THEY CALL YOU SOI? WHAT'S YOUR AGE? YOUR MEASUREMENTS? YOUR ADDRESS?♥
LISTEN, YOU ...
GRRRR
MASTER, YOU ARE ONE FAST WORKER.
GET AWAY, YOU LETCH !!
I SEE.
TAMAHOME, YOU GUYS MOVE ON!! SUBARU AND I'LL DEAL WITH HER!
WHAT !?
OUR LIVES ARE GETTING SHORTER BY THE SECOND... IF WE'RE GOING TO DIE, THEN WE CAN GO OUT IN BATTLE!

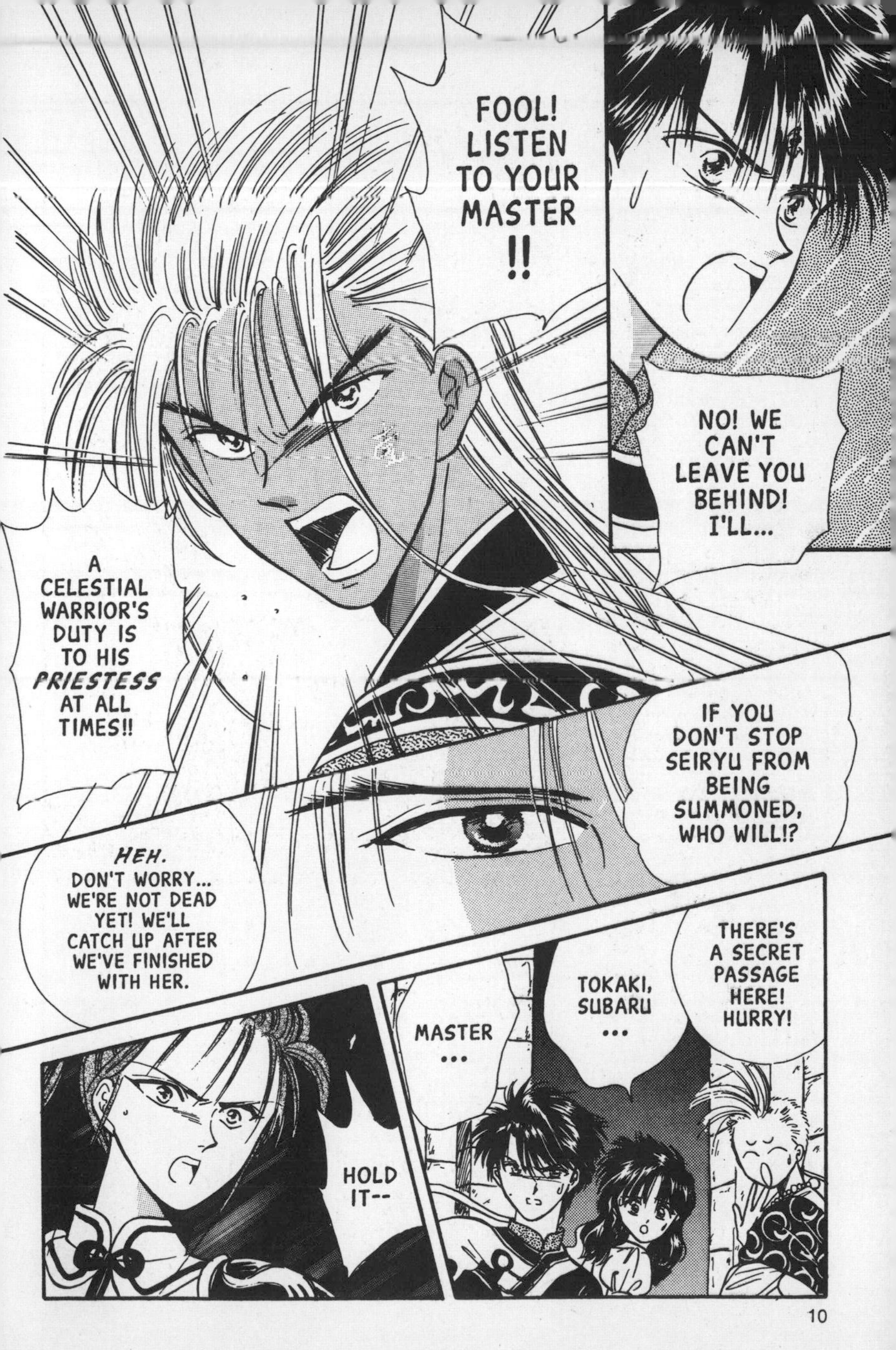

NO! WE CAN'T LEAVE YOU BEHIND! I'LL...
FOOL! LISTEN TO YOUR MASTER!!
A CELESTIAL WARRIOR'S DUTY IS TO HIS *PRIESTESS* AT ALL TIMES!!
IF YOU DON'T STOP SEIRYU FROM BEING SUMMONED, WHO WILL!?
HEH. DON'T WORRY... WE'RE NOT DEAD YET! WE'LL CATCH UP AFTER WE'VE FINISHED WITH HER.
THERE'S A SECRET PASSAGE HERE! HURRY!
TOKAKI, SUBARU...
MASTER...
HOLD IT--

Girlfriend

Hello, it's me Watase. I pulled an all-nighter, so I'm really exhausted! Lately, I've been pulling them several nights in a row. I've got dark rings under my eyes. Now, Positive attitude here! let's continue with my comments on the characters...
Oh, wait, before that, I want to thank all the fans who came to my book signing in Kyoto. At the "Comic One-Point Lesson," the participants bombarded me with questions like "Who does Nakago really love?";"What's Tasuki's history with women?"; "Who was the murderer of Chichiri's best friend?" I managed to respond to all of them, but I have to say they probed deeply. Also, thanks for all the gifts. The mini-Tama doll (Tamahome) someone made for me is now the idol of the entire staff here. He's super cute. Now if we only had one of Nakago. If we had all the characters covered we could "play house" with them!! My secret wish(?)

To continue... Regarding Mitsukake, I wanted someone macho. Someone you'd take one look at and say, "Wow, he's a man's man." I bet he'd be a really good husband. He's kind and calm. Many times I've wished I could just snuggle up against his back... (so large and inviting, a "snuggable" back!) I added the cat to emphasize his kindness. Big man with a kitty. Nice pair.

Speaking of pairs, I came up with Chiriko as a character to contrast with Mitsukake. The big man has to be paired up with a little kid. Of course, Chiriko has to be smart, but it turns out he's got a split personality. When his character appears, and he's wise, he can't recall being a dazed child.

To be continued →

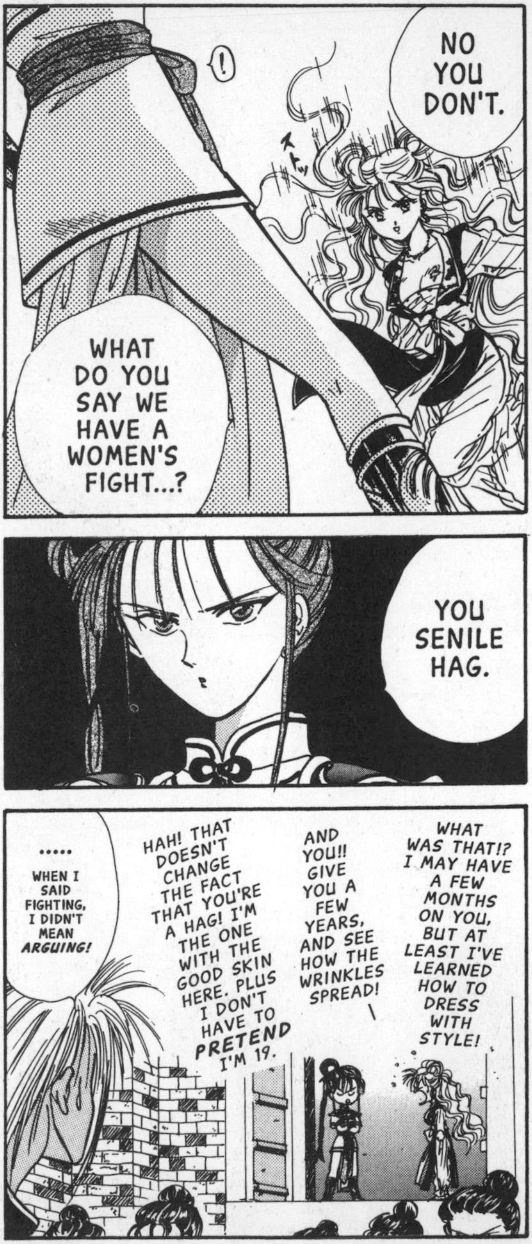
NO YOU DON'T.
!
WHAT DO YOU SAY WE HAVE A WOMEN'S FIGHT...?
YOU SENILE HAG.
WHAT WAS THAT!? I MAY HAVE A FEW MONTHS ON YOU, BUT AT LEAST I'VE LEARNED HOW TO DRESS WITH STYLE!
AND YOU!! GIVE YOU A FEW YEARS, AND SEE HOW THE WRINKLES SPREAD!
HAH! THAT DOESN'T CHANGE THE FACT THAT YOU'RE A HAG! I'M THE ONE WITH THE GOOD SKIN HERE. PLUS I DON'T HAVE TO PRETEND I'M 19.
..... WHEN I SAID FIGHTING, I DIDN'T MEAN ARGUING!

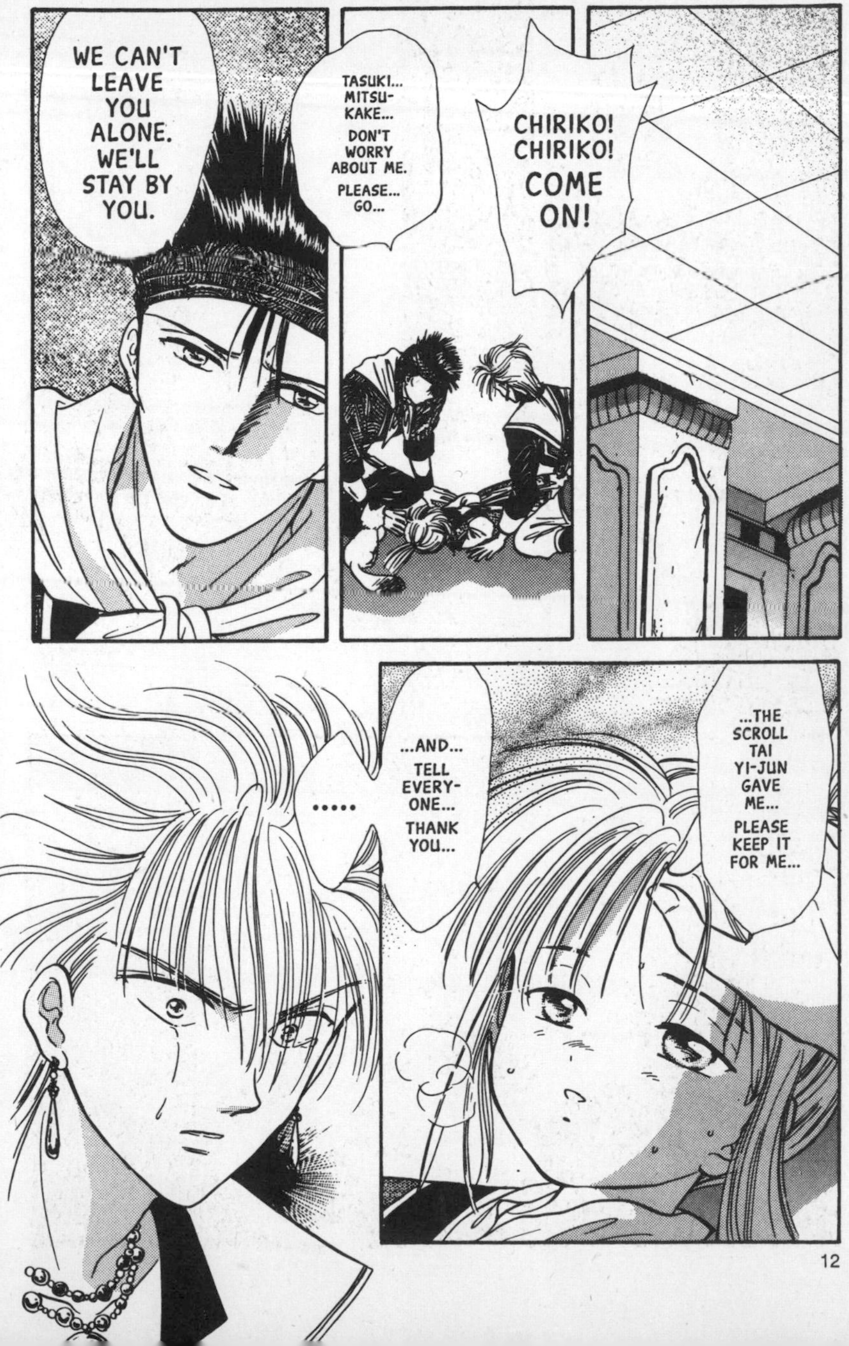
CHIRIKO! CHIRIKO! COME ON!
TASUKI... MITSU-KAKE... DON'T WORRY ABOUT ME. PLEASE... GO...
WE CAN'T LEAVE YOU ALONE. WE'LL STAY BY YOU.
...THE SCROLL TAI YI-JUN GAVE ME... PLEASE KEEP IT FOR ME...
...AND... TELL EVERY-ONE... THANK YOU...
.....

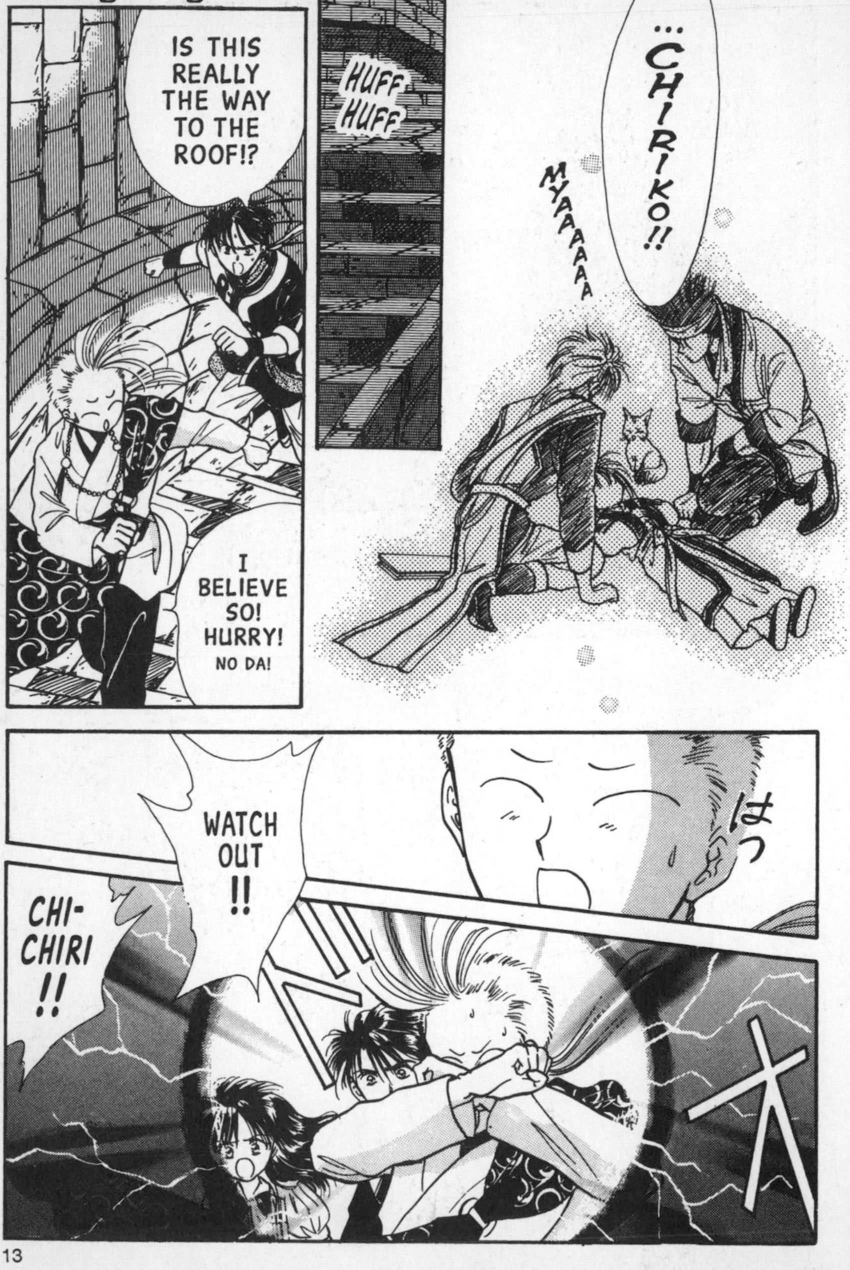
...CHIRIKO!!
MYAAAAAA
HUFF HUFF
IS THIS REALLY THE WAY TO THE ROOF!?
I BELIEVE SO! HURRY! NO DA!
はっ
WATCH OUT!!
CHI-CHIRI!!

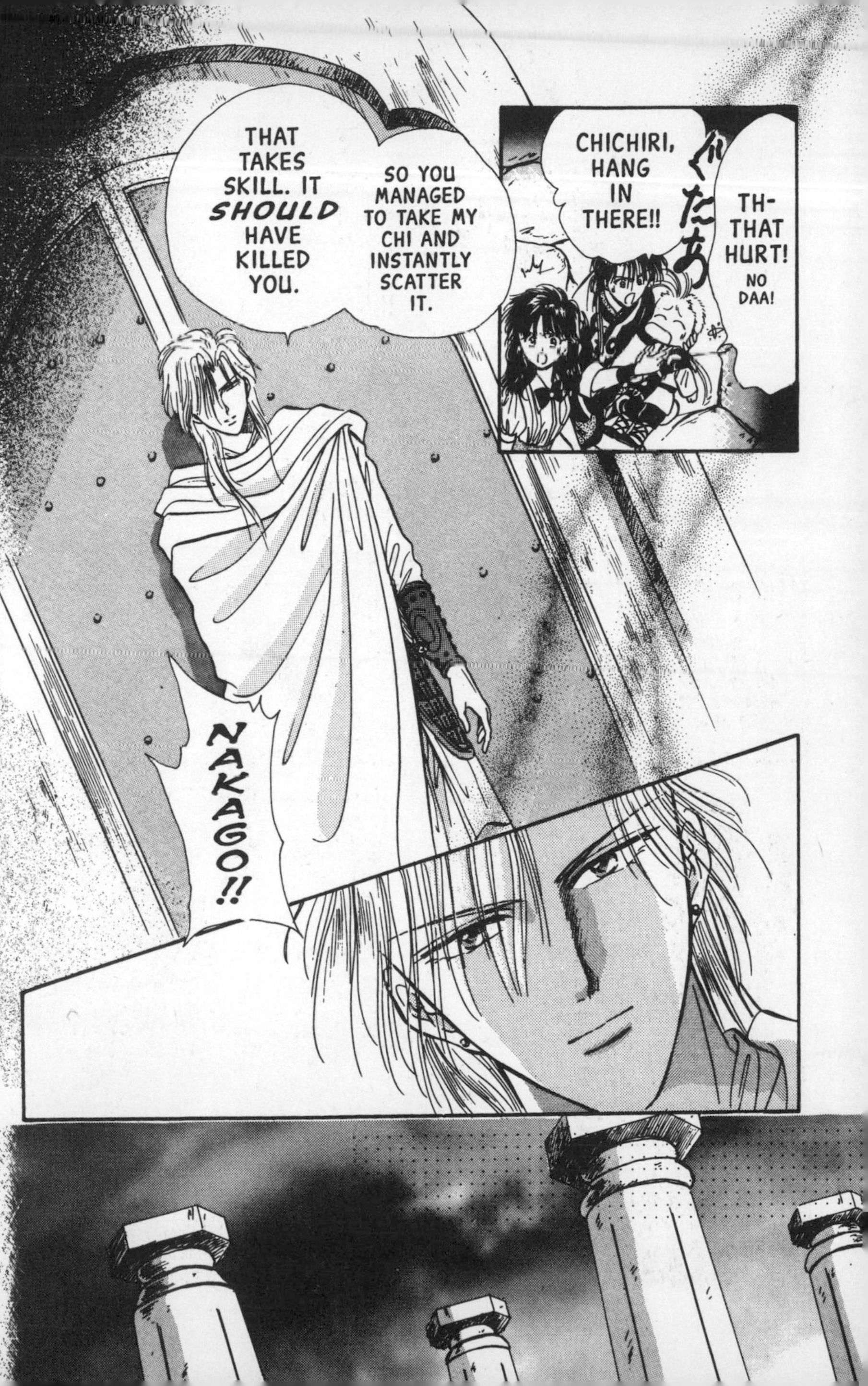
CHICHIRI, HANG IN THERE!!
ぐたぁ
TH- THAT HURT! NO DAA!
SO YOU MANAGED TO TAKE MY CHI AND INSTANTLY SCATTER IT.
THAT TAKES SKILL. IT ***SHOULD*** HAVE KILLED YOU.
NAKAGO!!

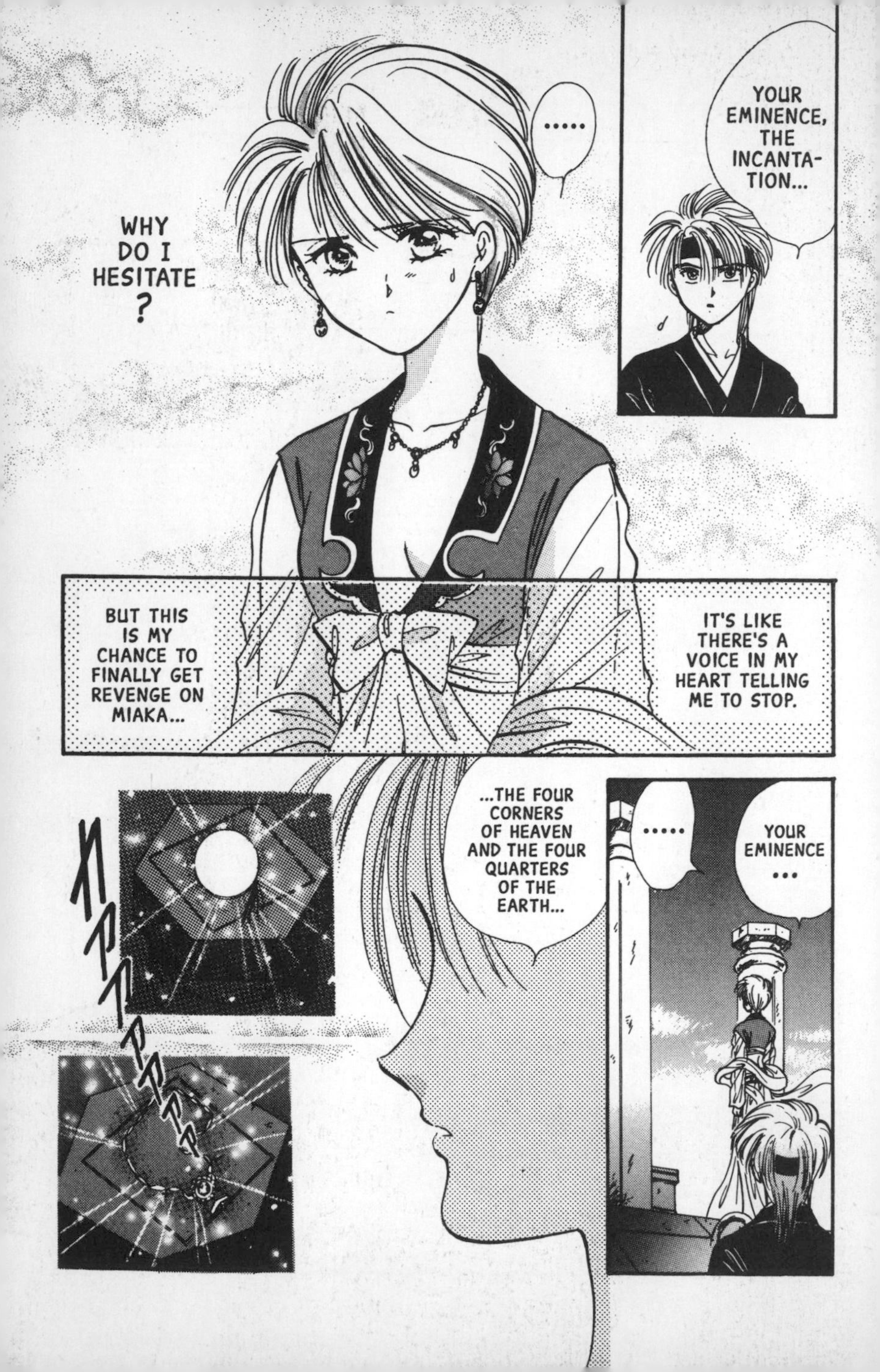
YOUR EMINENCE, THE INCANTATION...
.....
WHY DO I HESITATE?
IT'S LIKE THERE'S A VOICE IN MY HEART TELLING ME TO STOP.
BUT THIS IS MY CHANCE TO FINALLY GET REVENGE ON MIAKA...
YOUR EMINENCE...
.....
...THE FOUR CORNERS OF HEAVEN AND THE FOUR QUARTERS OF THE EARTH...

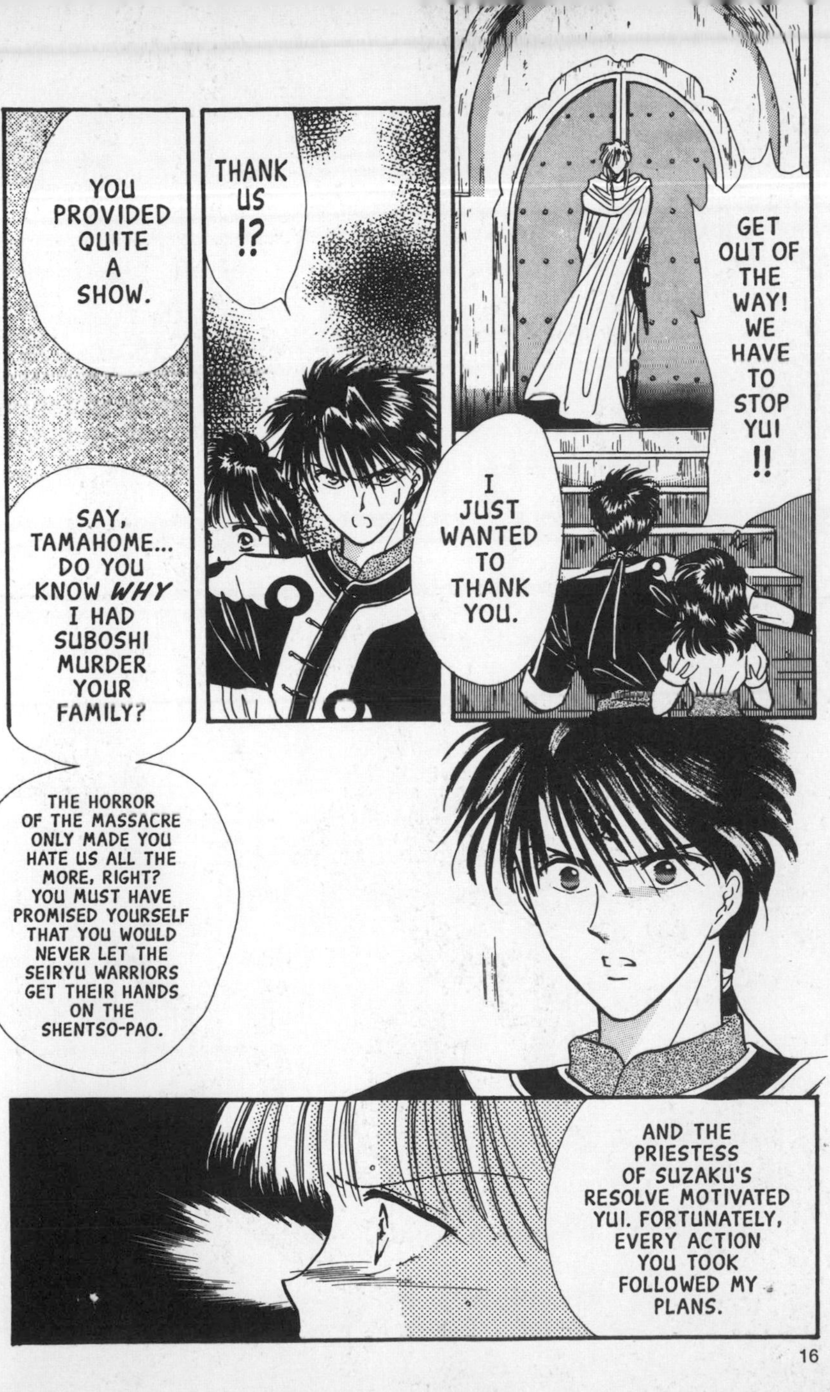
GET OUT OF THE WAY! WE HAVE TO STOP YUI!!
I JUST WANTED TO THANK YOU.
THANK US !?
YOU PROVIDED QUITE A SHOW.
SAY, TAMAHOME... DO YOU KNOW *WHY* I HAD SUBOSHI MURDER YOUR FAMILY?
THE HORROR OF THE MASSACRE ONLY MADE YOU HATE US ALL THE MORE, RIGHT? YOU MUST HAVE PROMISED YOURSELF THAT YOU WOULD NEVER LET THE SEIRYU WARRIORS GET THEIR HANDS ON THE SHENTSO-PAO.
AND THE PRIESTESS OF SUZAKU'S RESOLVE MOTIVATED YUI. FORTUNATELY, EVERY ACTION YOU TOOK FOLLOWED MY PLANS.

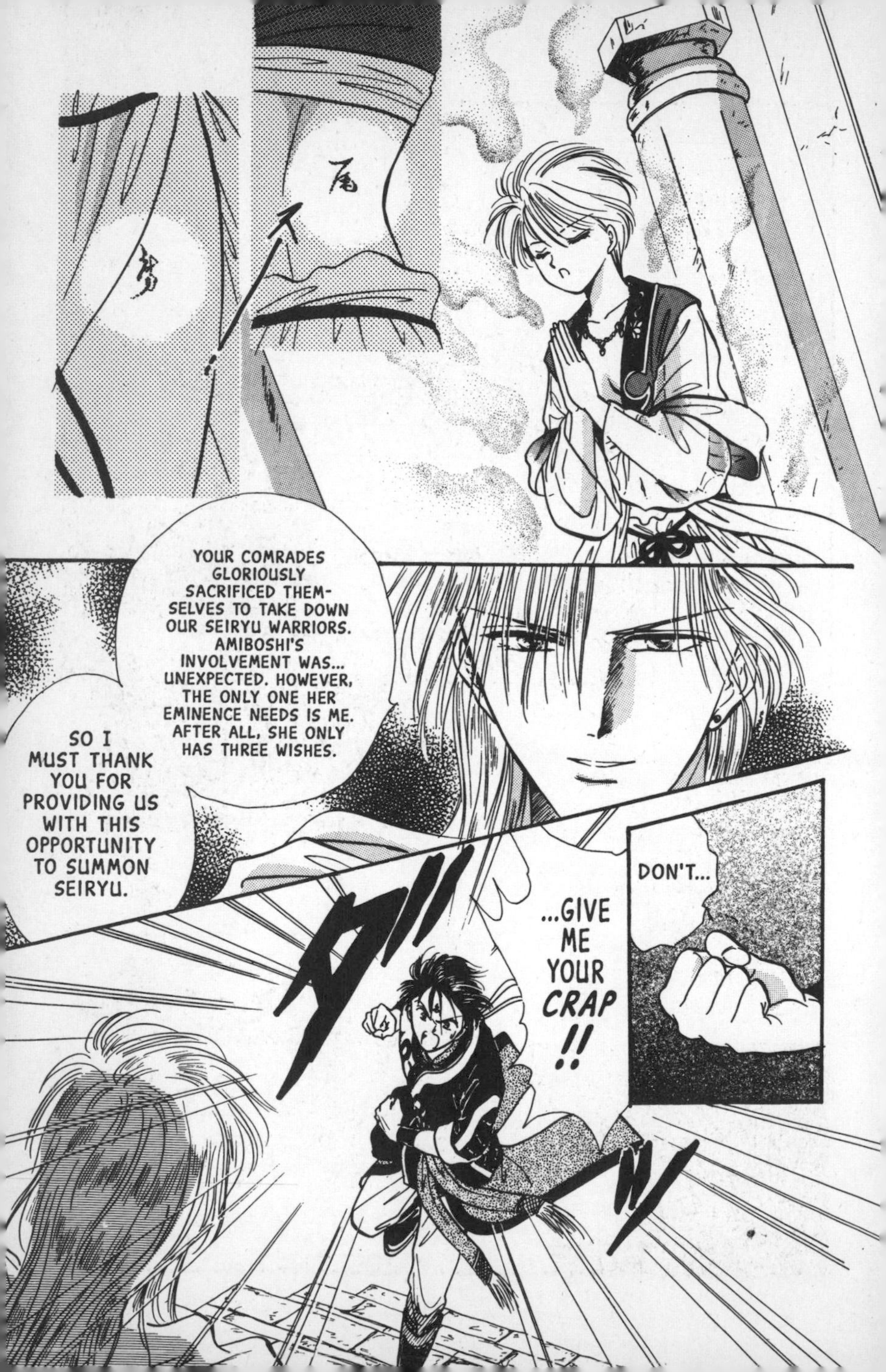
YOUR COMRADES GLORIOUSLY SACRIFICED THEMSELVES TO TAKE DOWN OUR SEIRYU WARRIORS. AMIBOSHI'S INVOLVEMENT WAS... UNEXPECTED. HOWEVER, THE ONLY ONE HER EMINENCE NEEDS IS ME. AFTER ALL, SHE ONLY HAS THREE WISHES.
SO I MUST THANK YOU FOR PROVIDING US WITH THIS OPPORTUNITY TO SUMMON SEIRYU.
DON'T...
...GIVE ME YOUR CRAP !!

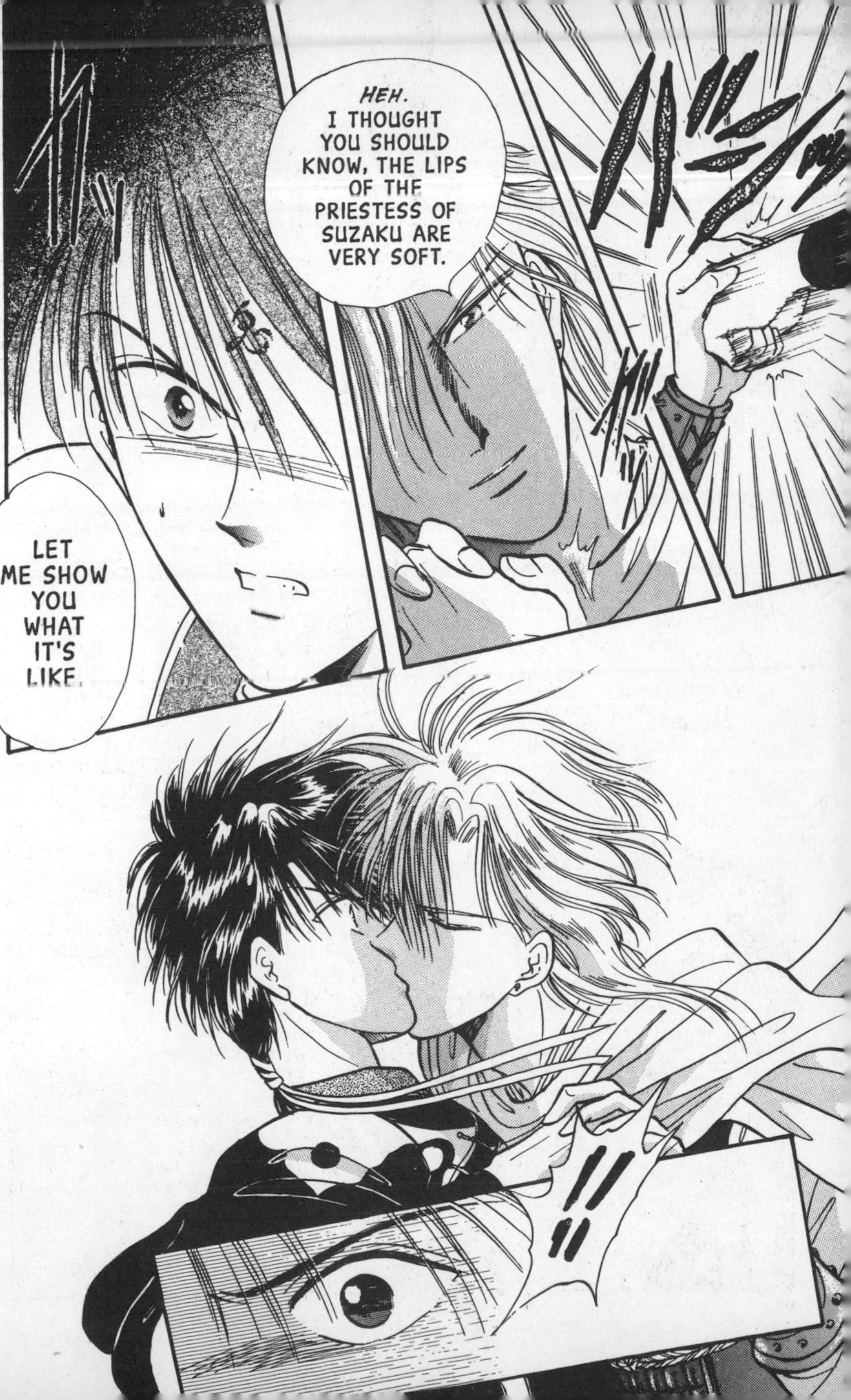
HEH.
I THOUGHT YOU SHOULD KNOW, THE LIPS OF THE PRIESTESS OF SUZAKU ARE VERY SOFT.
LET ME SHOW YOU WHAT IT'S LIKE.

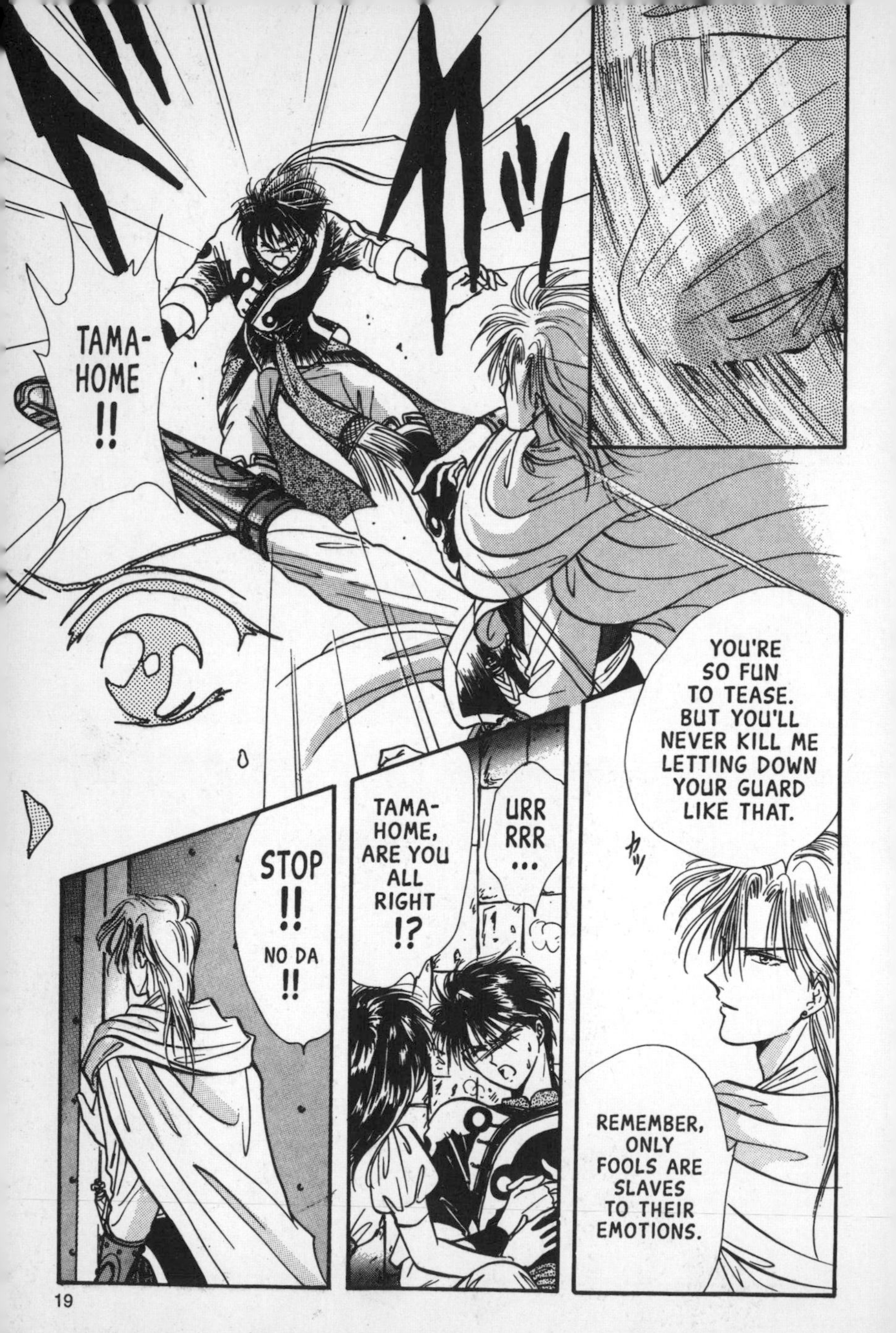
TAMA-HOME!!
YOU'RE SO FUN TO TEASE. BUT YOU'LL NEVER KILL ME LETTING DOWN YOUR GUARD LIKE THAT.
REMEMBER, ONLY FOOLS ARE SLAVES TO THEIR EMOTIONS.
URRRRR...
TAMA-HOME, ARE YOU ALL RIGHT!?
STOP!! NO DA!!

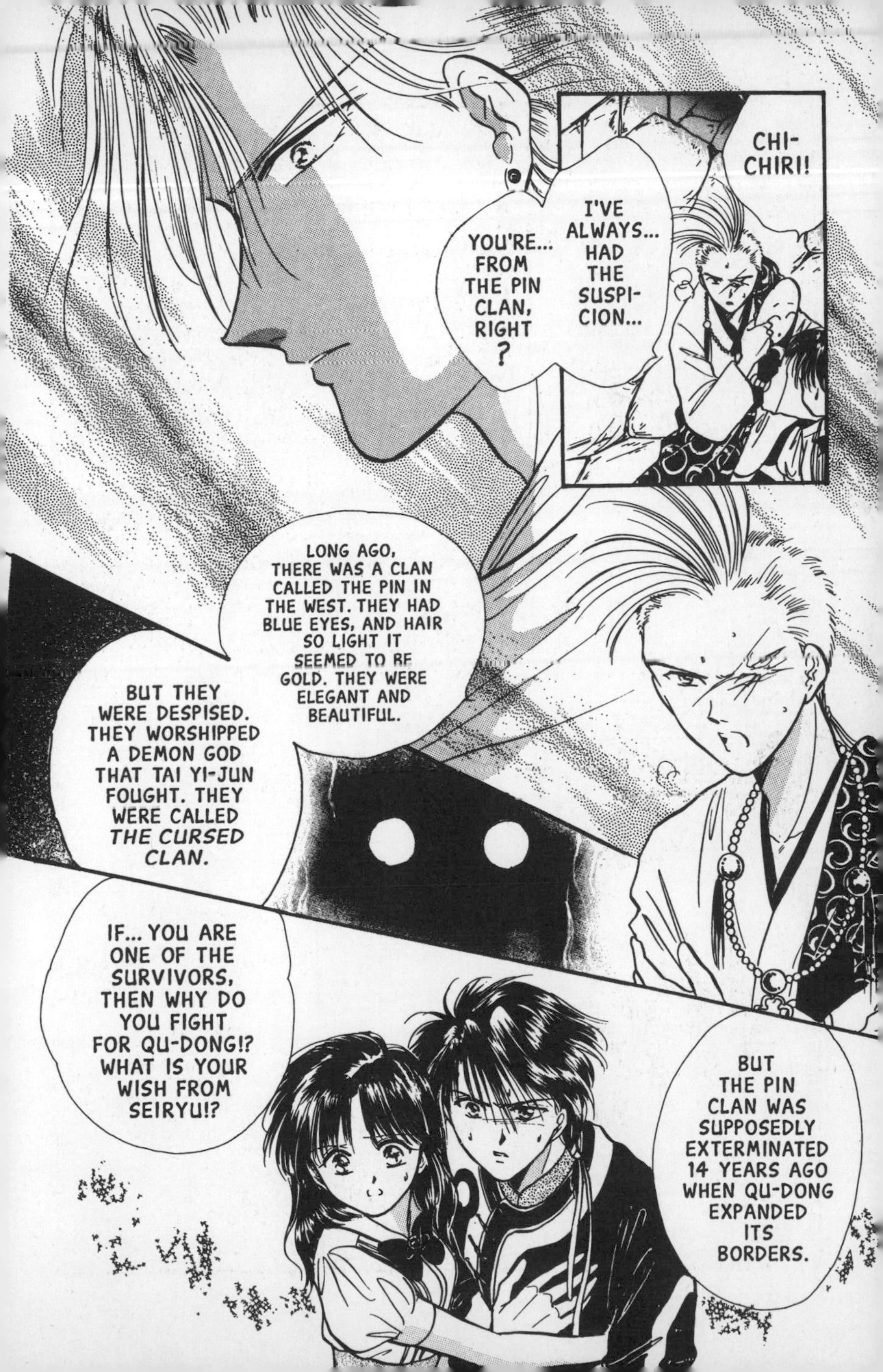
CHI-CHIRI!
I'VE ALWAYS... HAD THE SUSPICION...
YOU'RE... FROM THE PIN CLAN, RIGHT?
LONG AGO, THERE WAS A CLAN CALLED THE PIN IN THE WEST. THEY HAD BLUE EYES, AND HAIR SO LIGHT IT SEEMED TO BE GOLD. THEY WERE ELEGANT AND BEAUTIFUL.
BUT THEY WERE DESPISED. THEY WORSHIPPED A DEMON GOD THAT TAI YI-JUN FOUGHT. THEY WERE CALLED *THE CURSED CLAN.*
BUT THE PIN CLAN WAS SUPPOSEDLY EXTERMINATED 14 YEARS AGO WHEN QU-DONG EXPANDED ITS BORDERS.
IF... YOU ARE ONE OF THE SURVIVORS, THEN WHY DO YOU FIGHT FOR QU-DONG!? WHAT IS YOUR WISH FROM SEIRYU!?

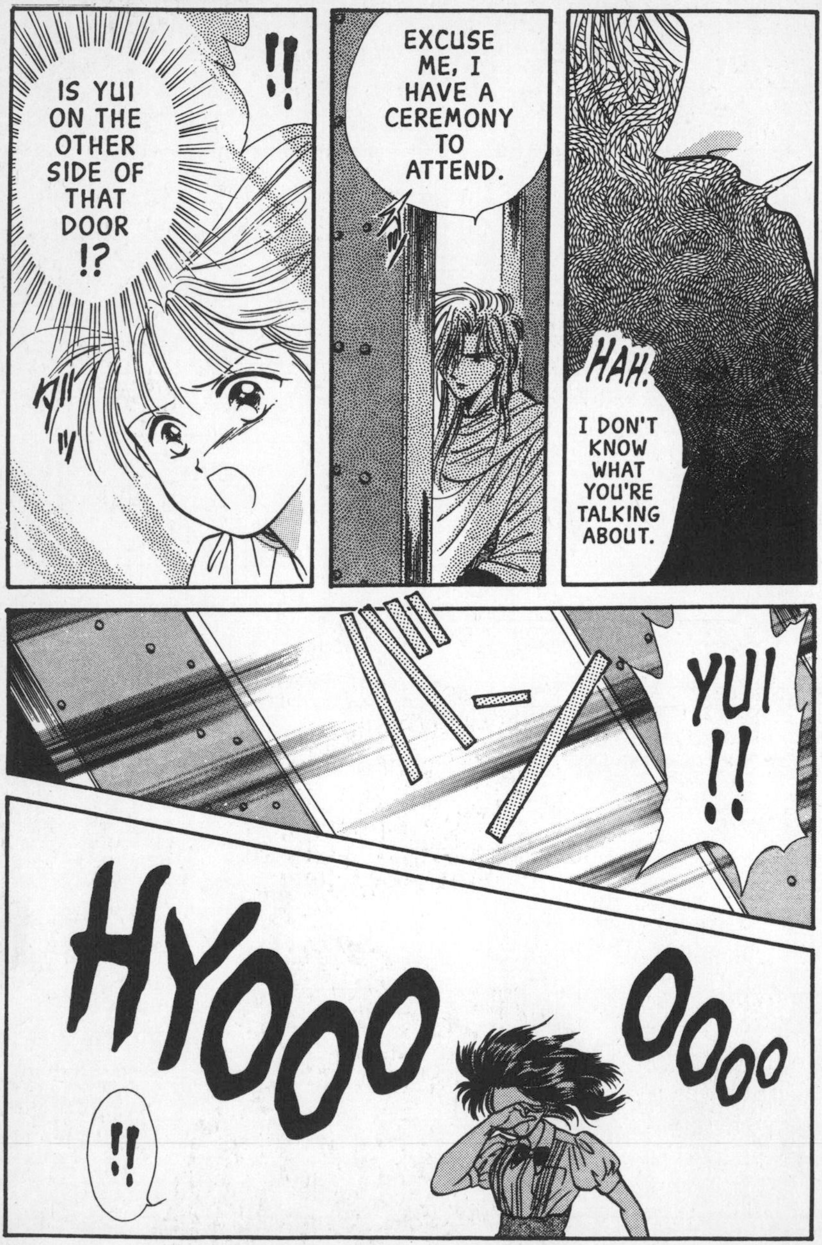
HAH.
I DON'T KNOW WHAT YOU'RE TALKING ABOUT.
EXCUSE ME, I HAVE A CEREMONY TO ATTEND.
!!
IS YUI ON THE OTHER SIDE OF THAT DOOR !?
YUI !!
HYOOO OOOO
!!

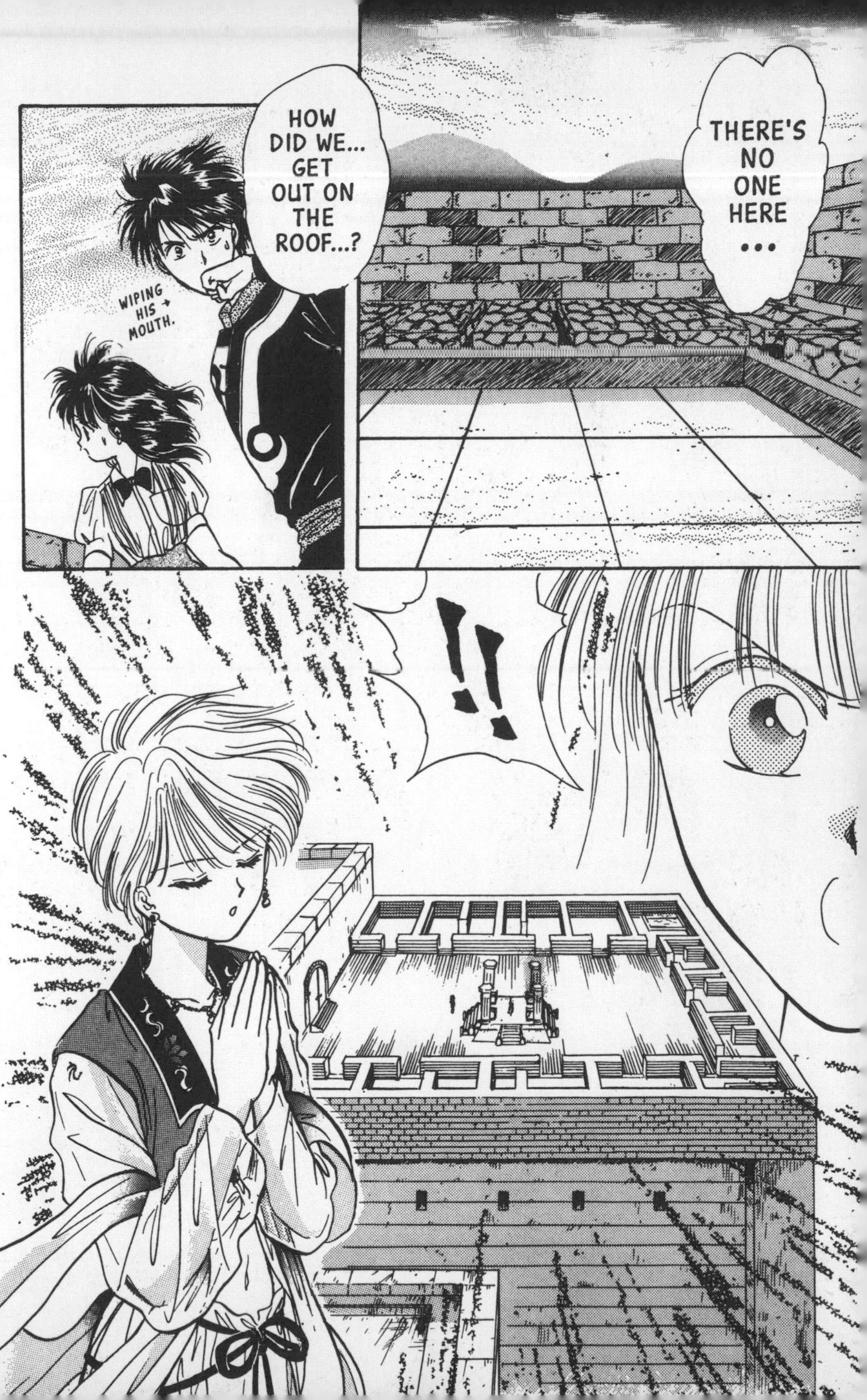
THERE'S NO ONE HERE ...
HOW DID WE... GET OUT ON THE ROOF...?
WIPING HIS MOUTH.
!!

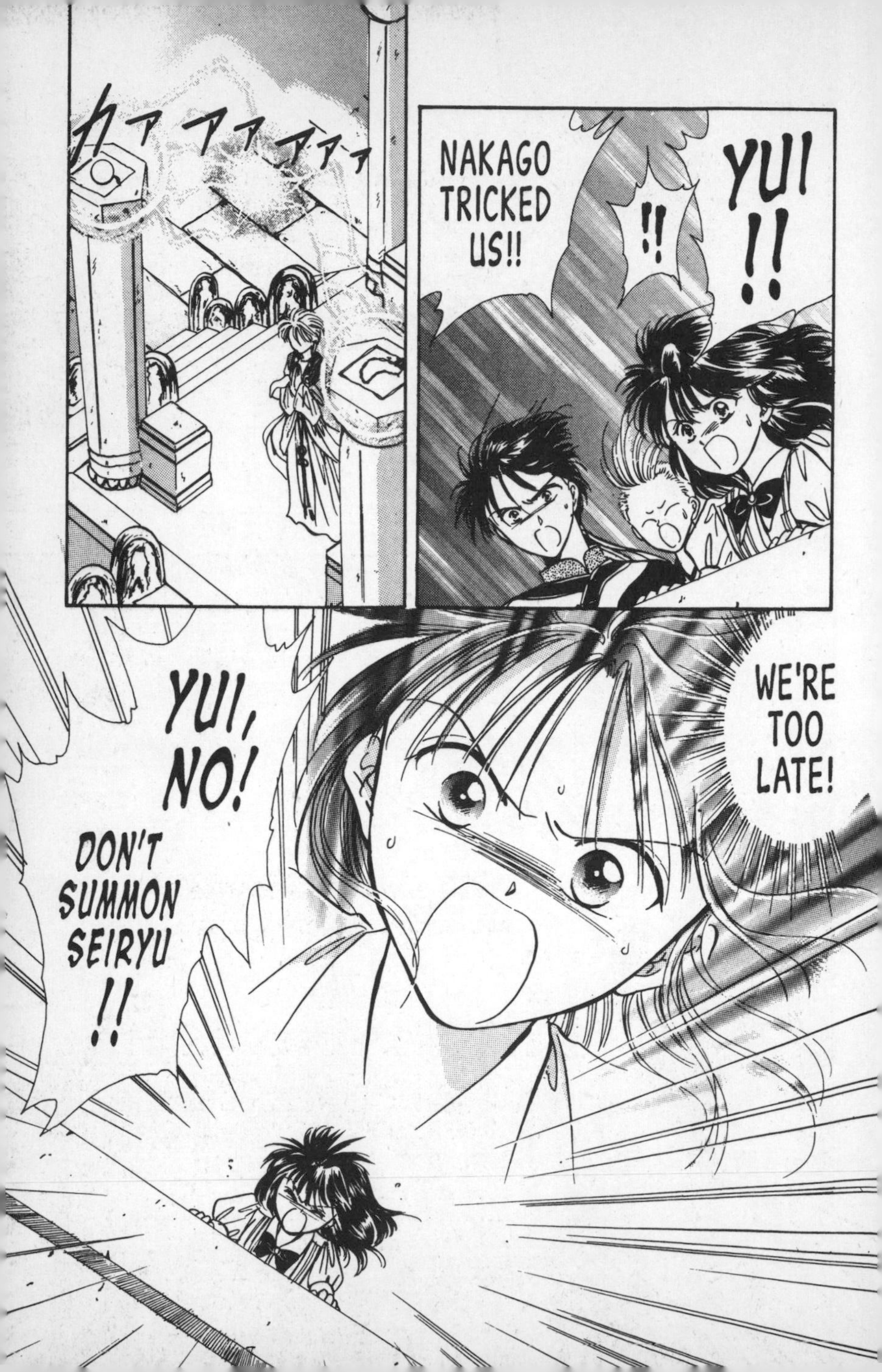
YUI!!
!!
NAKAGO TRICKED US!!
カァァァァァ
WE'RE TOO LATE!
YUI, NO!
DON'T SUMMON SEIRYU!!

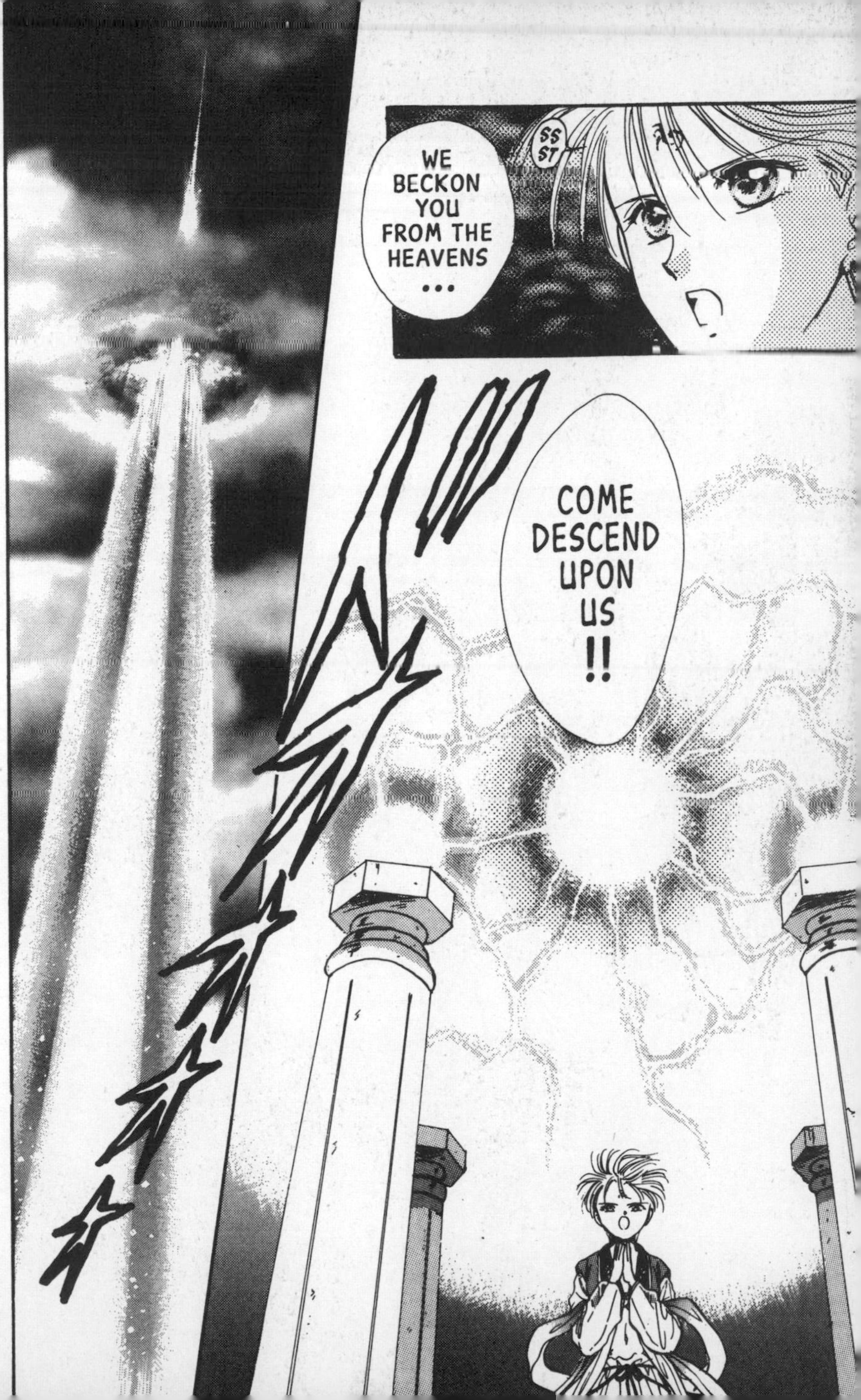
SS ST
WE BECKON YOU FROM THE HEAVENS ...
COME DESCEND UPON US !!

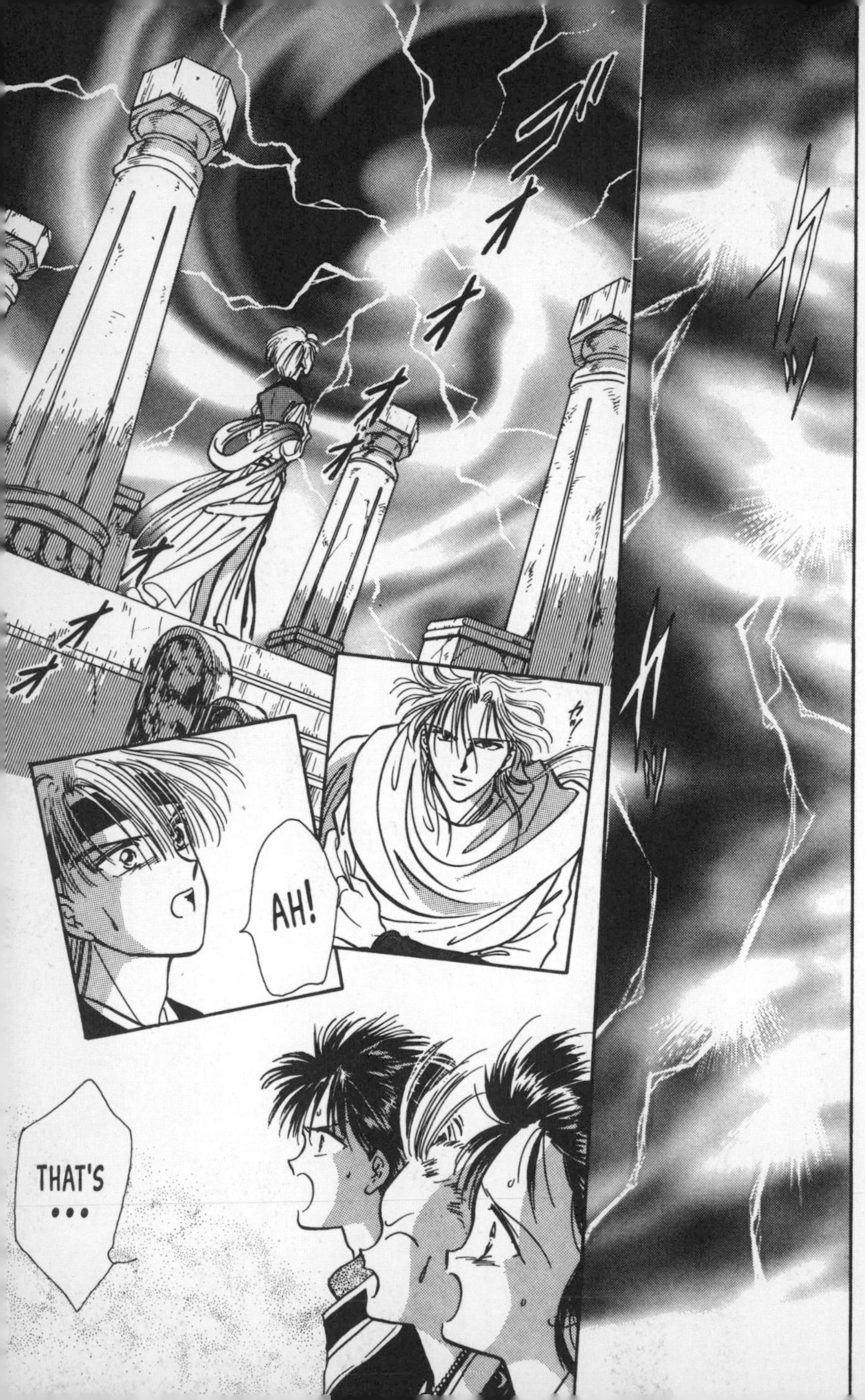
AH!
THAT'S ...

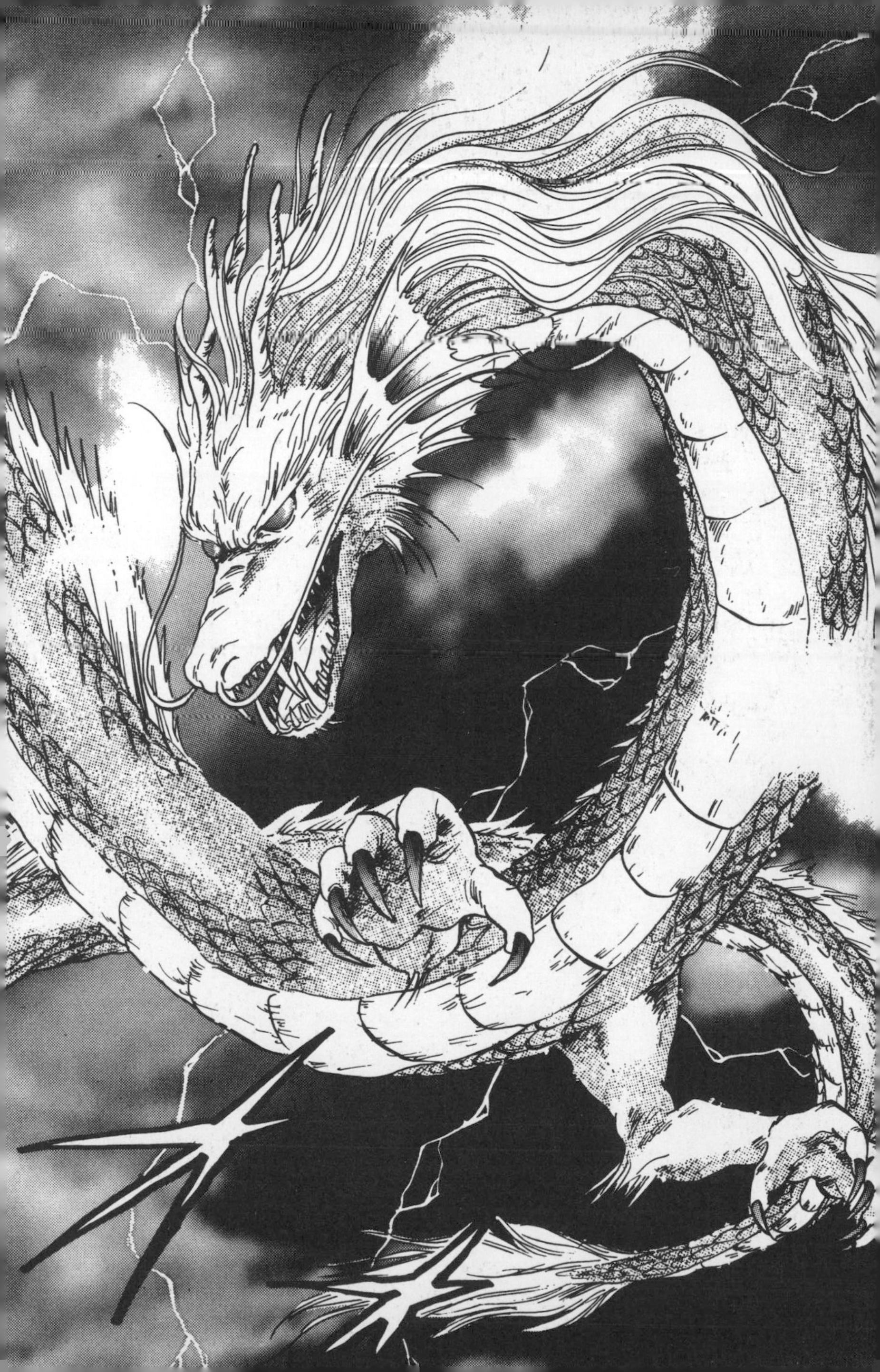

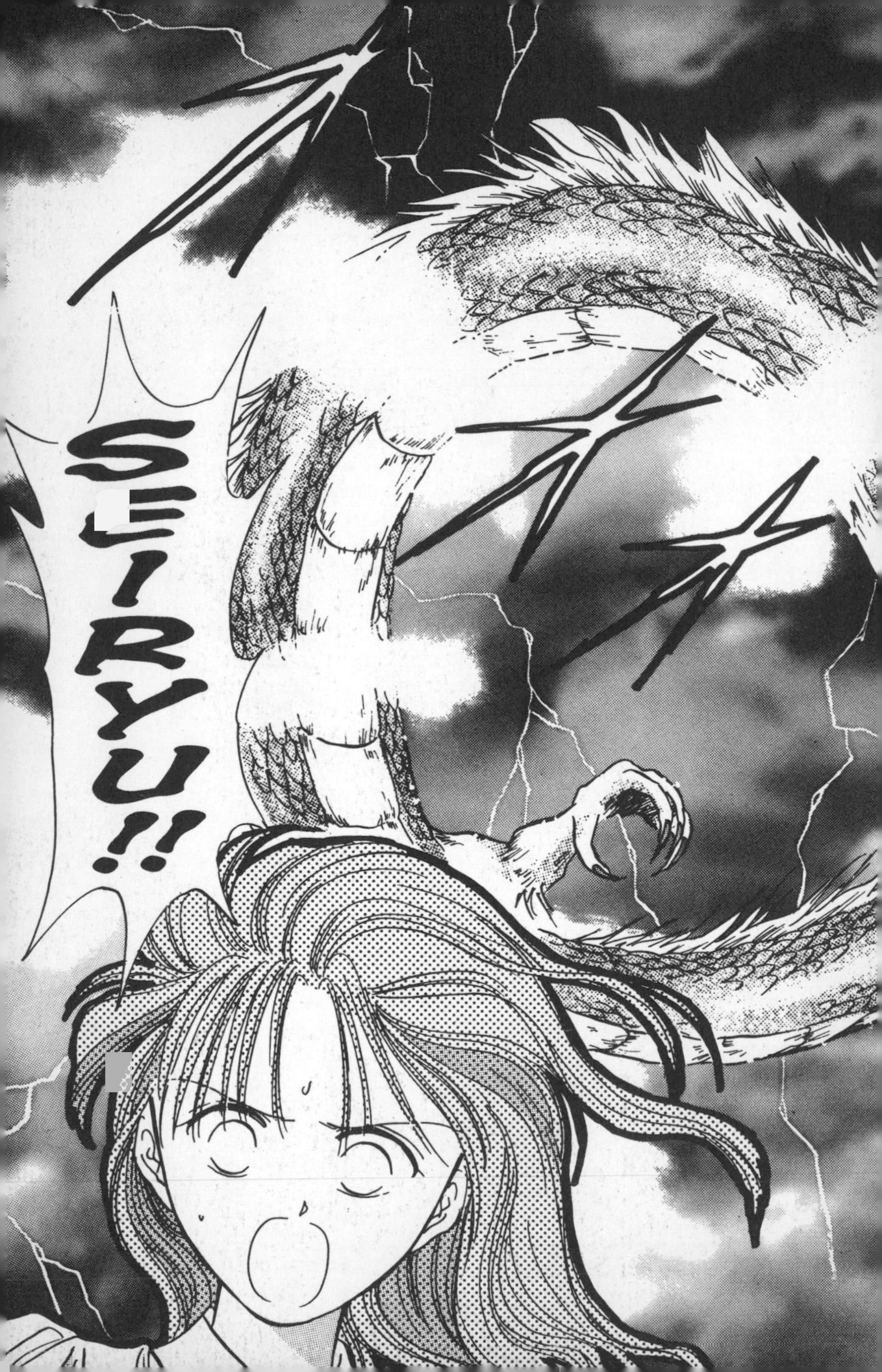
SEIRYU!!

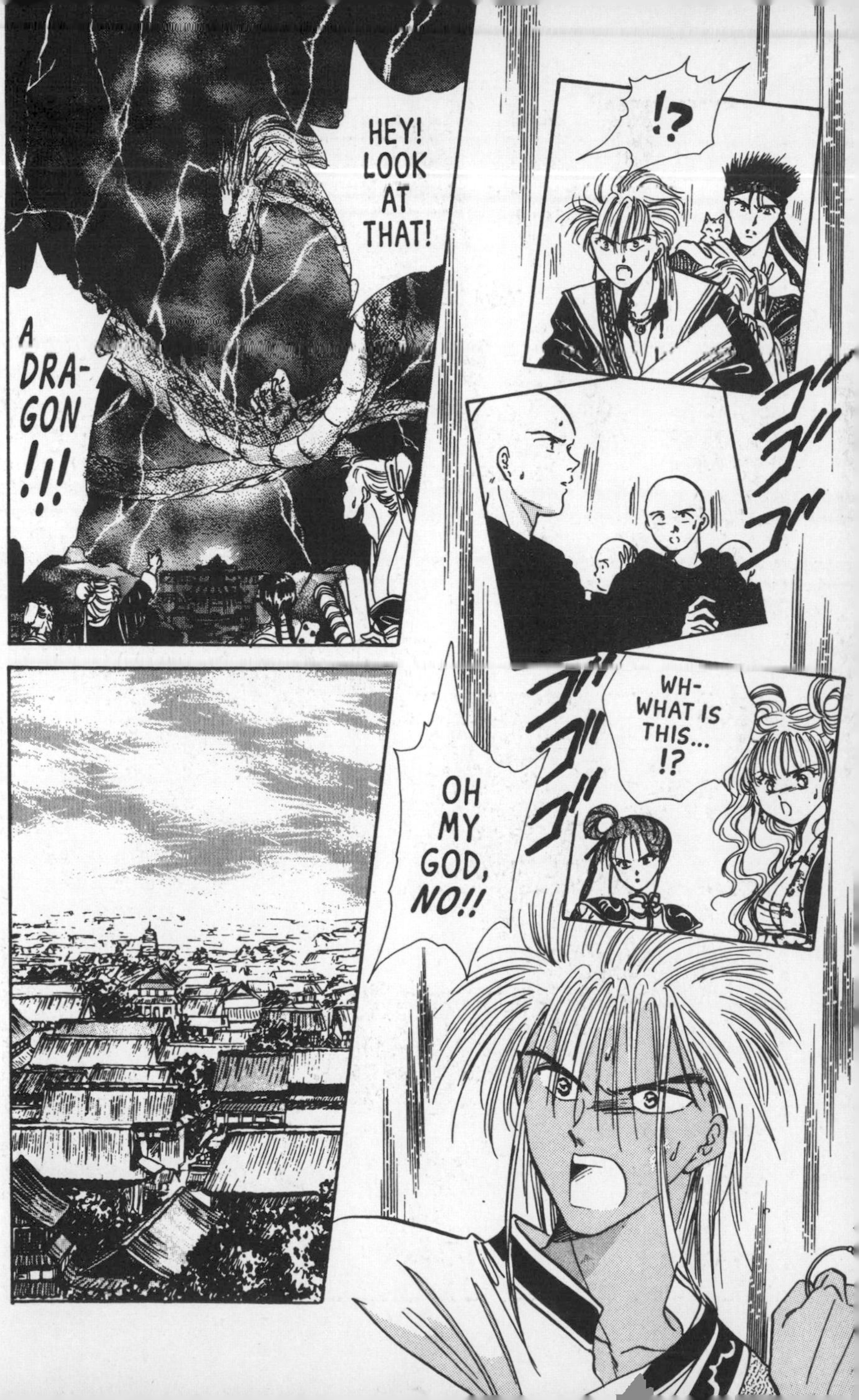
!?
ゴゴゴ
HEY! LOOK AT THAT!
A DRAGON!!!
ゴゴゴ
WH-WHAT IS THIS...!?
OH MY GOD, NO!!

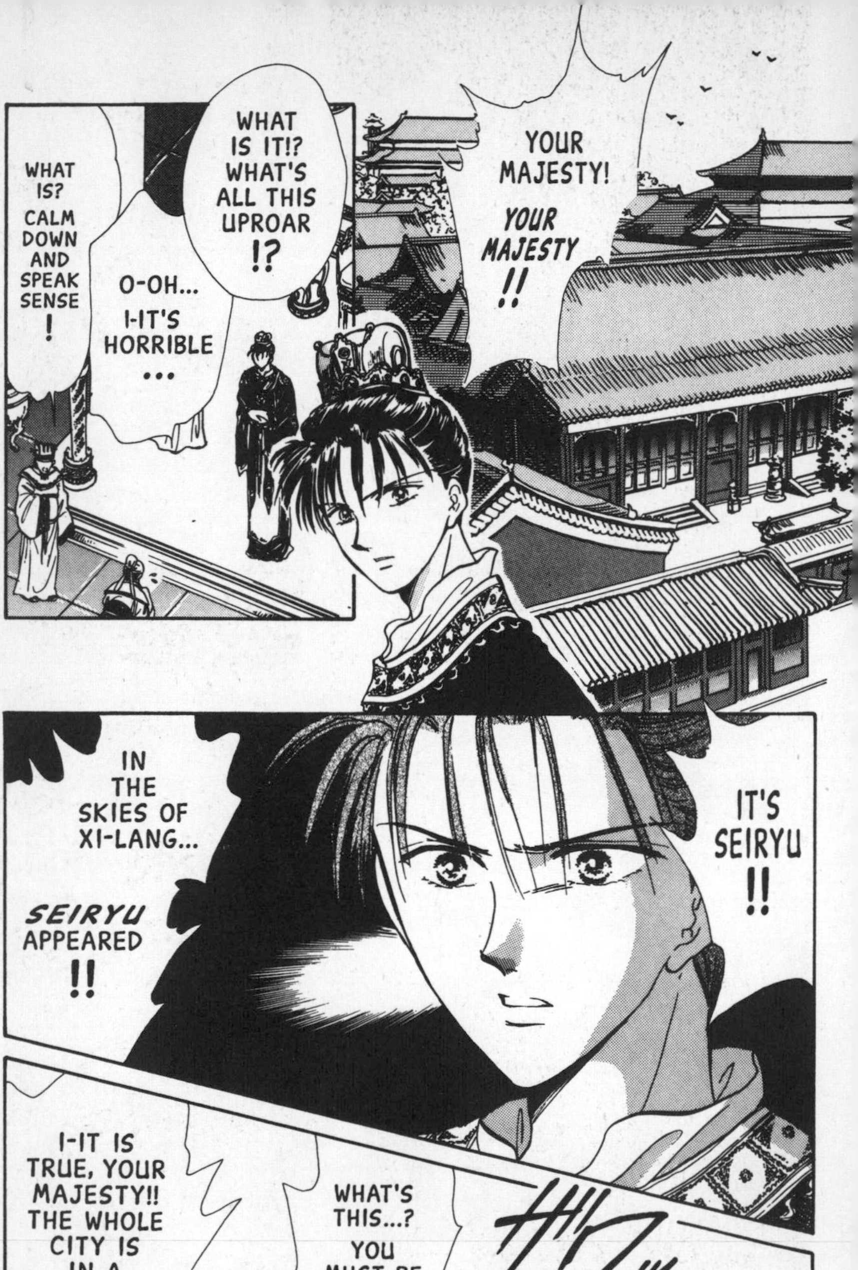
YOUR MAJESTY!
YOUR MAJESTY!!
WHAT IS IT!? WHAT'S ALL THIS UPROAR!?
O-OH... I-IT'S HORRIBLE...
WHAT IS? CALM DOWN AND SPEAK SENSE!
IT'S SEIRYU!!
IN THE SKIES OF XI-LANG...
SEIRYU APPEARED!!
WHAT'S THIS...?
YOU MUST BE JOKING!
I-IT IS TRUE, YOUR MAJESTY!! THE WHOLE CITY IS IN A PANIC!!

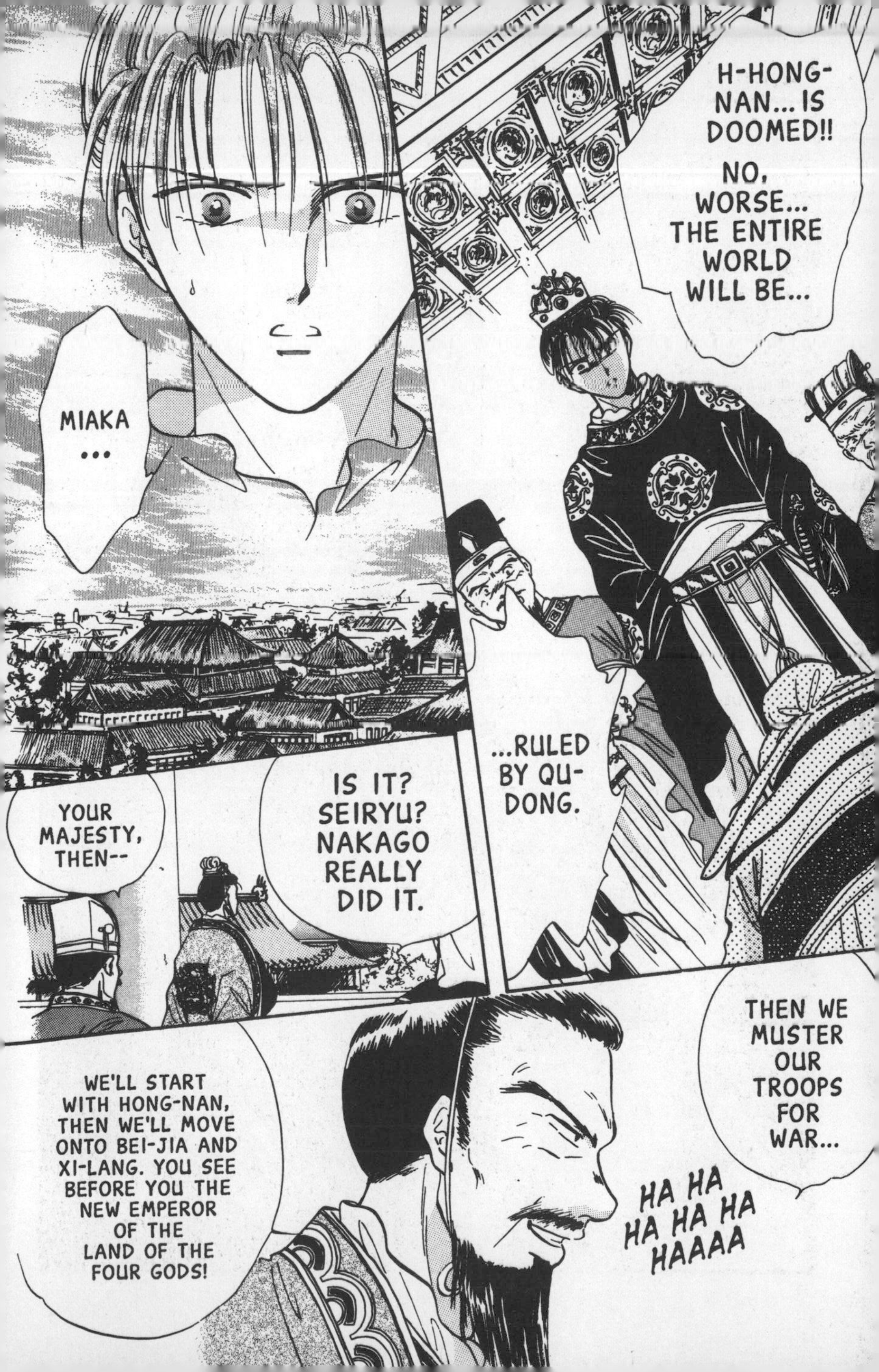
H-HONG-NAN... IS DOOMED!!
NO, WORSE... THE ENTIRE WORLD WILL BE...
...RULED BY QU-DONG.
MIAKA ...
IS IT? SEIRYU? NAKAGO REALLY DID IT.
YOUR MAJESTY, THEN--
THEN WE MUSTER OUR TROOPS FOR WAR...
WE'LL START WITH HONG-NAN, THEN WE'LL MOVE ONTO BEI-JIA AND XI-LANG. YOU SEE BEFORE YOU THE NEW EMPEROR OF THE LAND OF THE FOUR GODS!
HA HA HA HA HA HAAAA

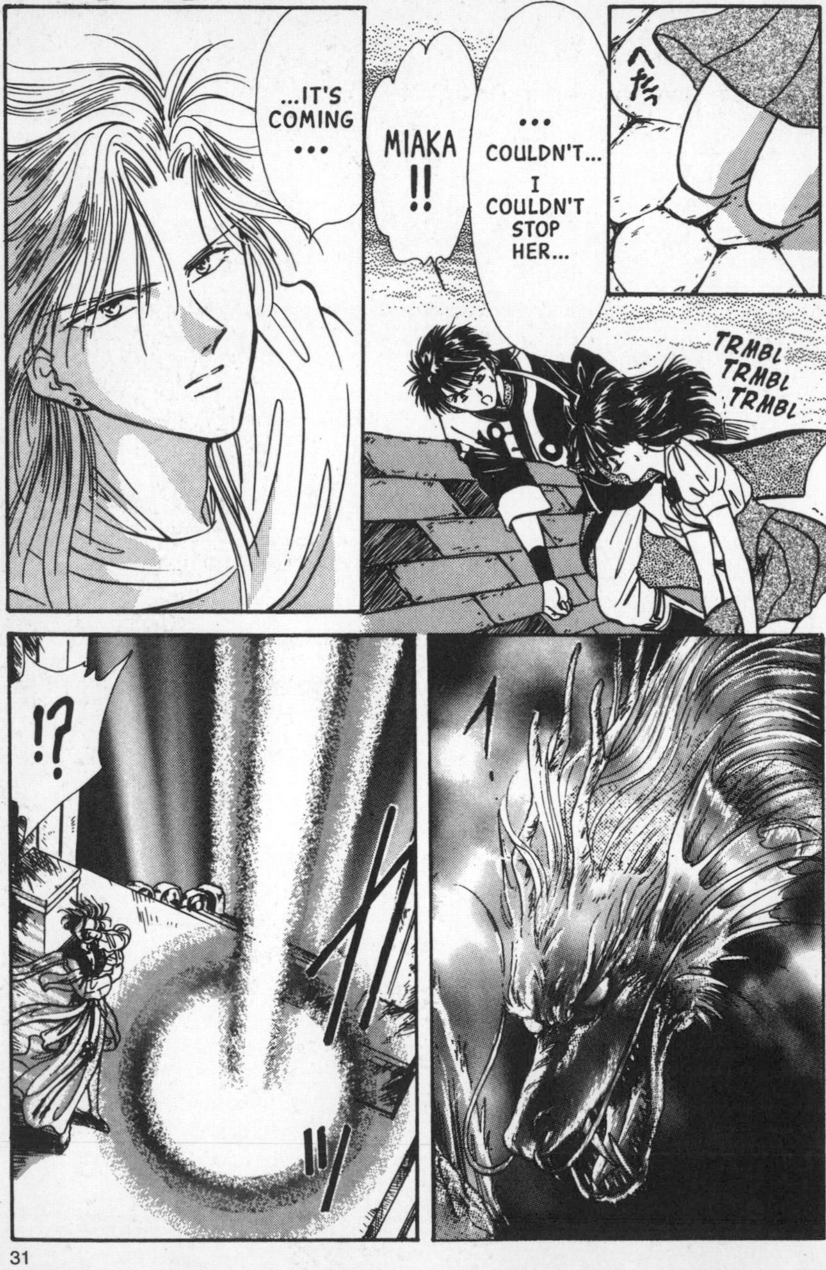
へたっ
... COULDN'T... I COULDN'T STOP HER...
MIAKA !!
TRMBL TRMBL TRMBL
...IT'S COMING ...
!?

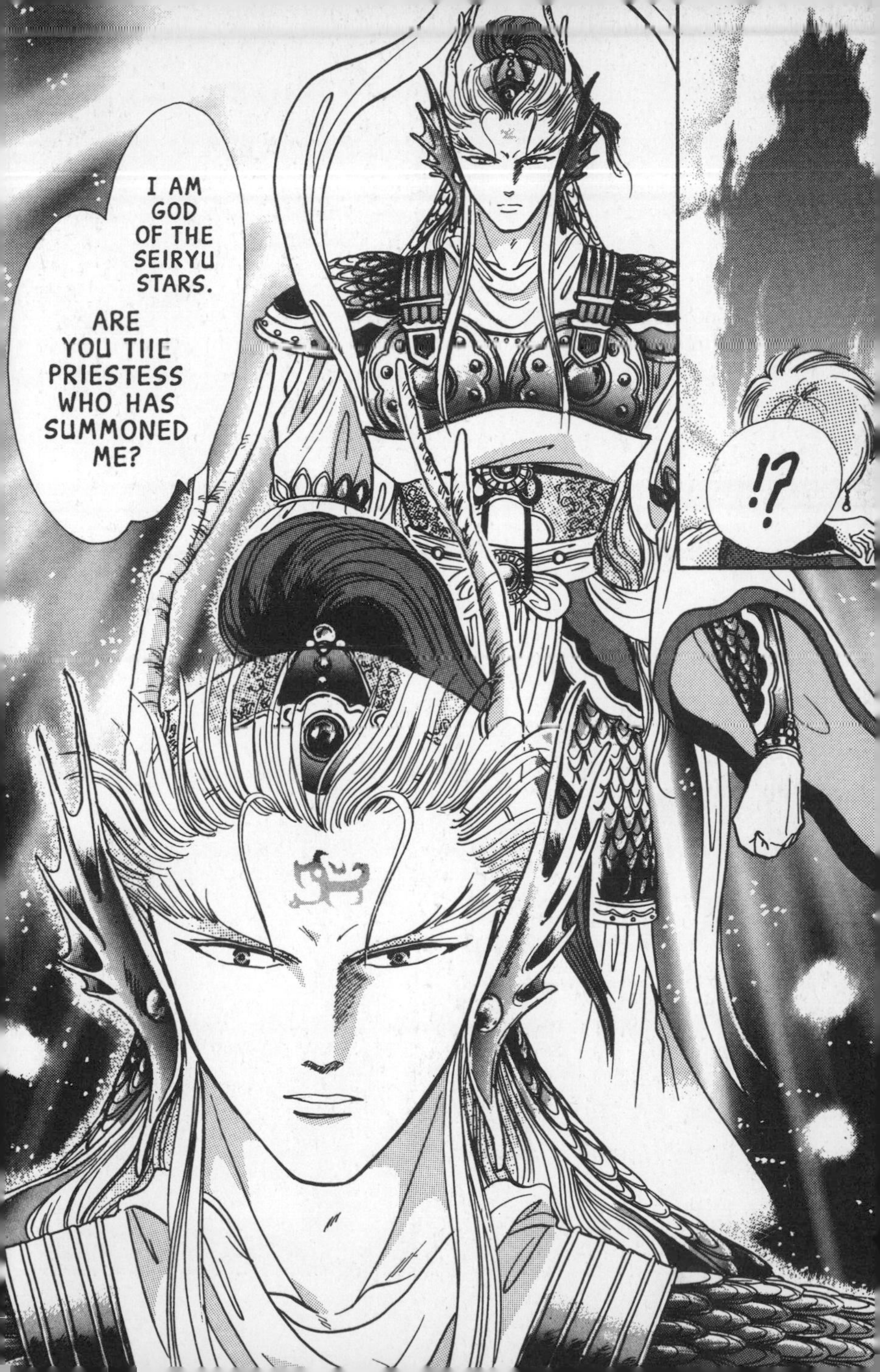
I AM GOD OF THE SEIRYU STARS.
ARE YOU THE PRIESTESS WHO HAS SUMMONED ME?
!?

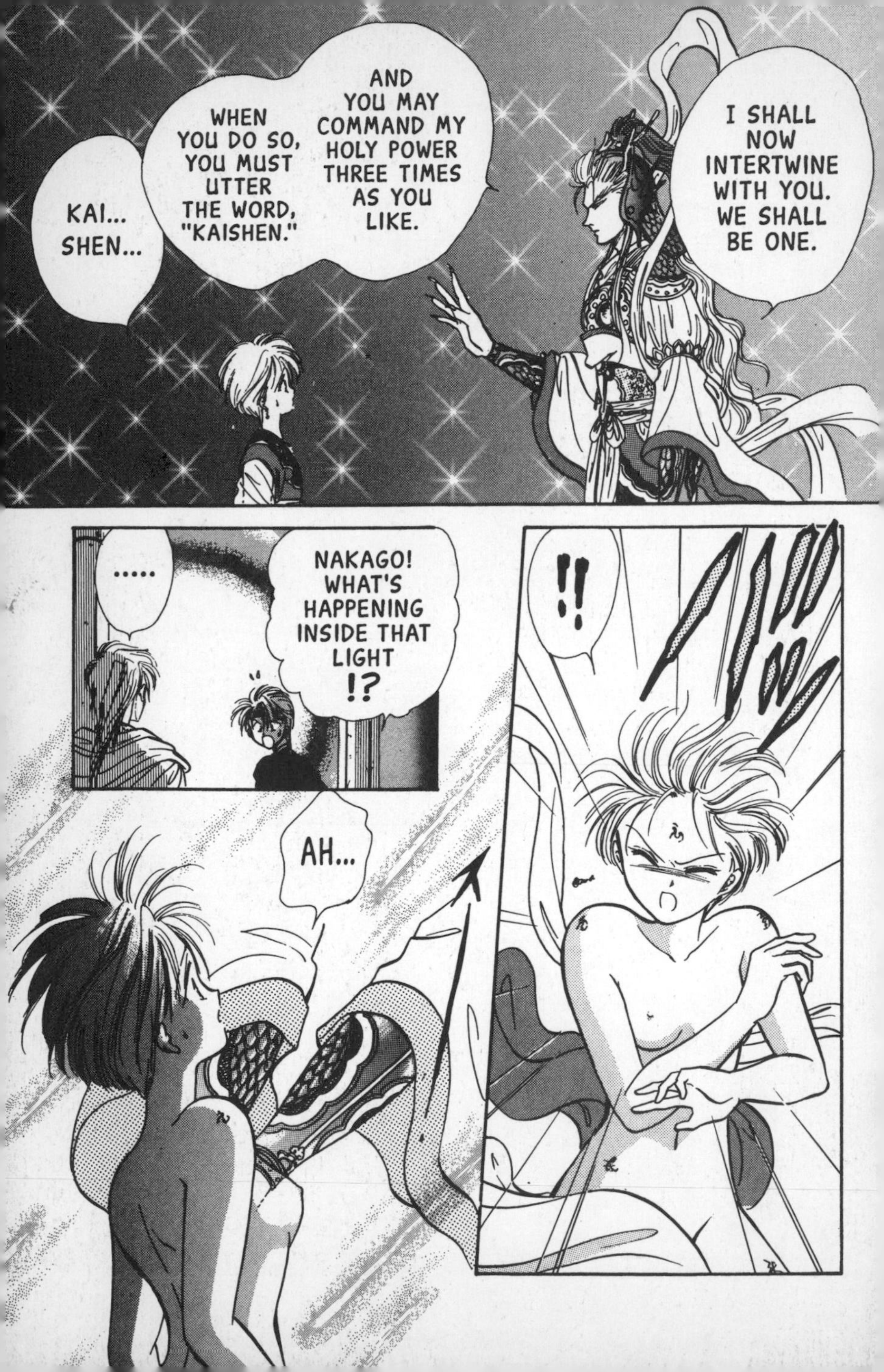
I SHALL NOW INTERTWINE WITH YOU. WE SHALL BE ONE.
AND YOU MAY COMMAND MY HOLY POWER THREE TIMES AS YOU LIKE.
WHEN YOU DO SO, YOU MUST UTTER THE WORD, "KAISHEN."
KAI... SHEN...
!!
NAKAGO! WHAT'S HAPPENING INSIDE THAT LIGHT !?
.....
AH...

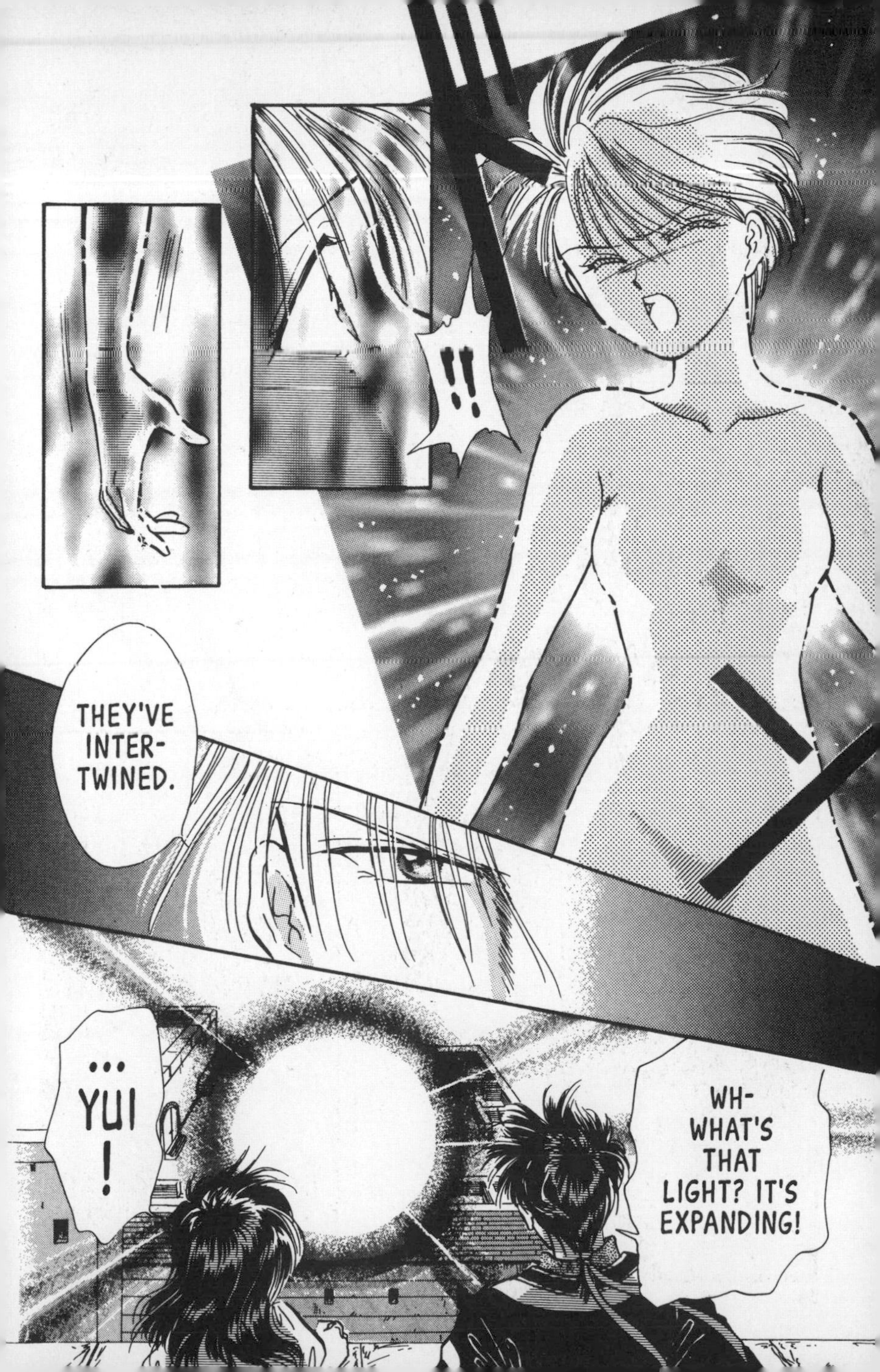
!!
THEY'VE INTER-TWINED.
WH- WHAT'S THAT LIGHT? IT'S EXPANDING!
...YUI!

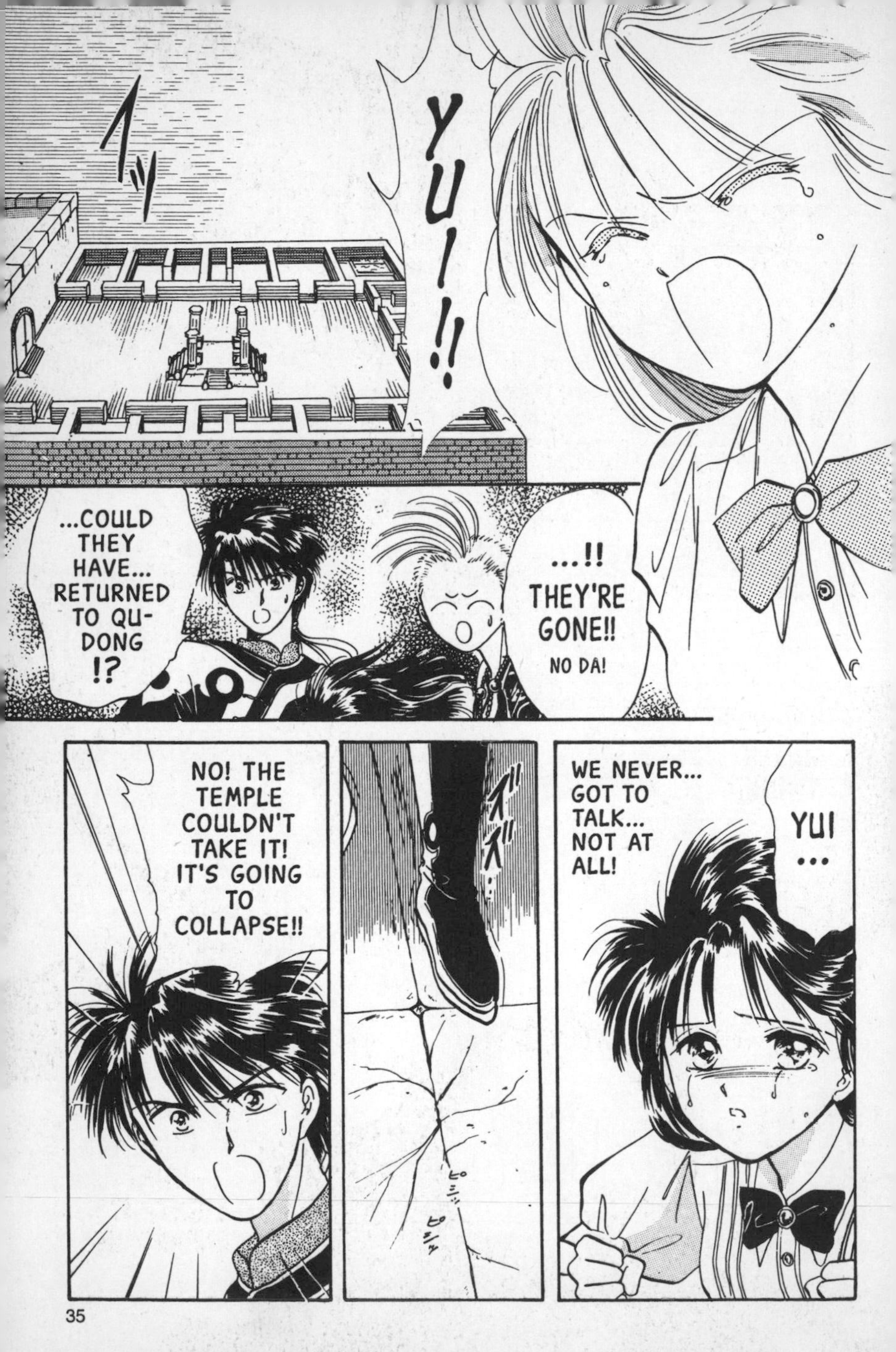
YUI!!
...!!
THEY'RE GONE!!
NO DA!
...COULD THEY HAVE... RETURNED TO QU-DONG!?
WE NEVER... GOT TO TALK... NOT AT ALL!
YUI...
NO! THE TEMPLE COULDN'T TAKE IT! IT'S GOING TO COLLAPSE!!

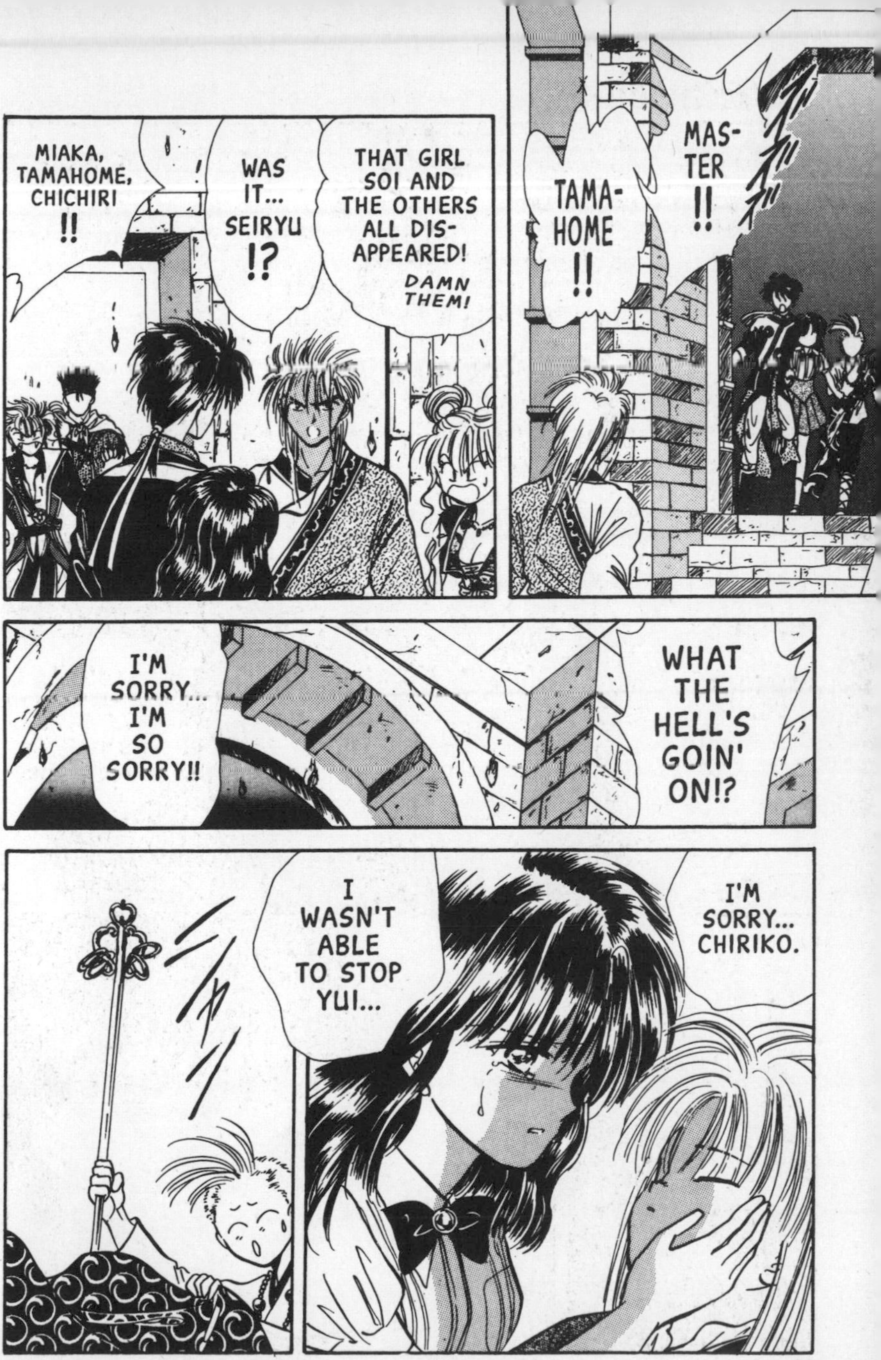
MASTER!!
TAMAHOME!!
THAT GIRL SOI AND THE OTHERS ALL DISAPPEARED!
DAMN THEM!
WAS IT... SEIRYU!?
MIAKA, TAMAHOME, CHICHIRI!!
WHAT THE HELL'S GOIN' ON!?
I'M SORRY... I'M SO SORRY!!
I'M SORRY... CHIRIKO.
I WASN'T ABLE TO STOP YUI...

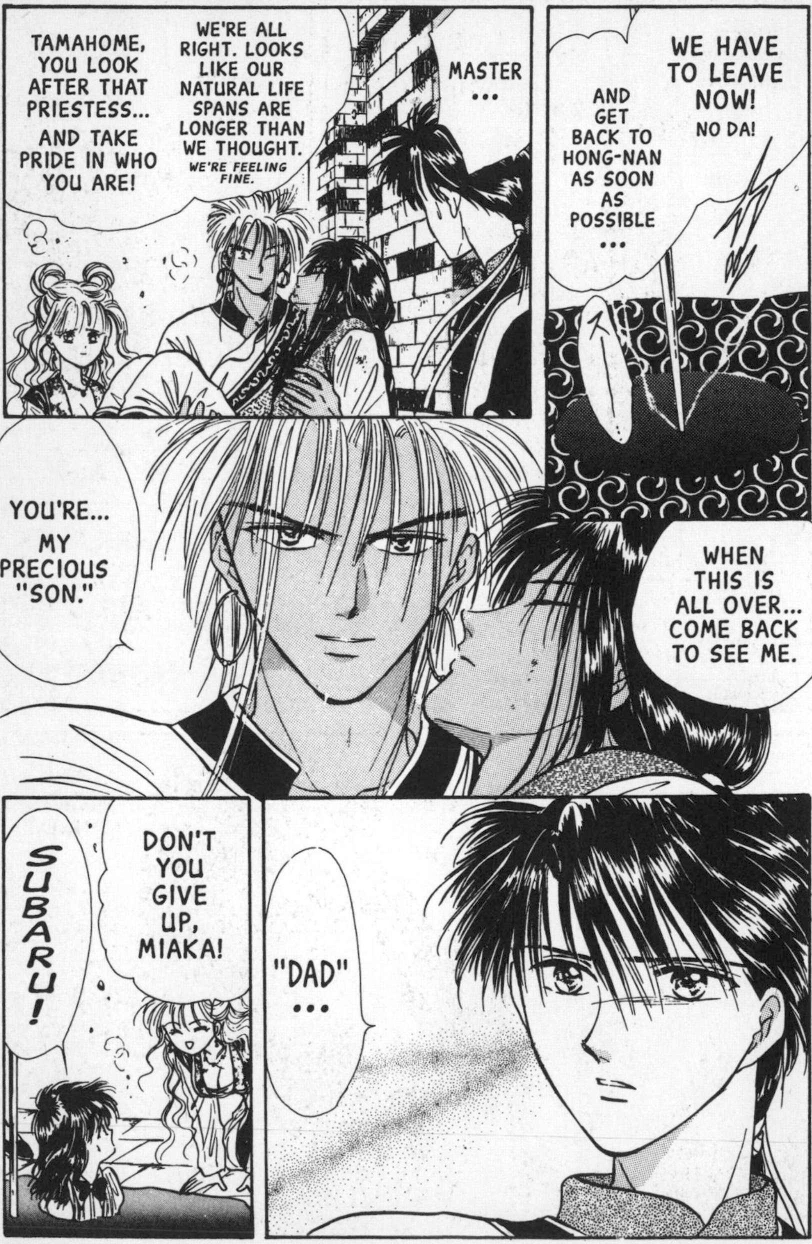
WE HAVE TO LEAVE NOW! NO DA!
AND GET BACK TO HONG-NAN AS SOON AS POSSIBLE...
MASTER...
WE'RE ALL RIGHT. LOOKS LIKE OUR NATURAL LIFE SPANS ARE LONGER THAN WE THOUGHT. WE'RE FEELING FINE.
TAMAHOME, YOU LOOK AFTER THAT PRIESTESS... AND TAKE PRIDE IN WHO YOU ARE!
WHEN THIS IS ALL OVER... COME BACK TO SEE ME.
YOU'RE... MY PRECIOUS "SON."
"DAD"...
DON'T YOU GIVE UP, MIAKA!
SUBARU!

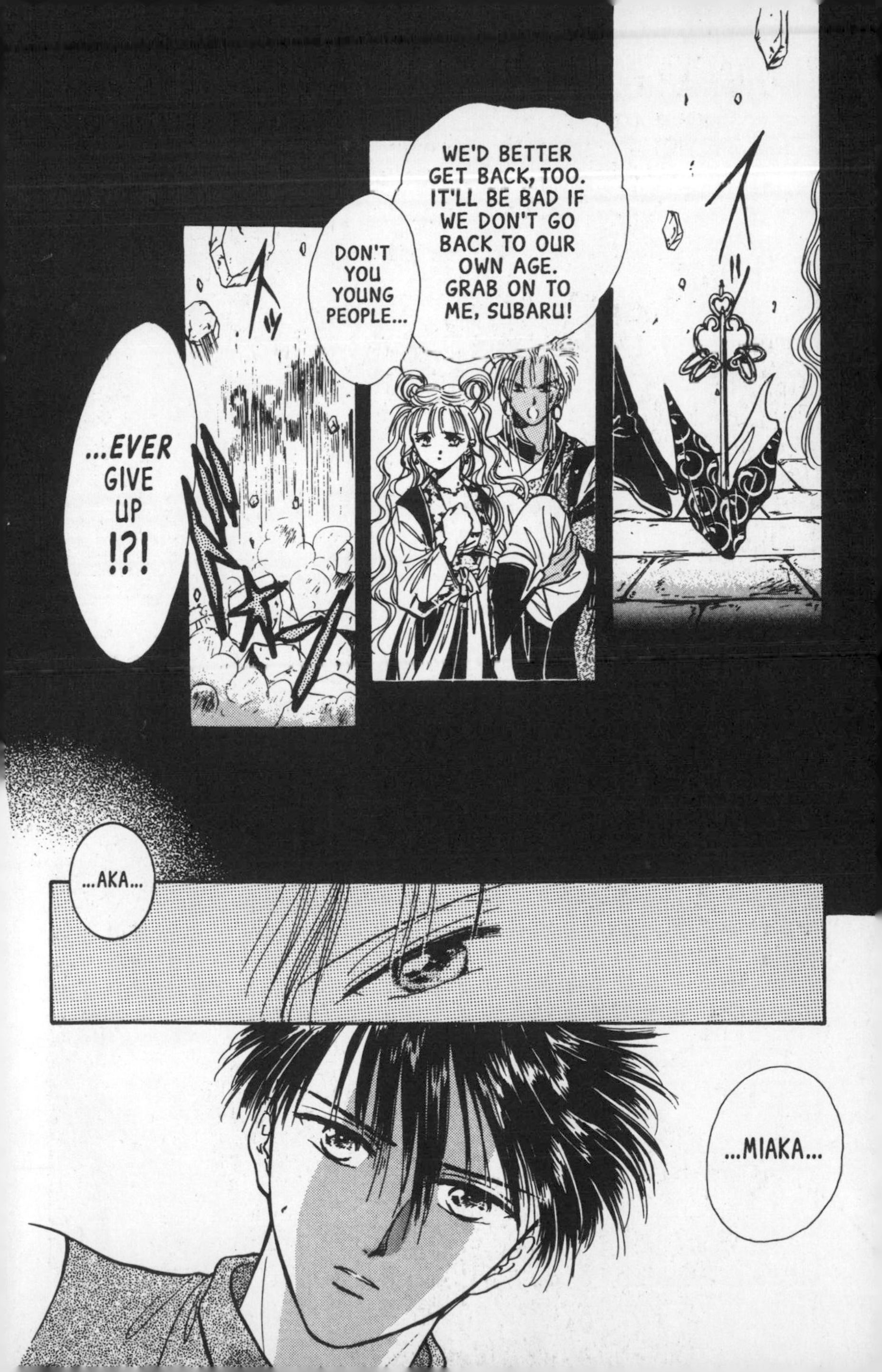
WE'D BETTER GET BACK, TOO. IT'LL BE BAD IF WE DON'T GO BACK TO OUR OWN AGE. GRAB ON TO ME, SUBARU!
DON'T YOU YOUNG PEOPLE...
...EVER GIVE UP !?!
...AKA...
...MIAKA...

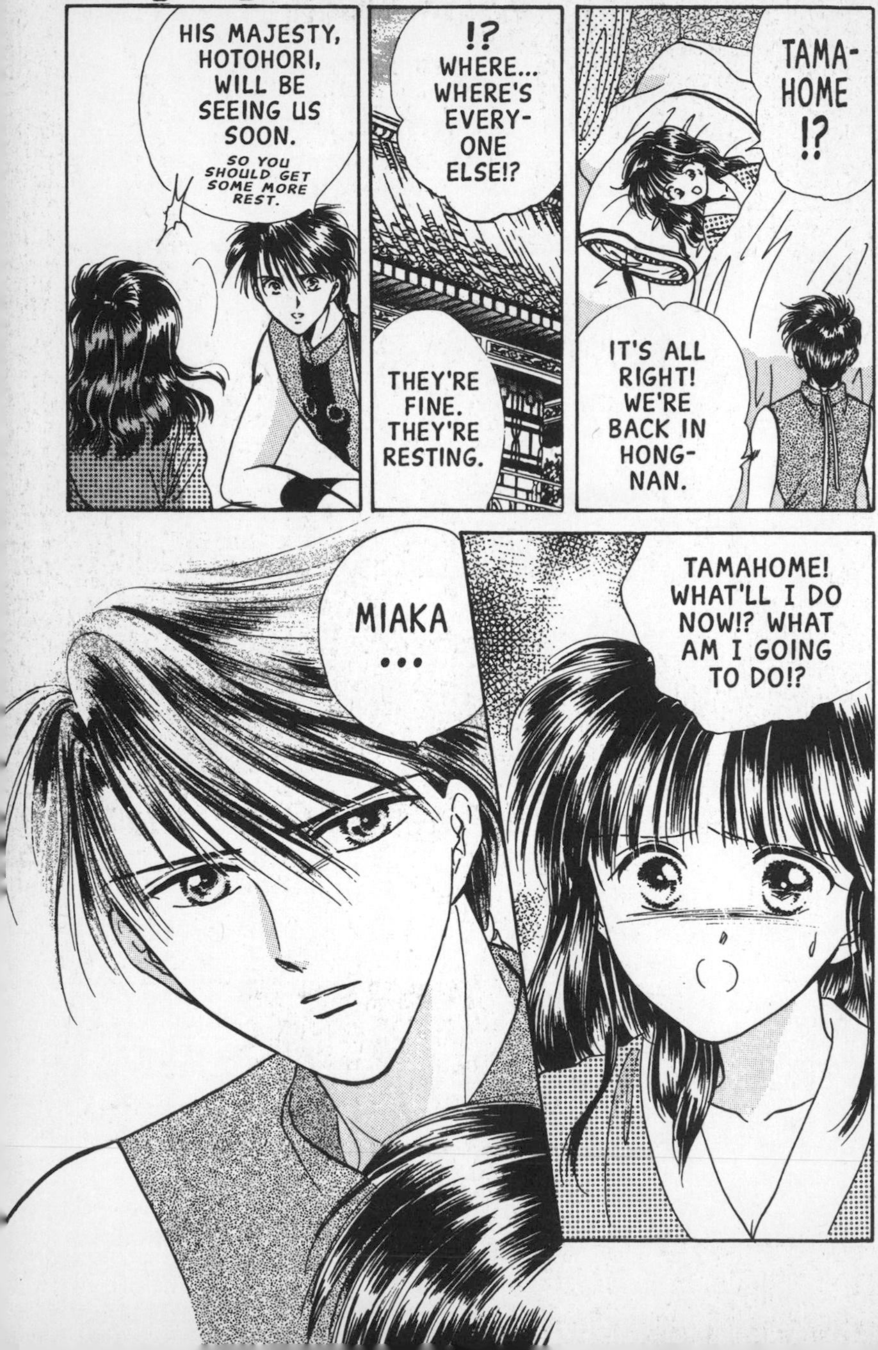
TAMA-HOME !?
IT'S ALL RIGHT! WE'RE BACK IN HONG-NAN.
!? WHERE... WHERE'S EVERY-ONE ELSE!?
THEY'RE FINE. THEY'RE RESTING.
HIS MAJESTY, HOTOHORI, WILL BE SEEING US SOON.
SO YOU SHOULD GET SOME MORE REST.
TAMAHOME! WHAT'LL I DO NOW!? WHAT AM I GOING TO DO!?
MIAKA ...

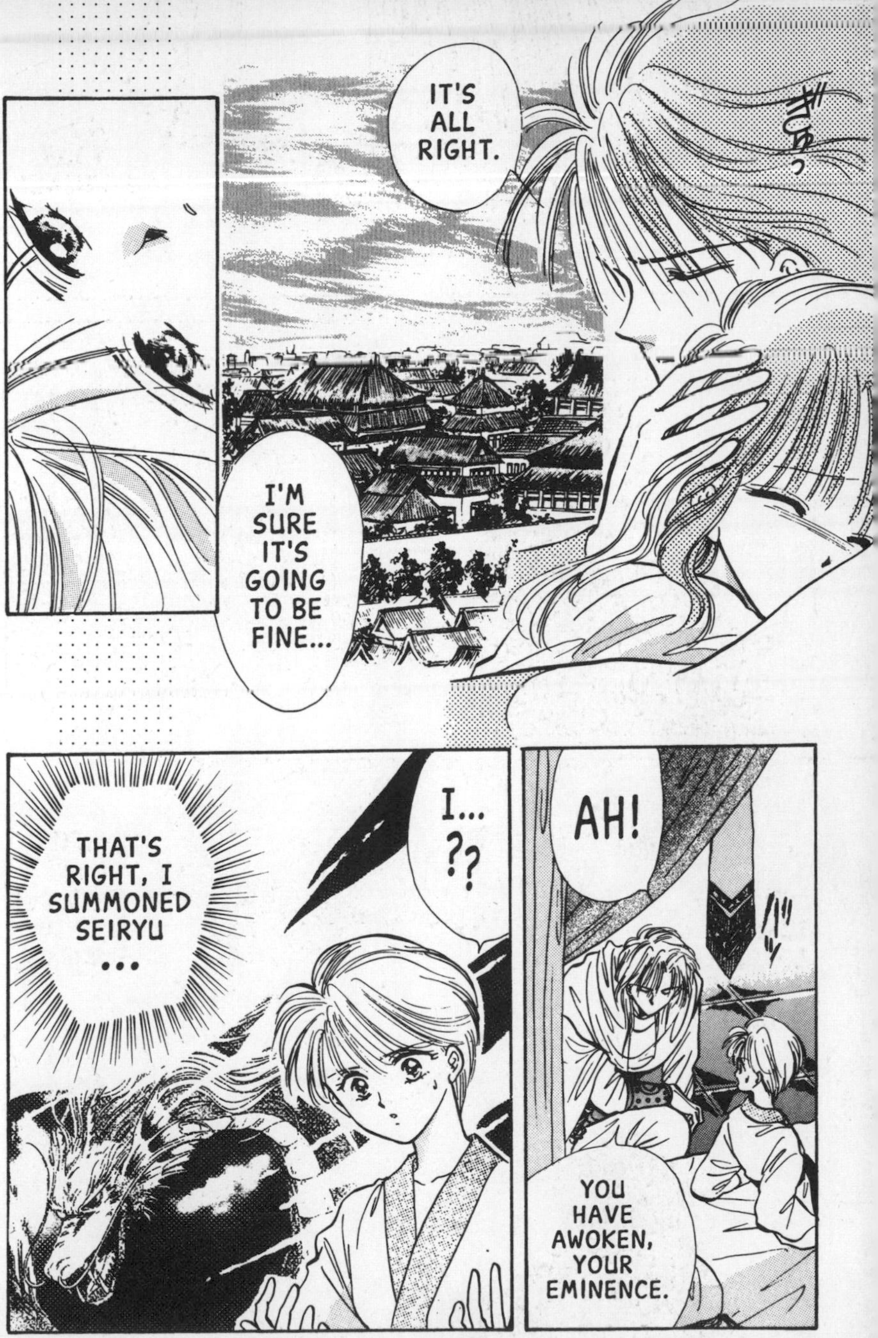
IT'S ALL RIGHT.
I'M SURE IT'S GOING TO BE FINE...
AH!
YOU HAVE AWOKEN, YOUR EMINENCE.
I... ??
THAT'S RIGHT, I SUMMONED SEIRYU ...

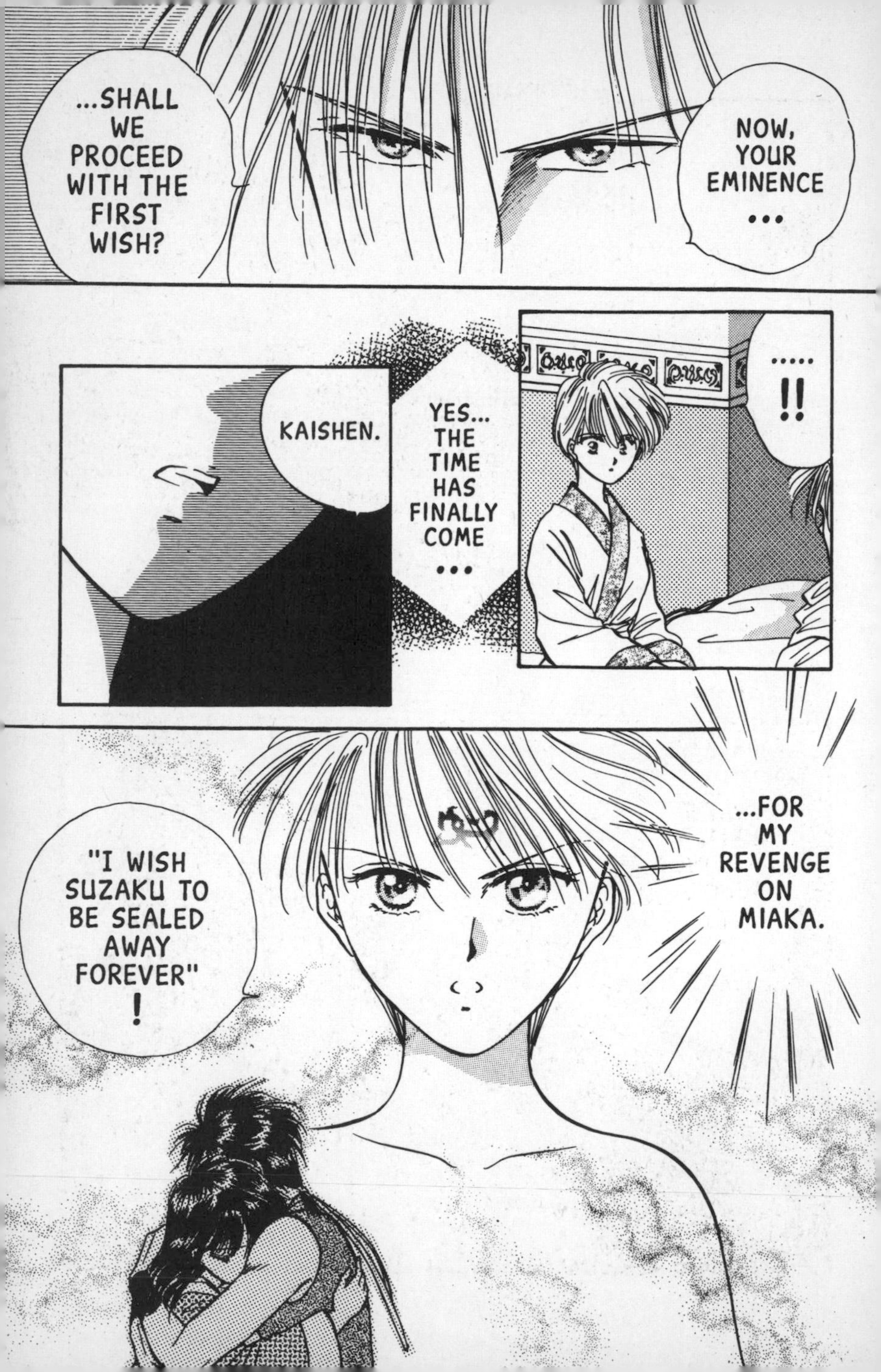
NOW, YOUR EMINENCE...
...SHALL WE PROCEED WITH THE FIRST WISH?
.....!!
YES... THE TIME HAS FINALLY COME...
KAISHEN.
...FOR MY REVENGE ON MIAKA.
"I WISH SUZAKU TO BE SEALED AWAY FOREVER"!

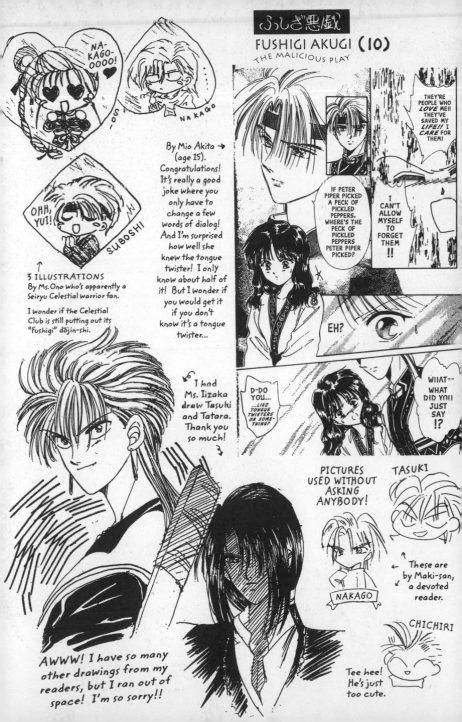

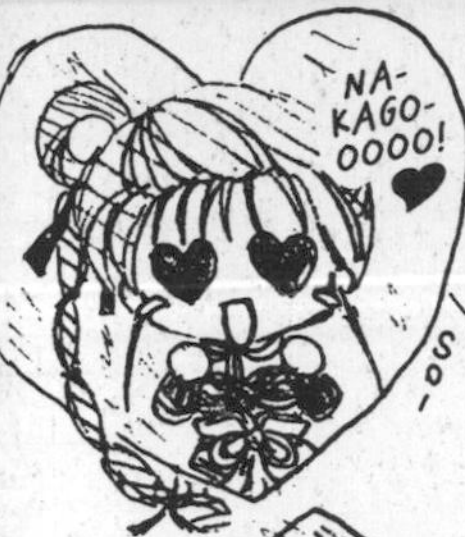
NA-KAGO-OOOO! ♥

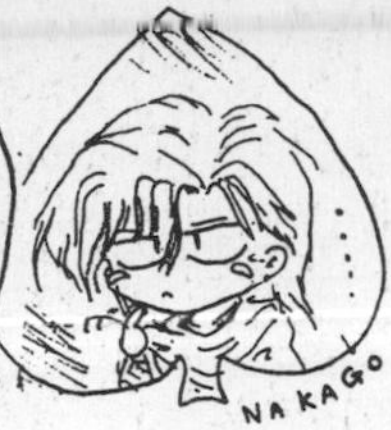
NAKAGO

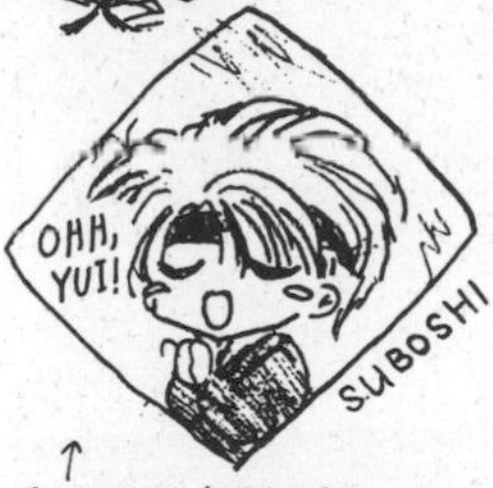
OHH, YUI!
SUBOSHI

↑
3 ILLUSTRATIONS
By Ms. Ono who's apparently a Seiryu Celestial warrior fan.

I wonder if the Celestial Club is still putting out its "Fushigi" dōjin-shi.

By Mio Akita → (age 15). Congratulations! It's really a good joke where you only have to change a few words of dialog! And I'm surprised how well she knew the tongue twister! I only know about half of it! But I wonder if you would get it if you don't know it's a tongue twister...

ふしぎ悪戯

FUSHIGI AKUGI (10)

THE MALICIOUS PLAY

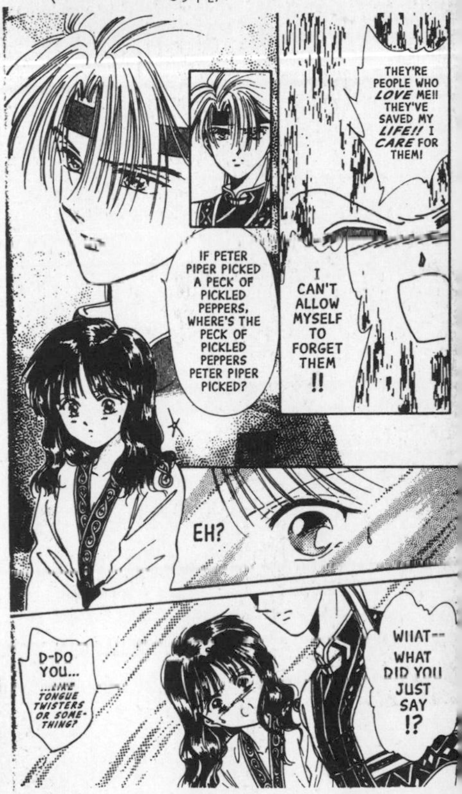
THEY'RE PEOPLE WHO LOVE ME!! THEY'VE SAVED MY LIFE!! I CARE FOR THEM!
I CAN'T ALLOW MYSELF TO FORGET THEM !!
IF PETER PIPER PICKED A PECK OF PICKLED PEPPERS, WHERE'S THE PECK OF PICKLED PEPPERS PETER PIPER PICKED?
EH?
WHAT-- WHAT DID YOU JUST SAY !?
D-DO YOU... ...LIKE TONGUE TWISTERS OR SOME-THING?

↶ I had Ms. Izaka draw Tasuki and Tatara. Thank you so much! ⤵

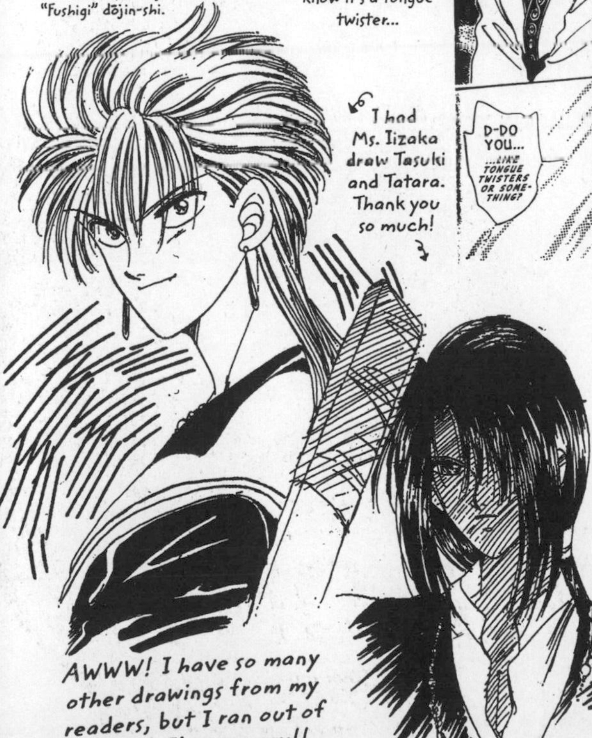

AWWW! I have so many other drawings from my readers, but I ran out of space! I'm so sorry!!

PICTURES USED WITHOUT ASKING ANYBODY!

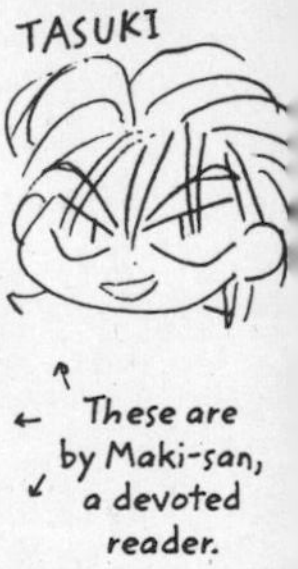
TASUKI

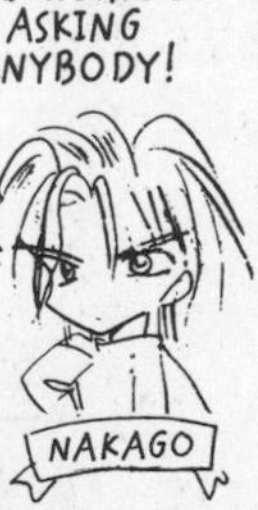
NAKAGO

These are by Maki-san, a devoted reader.

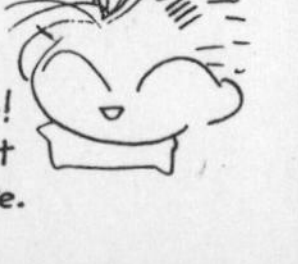
CHICHIRI

Tee hee! He's just too cute.

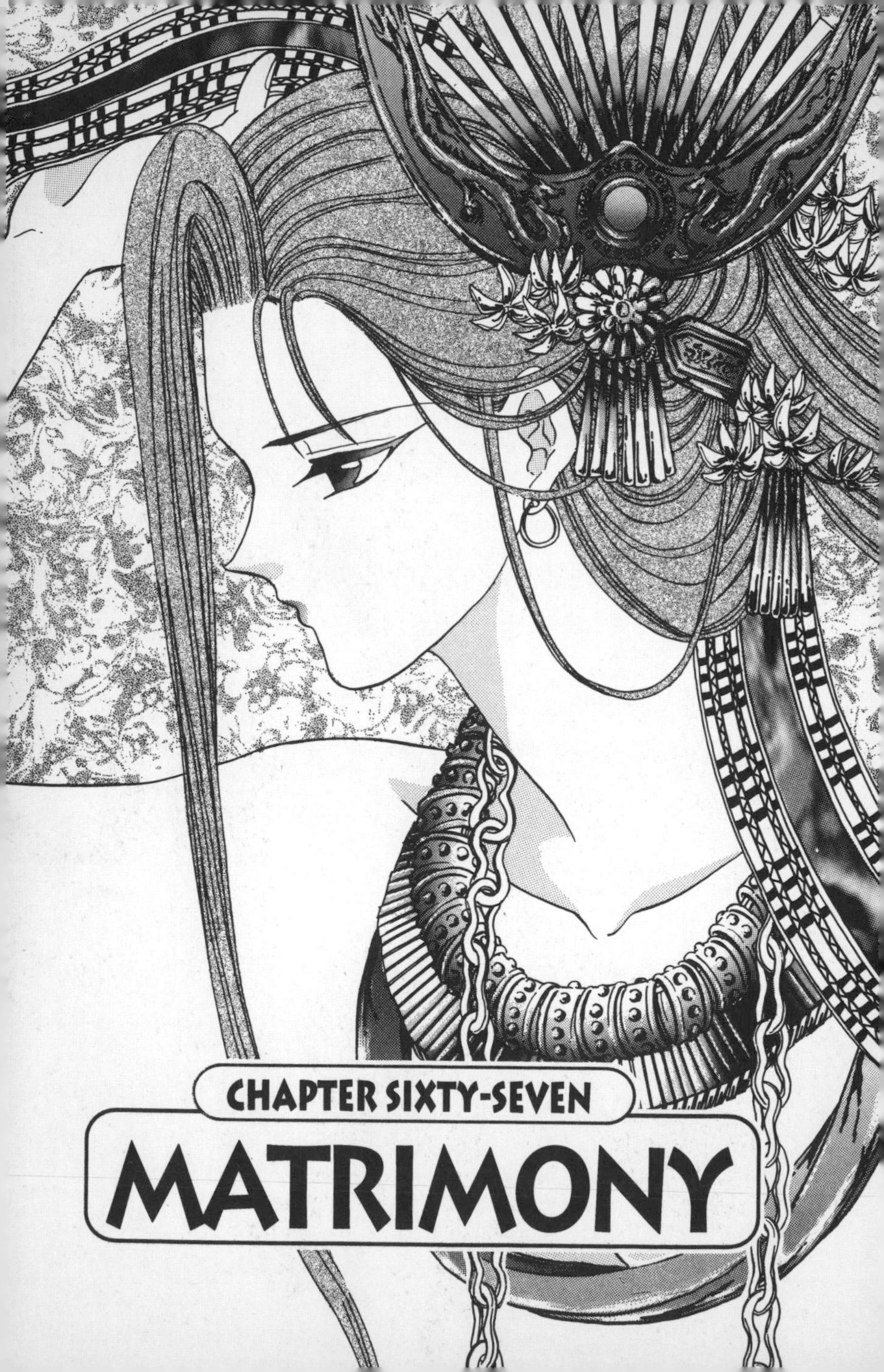
CHAPTER SIXTY-SEVEN
MATRIMONY

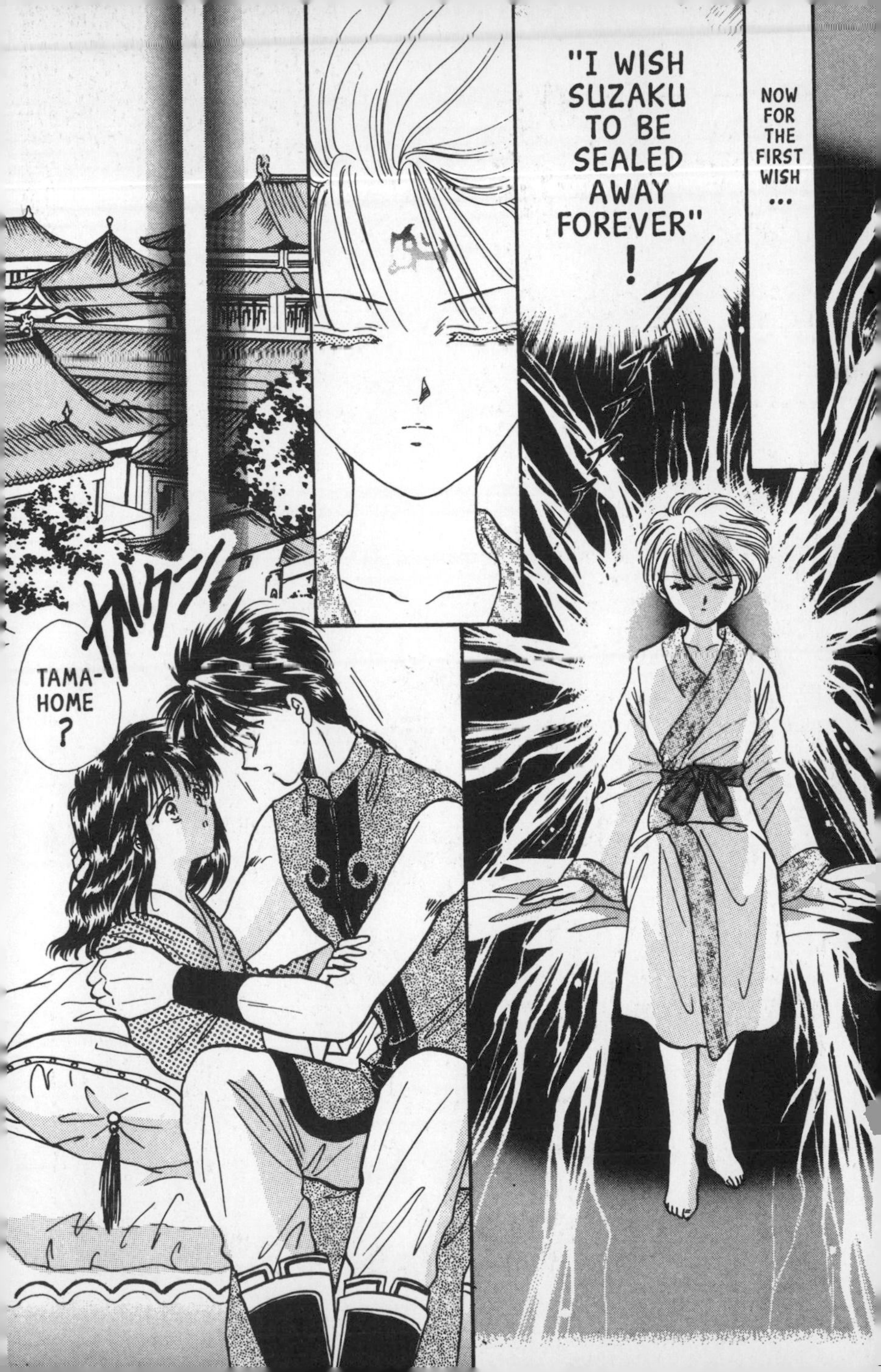
NOW FOR THE FIRST WISH ...
"I WISH SUZAKU TO BE SEALED AWAY FOREVER" !
TAMA-HOME ?

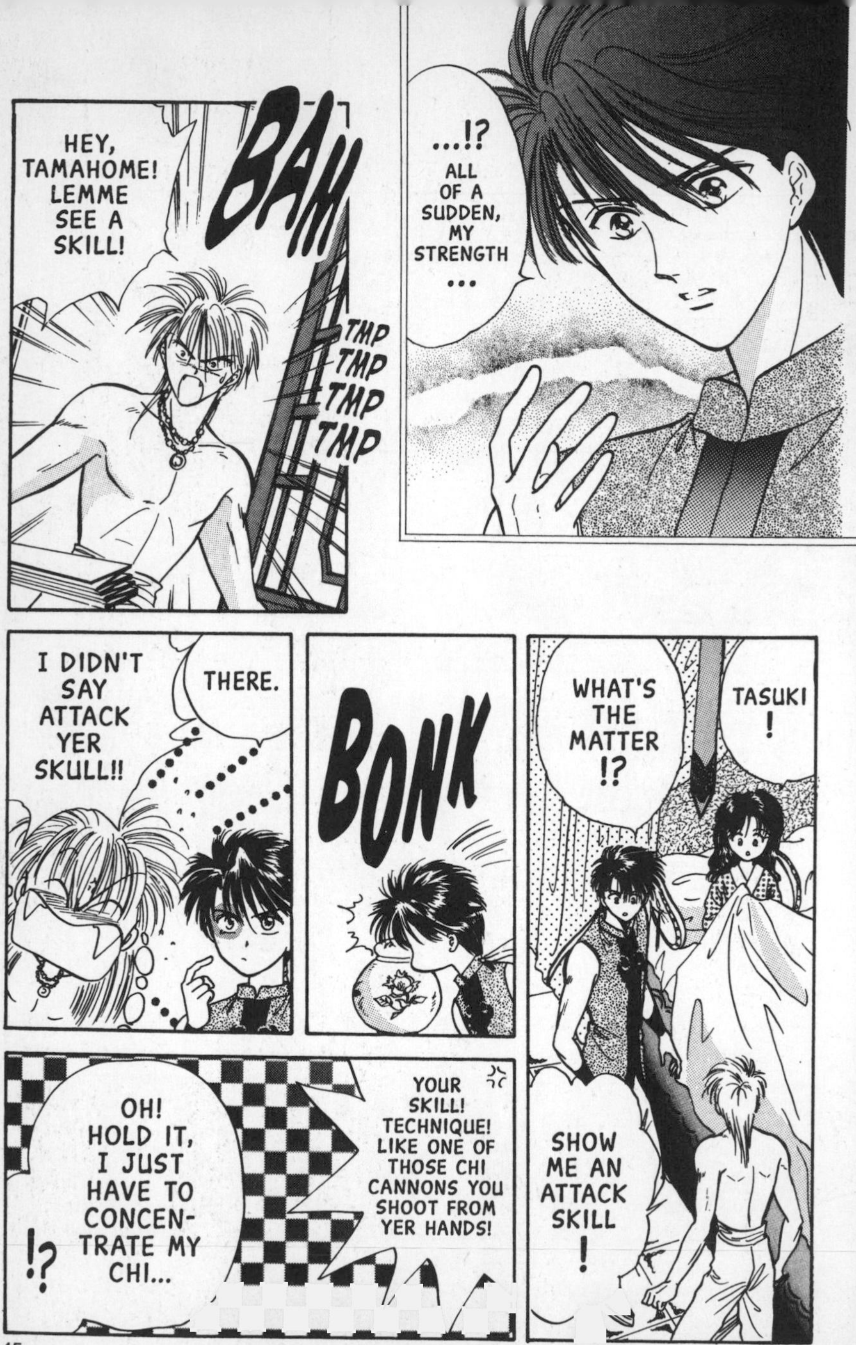
...!?
ALL OF A SUDDEN, MY STRENGTH...
HEY, TAMAHOME! LEMME SEE A SKILL!
BAH
TMP TMP TMP TMP
BONK
THERE.
I DIDN'T SAY ATTACK YER SKULL!!
TASUKI!
WHAT'S THE MATTER!?
SHOW ME AN ATTACK SKILL!
YOUR SKILL! TECHNIQUE! LIKE ONE OF THOSE CHI CANNONS YOU SHOOT FROM YER HANDS!
OH! HOLD IT, I JUST HAVE TO CONCEN-TRATE MY CHI...
!?

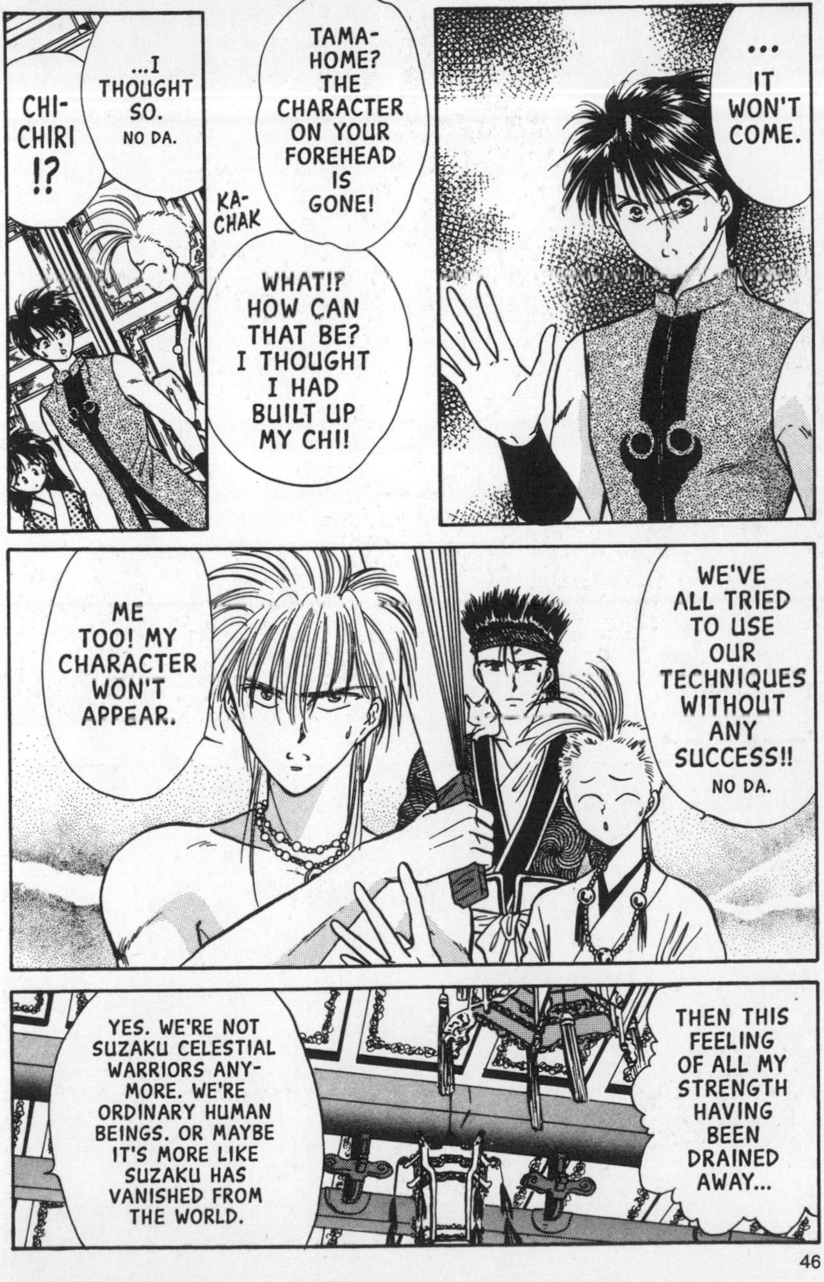
... IT WON'T COME.
TAMA-HOME? THE CHARACTER ON YOUR FOREHEAD IS GONE!
WHAT!? HOW CAN THAT BE? I THOUGHT I HAD BUILT UP MY CHI!
KA-CHAK
...I THOUGHT SO. NO DA.
CHI-CHIRI !?
WE'VE ALL TRIED TO USE OUR TECHNIQUES WITHOUT ANY SUCCESS!! NO DA.
ME TOO! MY CHARACTER WON'T APPEAR.
THEN THIS FEELING OF ALL MY STRENGTH HAVING BEEN DRAINED AWAY...
YES. WE'RE NOT SUZAKU CELESTIAL WARRIORS ANY-MORE. WE'RE ORDINARY HUMAN BEINGS. OR MAYBE IT'S MORE LIKE SUZAKU HAS VANISHED FROM THE WORLD.

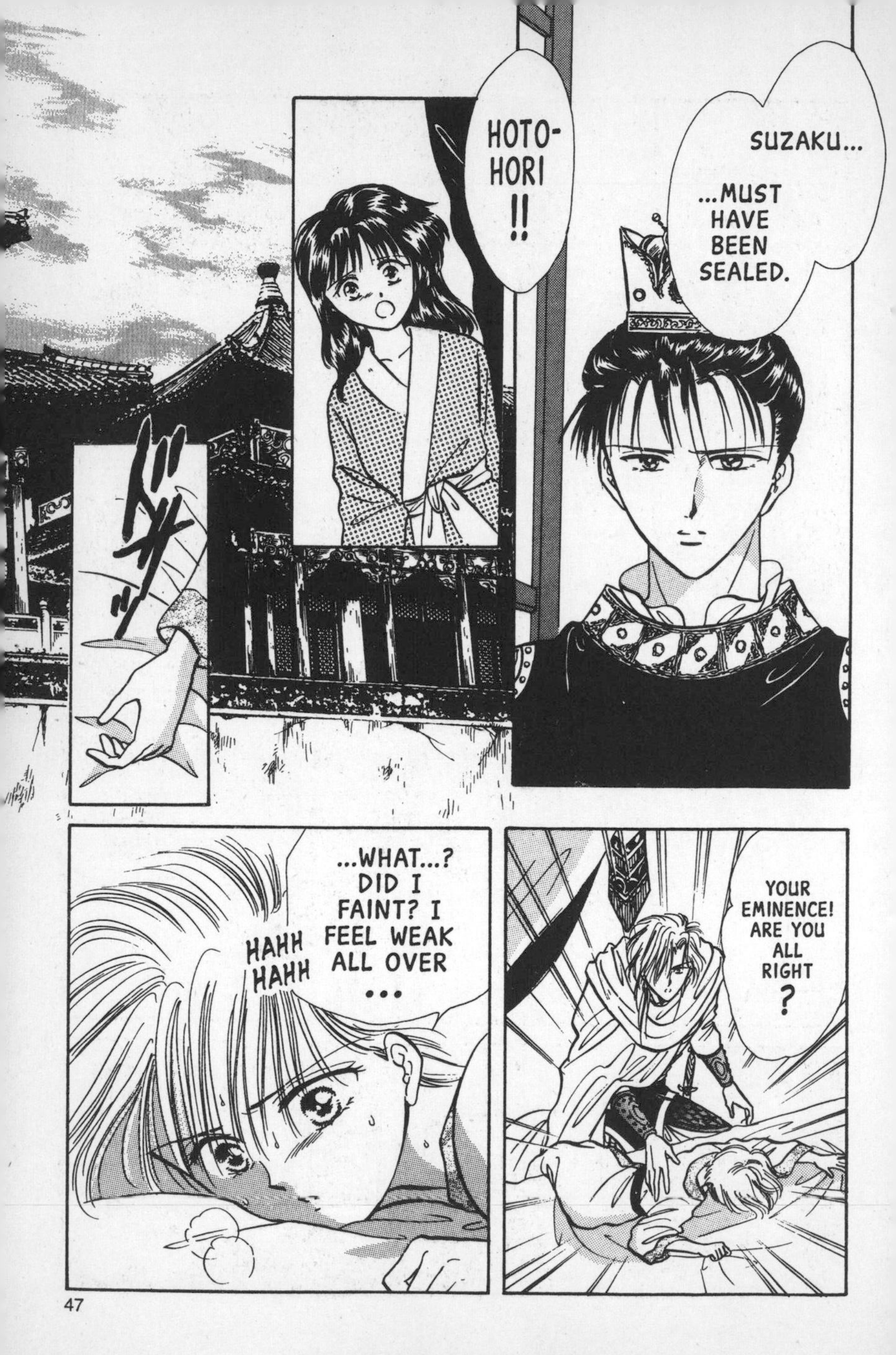
SUZAKU... ...MUST HAVE BEEN SEALED.
HOTO-HORI !!
ドサッ
YOUR EMINENCE! ARE YOU ALL RIGHT ?
...WHAT...? DID I FAINT? I FEEL WEAK ALL OVER ...
HAHH HAHH

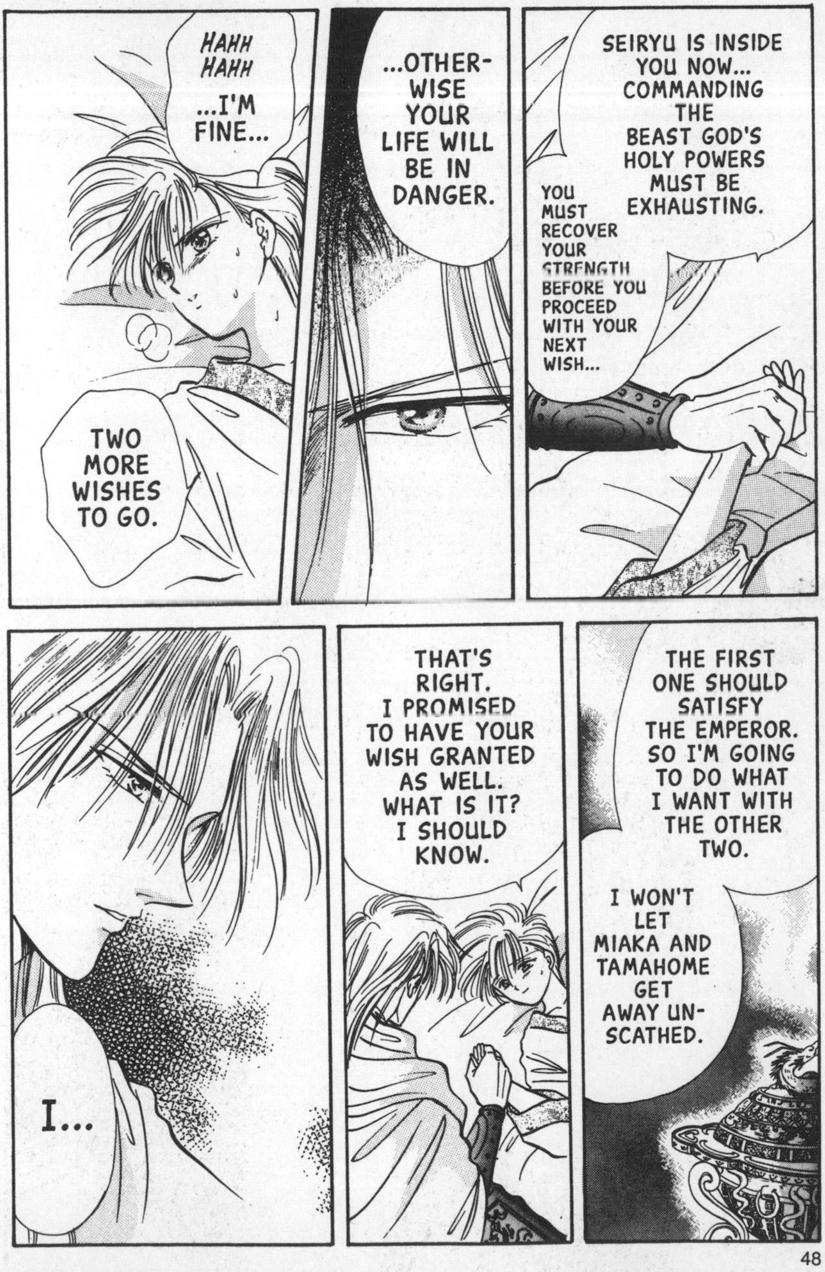
SEIRYU IS INSIDE YOU NOW... COMMANDING THE BEAST GOD'S HOLY POWERS MUST BE EXHAUSTING.
YOU MUST RECOVER YOUR STRENGTH BEFORE YOU PROCEED WITH YOUR NEXT WISH...
...OTHER-WISE YOUR LIFE WILL BE IN DANGER.
HAHH HAHH ...I'M FINE...
TWO MORE WISHES TO GO.
THE FIRST ONE SHOULD SATISFY THE EMPEROR. SO I'M GOING TO DO WHAT I WANT WITH THE OTHER TWO.
I WON'T LET MIAKA AND TAMAHOME GET AWAY UN-SCATHED.
THAT'S RIGHT. I PROMISED TO HAVE YOUR WISH GRANTED AS WELL. WHAT IS IT? I SHOULD KNOW.
I...

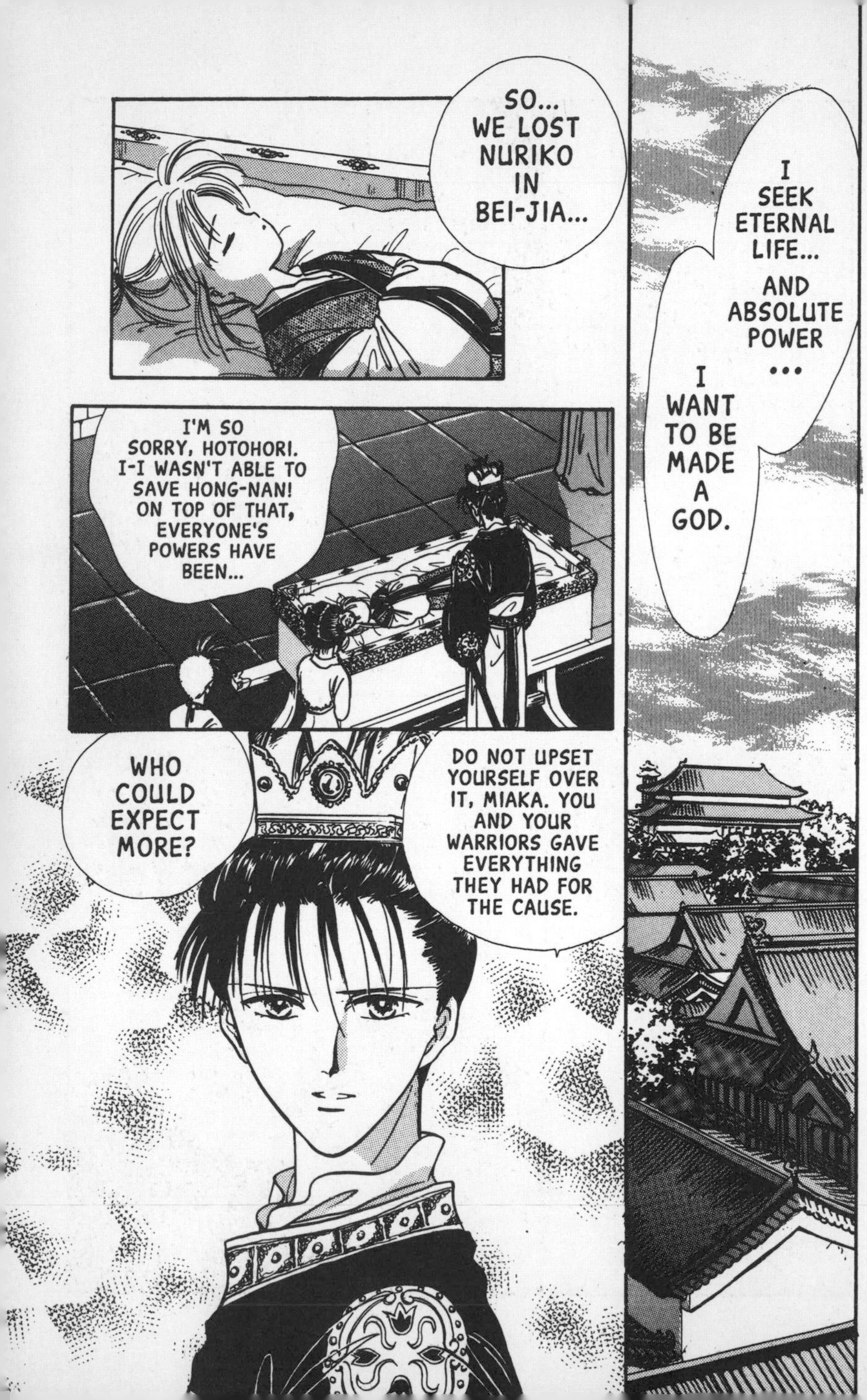
I SEEK ETERNAL LIFE... AND ABSOLUTE POWER...
I WANT TO BE MADE A GOD.
SO... WE LOST NURIKO IN BEI-JIA...
I'M SO SORRY, HOTOHORI. I-I WASN'T ABLE TO SAVE HONG-NAN! ON TOP OF THAT, EVERYONE'S POWERS HAVE BEEN...
DO NOT UPSET YOURSELF OVER IT, MIAKA. YOU AND YOUR WARRIORS GAVE EVERYTHING THEY HAD FOR THE CAUSE.
WHO COULD EXPECT MORE?

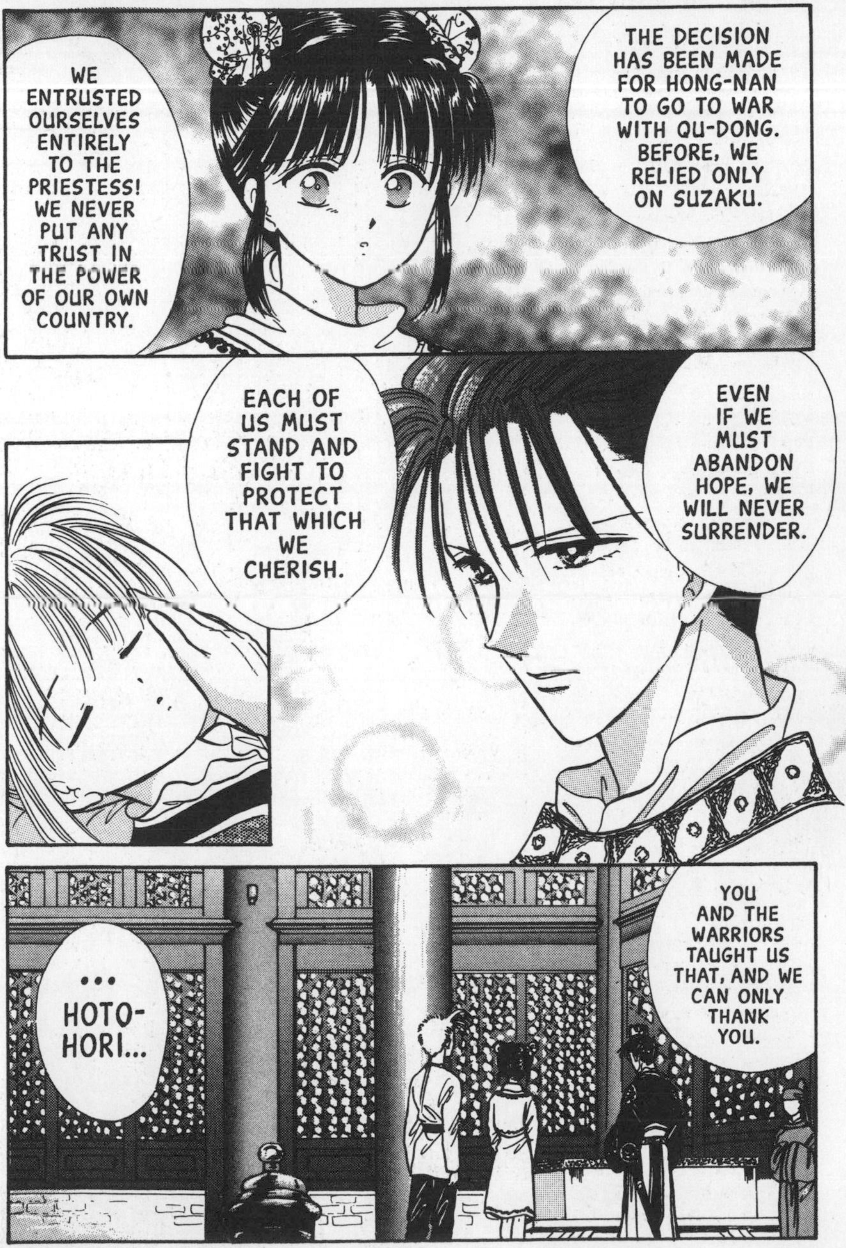
THE DECISION HAS BEEN MADE FOR HONG-NAN TO GO TO WAR WITH QU-DONG. BEFORE, WE RELIED ONLY ON SUZAKU.
WE ENTRUSTED OURSELVES ENTIRELY TO THE PRIESTESS! WE NEVER PUT ANY TRUST IN THE POWER OF OUR OWN COUNTRY.
EVEN IF WE MUST ABANDON HOPE, WE WILL NEVER SURRENDER.
EACH OF US MUST STAND AND FIGHT TO PROTECT THAT WHICH WE CHERISH.
YOU AND THE WARRIORS TAUGHT US THAT, AND WE CAN ONLY THANK YOU.
... HOTO-HORI...

Girlfriend

When he's a crybaby without his character, he can recall his wise self. So that must've been hard on him. The real Chiriko might in fact be the spacey one... By the way, I think I'm like Chiriko. I don't resemble him in terms of his height or intelligence, but when it comes to manga it's like I'm in a trance. My mind can't concentrate on anything else... No, really! They actually call me spacey. I swear, it's like I'm a different person. *Scary!*

Now, on to the Seiryu celestial warriors. *Hmm, hmm...* Nakago! The first Seiryu I came up with. I made him (look like a) blond to contrast him against Tamahome...his greatest rival. The "armor" also just came to me, so that became his outfit. And that's when he became a general. Come to think of it now, I think that armor protecting his "heart" represents his personality. But I didn't expect him to be so active in the story. He even kisses Tama! He was doing it to spite Miaka's and Tama's relationship. That feeling comes as naturally to him as eating, so he doesn't have to think twice about it. But I'm glad he's become popular lately. I like him! His foolishness is cute. Manato from "Prepubescence" used to be my favorite male character, but to be honest, Nakago's right up there with him. Basically, though, I like them all.

Amiboshi's very popular. According to the CD survey, he was ranked at No. 5. I got a lot of flack when he betrayed the Suzaku Warriors. (Or was it because he supposedly died?) *At the time...*

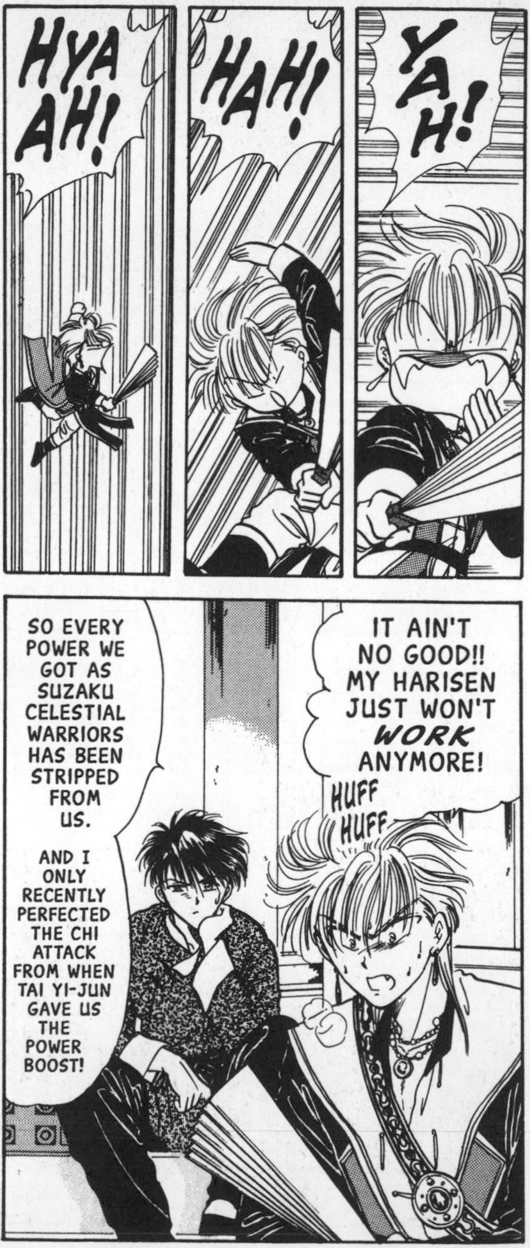
YAH!
HAH!
HYAAH!
IT AIN'T NO GOOD!! MY HARISEN JUST WON'T *WORK* ANYMORE!
HUFF HUFF
SO EVERY POWER WE GOT AS SUZAKU CELESTIAL WARRIORS HAS BEEN STRIPPED FROM US.
AND I ONLY RECENTLY PERFECTED THE CHI ATTACK FROM WHEN TAI YI-JUN GAVE US THE POWER BOOST!

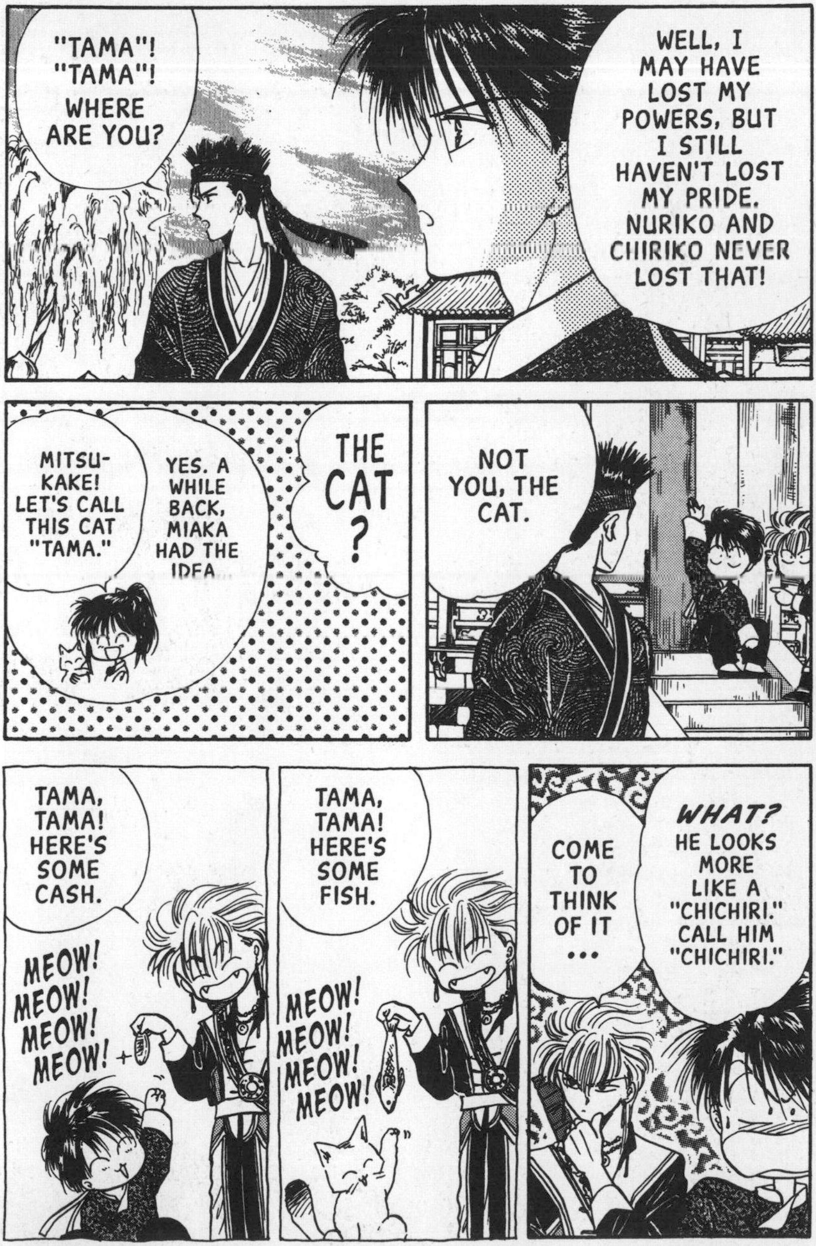
WELL, I MAY HAVE LOST MY POWERS, BUT I STILL HAVEN'T LOST MY PRIDE. NURIKO AND CHIRIKO NEVER LOST THAT!
"TAMA"! "TAMA"! WHERE ARE YOU?
NOT YOU, THE CAT.
THE CAT ?
YES. A WHILE BACK, MIAKA HAD THE IDEA...
MITSU-KAKE! LET'S CALL THIS CAT "TAMA."
WHAT? HE LOOKS MORE LIKE A "CHICHIRI." CALL HIM "CHICHIRI."
COME TO THINK OF IT ...
TAMA, TAMA! HERE'S SOME FISH.
MEOW! MEOW! MEOW! MEOW!
TAMA, TAMA! HERE'S SOME CASH.
MEOW! MEOW! MEOW! MEOW!

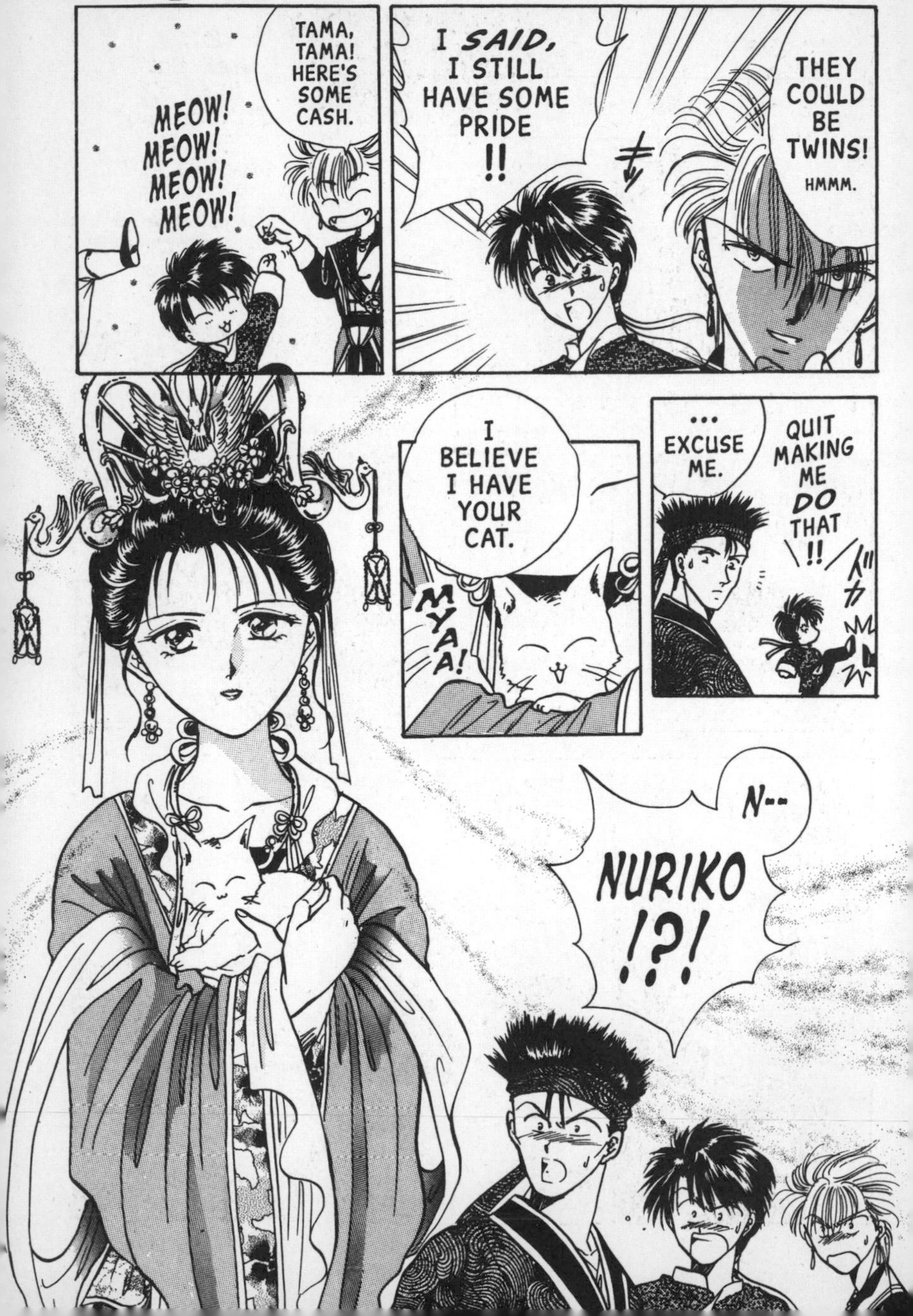
I SAID, I STILL HAVE SOME PRIDE !!
THEY COULD BE TWINS!
HMMM.
TAMA, TAMA! HERE'S SOME CASH.
MEOW! MEOW! MEOW! MEOW!
... EXCUSE ME.
QUIT MAKING ME DO THAT !!
I BELIEVE I HAVE YOUR CAT.
MYAA!
N--
NURIKO !?!

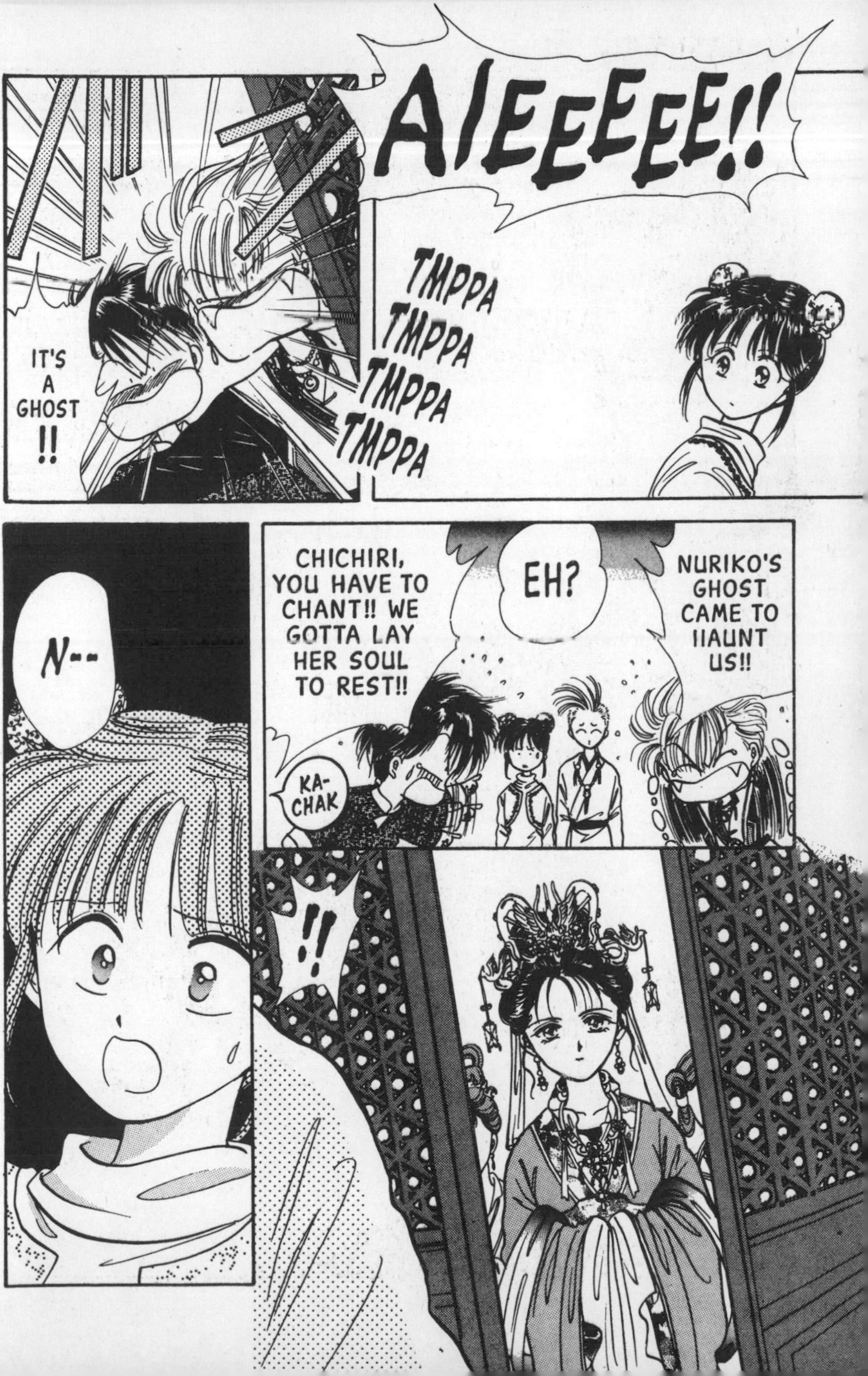

IT'S A GHOST !!
AIEEEEE!!
TMPPA TMPPA TMPPA TMPPA
CHICHIRI, YOU HAVE TO CHANT!! WE GOTTA LAY HER SOUL TO REST!!
EH?
NURIKO'S GHOST CAME TO HAUNT US!!
KA-CHAK
N--
!!

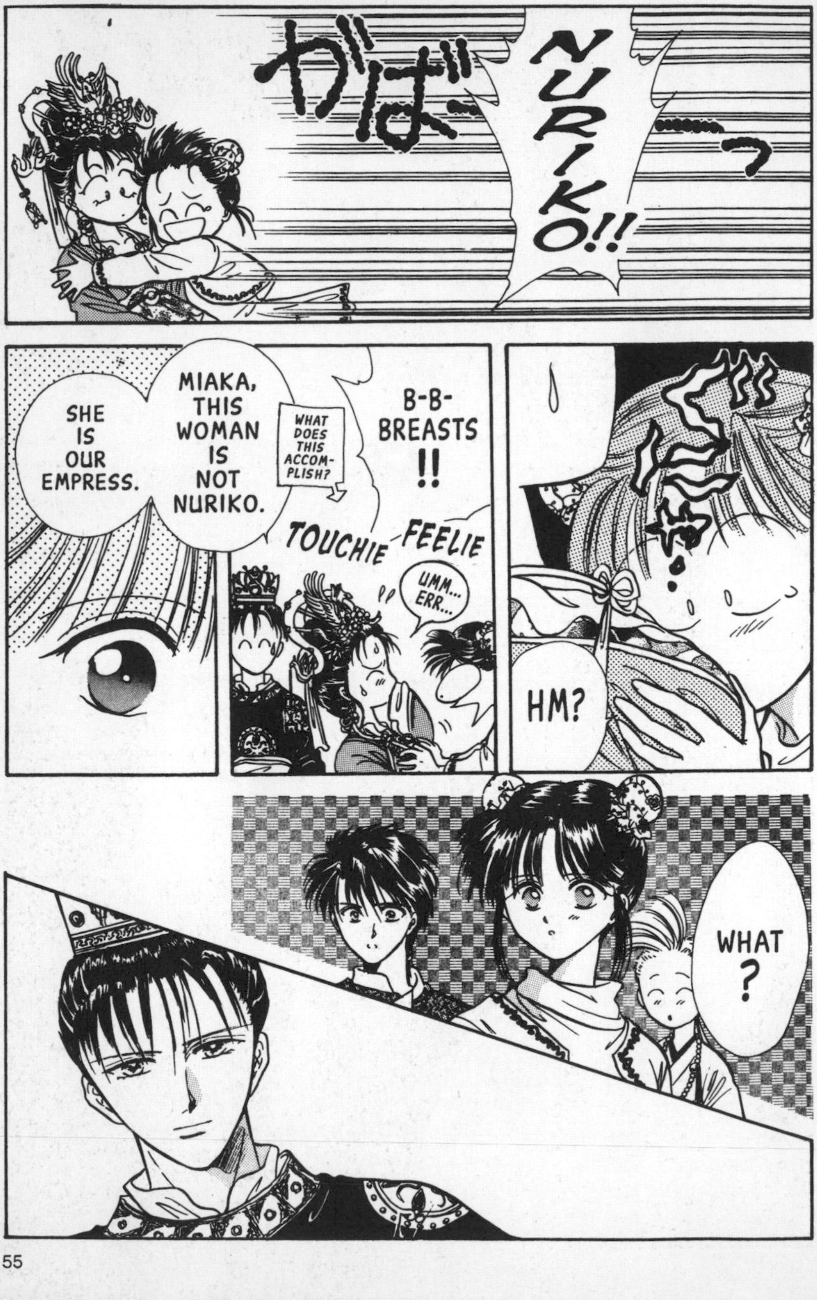

がばー
NURIKO!!
HM?
B-B-BREASTS!!
WHAT DOES THIS ACCOMPLISH?
TOUCHIE FEELIE
UMM... ERR...
MIAKA, THIS WOMAN IS NOT NURIKO.
SHE IS OUR EMPRESS.
WHAT?

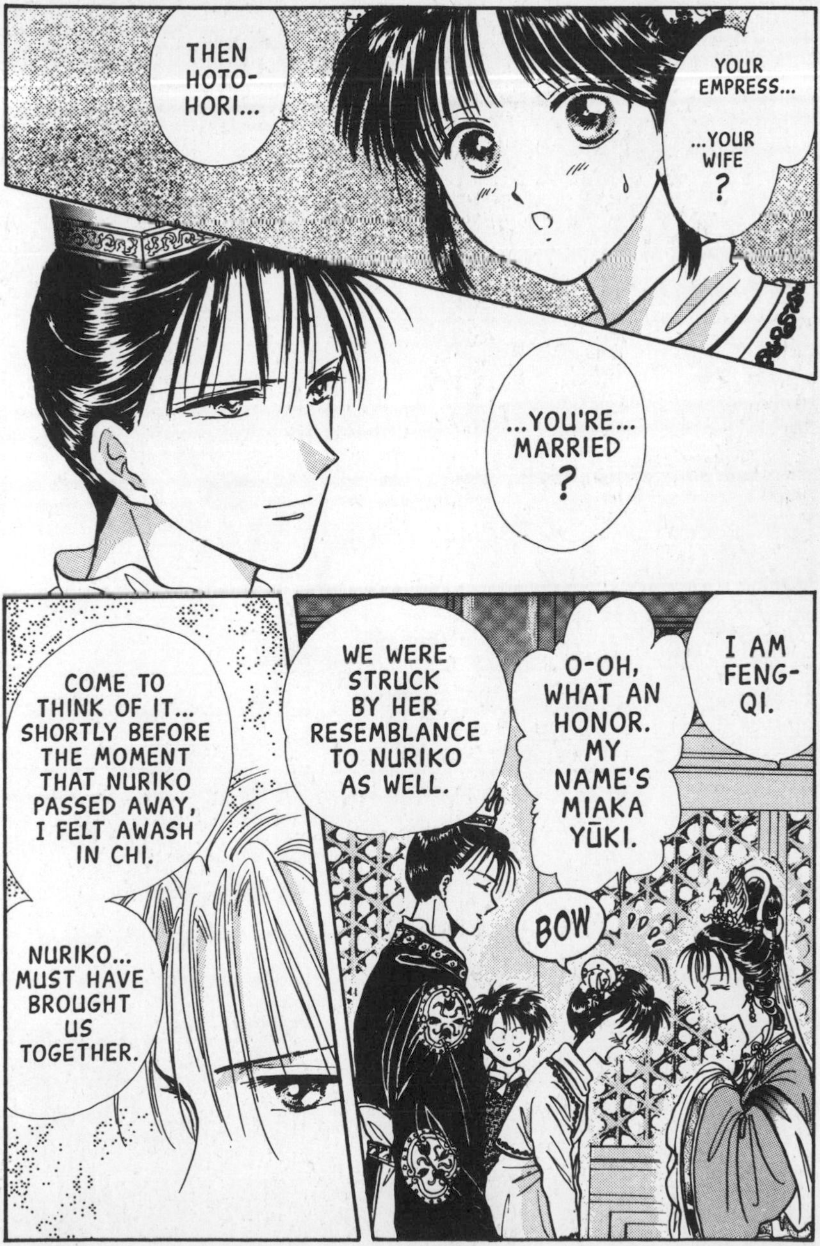
YOUR EMPRESS...
...YOUR WIFE ?
THEN HOTO-HORI...
...YOU'RE... MARRIED ?
I AM FENG-QI.
O-OH, WHAT AN HONOR. MY NAME'S MIAKA YŪKI.
BOW
WE WERE STRUCK BY HER RESEMBLANCE TO NURIKO AS WELL.
COME TO THINK OF IT... SHORTLY BEFORE THE MOMENT THAT NURIKO PASSED AWAY, I FELT AWASH IN CHI.
NURIKO... MUST HAVE BROUGHT US TOGETHER.

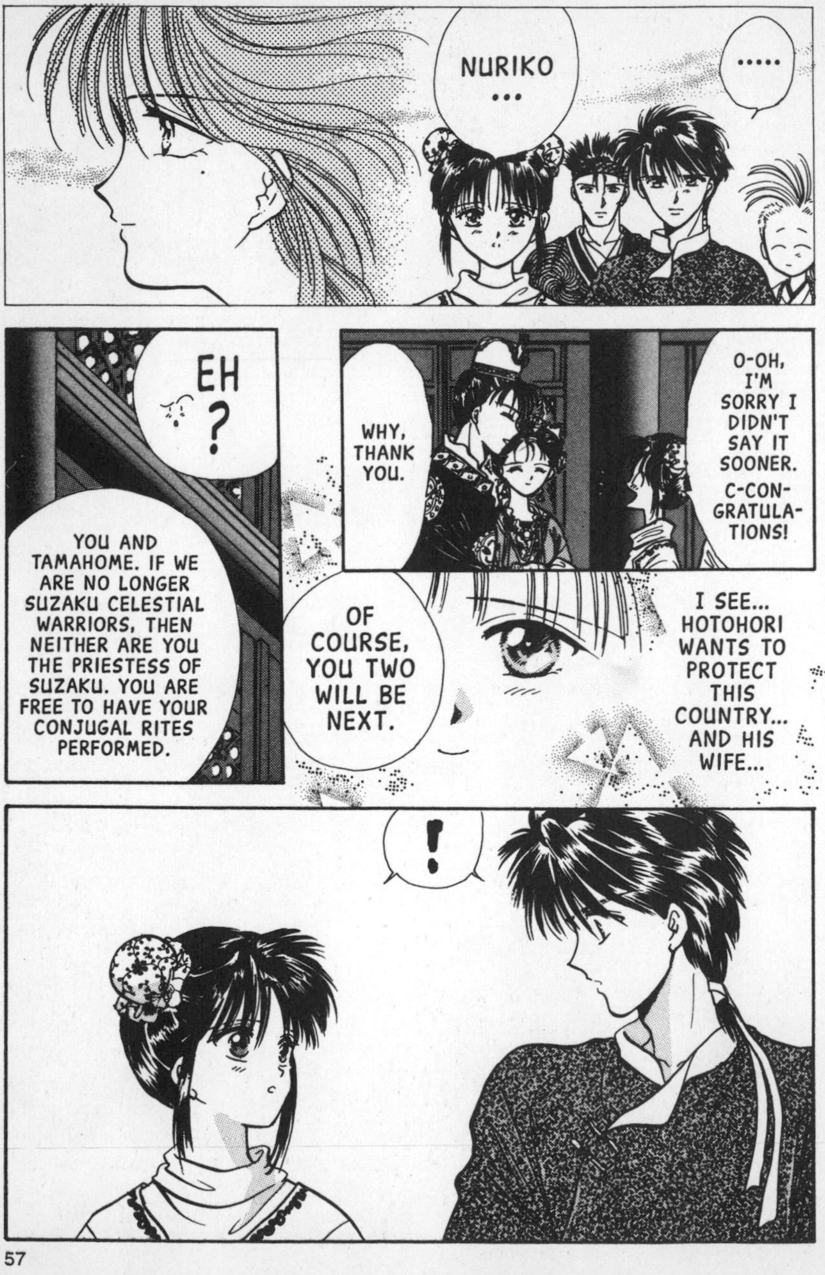
.....
NURIKO ...
O-OH, I'M SORRY I DIDN'T SAY IT SOONER. C-CONGRATULATIONS!
WHY, THANK YOU.
I SEE... HOTOHORI WANTS TO PROTECT THIS COUNTRY... AND HIS WIFE...
OF COURSE, YOU TWO WILL BE NEXT.
EH ?
YOU AND TAMAHOME. IF WE ARE NO LONGER SUZAKU CELESTIAL WARRIORS, THEN NEITHER ARE YOU THE PRIESTESS OF SUZAKU. YOU ARE FREE TO HAVE YOUR CONJUGAL RITES PERFORMED.
!

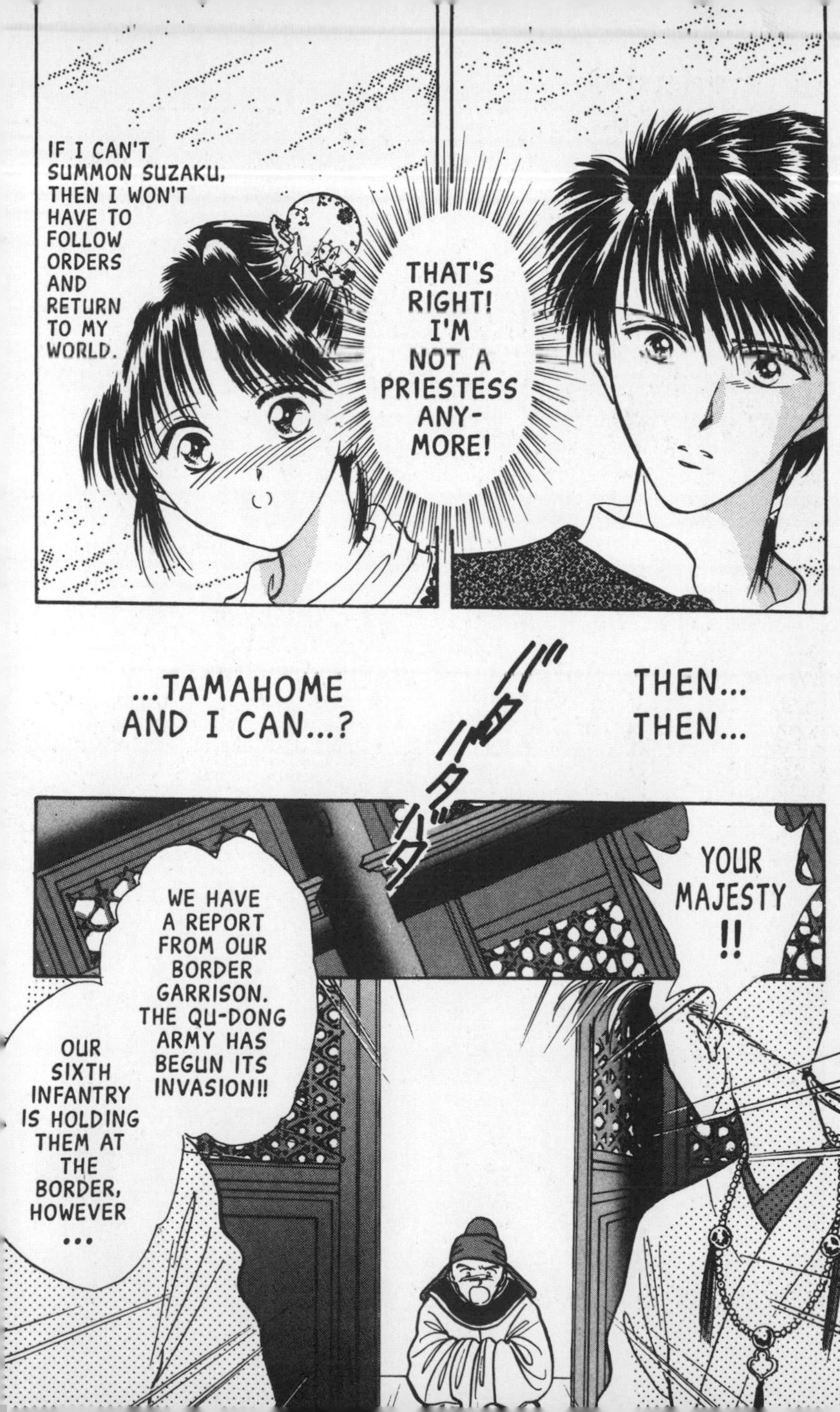
IF I CAN'T SUMMON SUZAKU, THEN I WON'T HAVE TO FOLLOW ORDERS AND RETURN TO MY WORLD.
THAT'S RIGHT! I'M NOT A PRIESTESS ANY-MORE!
THEN... THEN...
...TAMAHOME AND I CAN...?
YOUR MAJESTY !!
WE HAVE A REPORT FROM OUR BORDER GARRISON. THE QU-DONG ARMY HAS BEGUN ITS INVASION!!
OUR SIXTH INFANTRY IS HOLDING THEM AT THE BORDER, HOWEVER ...

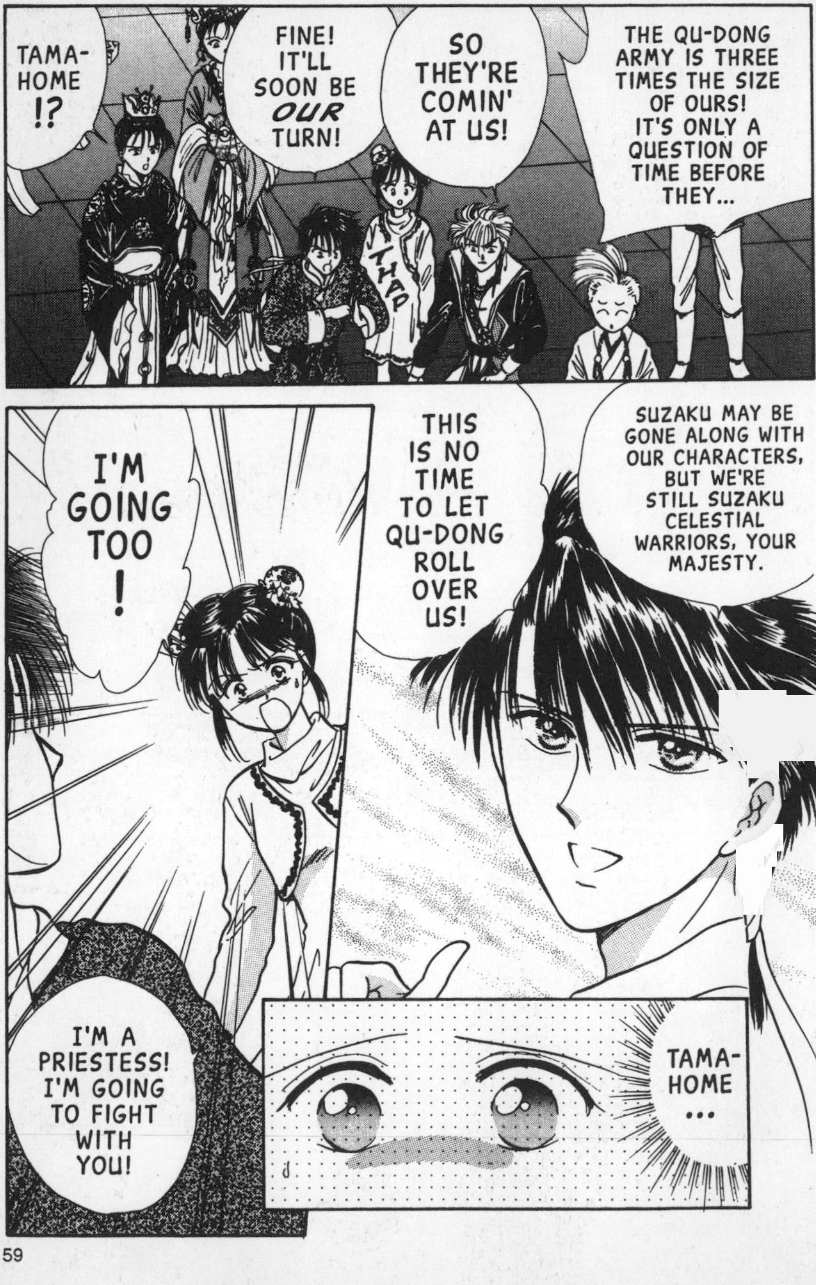
THE QU-DONG ARMY IS THREE TIMES THE SIZE OF OURS! IT'S ONLY A QUESTION OF TIME BEFORE THEY...
SO THEY'RE COMIN' AT US!
FINE! IT'LL SOON BE *OUR* TURN!
THAP
TAMA-HOME !?
SUZAKU MAY BE GONE ALONG WITH OUR CHARACTERS, BUT WE'RE STILL SUZAKU CELESTIAL WARRIORS, YOUR MAJESTY.
THIS IS NO TIME TO LET QU-DONG ROLL OVER US!
TAMA-HOME ...
I'M GOING TOO !
I'M A PRIESTESS! I'M GOING TO FIGHT WITH YOU!

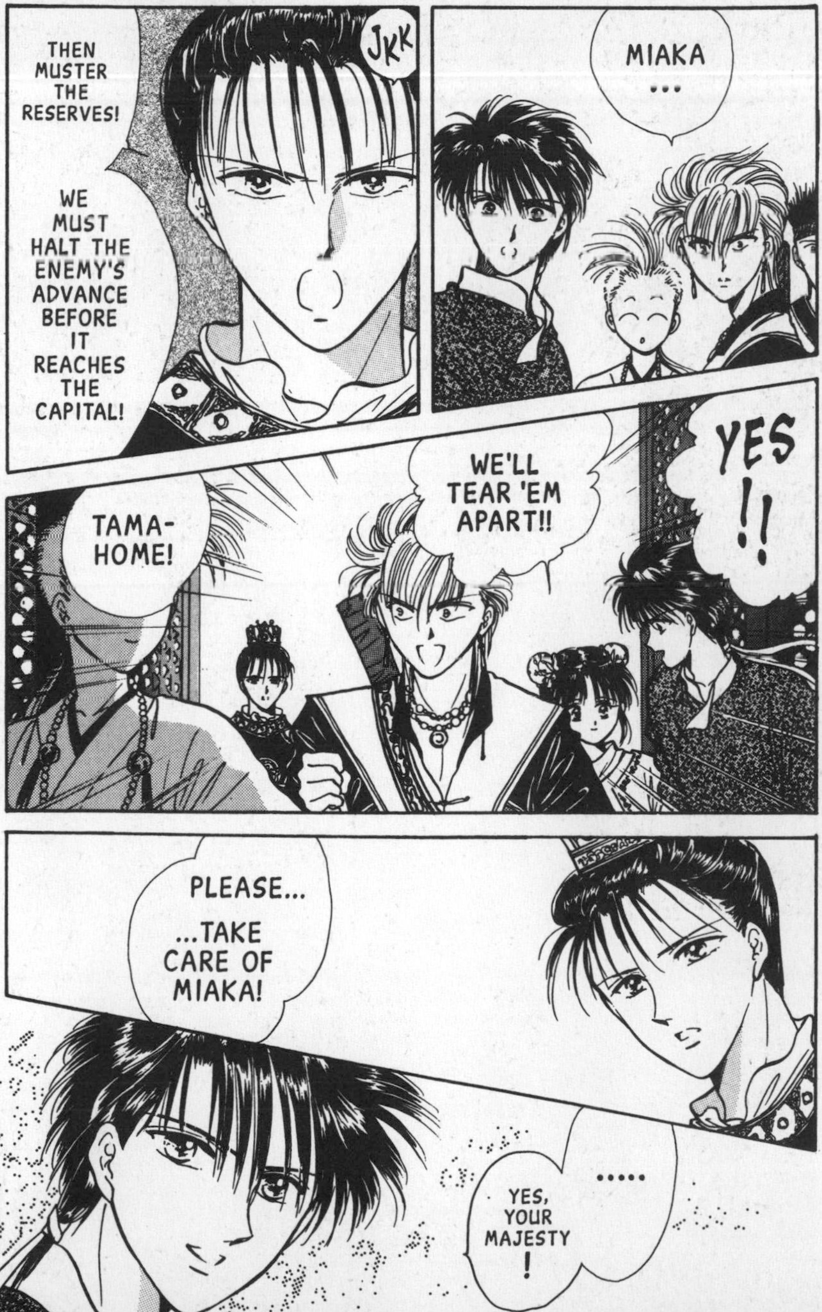
MIAKA ...
JKK
THEN MUSTER THE RESERVES!
WE MUST HALT THE ENEMY'S ADVANCE BEFORE IT REACHES THE CAPITAL!
YES !!
WE'LL TEAR 'EM APART!!
TAMA-HOME!
PLEASE... ...TAKE CARE OF MIAKA!
.....
YES, YOUR MAJESTY !

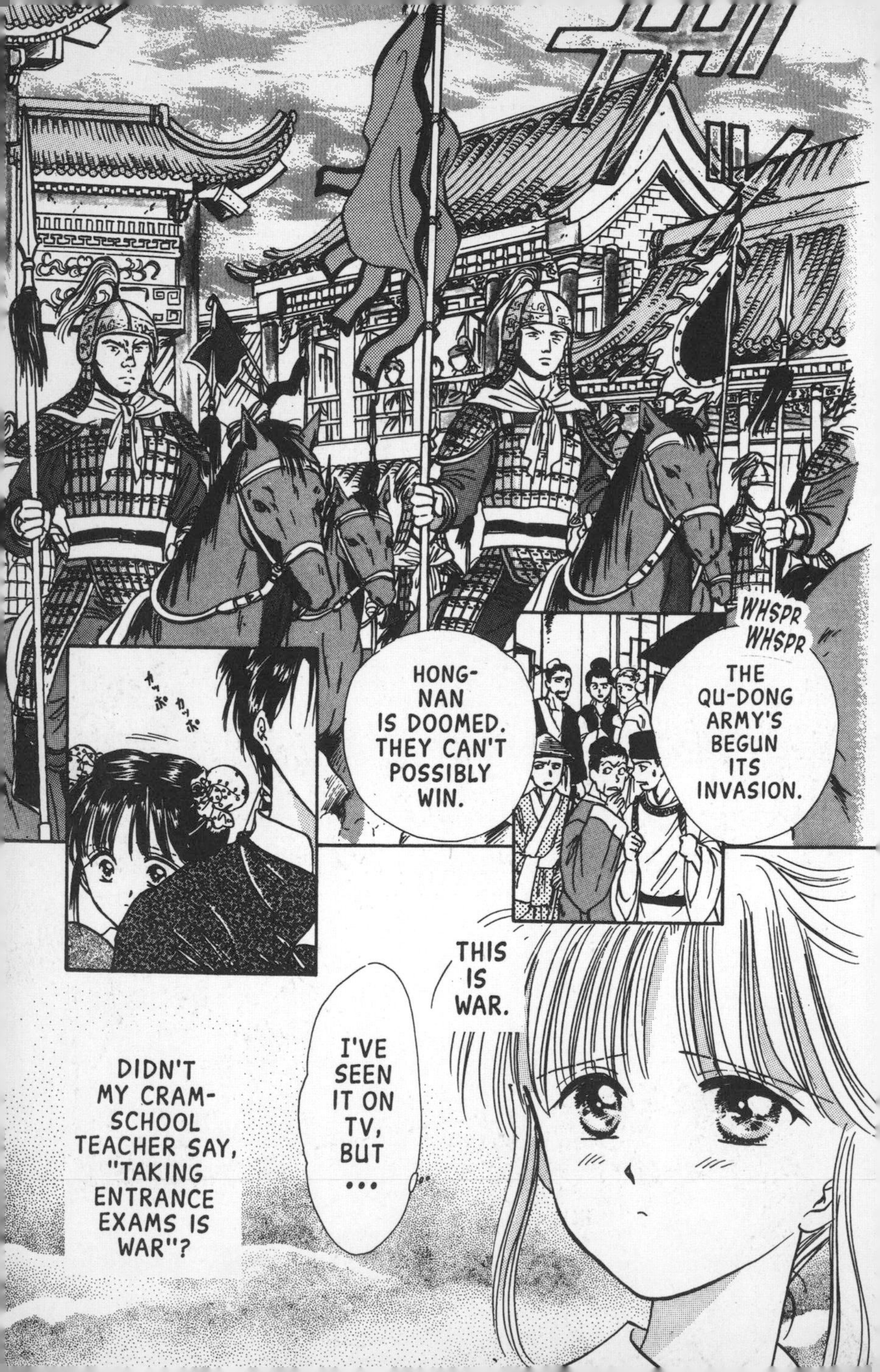
WHSPR WHSPR
THE QU-DONG ARMY'S BEGUN ITS INVASION.
HONG-NAN IS DOOMED. THEY CAN'T POSSIBLY WIN.
THIS IS WAR.
I'VE SEEN IT ON TV, BUT...
DIDN'T MY CRAM-SCHOOL TEACHER SAY, "TAKING ENTRANCE EXAMS IS WAR"?

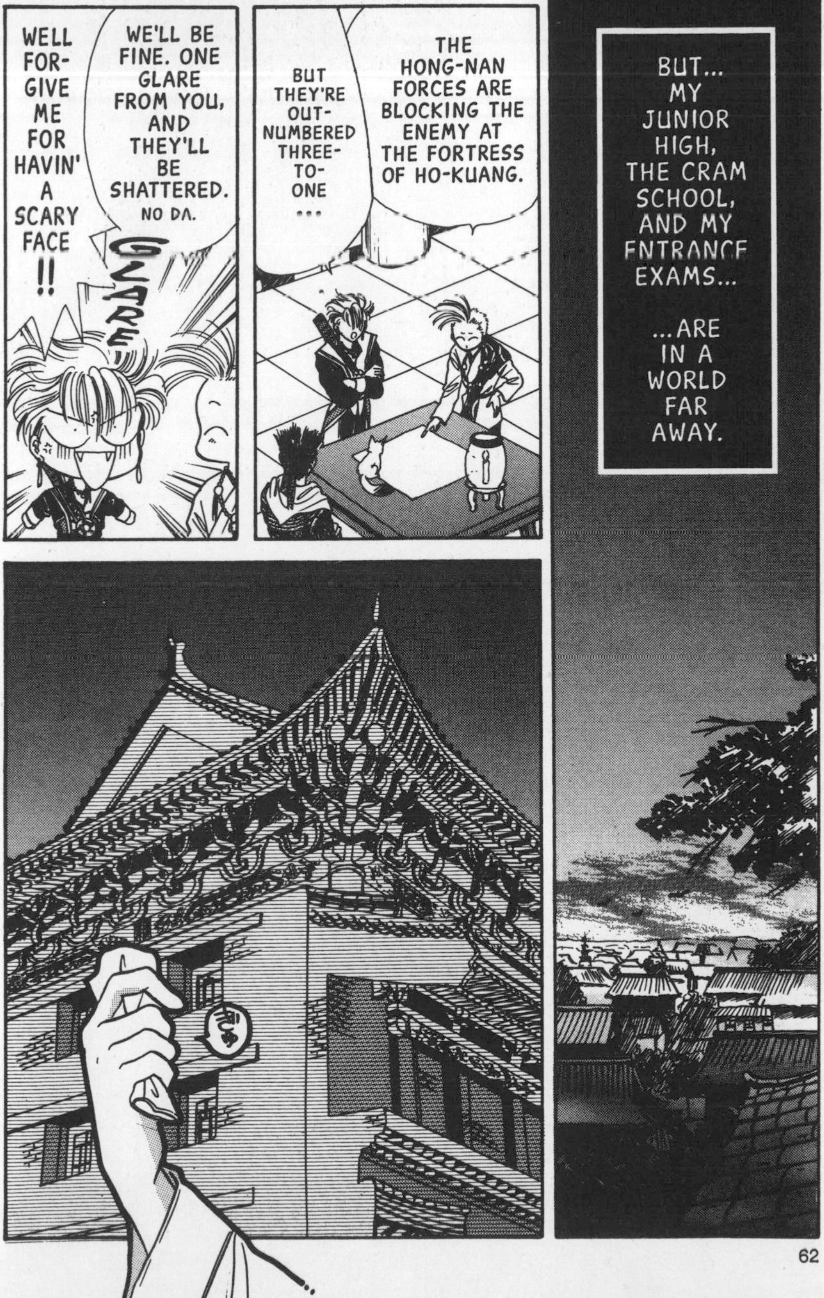
BUT... MY JUNIOR HIGH, THE CRAM SCHOOL, AND MY ENTRANCE EXAMS...
...ARE IN A WORLD FAR AWAY.
THE HONG-NAN FORCES ARE BLOCKING THE ENEMY AT THE FORTRESS OF HO-KUANG.
BUT THEY'RE OUT-NUMBERED THREE-TO-ONE ...
WE'LL BE FINE. ONE GLARE FROM YOU, AND THEY'LL BE SHATTERED. NO DA.
WELL FOR-GIVE ME FOR HAVIN' A SCARY FACE !!
GLARE

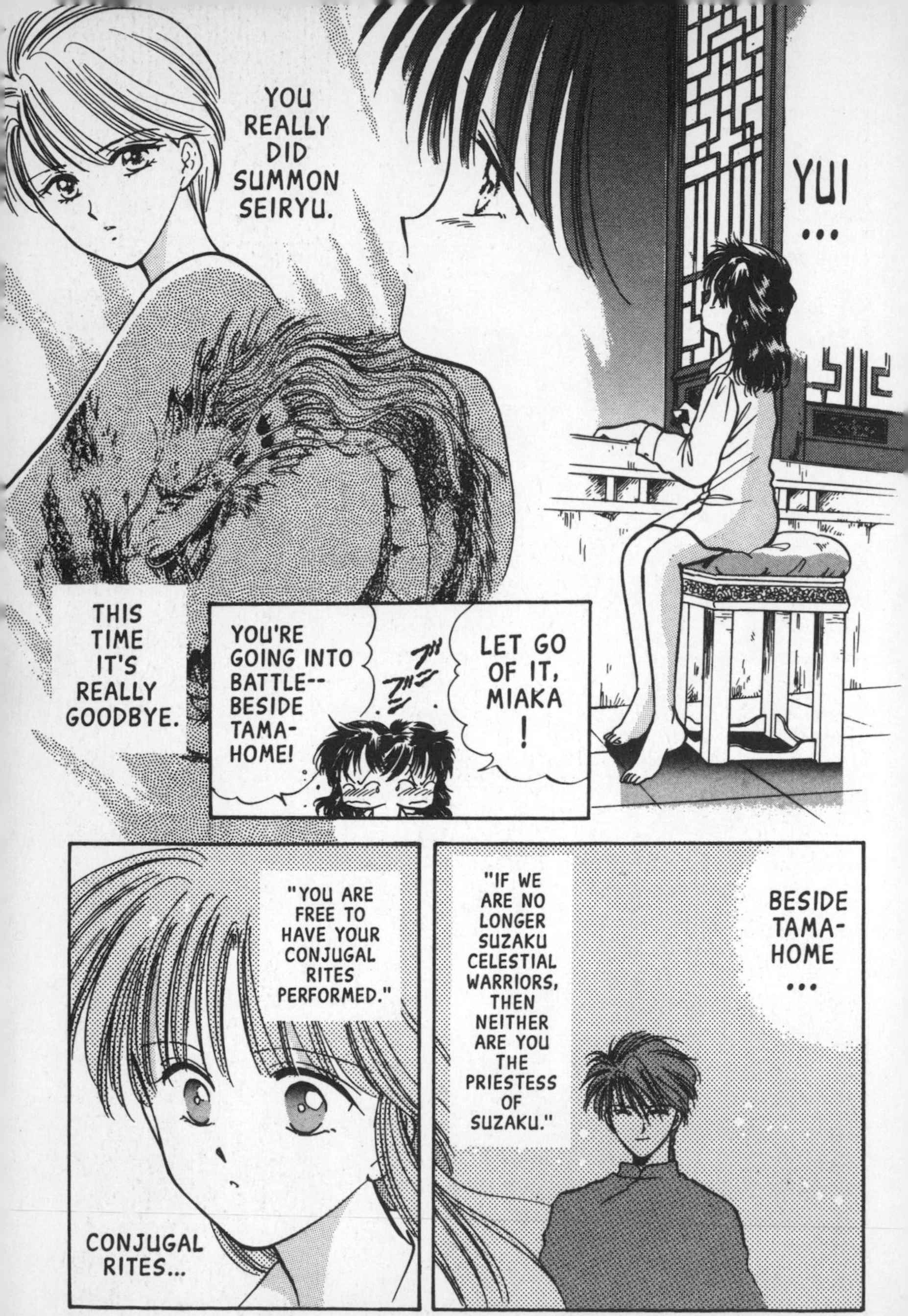
YUI...
YOU REALLY DID SUMMON SEIRYU.
THIS TIME IT'S REALLY GOODBYE.
LET GO OF IT, MIAKA!
YOU'RE GOING INTO BATTLE--BESIDE TAMA-HOME!
BESIDE TAMA-HOME...
"IF WE ARE NO LONGER SUZAKU CELESTIAL WARRIORS, THEN NEITHER ARE YOU THE PRIESTESS OF SUZAKU."
"YOU ARE FREE TO HAVE YOUR CONJUGAL RITES PERFORMED."
CONJUGAL RITES...

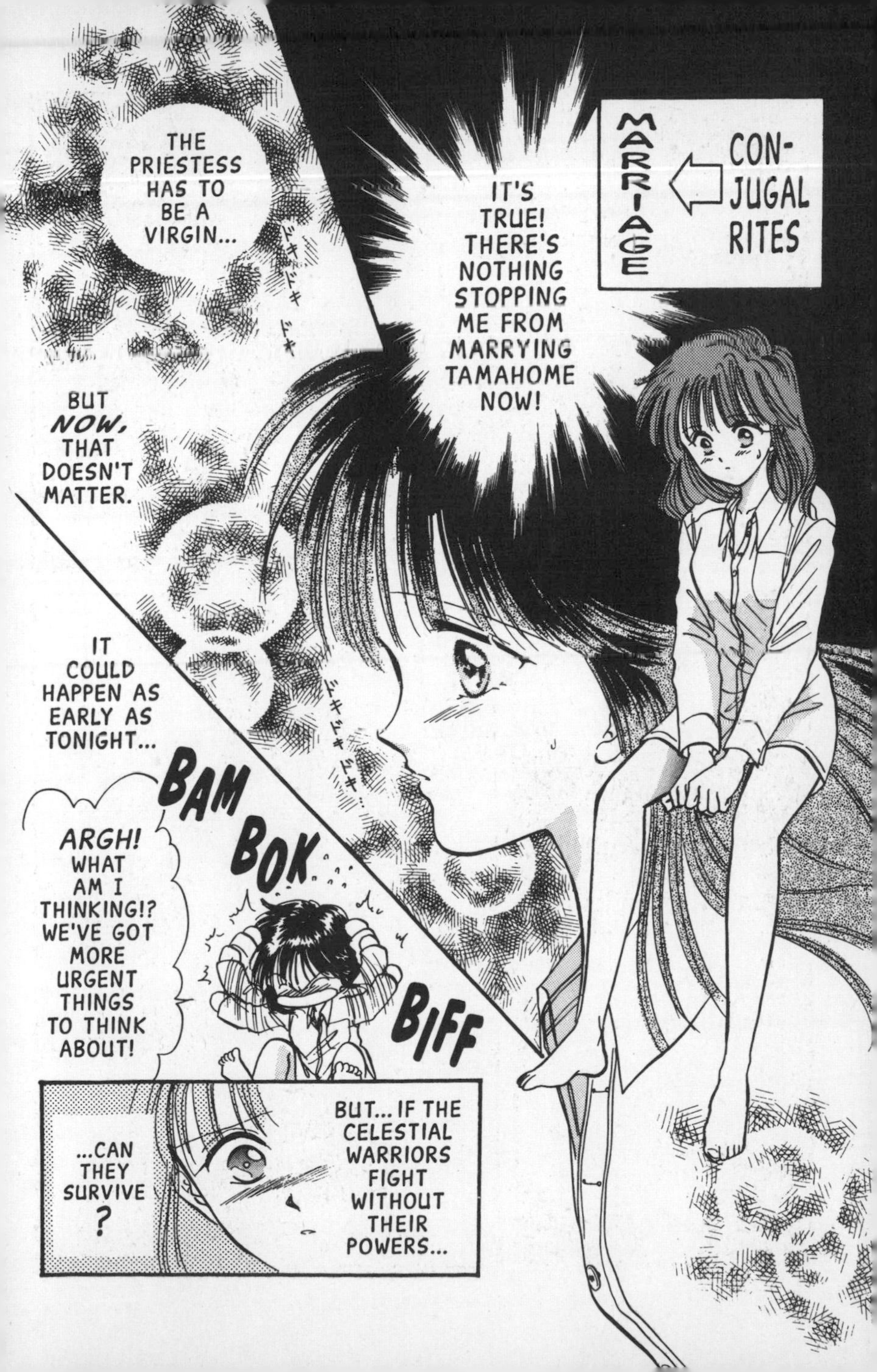
MARRIAGE
CON-JUGAL RITES
IT'S TRUE! THERE'S NOTHING STOPPING ME FROM MARRYING TAMAHOME NOW!
THE PRIESTESS HAS TO BE A VIRGIN...
ドキドキ ドキ
BUT *NOW,* THAT DOESN'T MATTER.
IT COULD HAPPEN AS EARLY AS TONIGHT...
ドキドキドキ...
BAM
BOK
BIFF
ARGH! WHAT AM I THINKING!? WE'VE GOT MORE URGENT THINGS TO THINK ABOUT!
BUT... IF THE CELESTIAL WARRIORS FIGHT WITHOUT THEIR POWERS...
...CAN THEY SURVIVE?

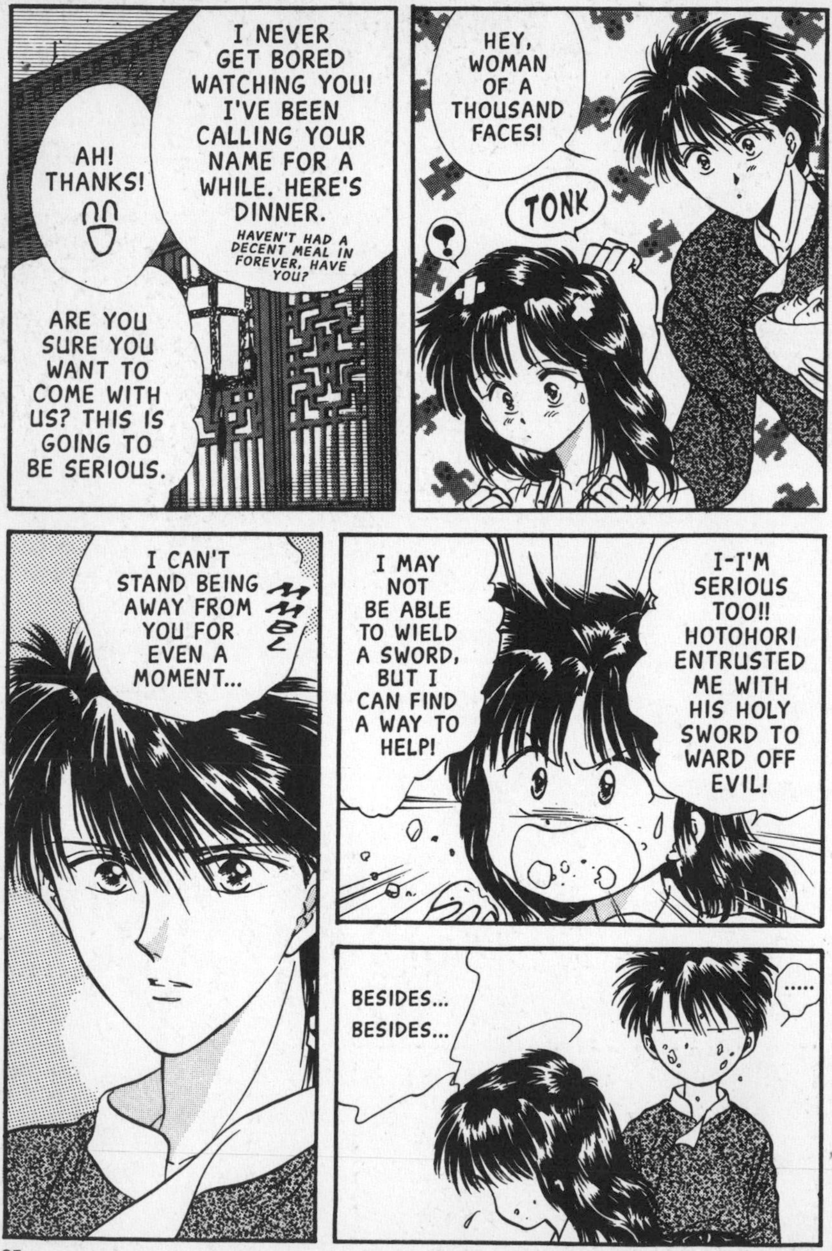
HEY, WOMAN OF A THOUSAND FACES!
TONK
?
I NEVER GET BORED WATCHING YOU! I'VE BEEN CALLING YOUR NAME FOR A WHILE. HERE'S DINNER.
HAVEN'T HAD A DECENT MEAL IN FOREVER, HAVE YOU?
AH! THANKS!
ARE YOU SURE YOU WANT TO COME WITH US? THIS IS GOING TO BE SERIOUS.
I-I'M SERIOUS TOO!! HOTOHORI ENTRUSTED ME WITH HIS HOLY SWORD TO WARD OFF EVIL!
I MAY NOT BE ABLE TO WIELD A SWORD, BUT I CAN FIND A WAY TO HELP!
.....
BESIDES... BESIDES...
I CAN'T STAND BEING AWAY FROM YOU FOR EVEN A MOMENT...
MMBL

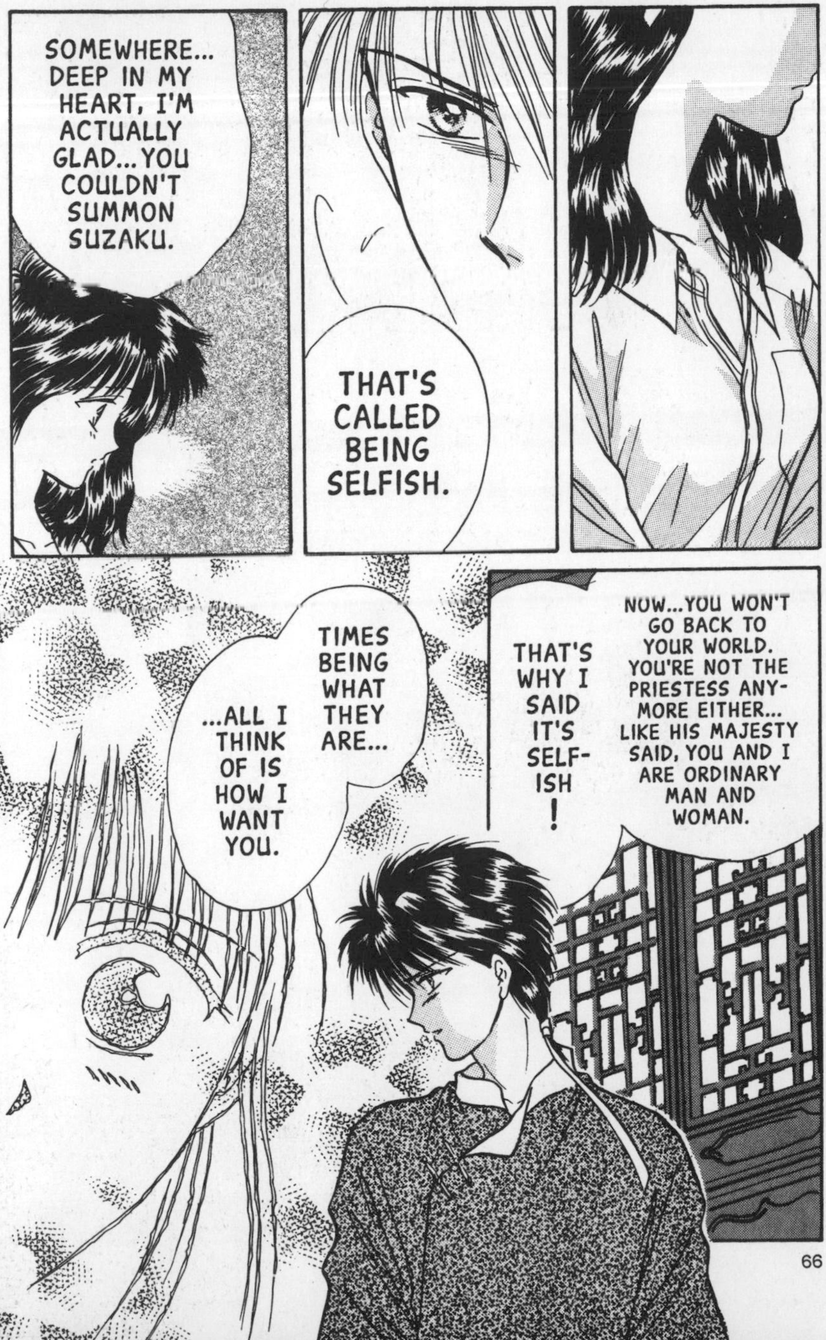
SOMEWHERE... DEEP IN MY HEART, I'M ACTUALLY GLAD... YOU COULDN'T SUMMON SUZAKU.
THAT'S CALLED BEING SELFISH.
NOW... YOU WON'T GO BACK TO YOUR WORLD. YOU'RE NOT THE PRIESTESS ANY-MORE EITHER... LIKE HIS MAJESTY SAID, YOU AND I ARE ORDINARY MAN AND WOMAN.
THAT'S WHY I SAID IT'S SELF-ISH!
TIMES BEING WHAT THEY ARE...
...ALL I THINK OF IS HOW I WANT YOU.

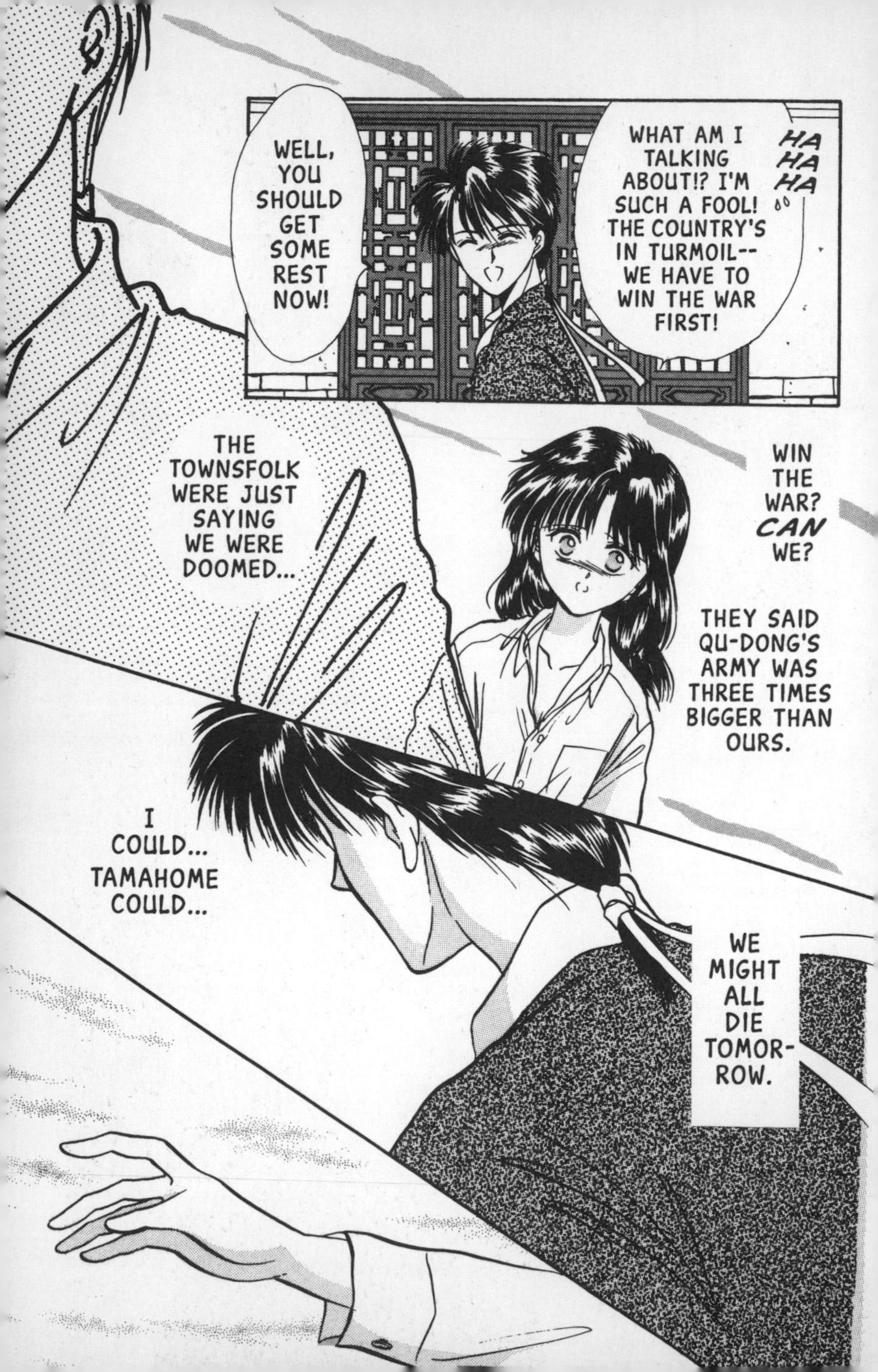

WHAT AM I TALKING ABOUT!? I'M SUCH A FOOL! THE COUNTRY'S IN TURMOIL-- WE HAVE TO WIN THE WAR FIRST!
HA HA HA
WELL, YOU SHOULD GET SOME REST NOW!
WIN THE WAR? CAN WE?
THE TOWNSFOLK WERE JUST SAYING WE WERE DOOMED...
THEY SAID QU-DONG'S ARMY WAS THREE TIMES BIGGER THAN OURS.
WE MIGHT ALL DIE TOMOR-ROW.
I COULD... TAMAHOME COULD...

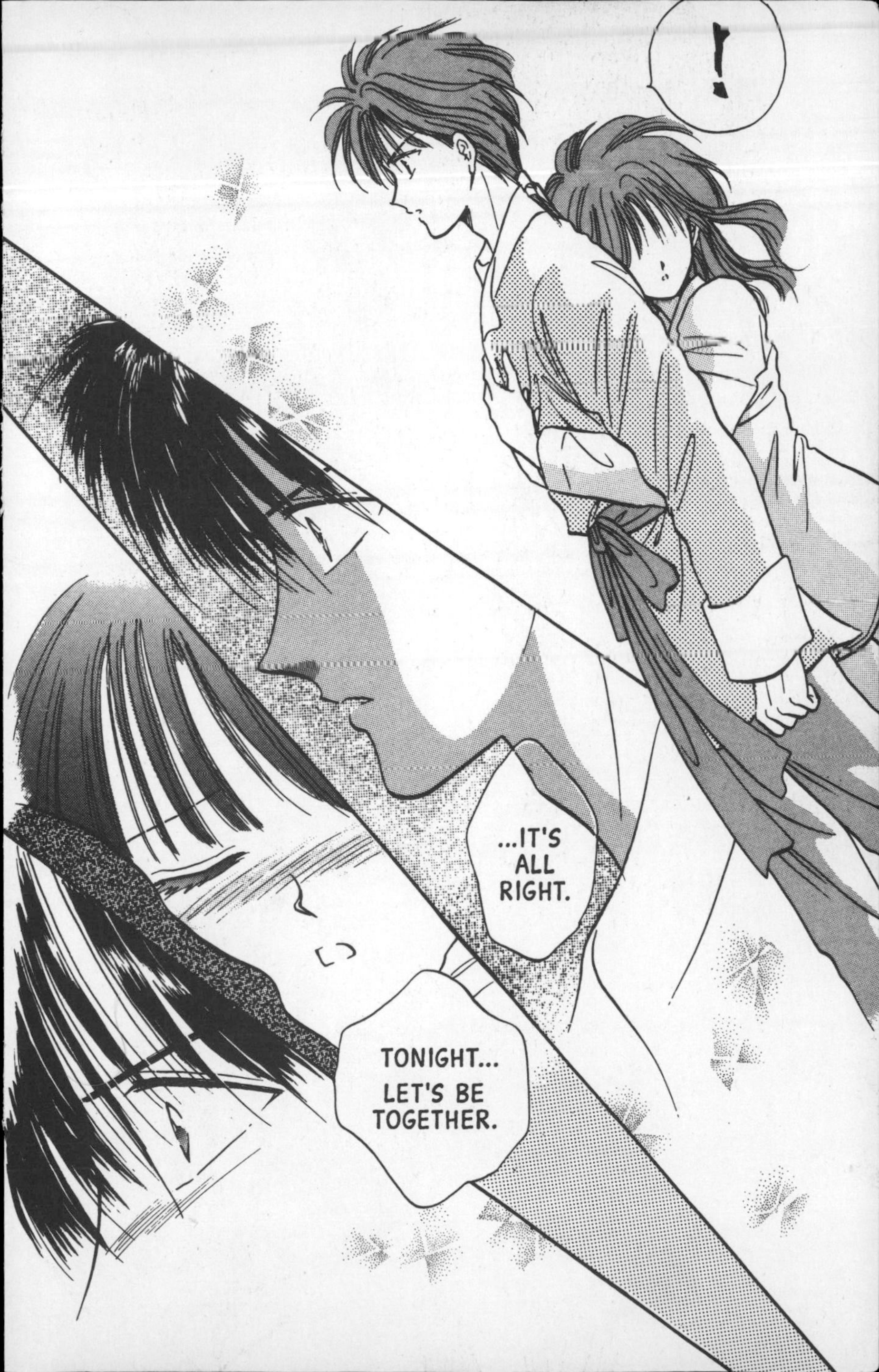
!
...IT'S ALL RIGHT.
TONIGHT... LET'S BE TOGETHER.

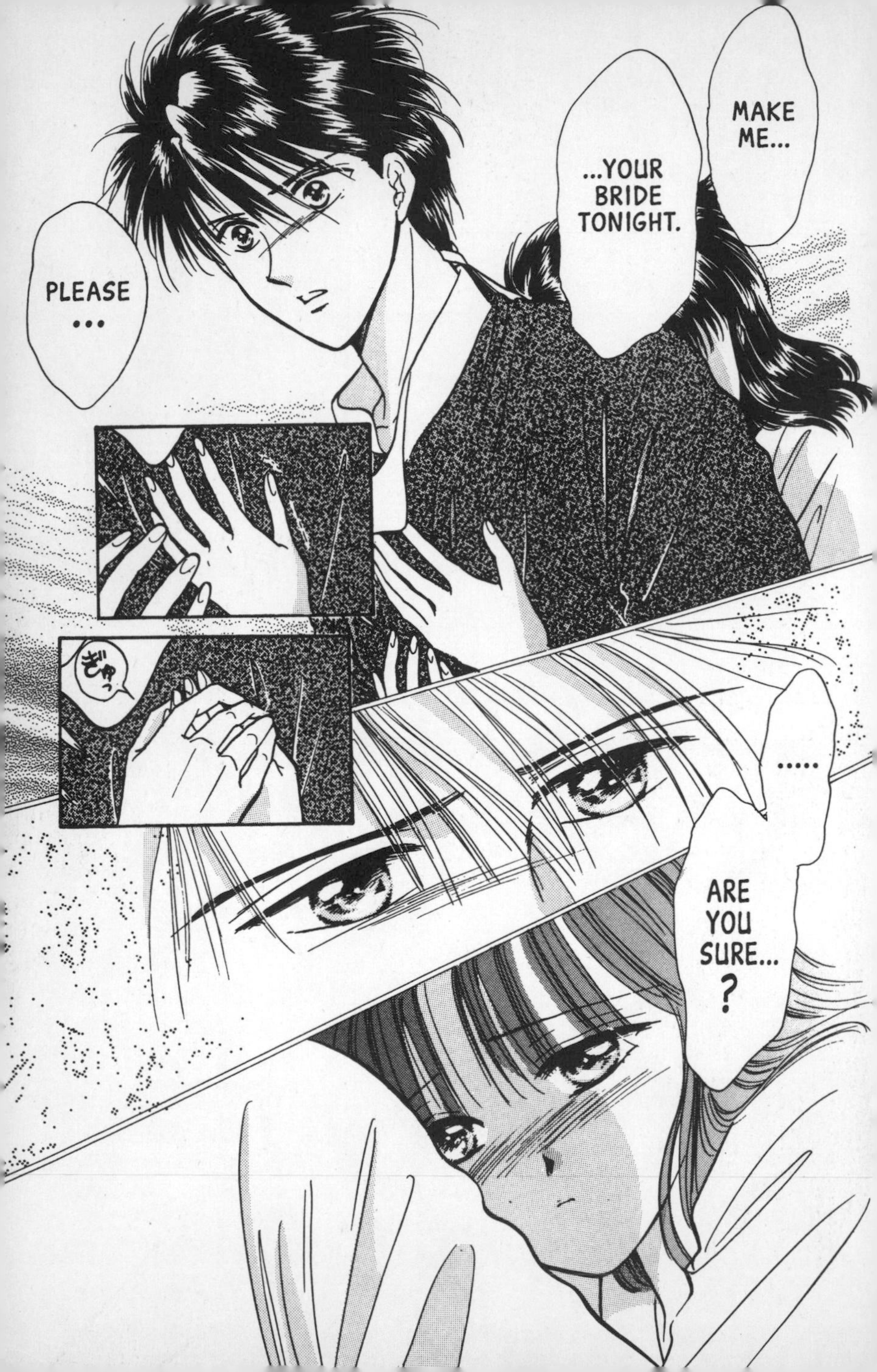
MAKE ME...
...YOUR BRIDE TONIGHT.
PLEASE ...
ぎゅっ
.....
ARE YOU SURE... ?

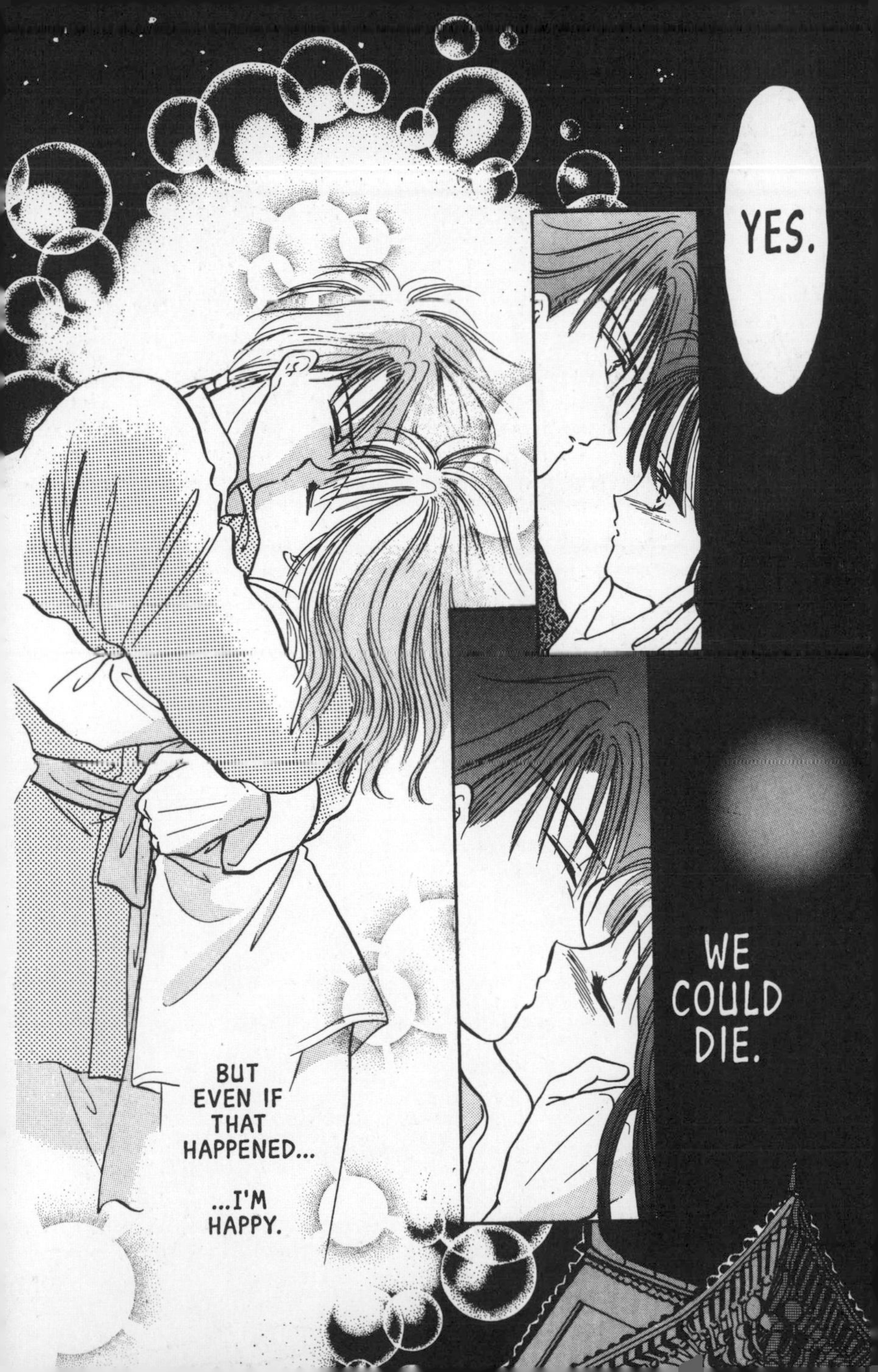
YES.
WE COULD DIE.
BUT EVEN IF THAT HAPPENED...
...I'M HAPPY.

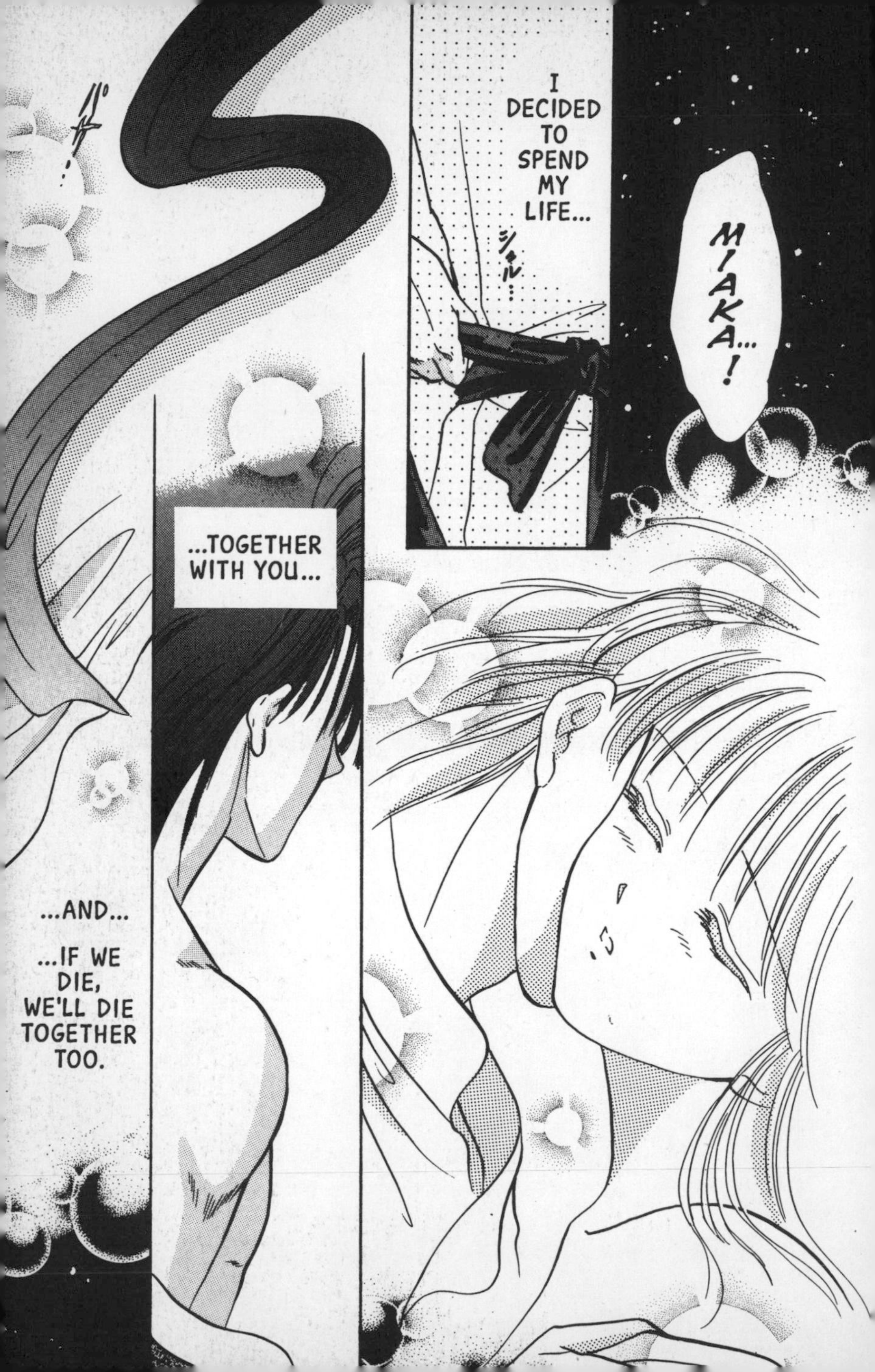
MIAKA...!
I DECIDED TO SPEND MY LIFE...
シュル…
...TOGETHER WITH YOU...
パサ…
...AND...
...IF WE DIE, WE'LL DIE TOGETHER TOO.

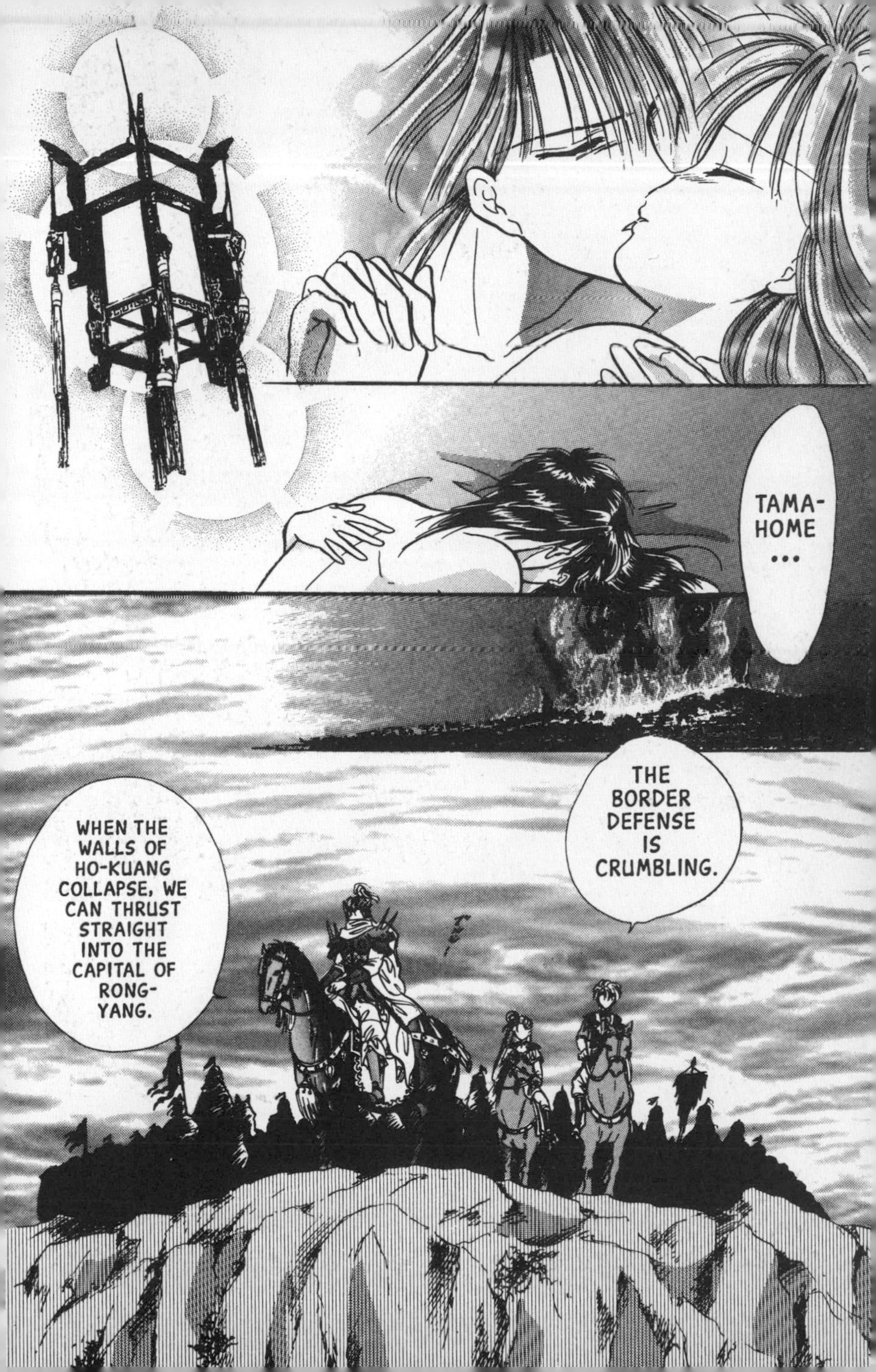
TAMA-
HOME
...
THE
BORDER
DEFENSE
IS
CRUMBLING.
WHEN THE
WALLS OF
HO-KUANG
COLLAPSE, WE
CAN THRUST
STRAIGHT
INTO THE
CAPITAL OF
RONG-
YANG.

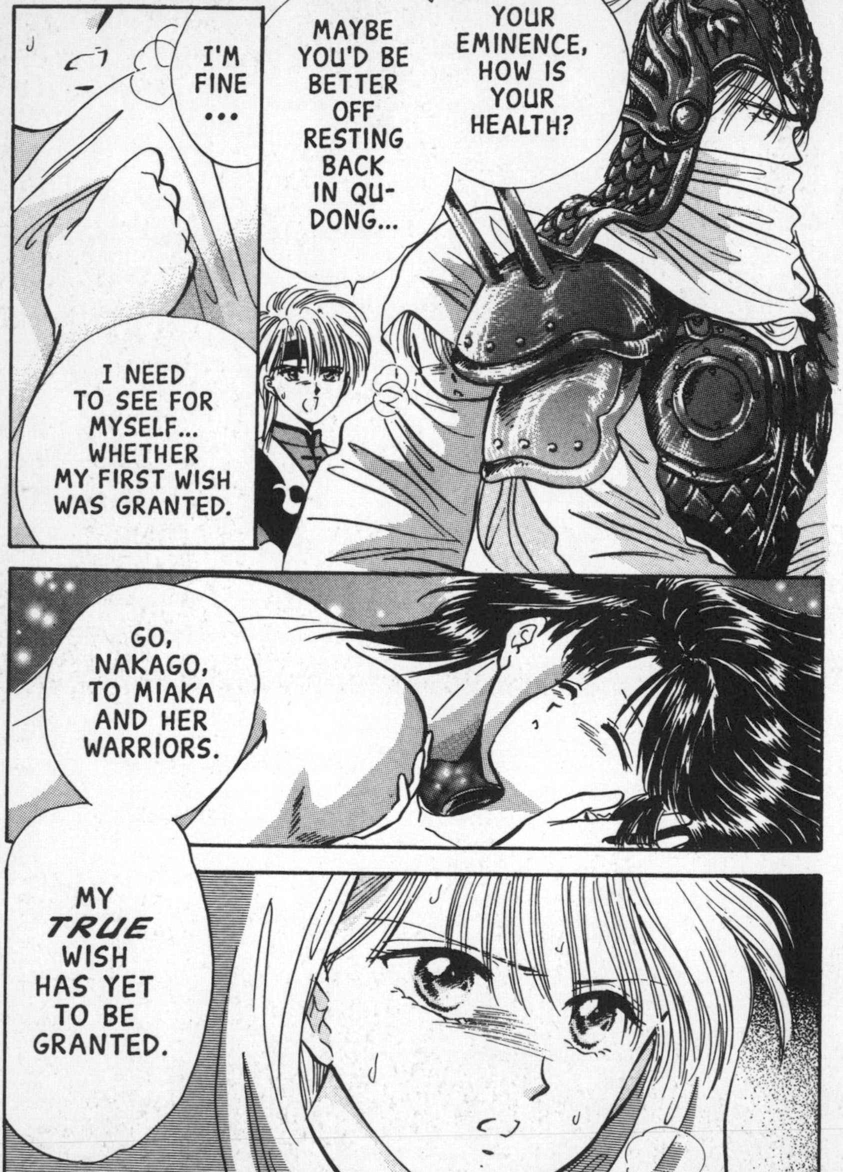
YOUR EMINENCE, HOW IS YOUR HEALTH?
MAYBE YOU'D BE BETTER OFF RESTING BACK IN QU-DONG...
I'M FINE ...
I NEED TO SEE FOR MYSELF... WHETHER MY FIRST WISH WAS GRANTED.
GO, NAKAGO, TO MIAKA AND HER WARRIORS.
MY *TRUE* WISH HAS YET TO BE GRANTED.

FUSHIGI YŪGI'S "?" PART 4

Q1: Are the celestial warriors' Chinese characters (kanji) always visible on their skin?

A: Not always. They show up when the warrior's chi is elevated. Once they're used to using their chi, they can make it appear by their own will. By the way, the colors for the celestial warriors' characters are also symbolic, Suzaku's being red and Seiryu's blue. Also, the font changed to *sōshotai* ("grass writing") after the warriors powered up. (I changed it 'cause it looks cool!)

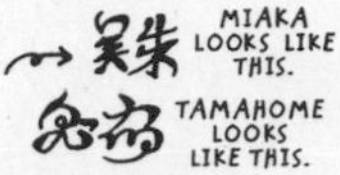
MIAKA LOOKS LIKE THIS.
TAMAHOME LOOKS LIKE THIS.

Q2: How does time pass for Miaka and Yui in the book? Are they growing up?

A: Time moves at the same rate for them as it does in the real world. Even if the characters in the book age over the course of many years, if it's only been a couple days in the real world, that's all that Miaka and Yui age. So having a change of clothes and underwear isn't that crucial for the girls, because in reality, they're only wearing their clothes for a couple days. So, "that time of the month" isn't an issue, either. If they'd spent a hundred years in the book, then maybe the day would come in the real world, but... Tamahome would be an old man by then.

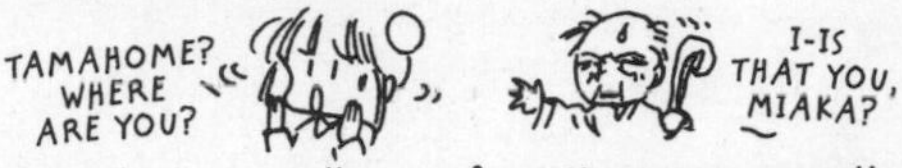
TAMAHOME? WHERE ARE YOU?
I-IS THAT YOU, MIAKA?

Q3: How is it that the celestial warriors all come from the same generation? Aren't there any who've died or ones that haven't been born yet?

A: It's destiny. (Quite simply.) There wouldn't be much point in them being so scattered over generations. The appearance of the Priestess would lose its significance. The Priestess and celestial warriors have a group destiny.

Q4: Did Tasuki ever have a girlfriend?

A: No. His older sisters picked on him, so he left, yelling, "I'm outta here!" and became a woman-hating delinquent. But he has had experience with women. As a bandit, he had to "take the pressure off," and so he has been to the pleasure quarters with Knei-Gong.

Q5: Why doesn't Tai Yi-Jun show up on the Seiryu side?

A: Tai Yi-Jun (the Emperor of the Heavens) imparts wisdom to celestial warriors, but this isn't the case with the Seiryu because they've allied themselves with the demon worshipped by Nakago. Just as Tai Yi-Jun claimed, the beautiful Daichi-san Mountain only appears like a barren rocky bluff when the wicked see it. Those with negative chi cannot even discern the existence of Tai Yi-Jun. By the way, Tai Yi-Jun assumes the guise of an old woman for humans.

Q6: Warning from a Nuriko fan! Many of her drawings are missing her mole!!

A: The moles were lost in the printing process because they were so small. I made sure she always had one in the original art. Also, there's a typographical error for Suboshi (in the Japanese original) where the word "*masaka*" ("that can't be") was mistakenly spelled "*mamaka*." This occurred in the layout process -- I wrote them correctly in the original. So please let those slide.

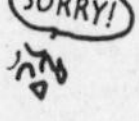
SORRY!

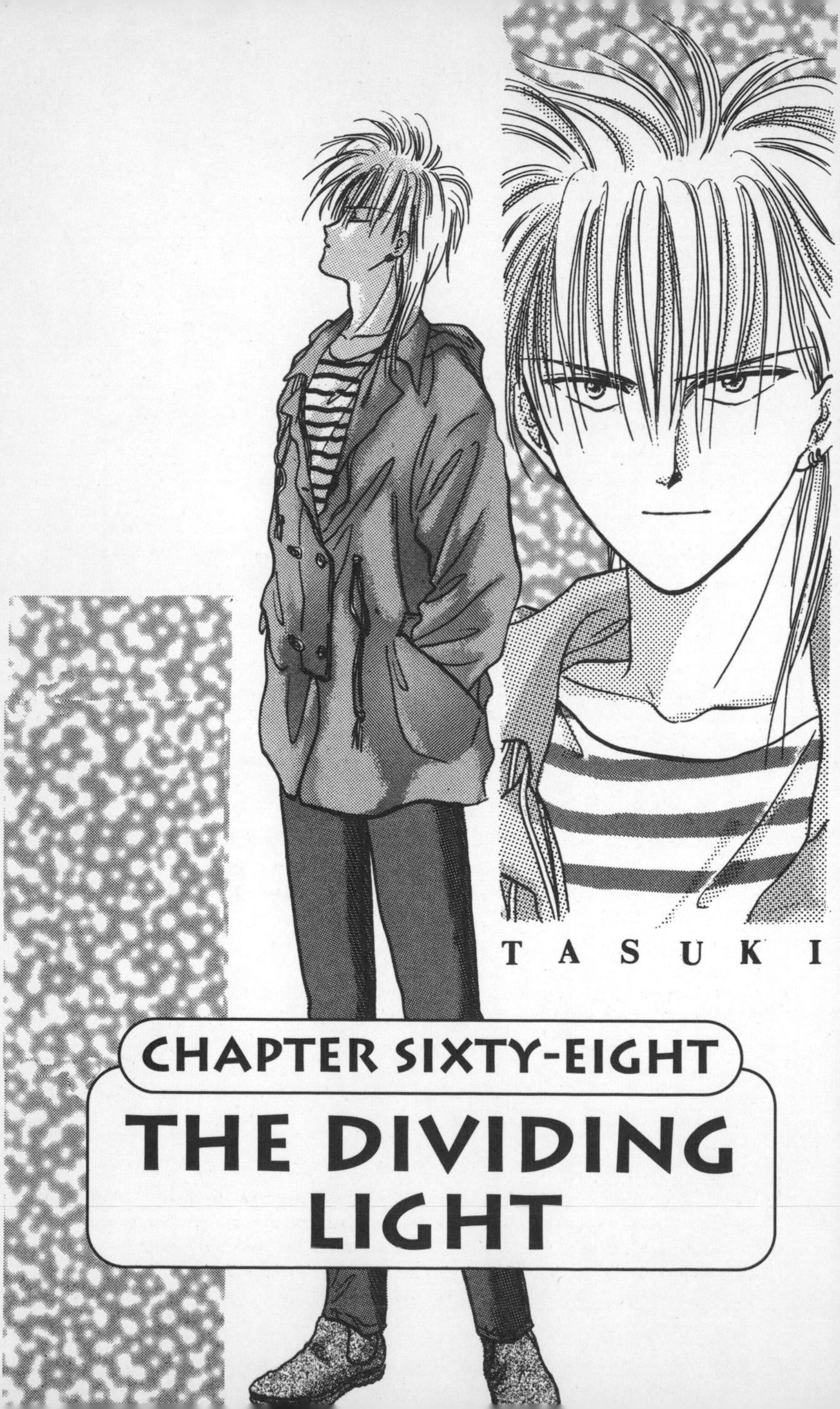
TASUKI

CHAPTER SIXTY-EIGHT

THE DIVIDING LIGHT

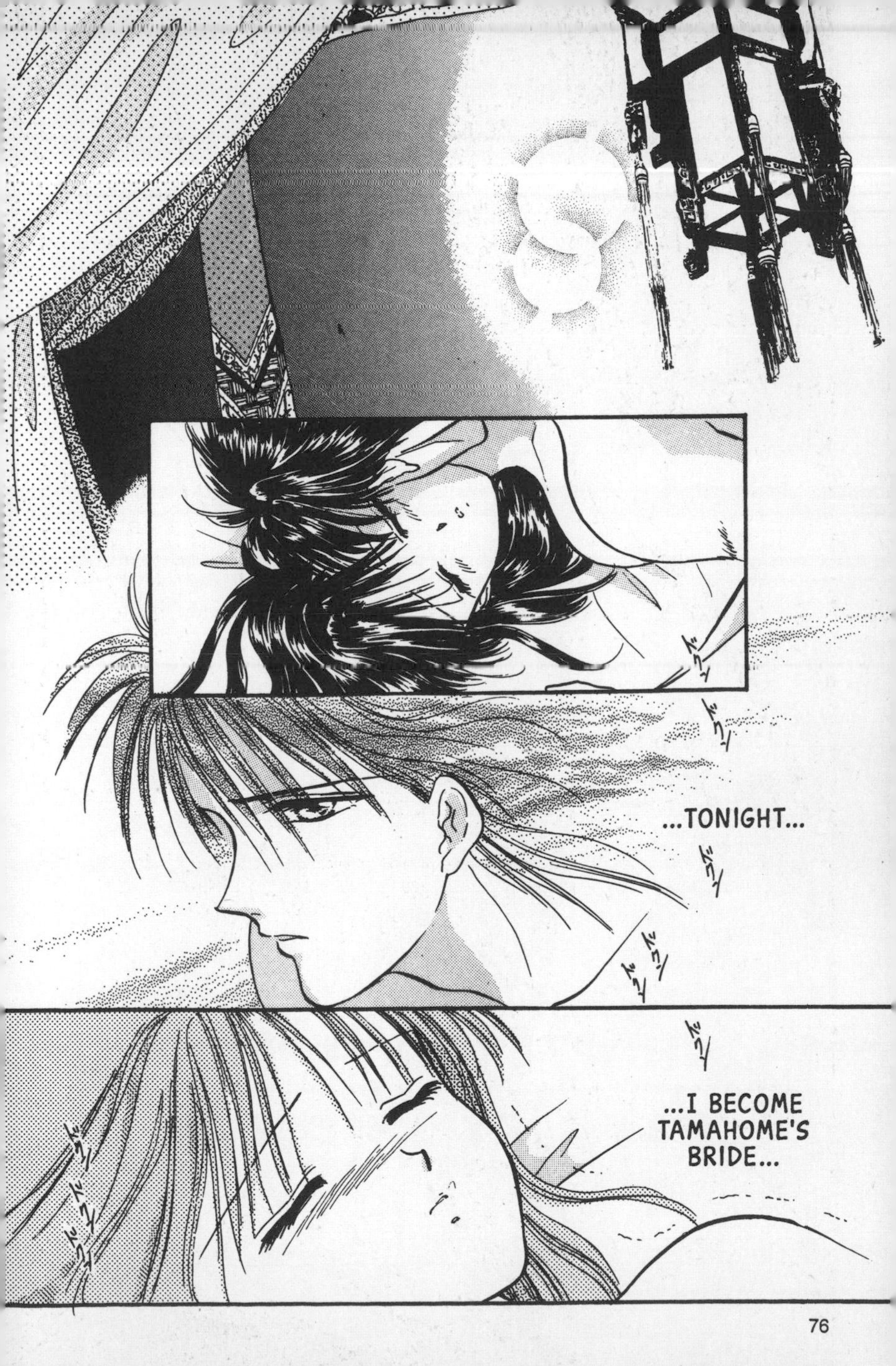
...TONIGHT...
...I BECOME TAMAHOME'S BRIDE...

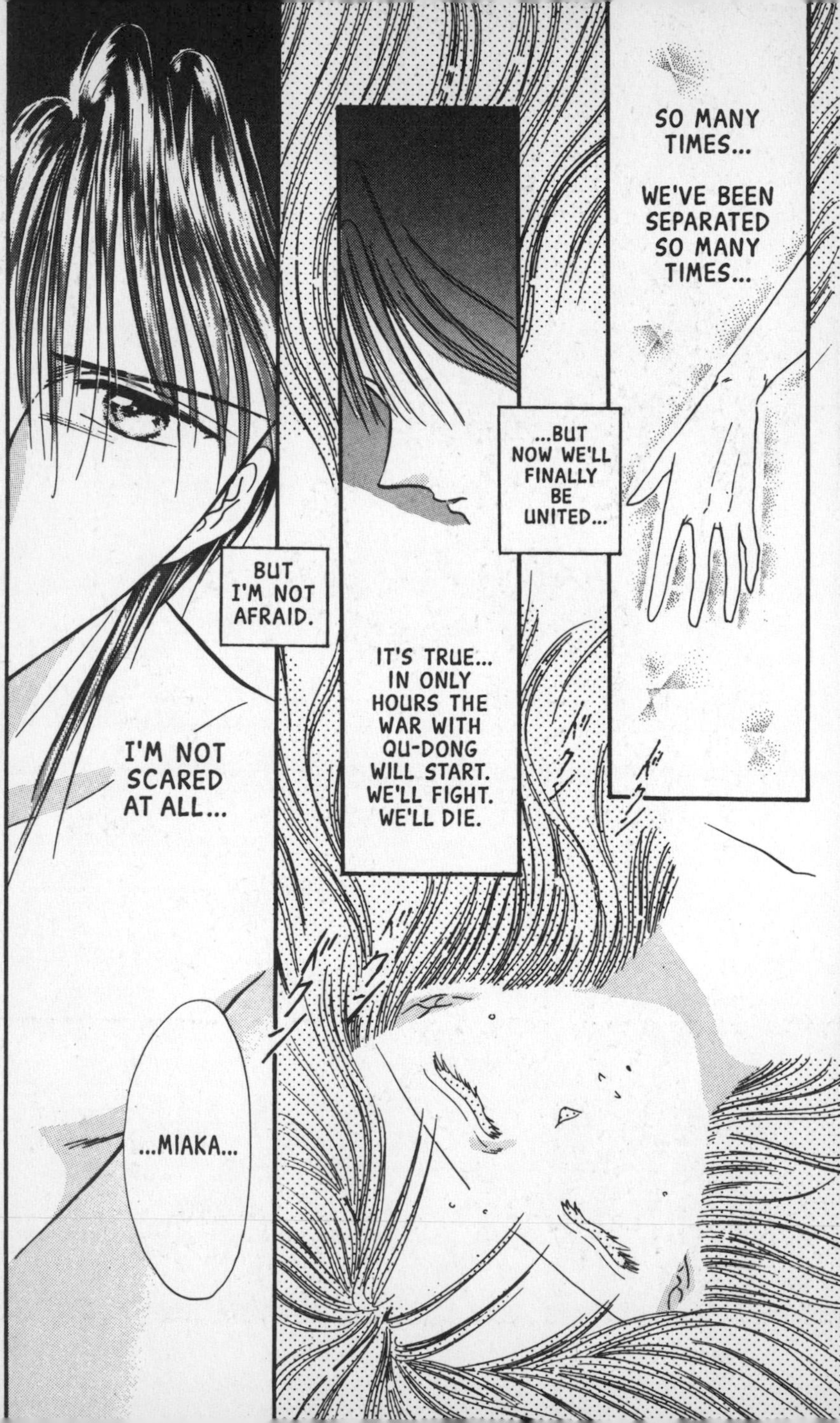
SO MANY TIMES...
WE'VE BEEN SEPARATED SO MANY TIMES...
...BUT NOW WE'LL FINALLY BE UNITED...
IT'S TRUE... IN ONLY HOURS THE WAR WITH QU-DONG WILL START. WE'LL FIGHT. WE'LL DIE.
BUT I'M NOT AFRAID.
I'M NOT SCARED AT ALL...
...MIAKA...

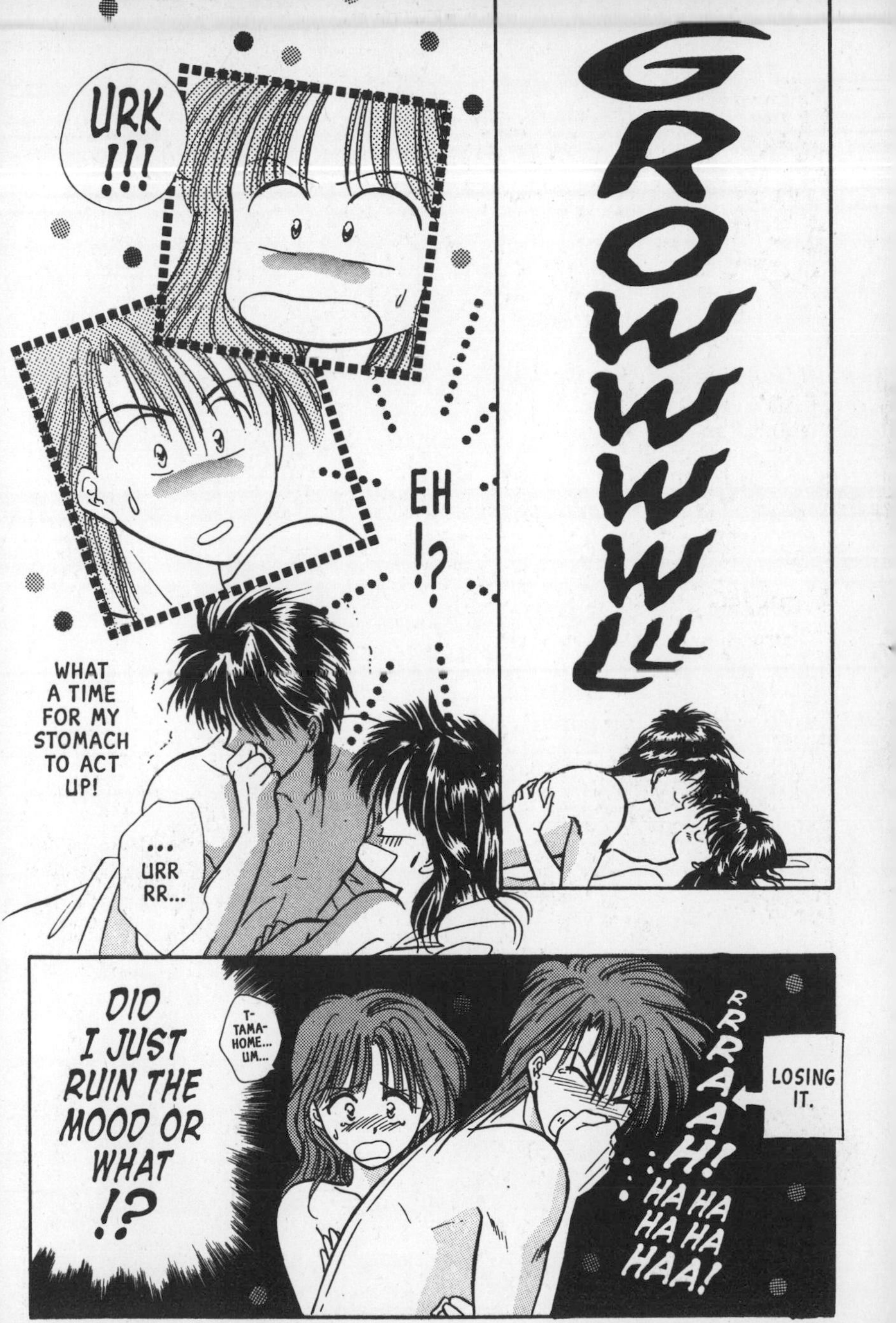
GROWWWWL
URK!!!
EH!?
WHAT A TIME FOR MY STOMACH TO ACT UP!
...URRRR...
RRRAAH! HAHA HAHA HAHA HAA!
LOSING IT.
T-TAMAHOME... UM...
DID I JUST RUIN THE MOOD OR WHAT!?

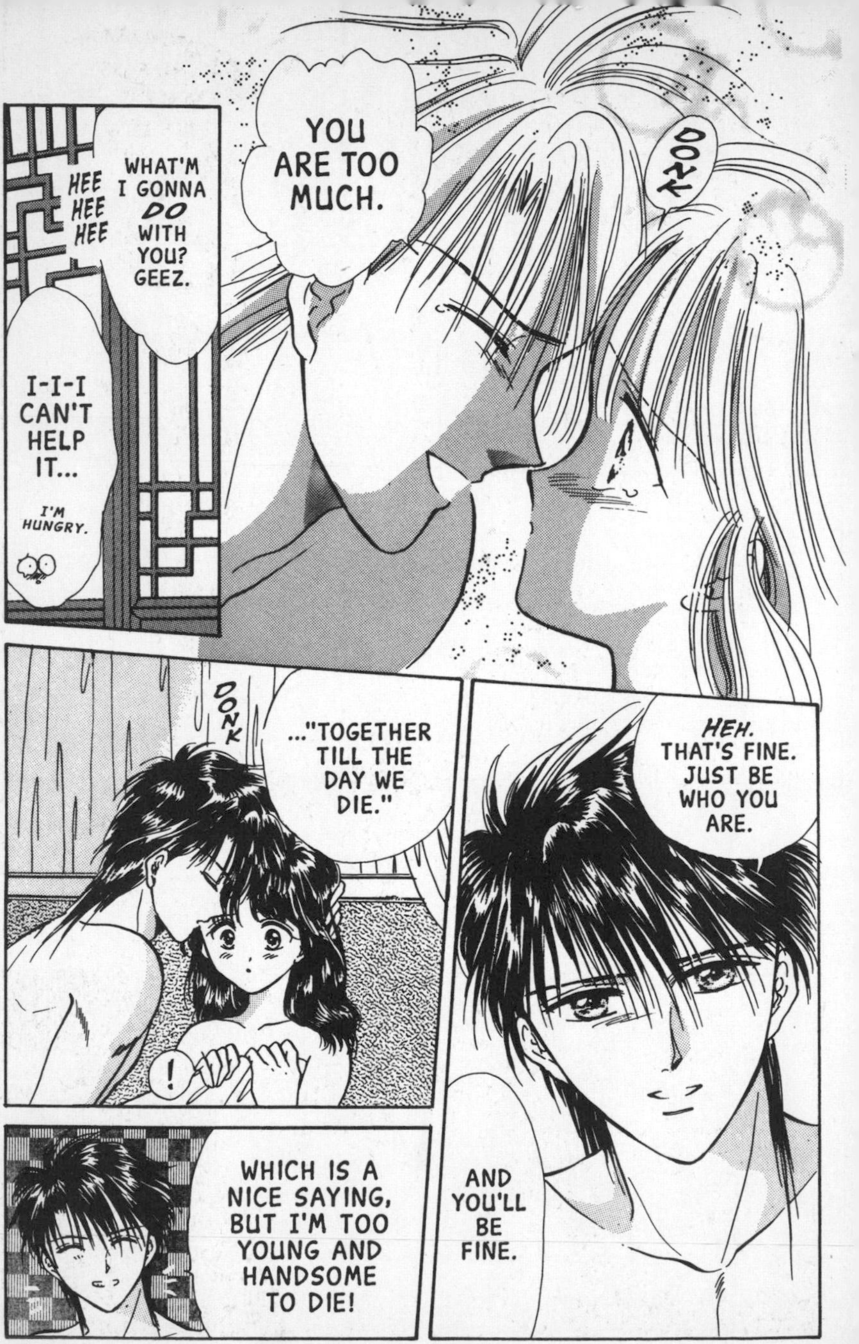
DONK
YOU ARE TOO MUCH.
HEE HEE HEE
WHAT'M I GONNA DO WITH YOU? GEEZ.
I-I-I CAN'T HELP IT...
I'M HUNGRY.
HEH. THAT'S FINE. JUST BE WHO YOU ARE.
AND YOU'LL BE FINE.
DONK
..."TOGETHER TILL THE DAY WE DIE."
!
WHICH IS A NICE SAYING, BUT I'M TOO YOUNG AND HANDSOME TO DIE!

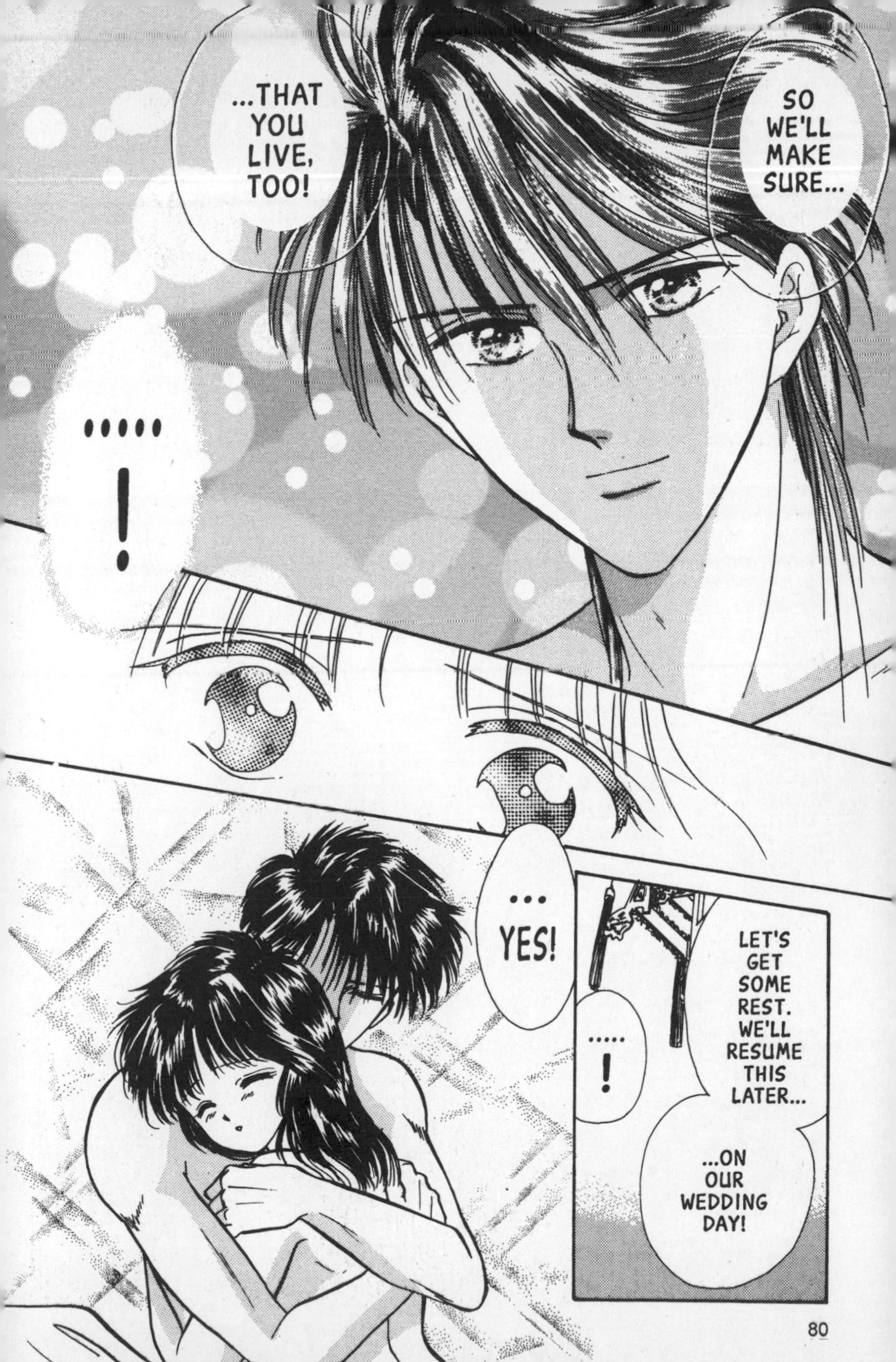
SO WE'LL MAKE SURE...
...THAT YOU LIVE, TOO!
.....!
... YES!
LET'S GET SOME REST. WE'LL RESUME THIS LATER...
...ON OUR WEDDING DAY!
.....!

But it turns out Amiboshi was having second thoughts during the ceremony. When Amiboshi and Miaka met the second time, and the village was attacked, he used his chi and his flute to annihilate the Qu-Dong soldiers and protect Miaka. He could have used that power at the ceremony, but he didn't. I also don't think his feelings for Miaka are romantic. *I think.* It's just that both of them are caring in the same way... He must have really been moved by what Miaka said to him right before he fell into the river. You know, that weird phase you go through right before falling in love? I think that's what it felt like for him.
By the way, he holds the flute in his left hand when he releases his chi. But when he plays it normally, it's in his right hand. He's ambidextrous.

Suboshi is identical to Amiboshi. *They're twins.* But Suboshi can rub some people the wrong way. He has an extreme personality. *He's too loyal!* He's a nice kid who'll fight to the death with anyone who threatens or attacks his older brother. He started out being a caring brother, but now, his feelings could almost be considered incestuous... Well, there's only an element of that, so I guess it's all right. *Of course it's not!* Suboshi's the only extreme one. Amiboshi's normal after all.
It's true that Suboshi has a crush on Yui. They're actually the same age, but Yui is mentally more mature...
I don't know how I came up with the idea that Suboshi and Amiboshi would be twins. They're exactly identical, but some readers have claimed, "I can see the difference in their eyes and their aura." That's true. Suboshi does have a look that's entirely absent from Amiboshi. *A difference in personality.*
In any case, the illustration in Volume 10 caused quite a stir...
I didn't mean it to be so sexual...

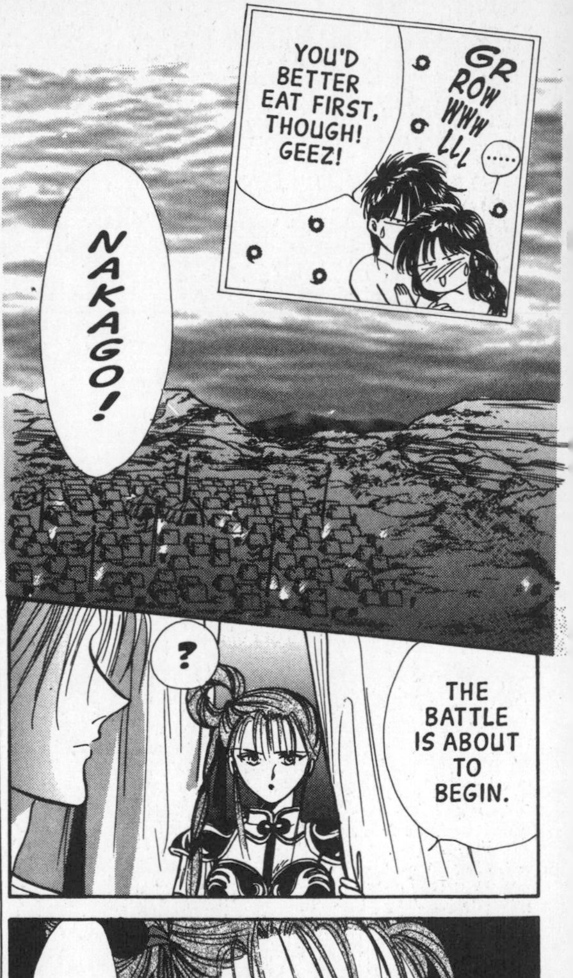
GRROWWWWLLL
.....
YOU'D BETTER EAT FIRST, THOUGH! GEEZ!
NAKAGO!
THE BATTLE IS ABOUT TO BEGIN.
?
.....
!!

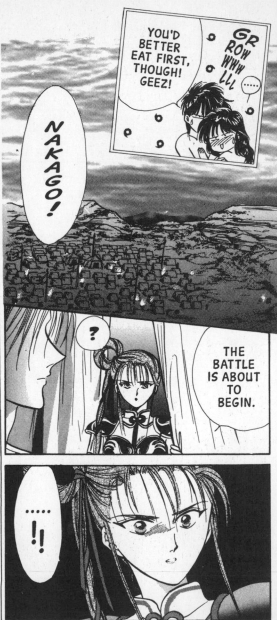

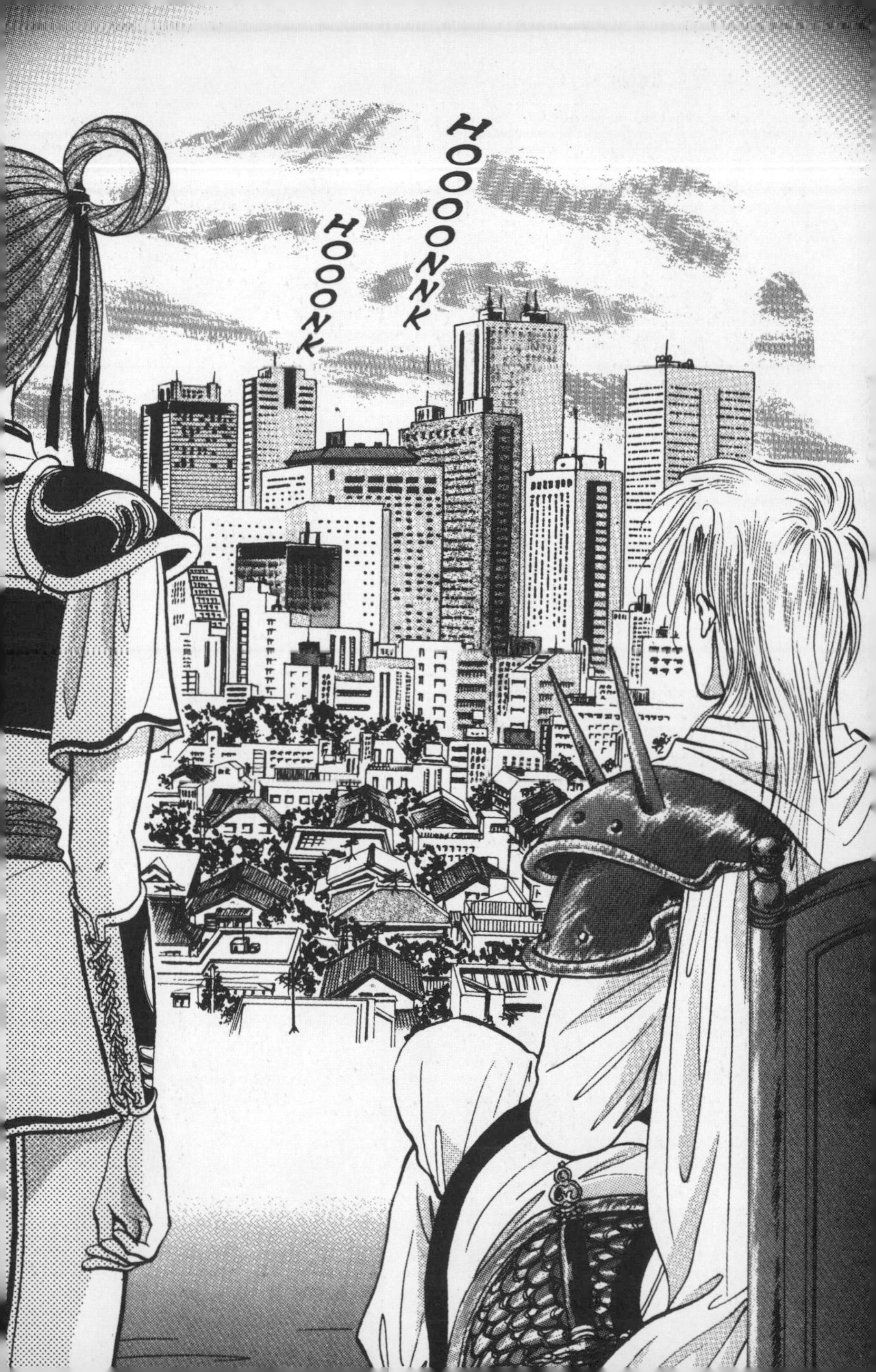
HOOOOONNK
HOOOONK

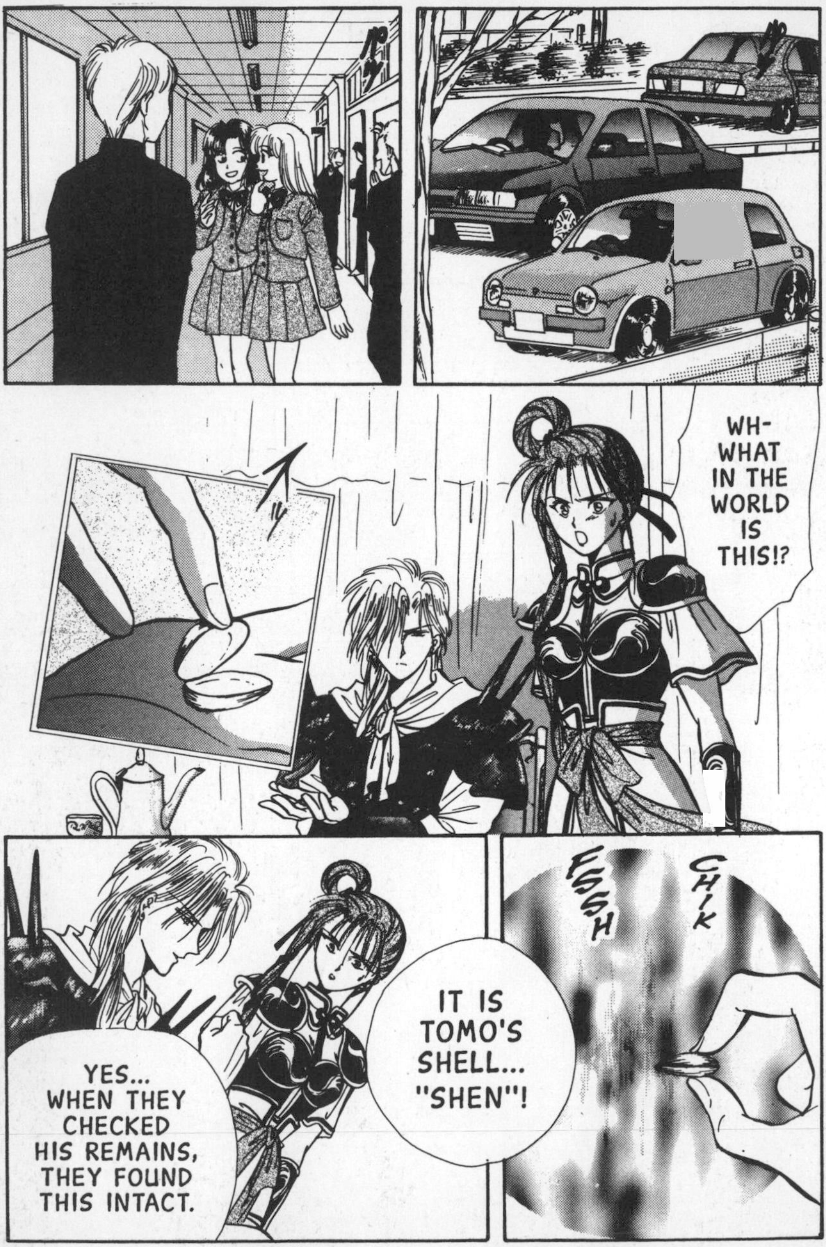
WH-
WHAT IN THE WORLD IS THIS!?
FSSH
CHIK
IT IS TOMO'S SHELL... "SHEN"!
YES... WHEN THEY CHECKED HIS REMAINS, THEY FOUND THIS INTACT.

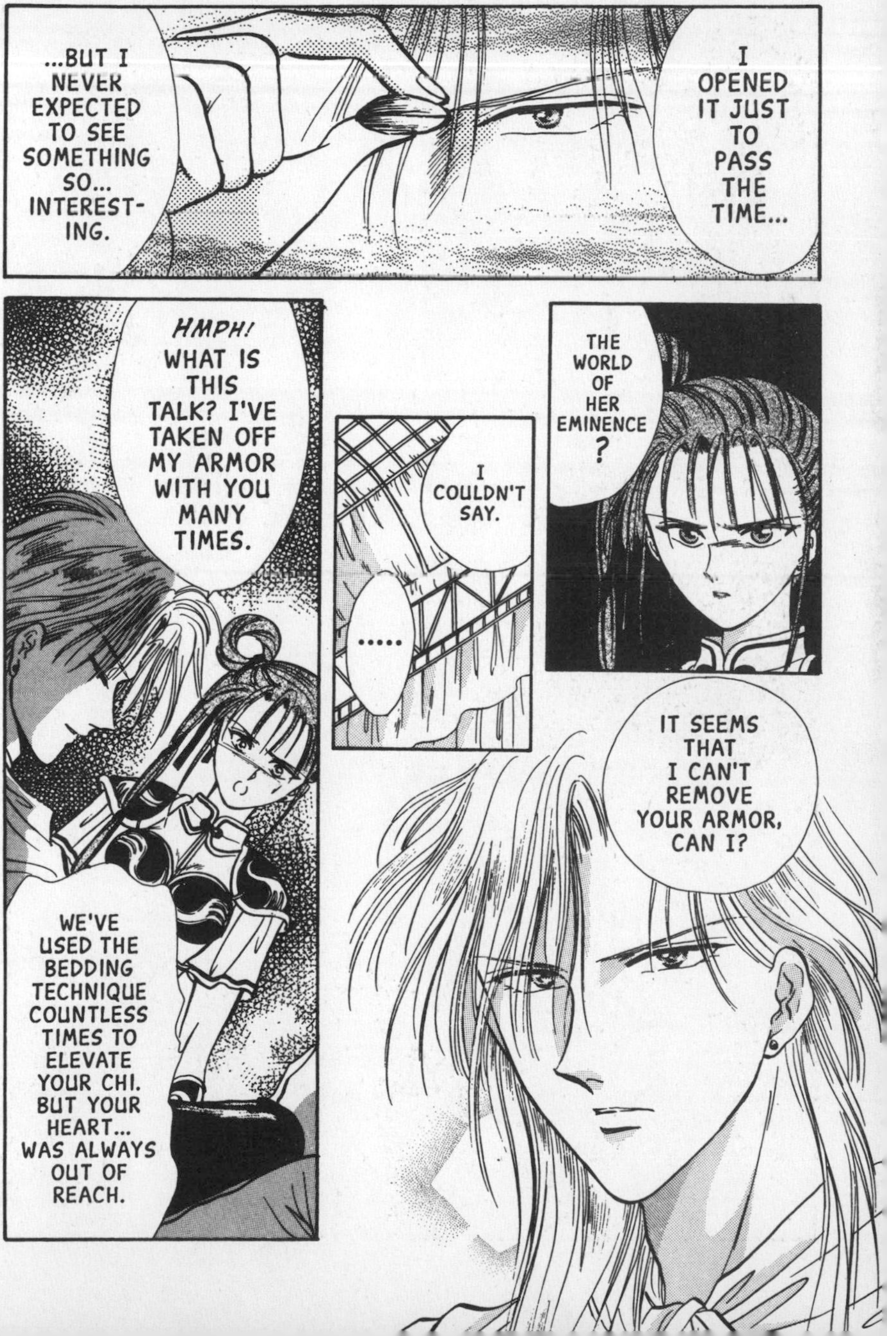
I OPENED IT JUST TO PASS THE TIME...
...BUT I NEVER EXPECTED TO SEE SOMETHING SO... INTEREST-ING.
THE WORLD OF HER EMINENCE?
I COULDN'T SAY.
......
IT SEEMS THAT I CAN'T REMOVE YOUR ARMOR, CAN I?
HMPH! WHAT IS THIS TALK? I'VE TAKEN OFF MY ARMOR WITH YOU MANY TIMES.
WE'VE USED THE BEDDING TECHNIQUE COUNTLESS TIMES TO ELEVATE YOUR CHI. BUT YOUR HEART... WAS ALWAYS OUT OF REACH.

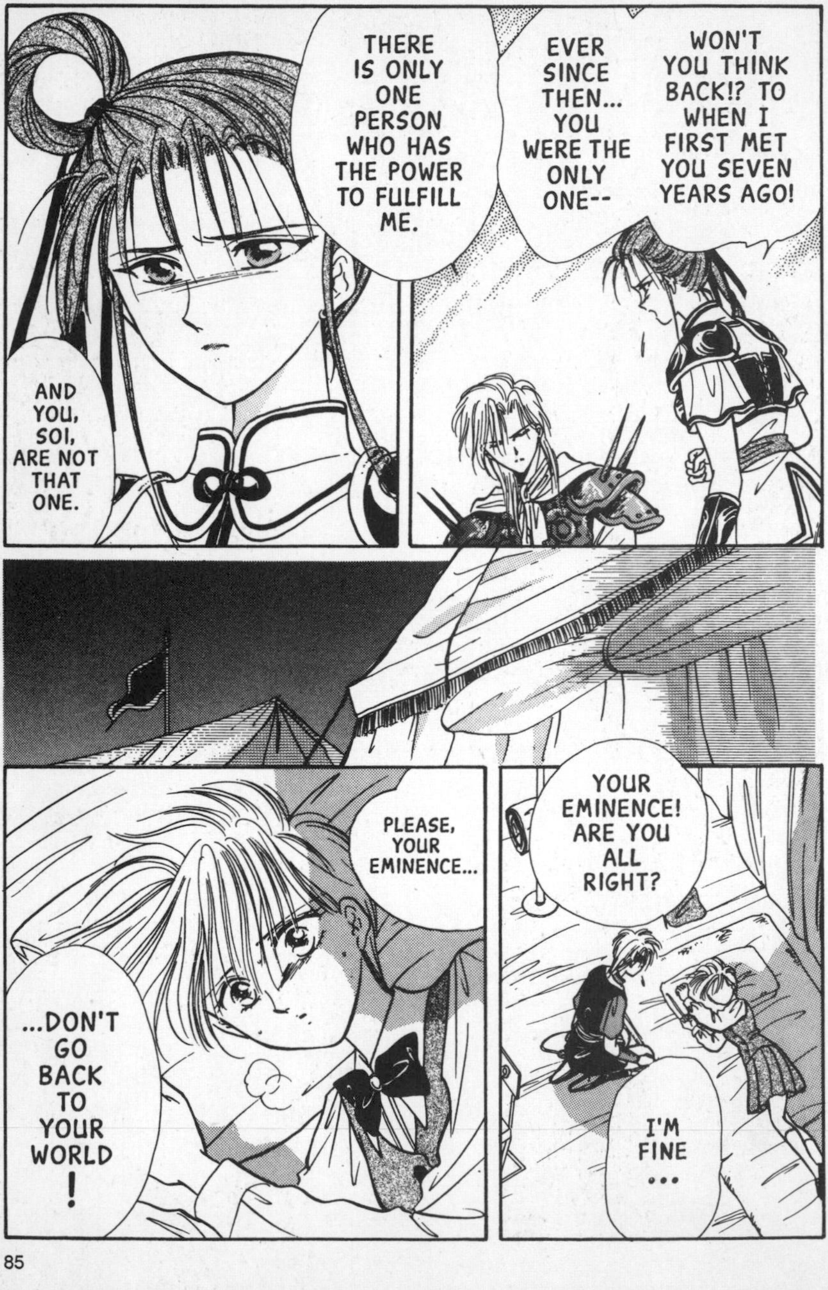
WON'T YOU THINK BACK!? TO WHEN I FIRST MET YOU SEVEN YEARS AGO!
EVER SINCE THEN... YOU WERE THE ONLY ONE--
THERE IS ONLY ONE PERSON WHO HAS THE POWER TO FULFILL ME.
AND YOU, SOI, ARE NOT THAT ONE.
YOUR EMINENCE! ARE YOU ALL RIGHT?
I'M FINE ...
PLEASE, YOUR EMINENCE...
...DON'T GO BACK TO YOUR WORLD!

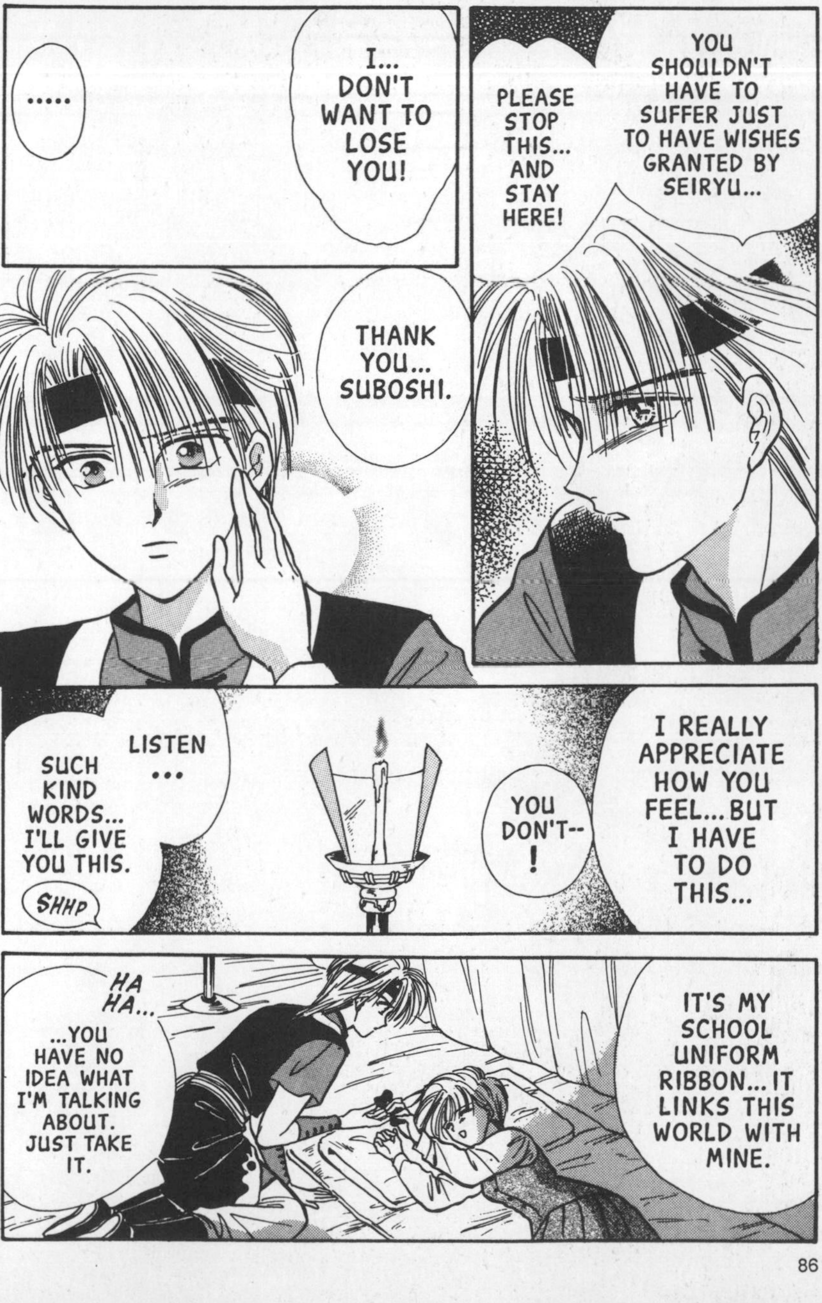
YOU SHOULDN'T HAVE TO SUFFER JUST TO HAVE WISHES GRANTED BY SEIRYU...
PLEASE STOP THIS... AND STAY HERE!
I... DON'T WANT TO LOSE YOU!
.....
THANK YOU... SUBOSHI.
I REALLY APPRECIATE HOW YOU FEEL...BUT I HAVE TO DO THIS...
YOU DON'T--!
LISTEN...
SUCH KIND WORDS... I'LL GIVE YOU THIS.
SHHP
IT'S MY SCHOOL UNIFORM RIBBON... IT LINKS THIS WORLD WITH MINE.
HA HA...
...YOU HAVE NO IDEA WHAT I'M TALKING ABOUT. JUST TAKE IT.

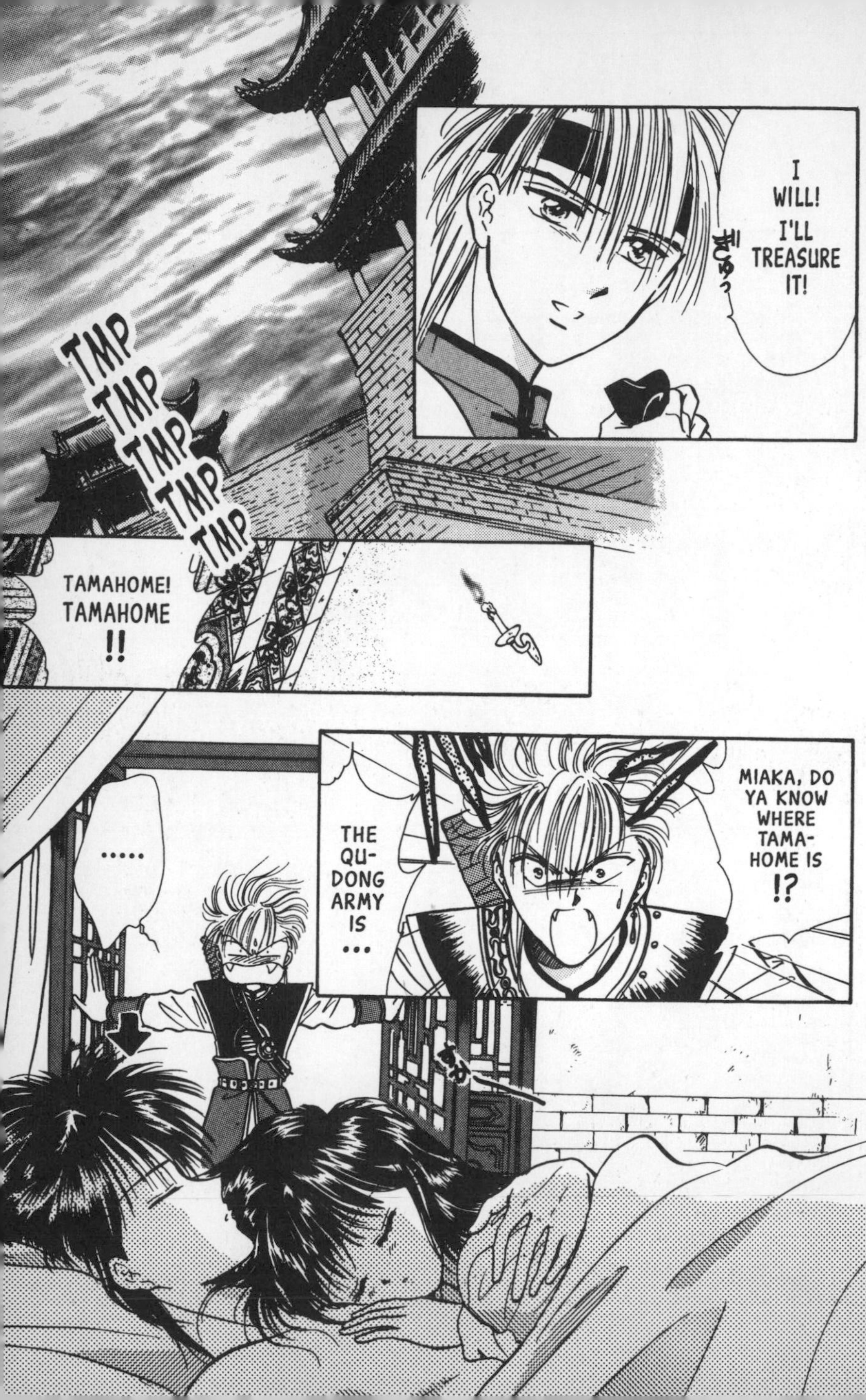
I WILL! I'LL TREASURE IT!
TMP TMP TMP TMP TMP
TAMAHOME! TAMAHOME !!
MIAKA, DO YA KNOW WHERE TAMA-HOME IS !?
THE QU-DONG ARMY IS ...
.....

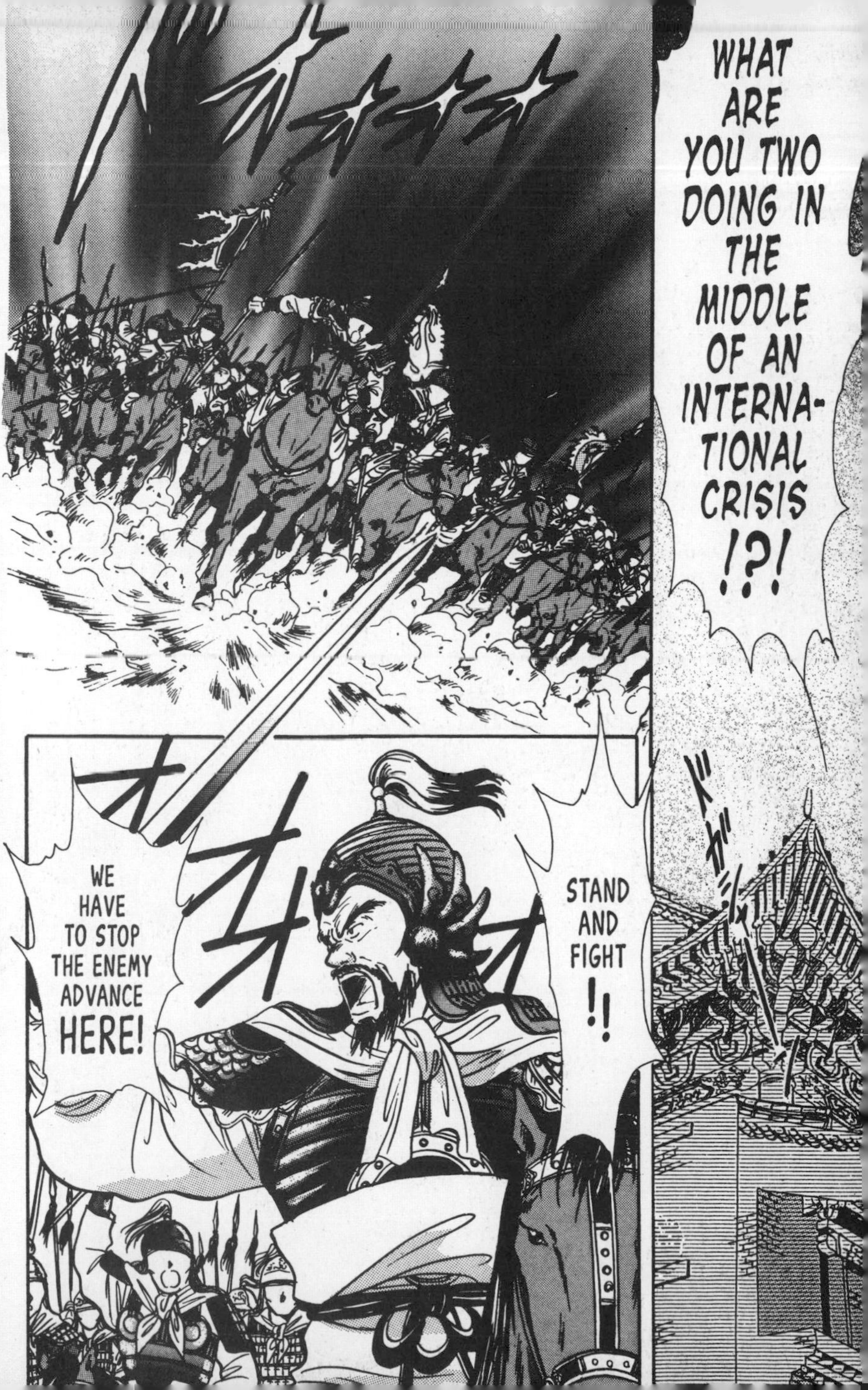
WHAT ARE YOU TWO DOING IN THE MIDDLE OF AN INTERNATIONAL CRISIS !?!
STAND AND FIGHT !!
WE HAVE TO STOP THE ENEMY ADVANCE HERE!

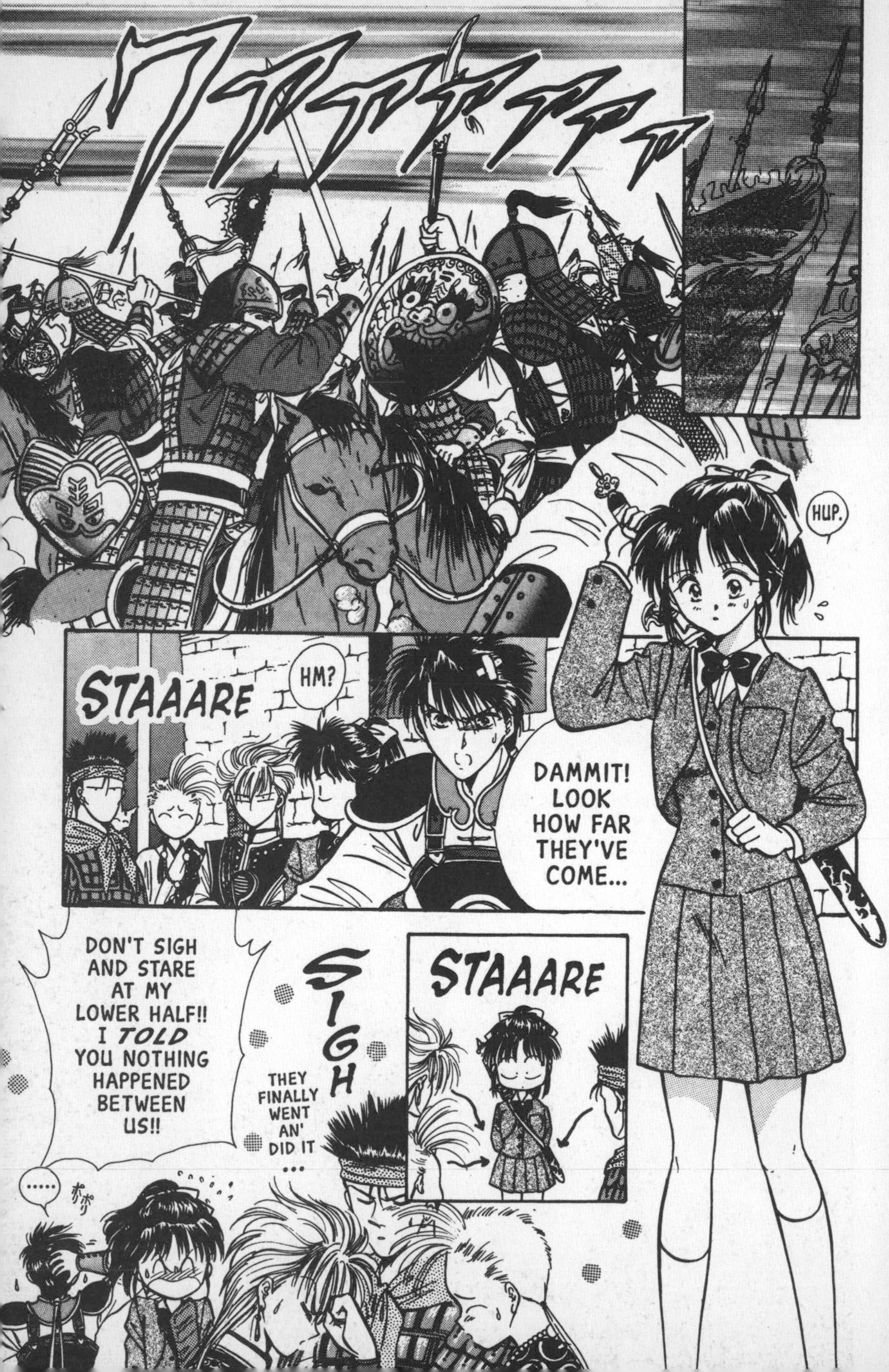
HUP.
HM?
STAAARE
DAMMIT! LOOK HOW FAR THEY'VE COME...
STAAARE
SIGH
THEY FINALLY WENT AN' DID IT ...
DON'T SIGH AND STARE AT MY LOWER HALF!! I *TOLD* YOU NOTHING HAPPENED BETWEEN US!!
......

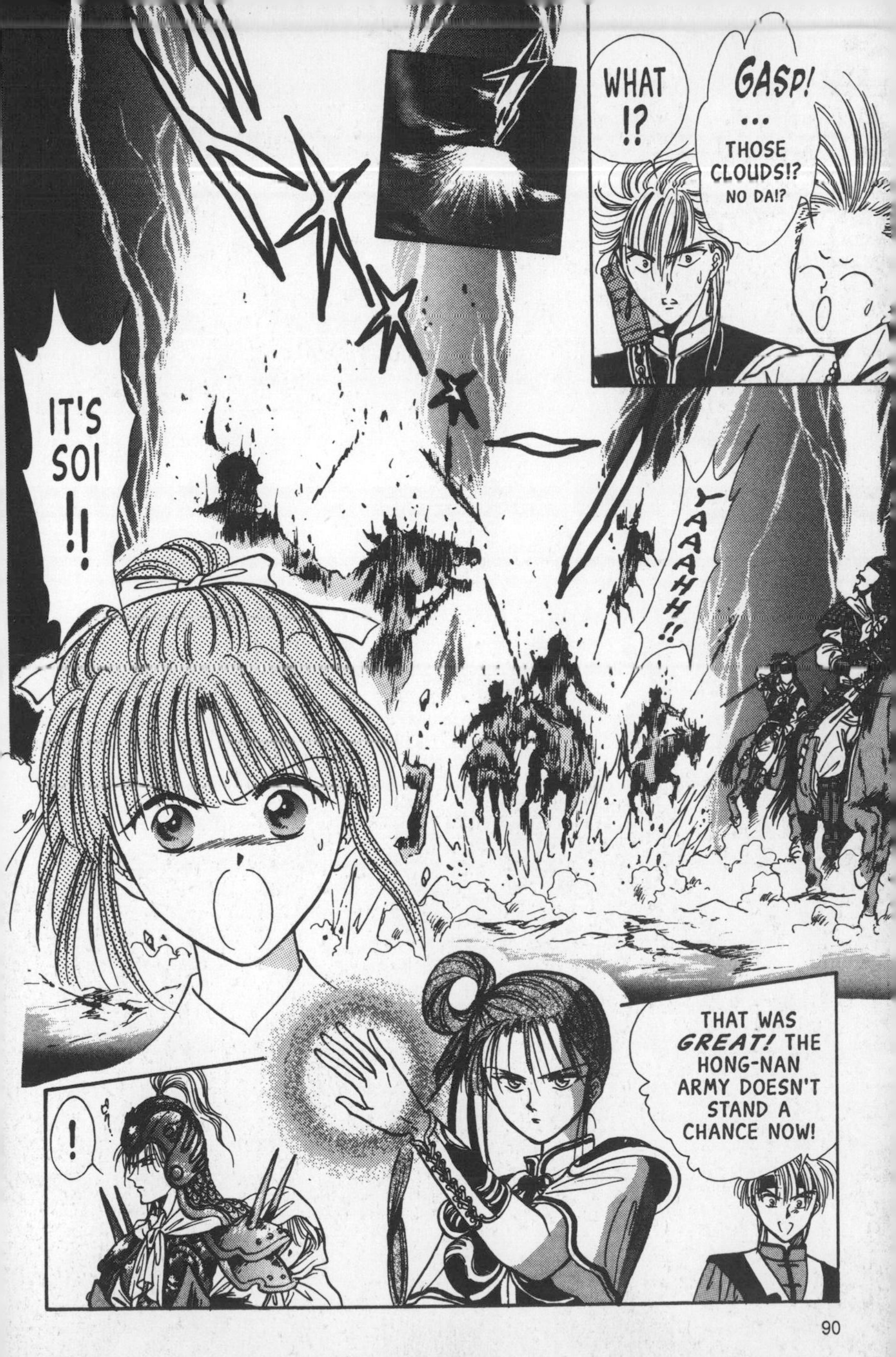
WHAT !?
GASP! ... THOSE CLOUDS!? NO DA!?
IT'S SOI !!
YAAAAHH!!
THAT WAS GREAT! THE HONG-NAN ARMY DOESN'T STAND A CHANCE NOW!
!

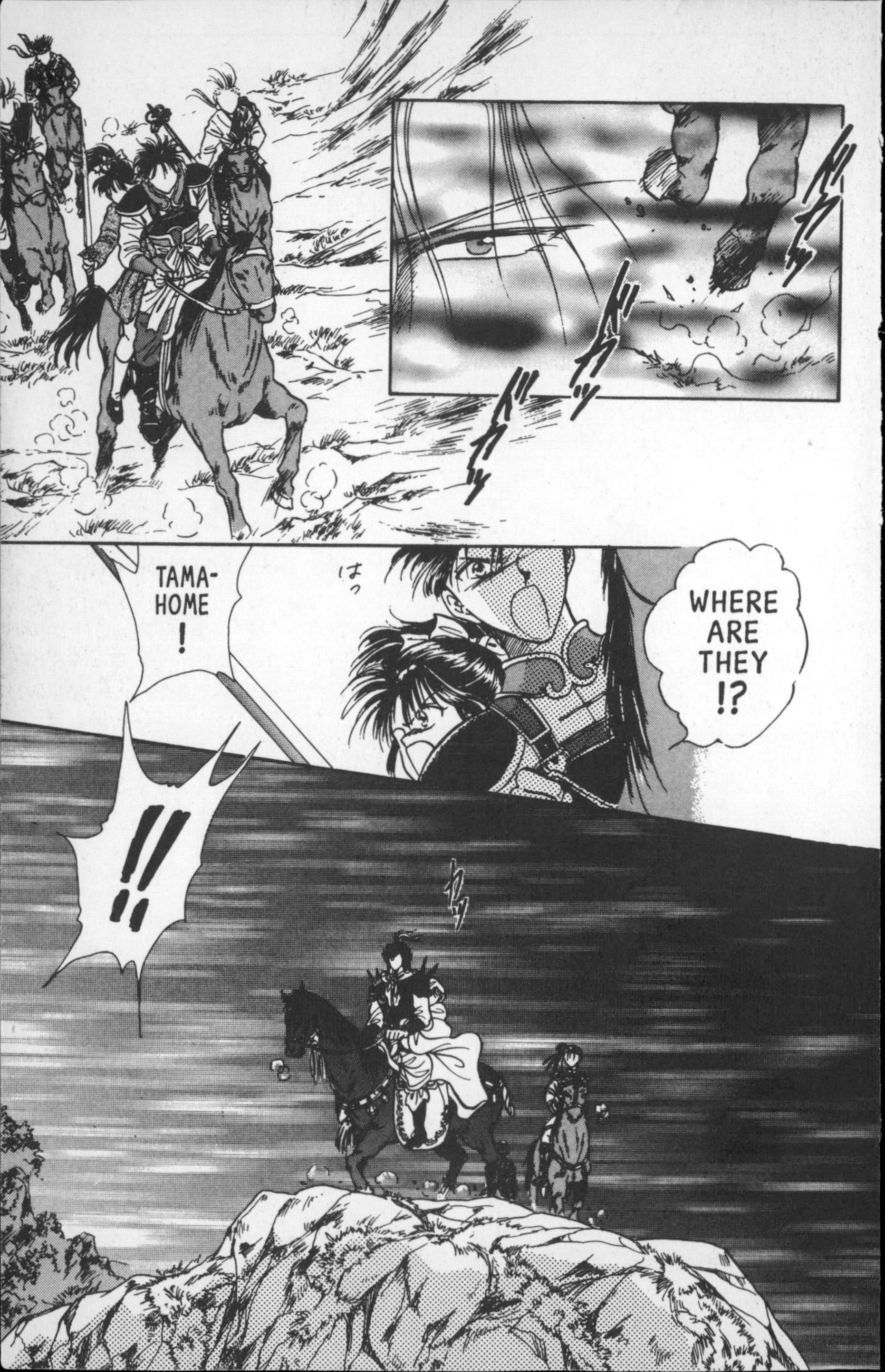
WHERE ARE THEY !?
はっ
TAMA-HOME !
!!

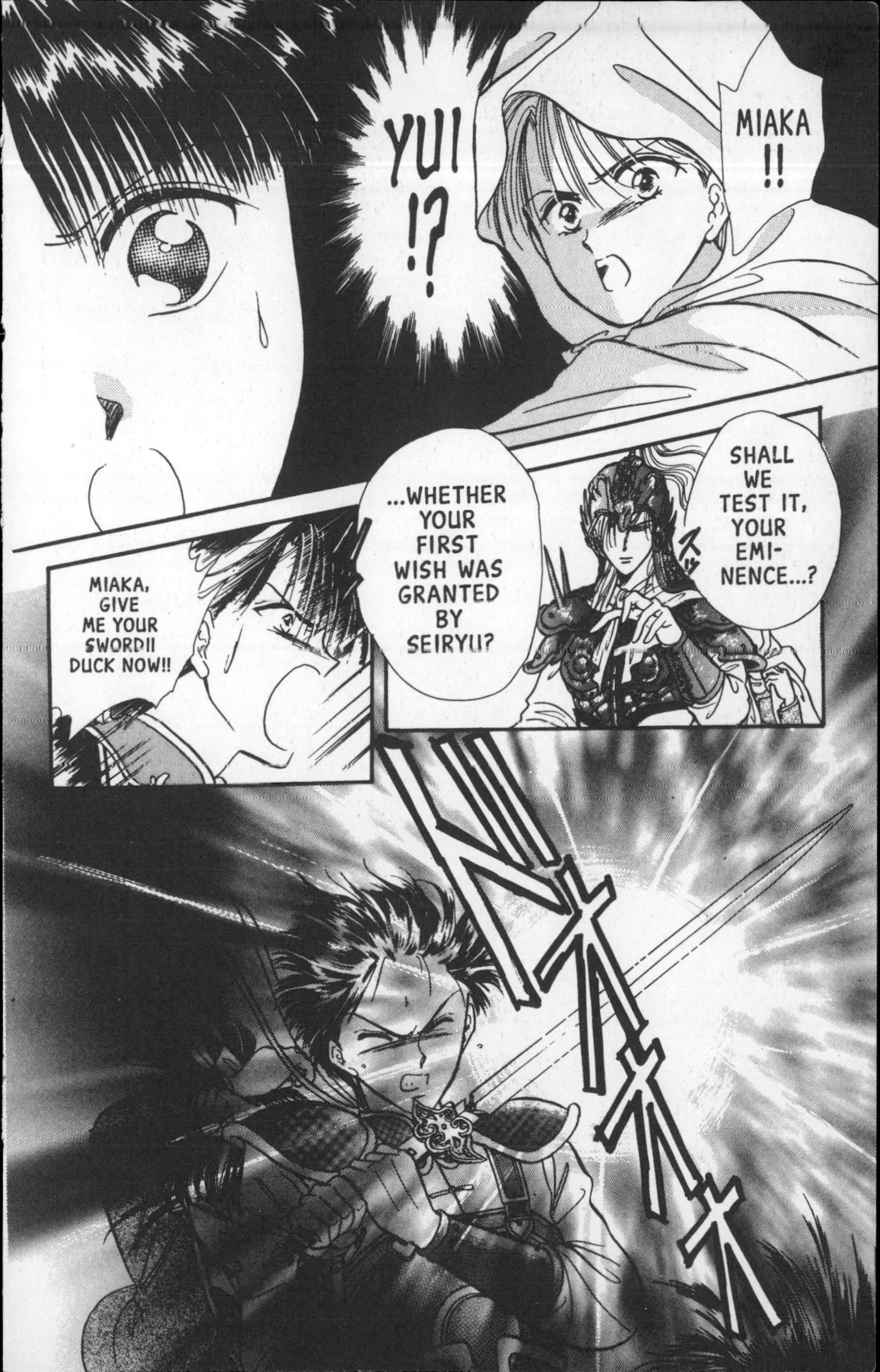
MIAKA !!
YUI !?
SHALL WE TEST IT, YOUR EMINENCE...?
...WHETHER YOUR FIRST WISH WAS GRANTED BY SEIRYU?
MIAKA, GIVE ME YOUR SWORD!! DUCK NOW!!

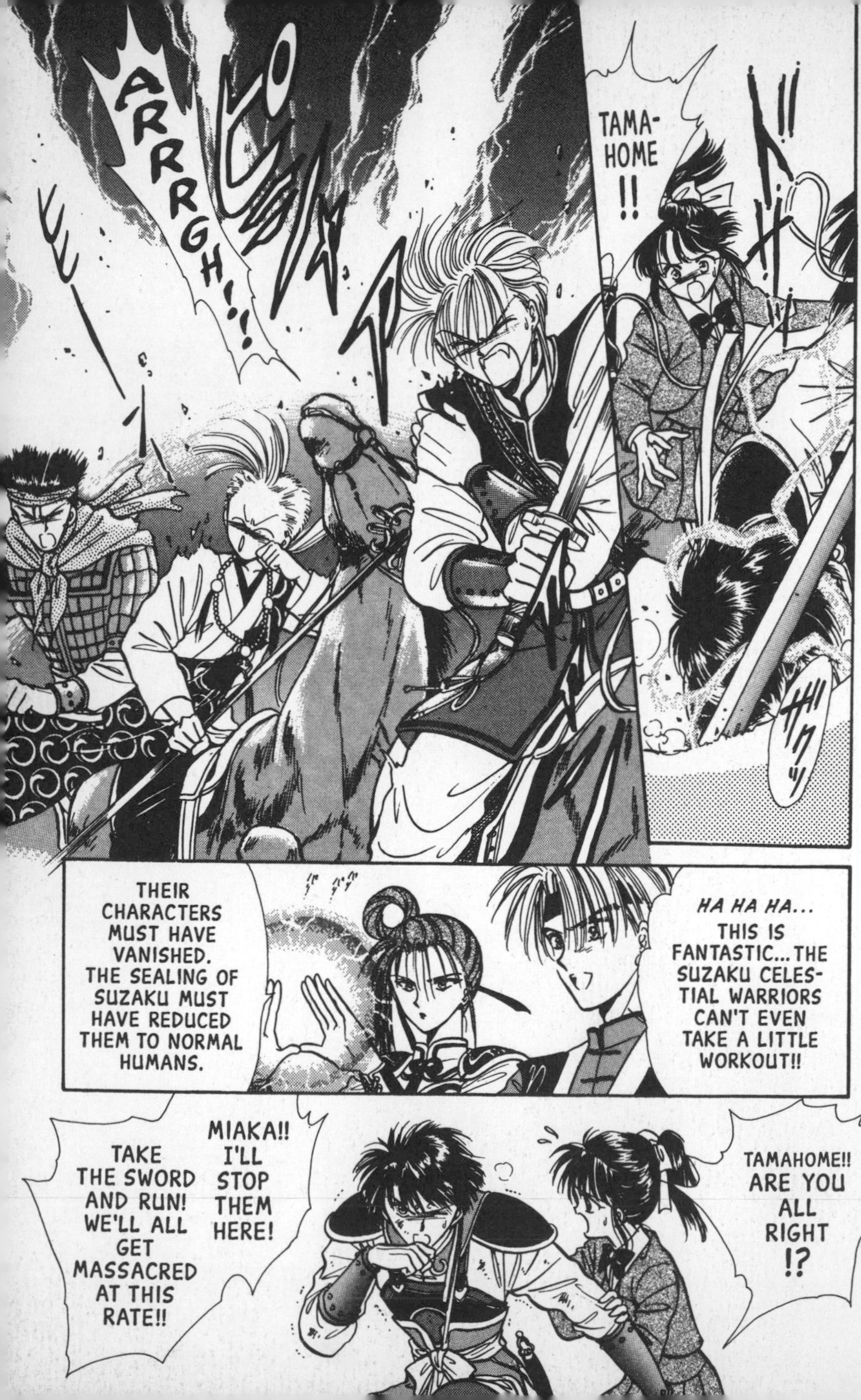
TAMA-HOME!!
ARRRGH!!!
HA HA HA... THIS IS FANTASTIC... THE SUZAKU CELESTIAL WARRIORS CAN'T EVEN TAKE A LITTLE WORKOUT!!
THEIR CHARACTERS MUST HAVE VANISHED. THE SEALING OF SUZAKU MUST HAVE REDUCED THEM TO NORMAL HUMANS.
TAMAHOME!! ARE YOU ALL RIGHT!?
MIAKA!! I'LL STOP THEM HERE!
TAKE THE SWORD AND RUN! WE'LL ALL GET MASSACRED AT THIS RATE!!

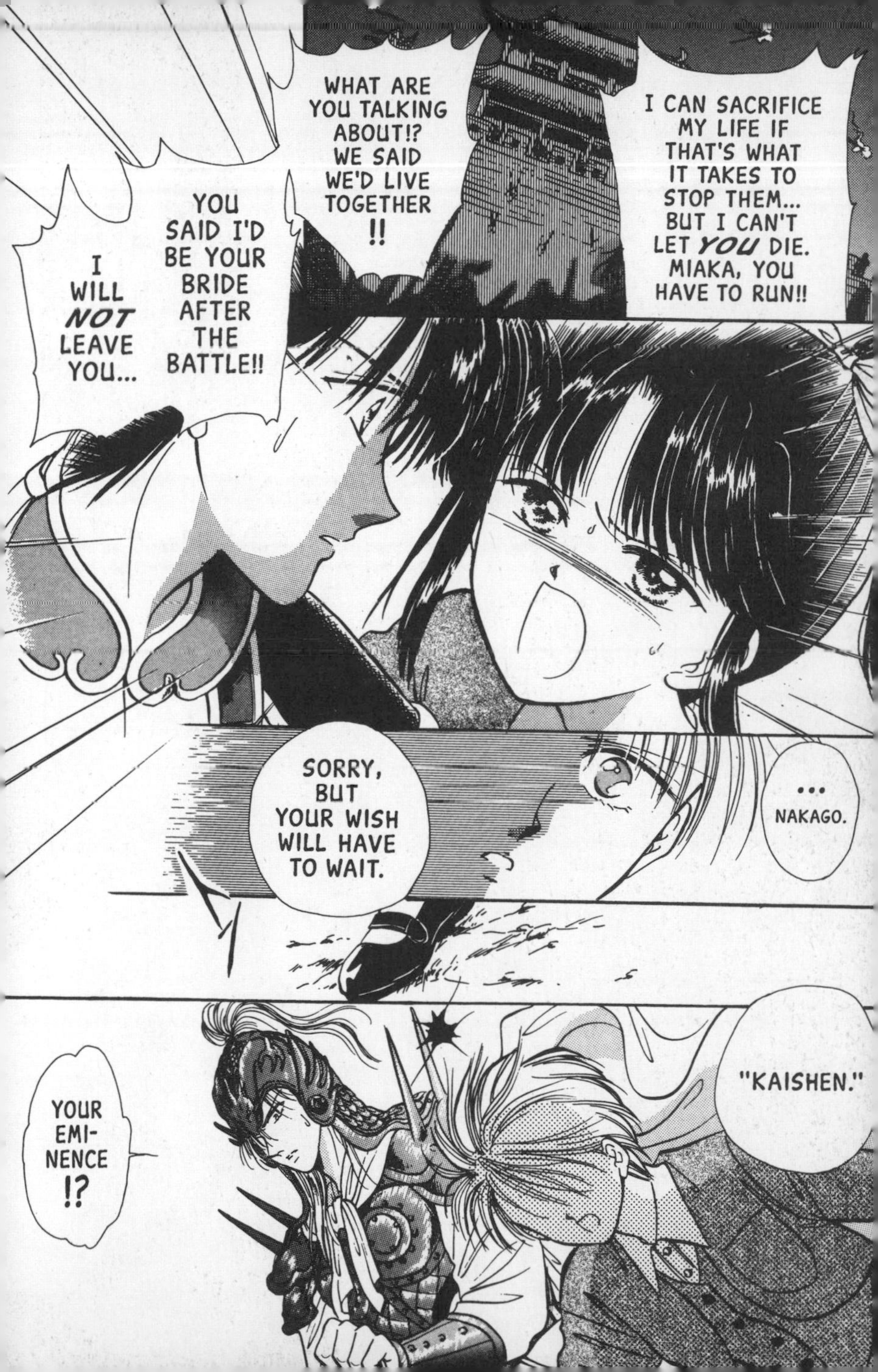
I CAN SACRIFICE MY LIFE IF THAT'S WHAT IT TAKES TO STOP THEM... BUT I CAN'T LET *YOU* DIE. MIAKA, YOU HAVE TO RUN!!
WHAT ARE YOU TALKING ABOUT!? WE SAID WE'D LIVE TOGETHER!!
YOU SAID I'D BE YOUR BRIDE AFTER THE BATTLE!!
I WILL *NOT* LEAVE YOU...
... NAKAGO.
SORRY, BUT YOUR WISH WILL HAVE TO WAIT.
"KAISHEN."
YOUR EMINENCE!?

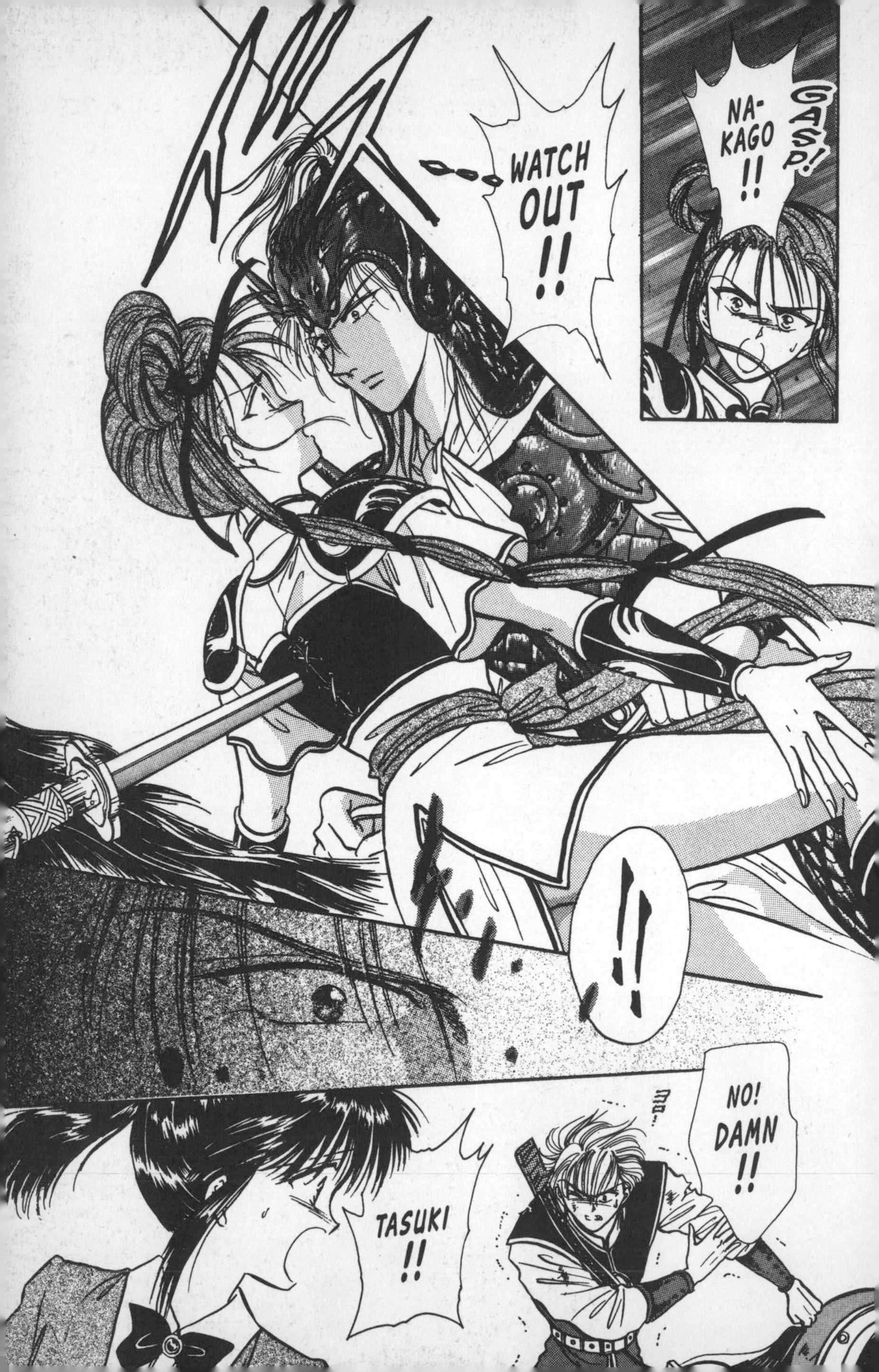
GASP!
NA-KAGO!!
...WATCH OUT!!
!!
...ma...
NO! DAMN!!
TASUKI!!

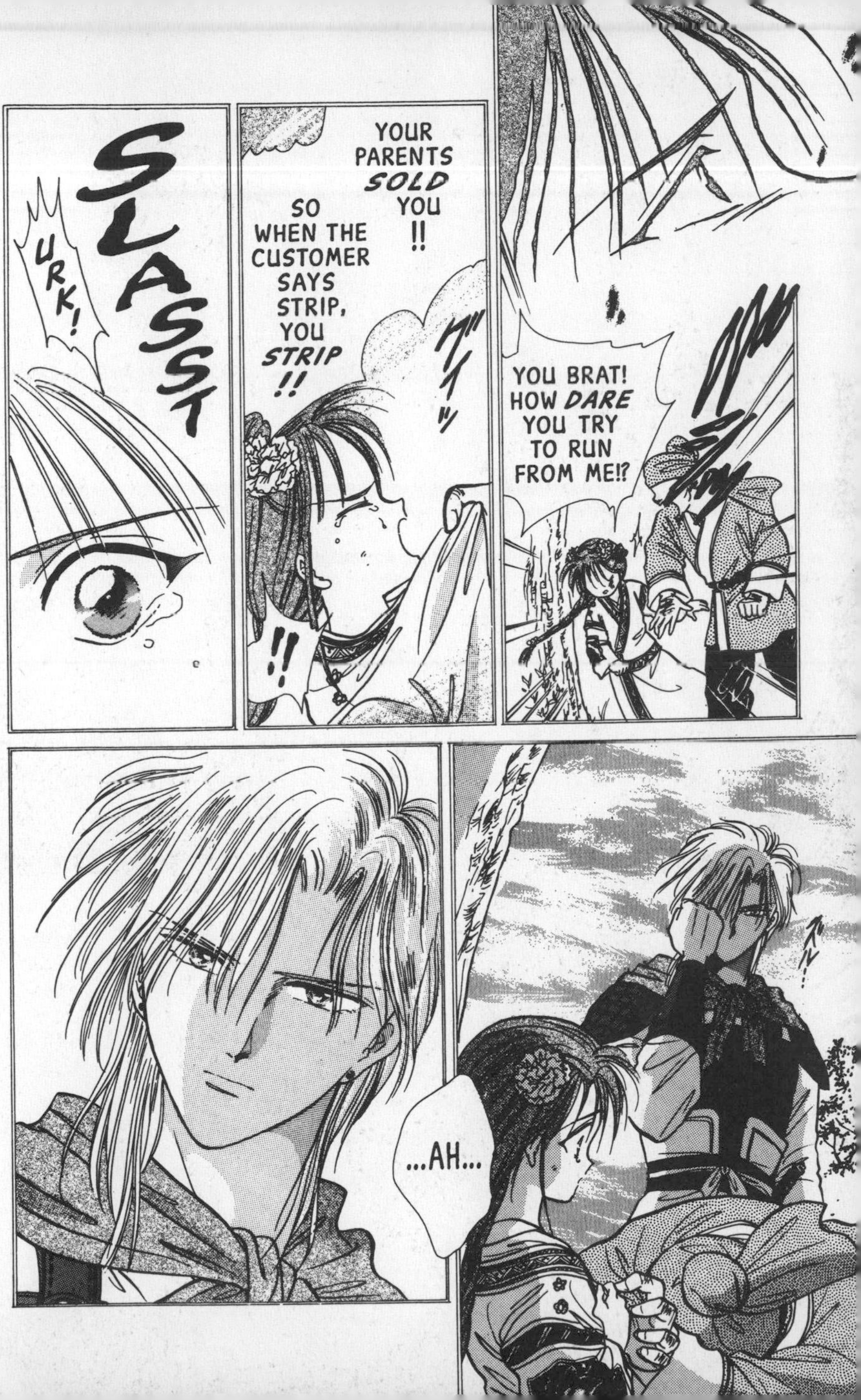
YOU BRAT! HOW DARE YOU TRY TO RUN FROM ME!?
YOUR PARENTS SOLD YOU !!
SO WHEN THE CUSTOMER SAYS STRIP, YOU STRIP !!
!!
SLASST
URK!
...AH...

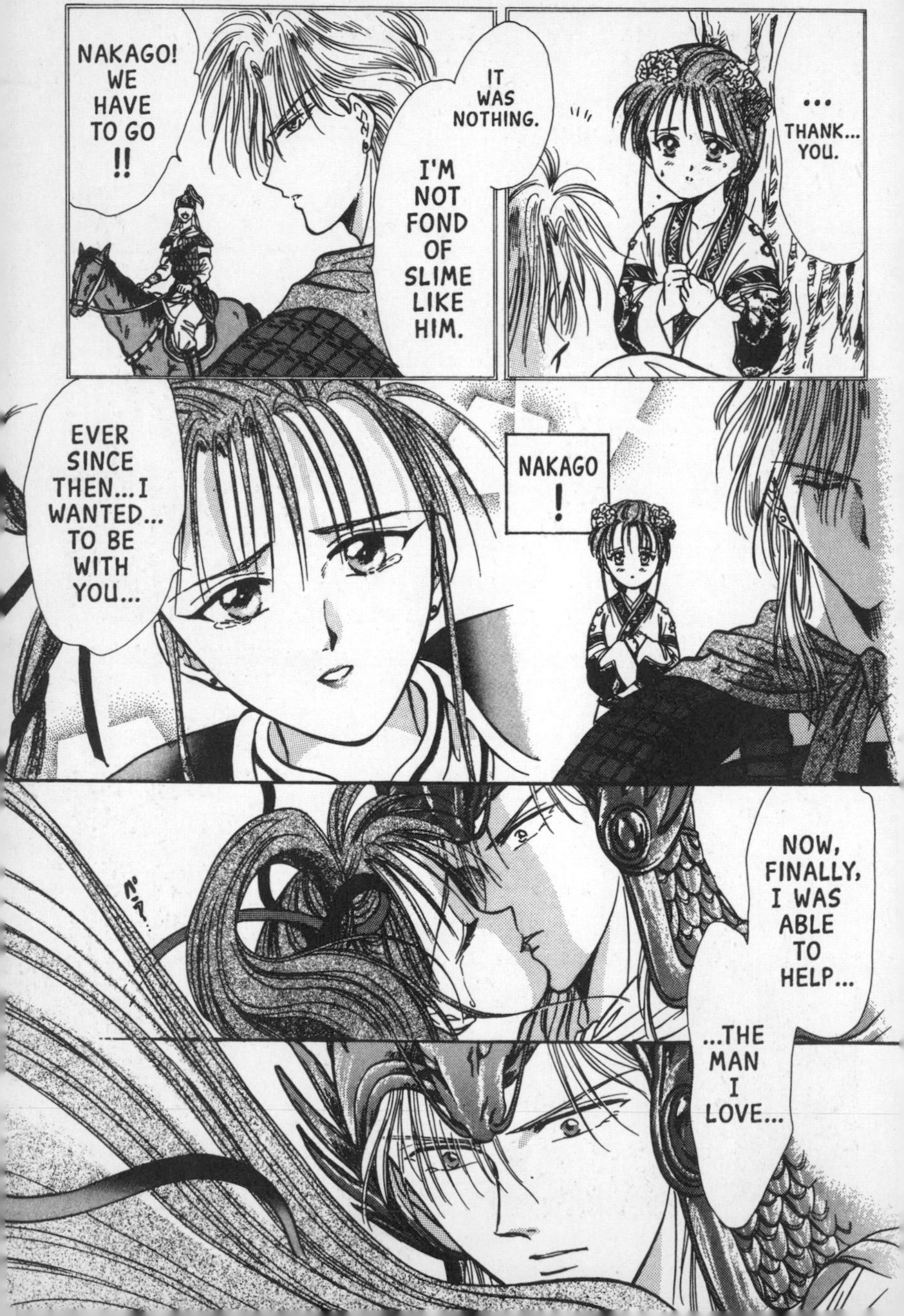
... THANK... YOU.
IT WAS NOTHING.
I'M NOT FOND OF SLIME LIKE HIM.
NAKAGO! WE HAVE TO GO!!
NAKAGO!
EVER SINCE THEN... I WANTED... TO BE WITH YOU...
NOW, FINALLY, I WAS ABLE TO HELP...
...THE MAN I LOVE...

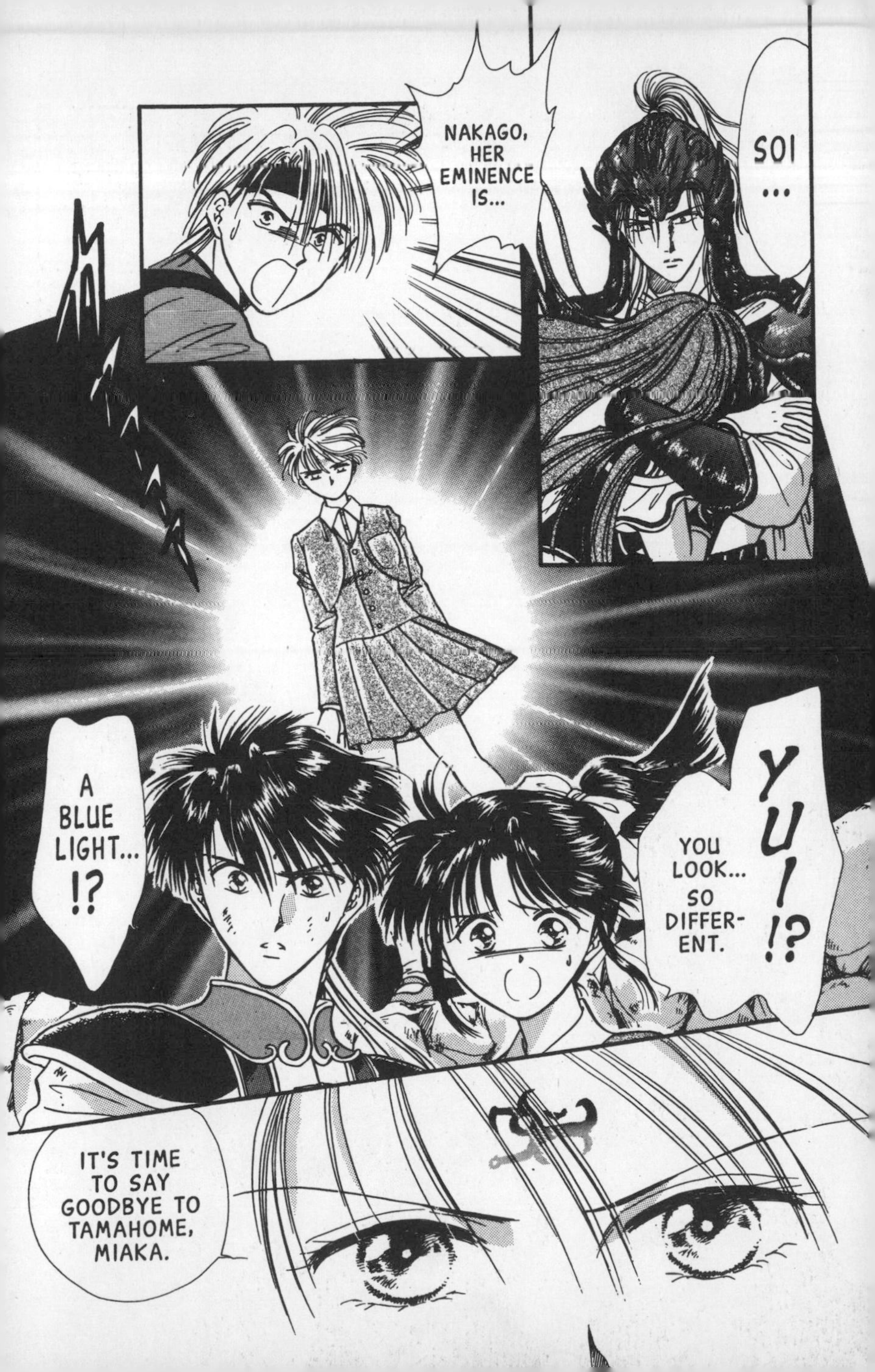
SOI ...
NAKAGO, HER EMINENCE IS...
YUI !?
YOU LOOK... SO DIFFERENT.
A BLUE LIGHT... !?
IT'S TIME TO SAY GOODBYE TO TAMAHOME, MIAKA.

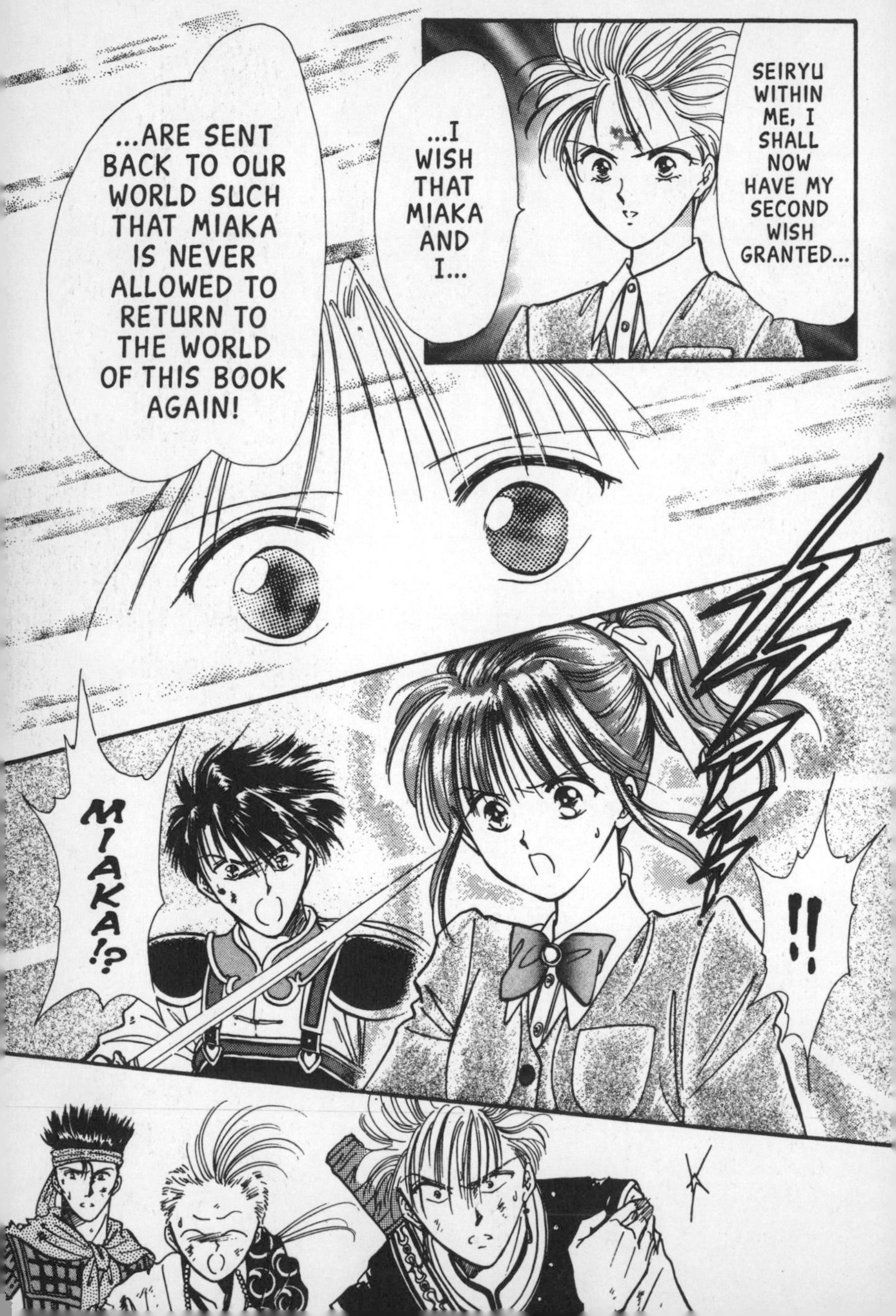
SEIRYU WITHIN ME, I SHALL NOW HAVE MY SECOND WISH GRANTED...
...I WISH THAT MIAKA AND I...
...ARE SENT BACK TO OUR WORLD SUCH THAT MIAKA IS NEVER ALLOWED TO RETURN TO THE WORLD OF THIS BOOK AGAIN!
!!
MIAKA!?

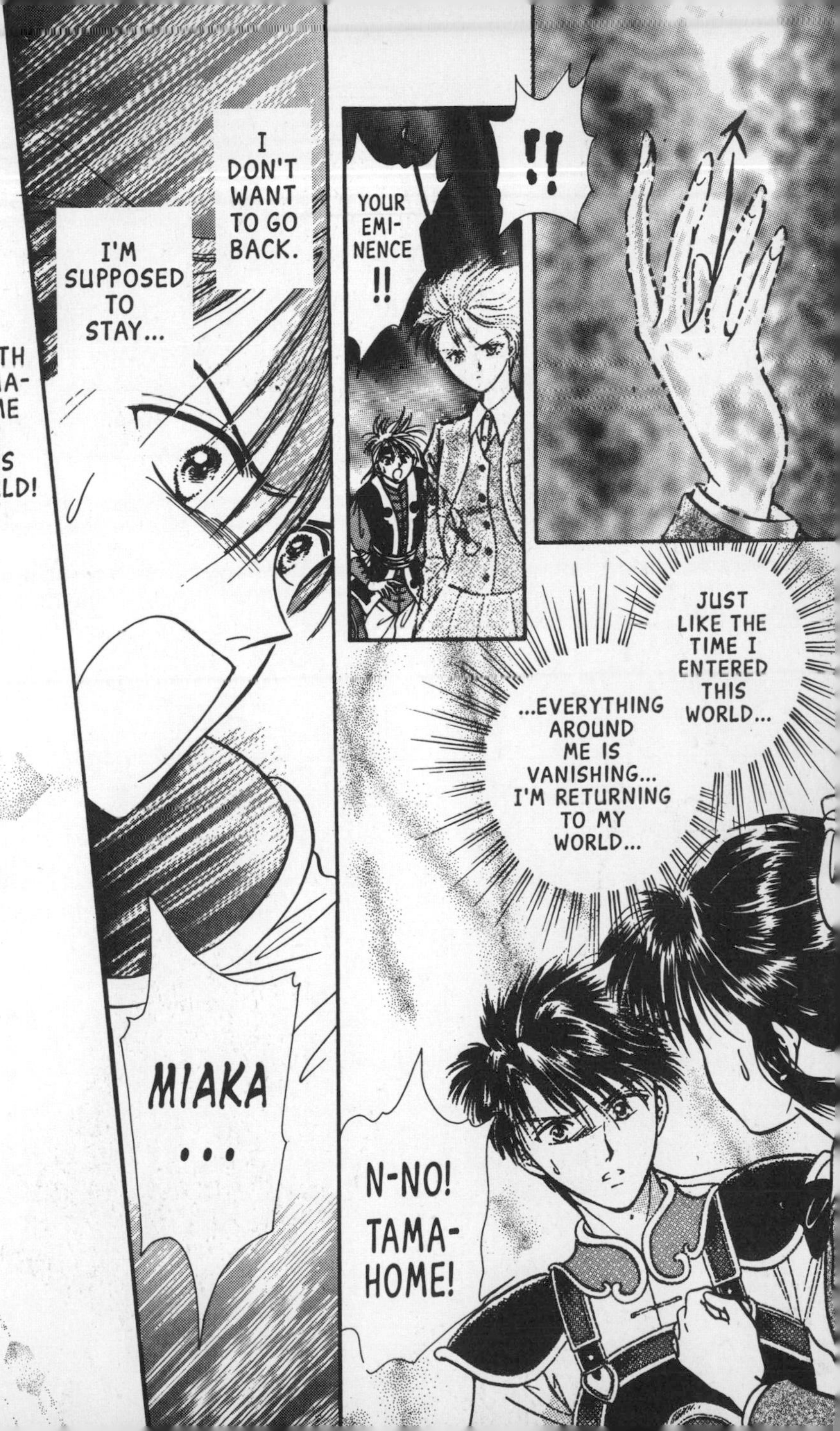
!!
YOUR EMINENCE !!
JUST LIKE THE TIME I ENTERED THIS WORLD...
...EVERYTHING AROUND ME IS VANISHING... I'M RETURNING TO MY WORLD...
N-NO! TAMA-HOME!
I DON'T WANT TO GO BACK.
I'M SUPPOSED TO STAY...
...WITH TAMA-HOME IN THIS WORLD!
MIAKA ...

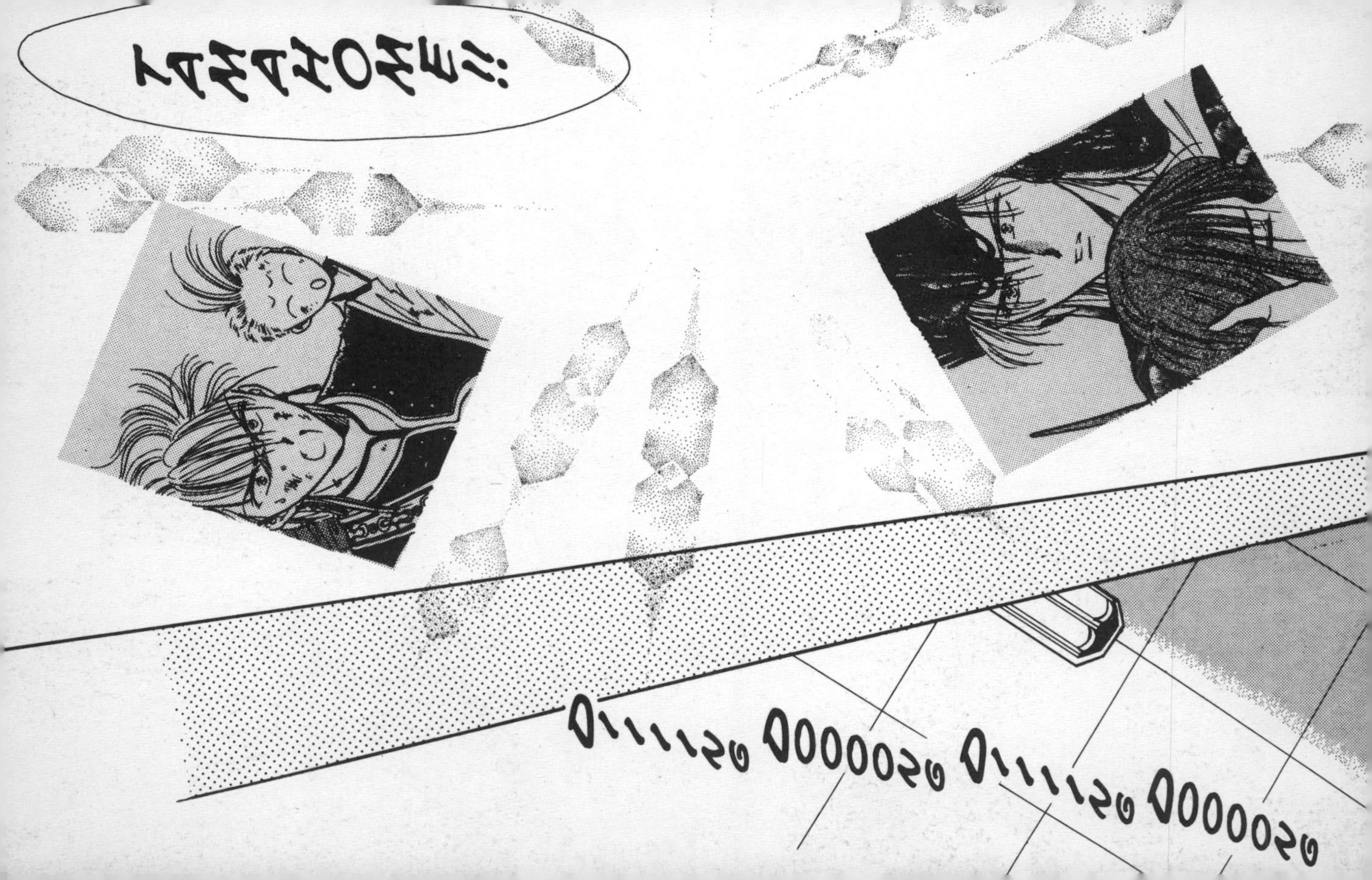
TAMAHOME!!
DIIIING DOOOONG DIIIING DOOOONG

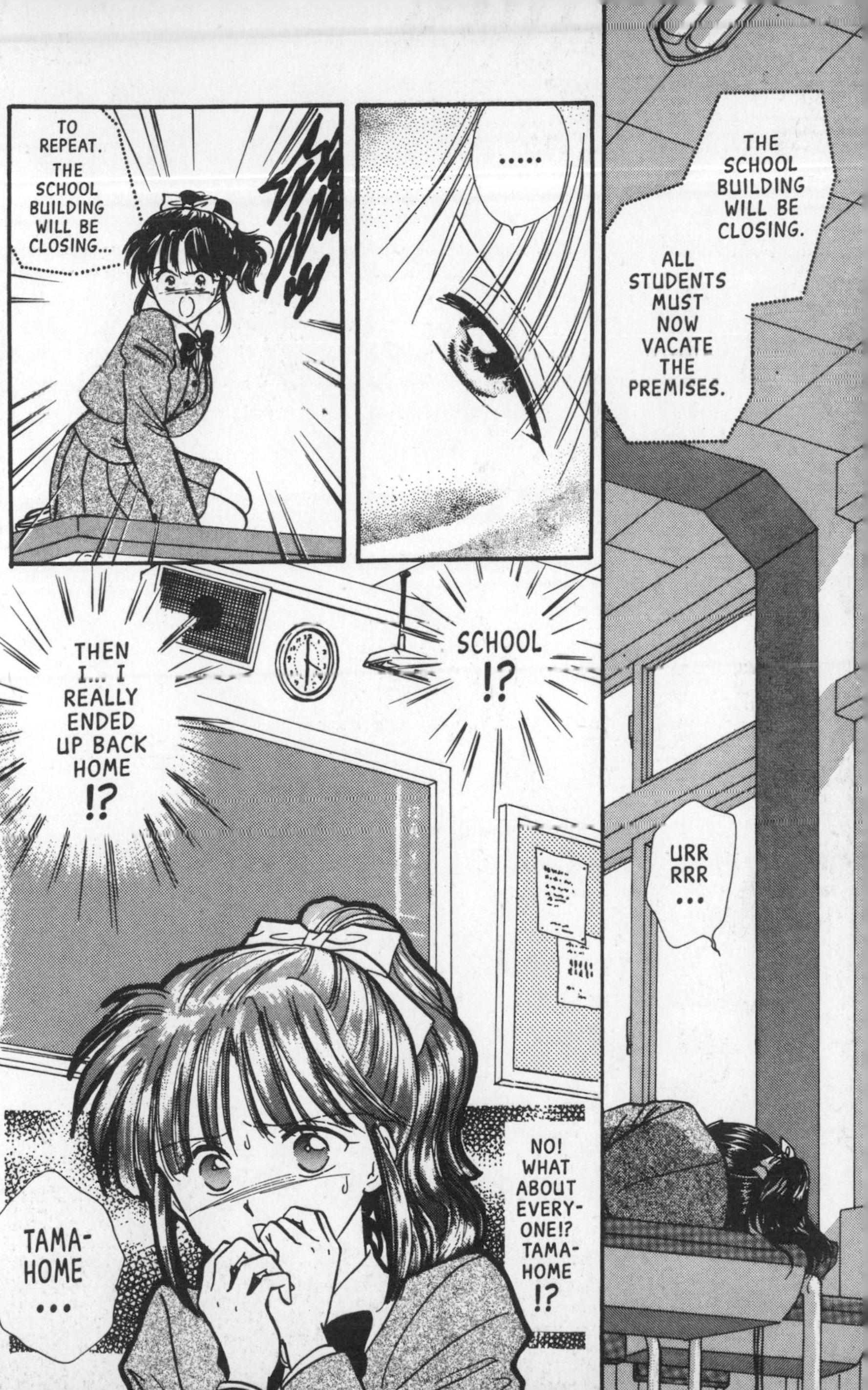
THE SCHOOL BUILDING WILL BE CLOSING.
ALL STUDENTS MUST NOW VACATE THE PREMISES.
URR RRR ...
.....
TO REPEAT. THE SCHOOL BUILDING WILL BE CLOSING...
SCHOOL !?
THEN I... I REALLY ENDED UP BACK HOME !?
NO! WHAT ABOUT EVERY-ONE!? TAMA-HOME !?
TAMA-HOME ...

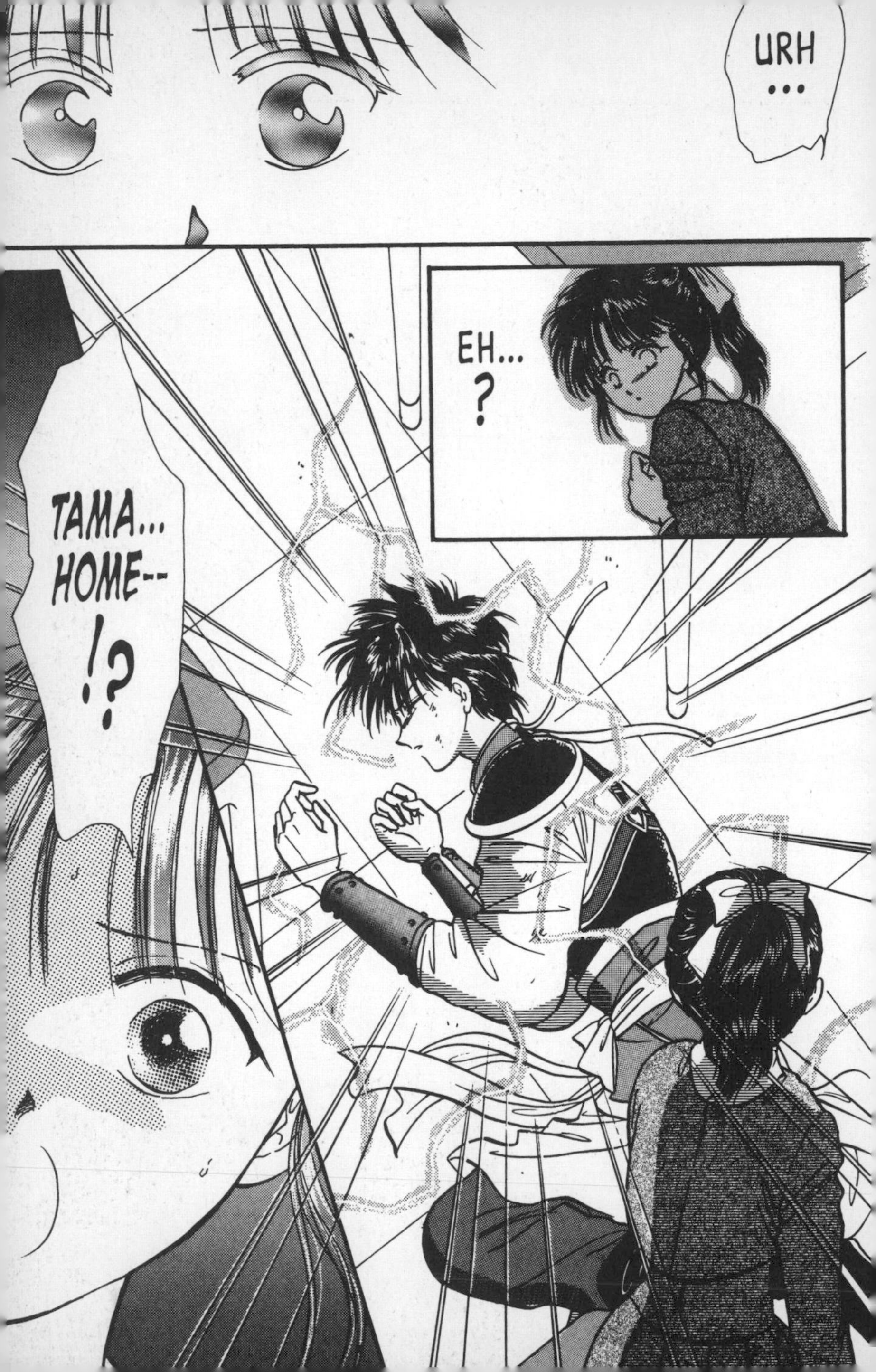
URH ...
EH... ?
TAMA... HOME-- !?

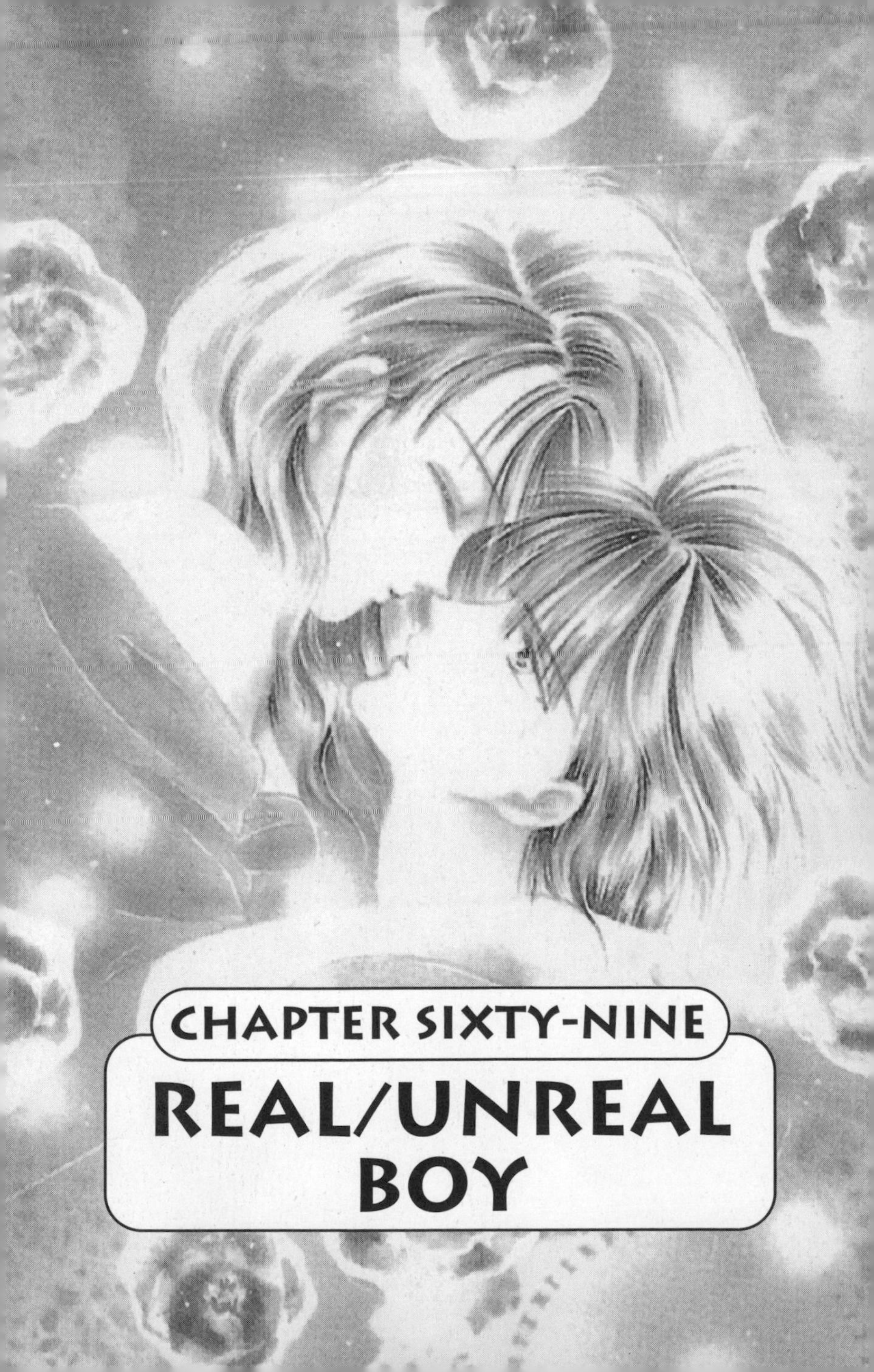
CHAPTER SIXTY-NINE
REAL/UNREAL
BOY

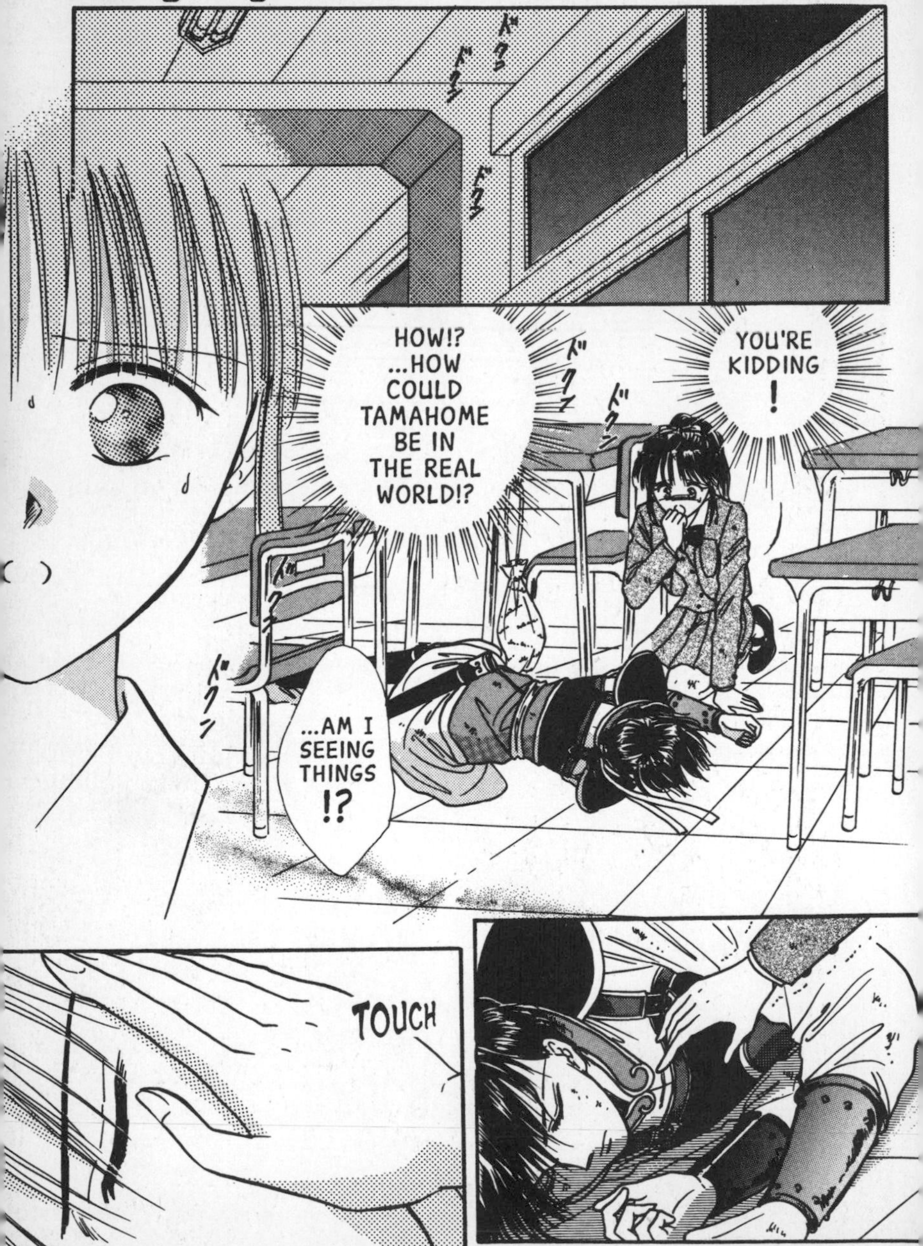
YOU'RE KIDDING!
HOW!? ...HOW COULD TAMAHOME BE IN THE REAL WORLD!?
...AM I SEEING THINGS!?
TOUCH

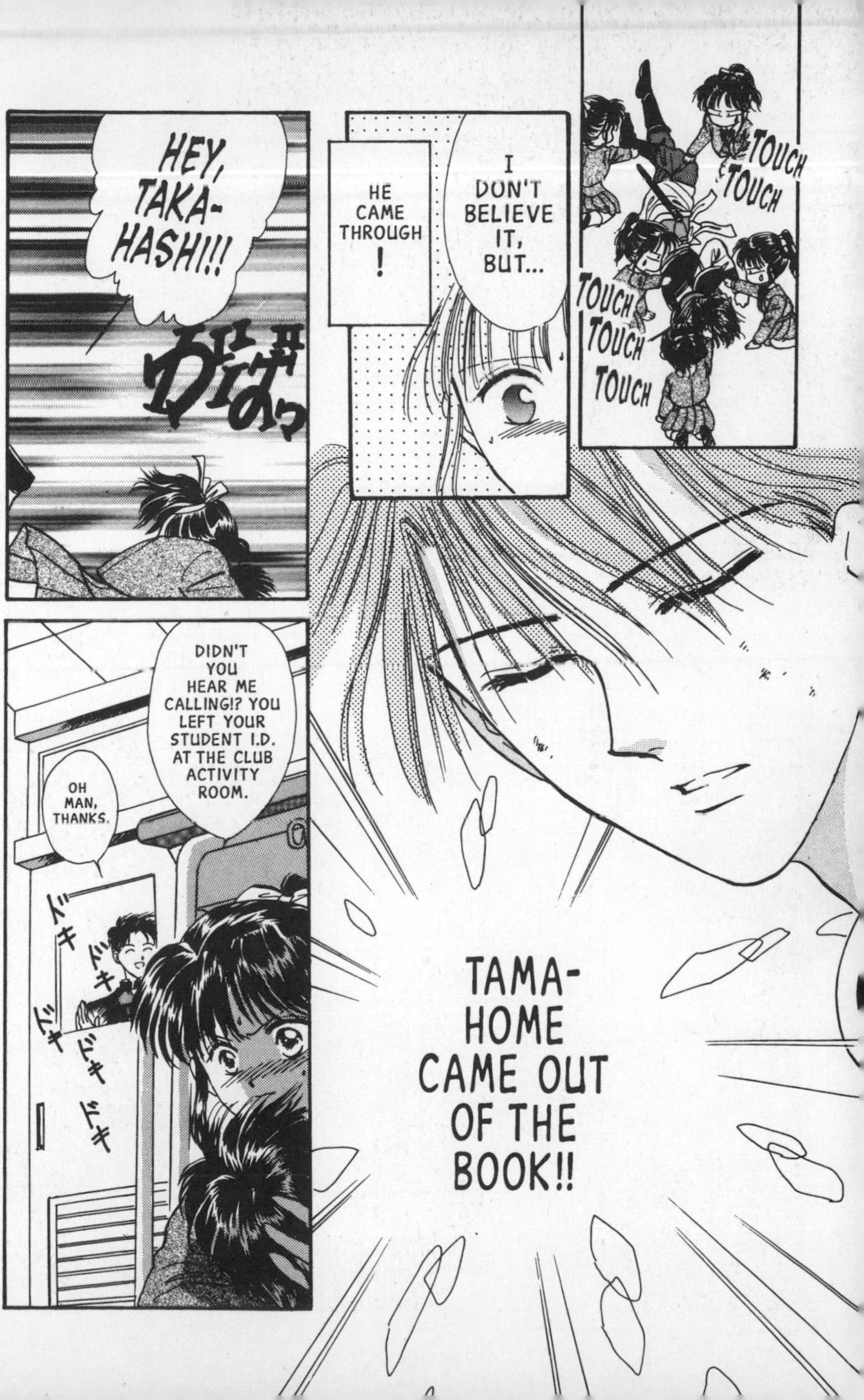

TOUCH TOUCH
TOUCH TOUCH TOUCH
I DON'T BELIEVE IT, BUT...
HE CAME THROUGH!
HEY, TAKA-HASHI!!!
TAMA-HOME CAME OUT OF THE BOOK!!
DIDN'T YOU HEAR ME CALLING!? YOU LEFT YOUR STUDENT I.D. AT THE CLUB ACTIVITY ROOM.
OH MAN, THANKS.
ドキ ドキ ドキ ドキ ドキ

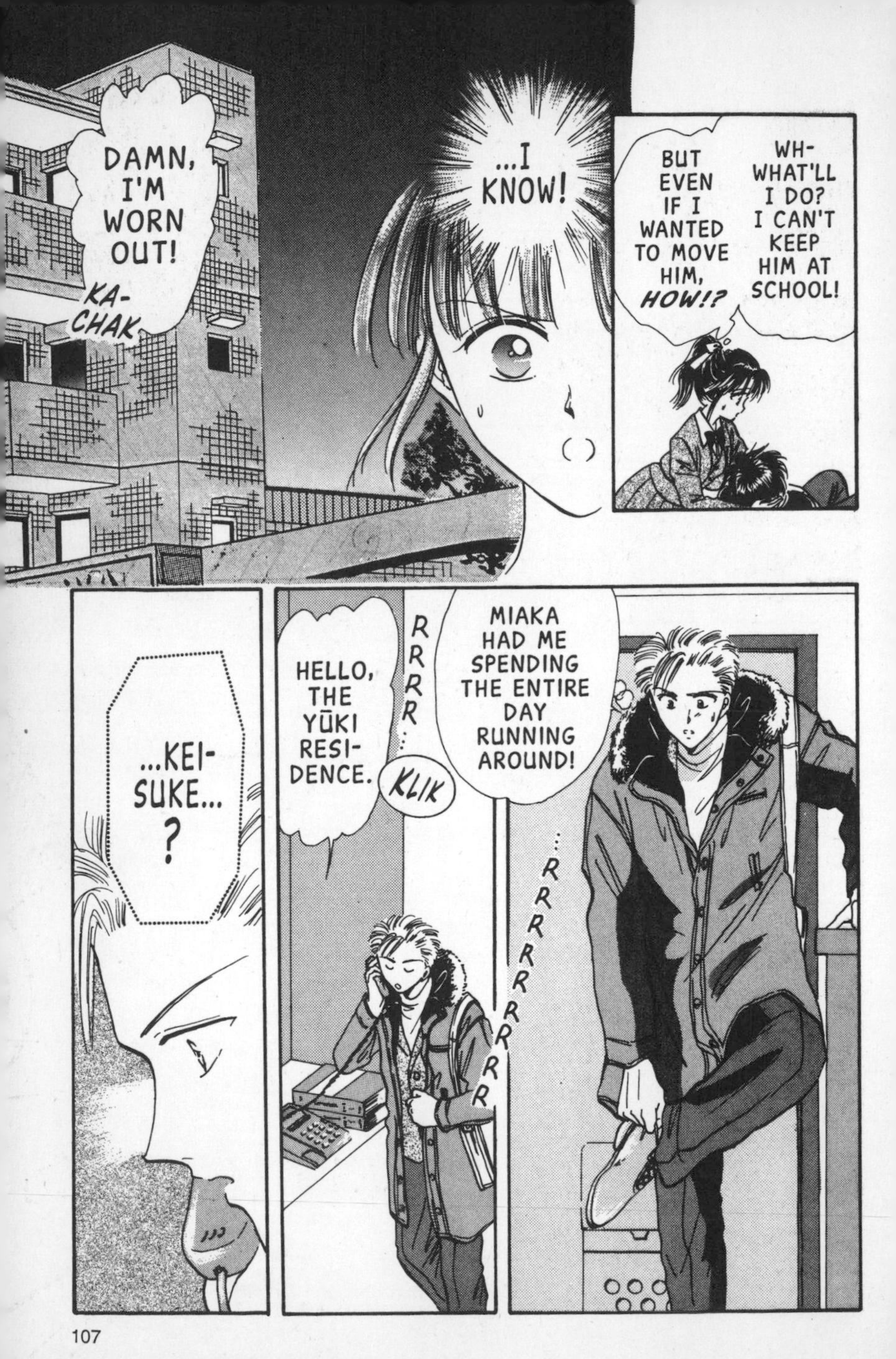
WH-WHAT'LL I DO? I CAN'T KEEP HIM AT SCHOOL!
BUT EVEN IF I WANTED TO MOVE HIM, HOW!?
...I KNOW!
DAMN, I'M WORN OUT!
KA-CHAK
MIAKA HAD ME SPENDING THE ENTIRE DAY RUNNING AROUND!
...RRRRRRRRR
RRRR...
KLIK
HELLO, THE YŪKI RESIDENCE.
...KEI-SUKE...?

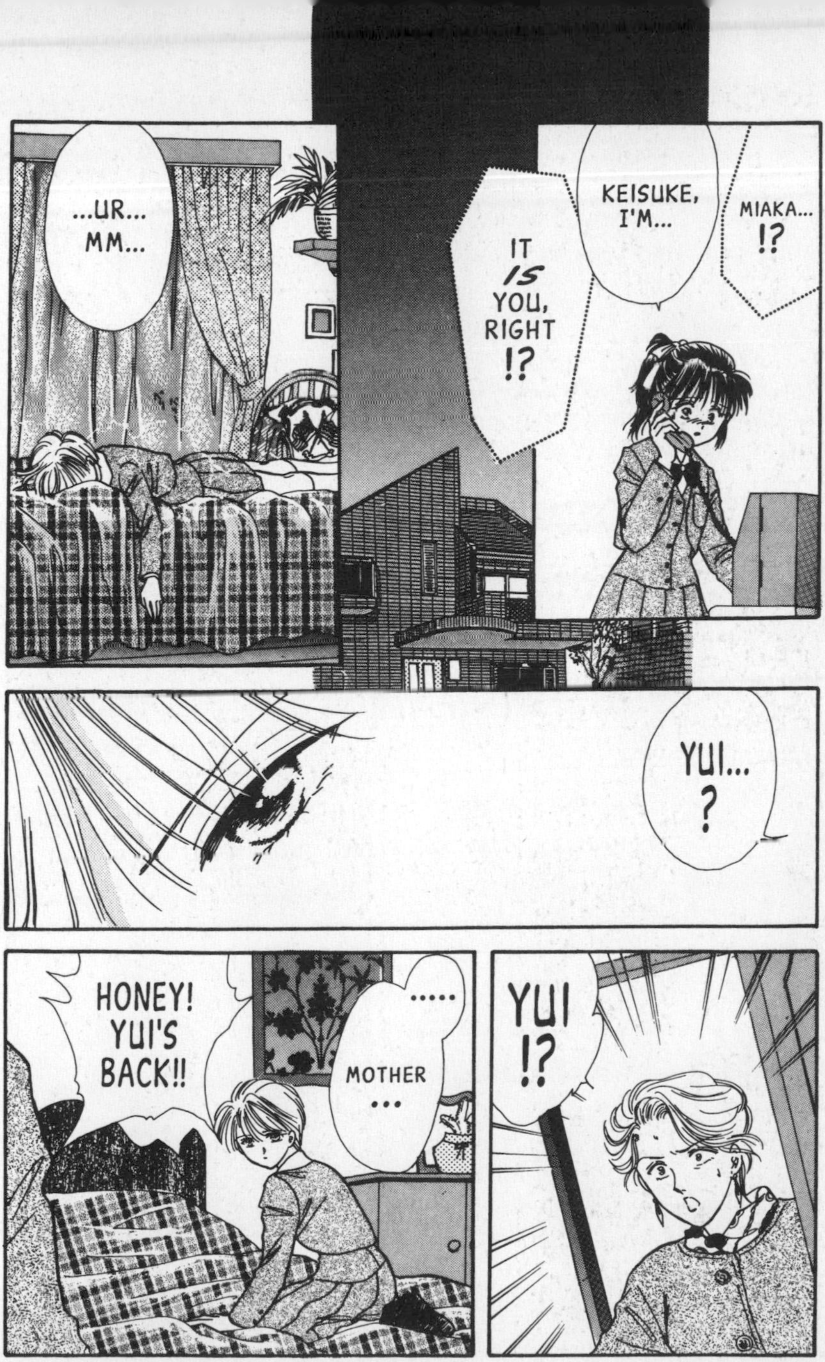
MIAKA... !?
KEISUKE, I'M...
IT IS YOU, RIGHT !?
...UR... MM...
YUI... ?
YUI !?
HONEY! YUI'S BACK!!
..... MOTHER ...

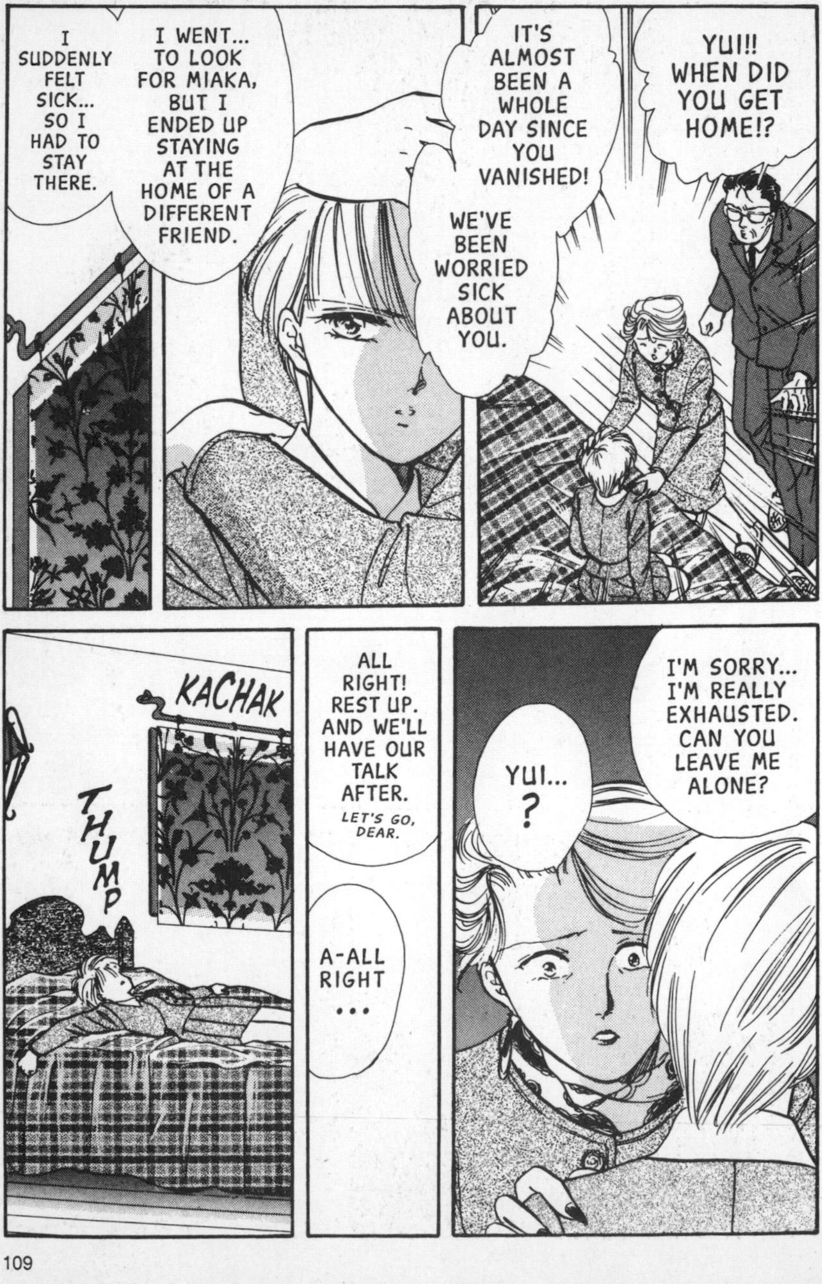
YUI!! WHEN DID YOU GET HOME!?
IT'S ALMOST BEEN A WHOLE DAY SINCE YOU VANISHED!
WE'VE BEEN WORRIED SICK ABOUT YOU.
I WENT... TO LOOK FOR MIAKA, BUT I ENDED UP STAYING AT THE HOME OF A DIFFERENT FRIEND.
I SUDDENLY FELT SICK... SO I HAD TO STAY THERE.
I'M SORRY... I'M REALLY EXHAUSTED. CAN YOU LEAVE ME ALONE?
YUI... ?
ALL RIGHT! REST UP. AND WE'LL HAVE OUR TALK AFTER.
LET'S GO, DEAR.
A-ALL RIGHT ...
KACHAK
THUMP

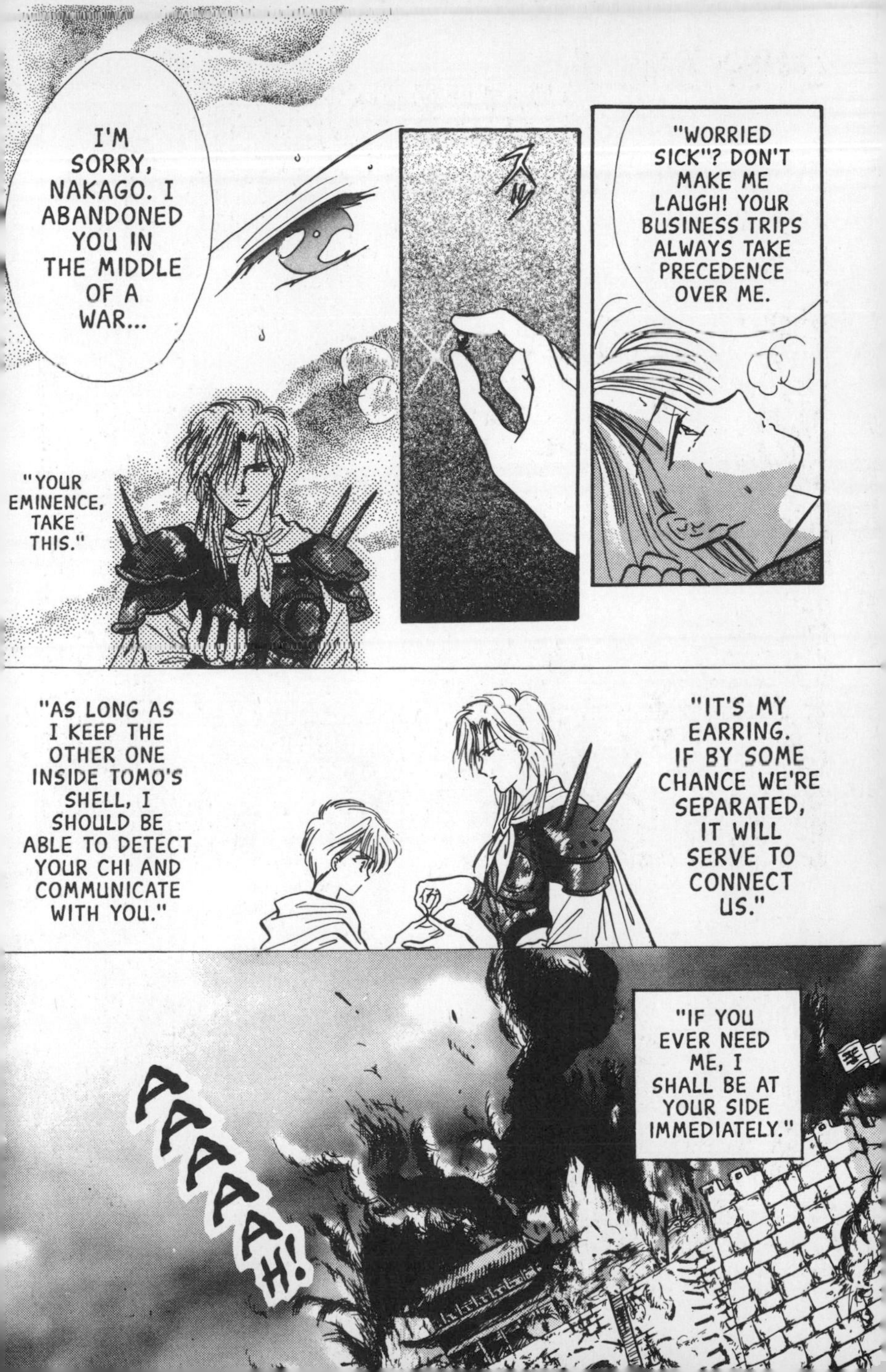
"WORRIED SICK"? DON'T MAKE ME LAUGH! YOUR BUSINESS TRIPS ALWAYS TAKE PRECEDENCE OVER ME.
I'M SORRY, NAKAGO. I ABANDONED YOU IN THE MIDDLE OF A WAR...
"YOUR EMINENCE, TAKE THIS."
"IT'S MY EARRING. IF BY SOME CHANCE WE'RE SEPARATED, IT WILL SERVE TO CONNECT US."
"AS LONG AS I KEEP THE OTHER ONE INSIDE TOMO'S SHELL, I SHOULD BE ABLE TO DETECT YOUR CHI AND COMMUNICATE WITH YOU."
"IF YOU EVER NEED ME, I SHALL BE AT YOUR SIDE IMMEDIATELY."
AAAAAH!

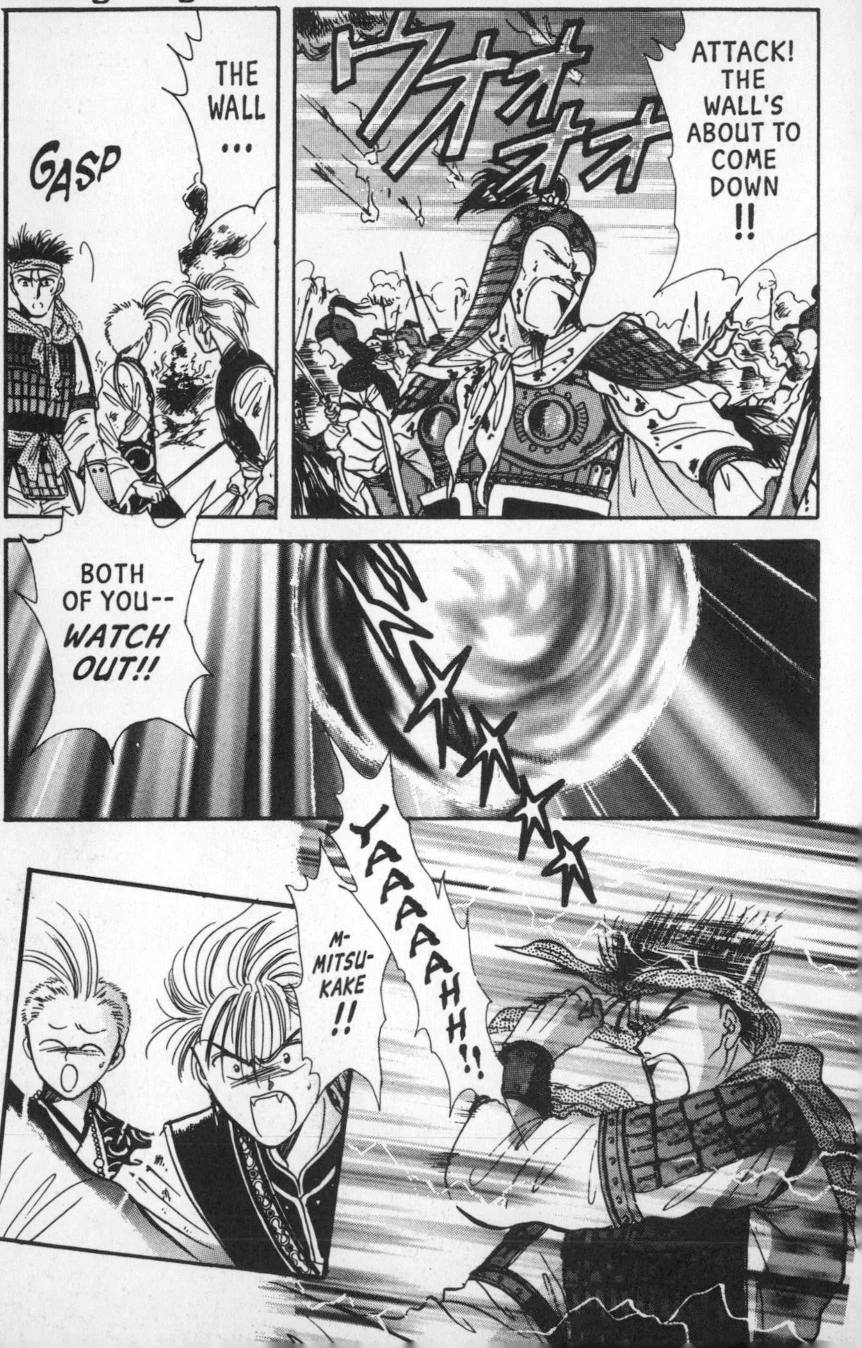
ATTACK! THE WALL'S ABOUT TO COME DOWN !!
THE WALL ...
GASP
BOTH OF YOU-- WATCH OUT!!
YAAAAAHH!!
M-MITSUKAKE !!

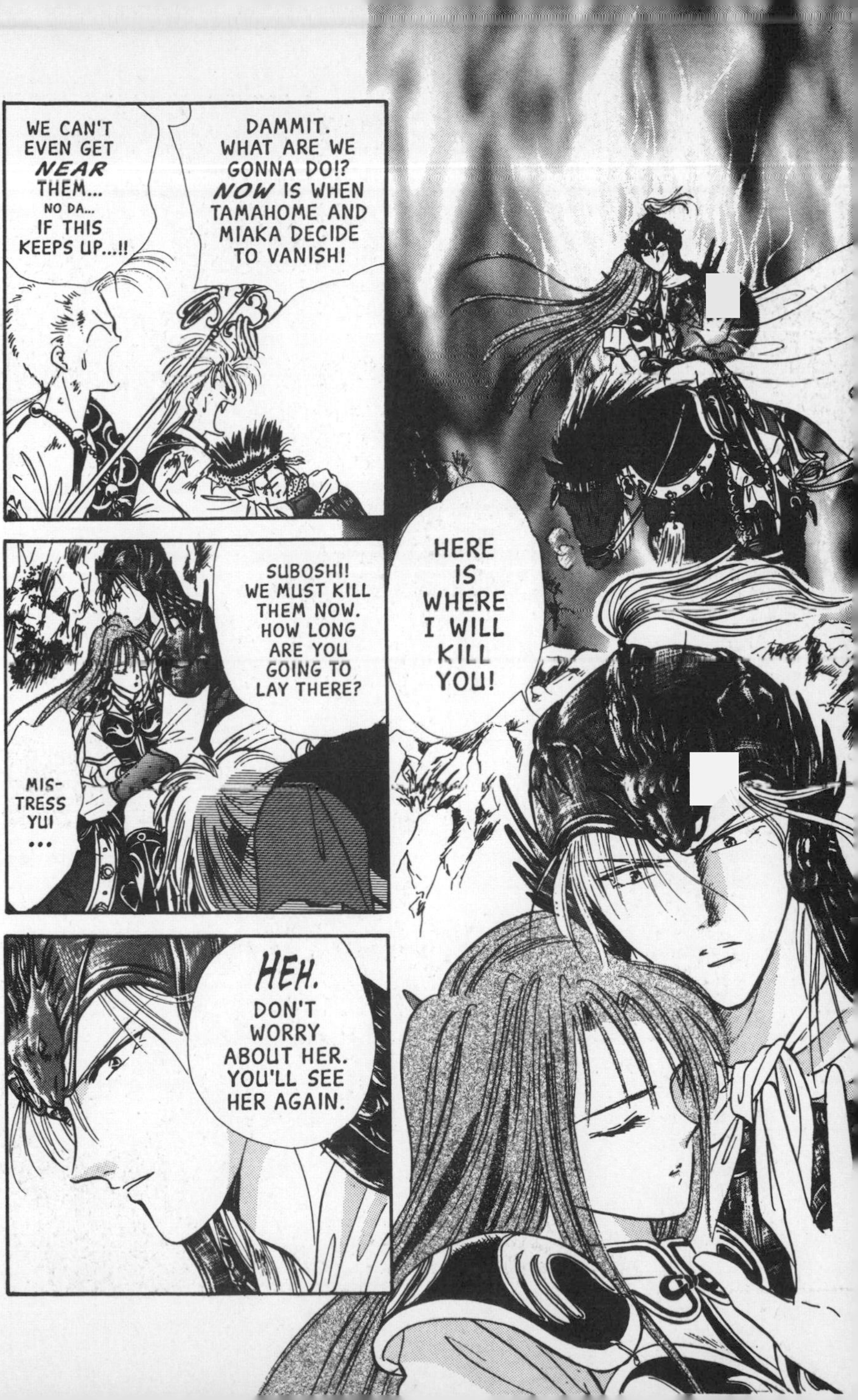
HERE IS WHERE I WILL KILL YOU!
DAMMIT. WHAT ARE WE GONNA DO!? NOW IS WHEN TAMAHOME AND MIAKA DECIDE TO VANISH!
WE CAN'T EVEN GET NEAR THEM... NO DA... IF THIS KEEPS UP...!!
SUBOSHI!! WE MUST KILL THEM NOW. HOW LONG ARE YOU GOING TO LAY THERE?
MISTRESS YUI...
HEH. DON'T WORRY ABOUT HER. YOU'LL SEE HER AGAIN.

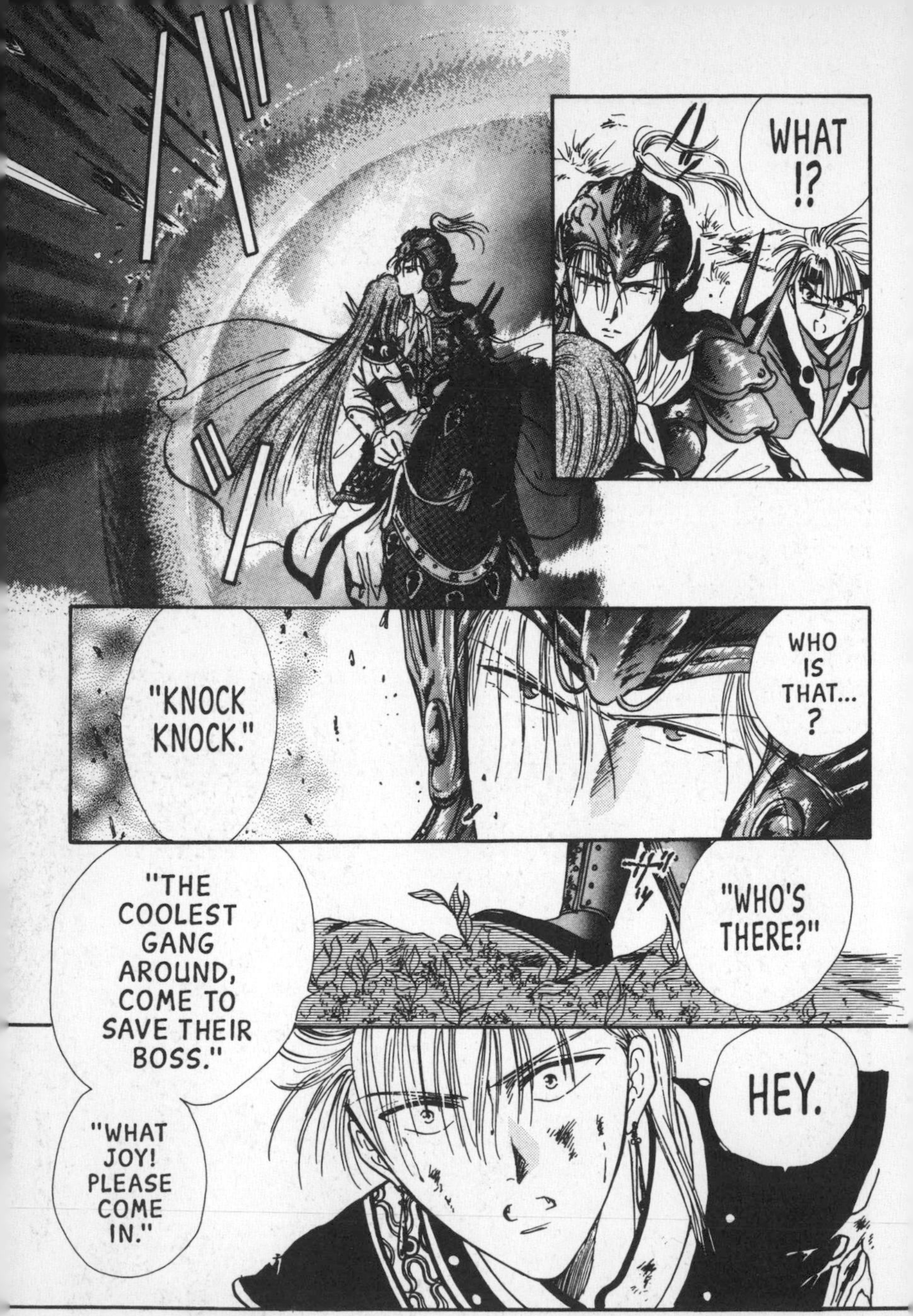
WHAT !?
WHO IS THAT... ?
"KNOCK KNOCK."
"WHO'S THERE?"
"THE COOLEST GANG AROUND, COME TO SAVE THEIR BOSS."
HEY.
"WHAT JOY! PLEASE COME IN."

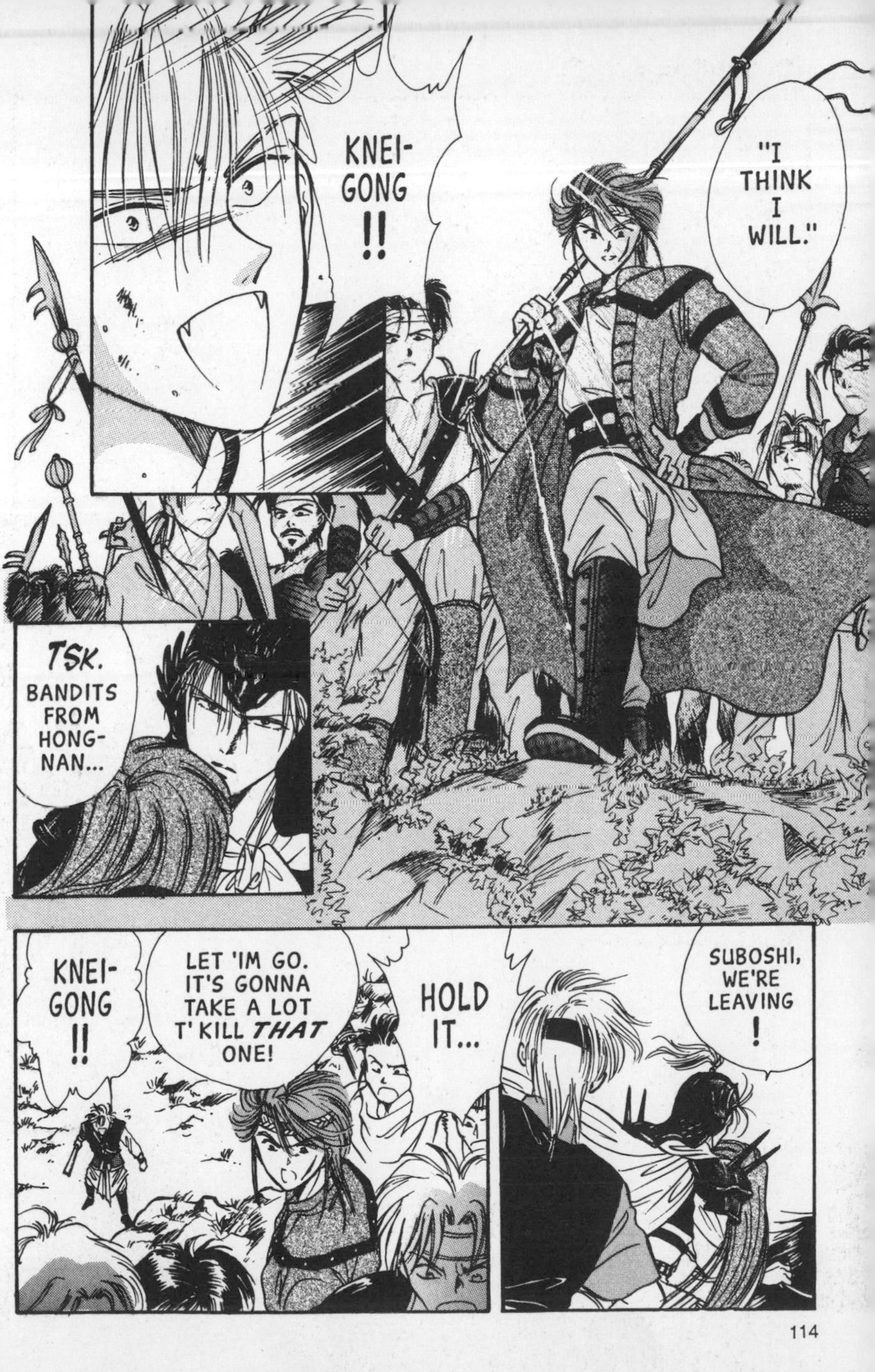
"I THINK I WILL."
KNEI-GONG!!
TSK. BANDITS FROM HONG-NAN...
SUBOSHI, WE'RE LEAVING!
HOLD IT...
LET 'IM GO. IT'S GONNA TAKE A LOT T' KILL *THAT* ONE!
KNEI-GONG!!

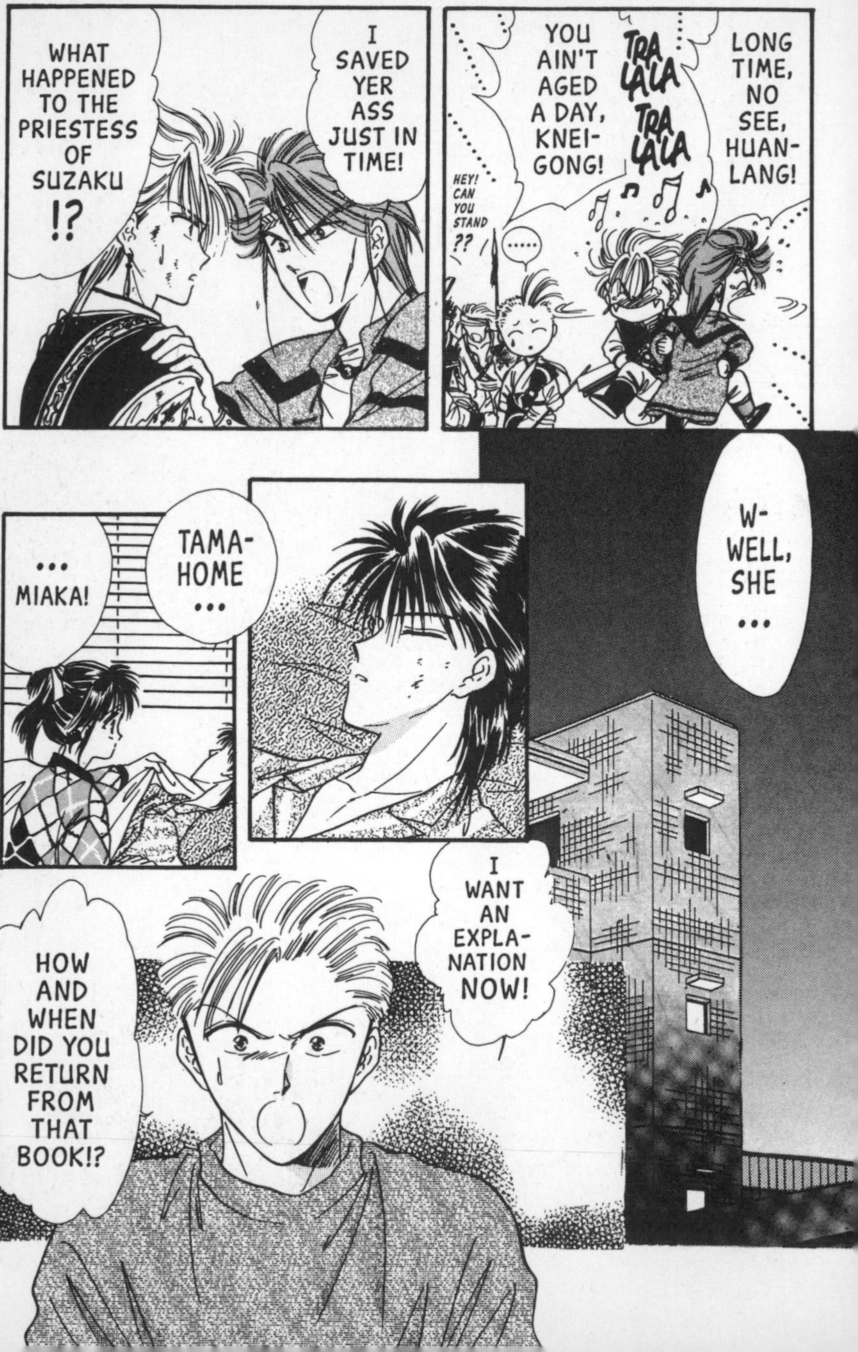
LONG TIME, NO SEE, HUAN-LANG!
TRA LA LA TRA LA LA
YOU AIN'T AGED A DAY, KNEI-GONG!
HEY! CAN YOU STAND ??
......
I SAVED YER ASS JUST IN TIME!
WHAT HAPPENED TO THE PRIESTESS OF SUZAKU !?
W-WELL, SHE ...
TAMA-HOME ...
... MIAKA!
I WANT AN EXPLANATION NOW!
HOW AND WHEN DID YOU RETURN FROM THAT BOOK!?

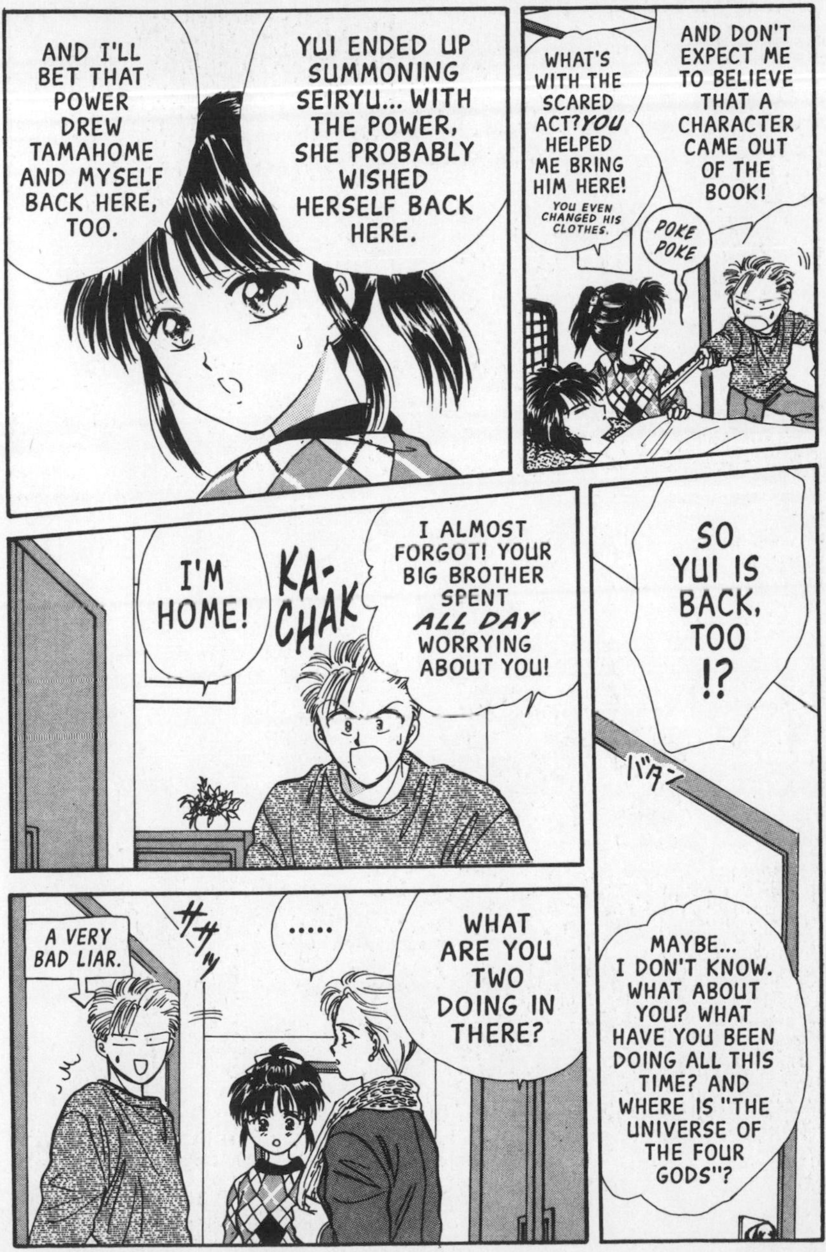

WHAT'S WITH THE SCARED ACT? *YOU* HELPED ME BRING HIM HERE!
YOU EVEN CHANGED HIS CLOTHES.
AND DON'T EXPECT ME TO BELIEVE THAT A CHARACTER CAME OUT OF THE BOOK!
POKE POKE
YUI ENDED UP SUMMONING SEIRYU... WITH THE POWER, SHE PROBABLY WISHED HERSELF BACK HERE.
AND I'LL BET THAT POWER DREW TAMAHOME AND MYSELF BACK HERE, TOO.
SO YUI IS BACK, TOO !?
バタン
MAYBE... I DON'T KNOW. WHAT ABOUT YOU? WHAT HAVE YOU BEEN DOING ALL THIS TIME? AND WHERE IS "THE UNIVERSE OF THE FOUR GODS"?
I ALMOST FORGOT! YOUR BIG BROTHER SPENT *ALL DAY* WORRYING ABOUT YOU!
KA-CHAK
I'M HOME!
WHAT ARE YOU TWO DOING IN THERE?
.....
ザザッ
A VERY BAD LIAR.

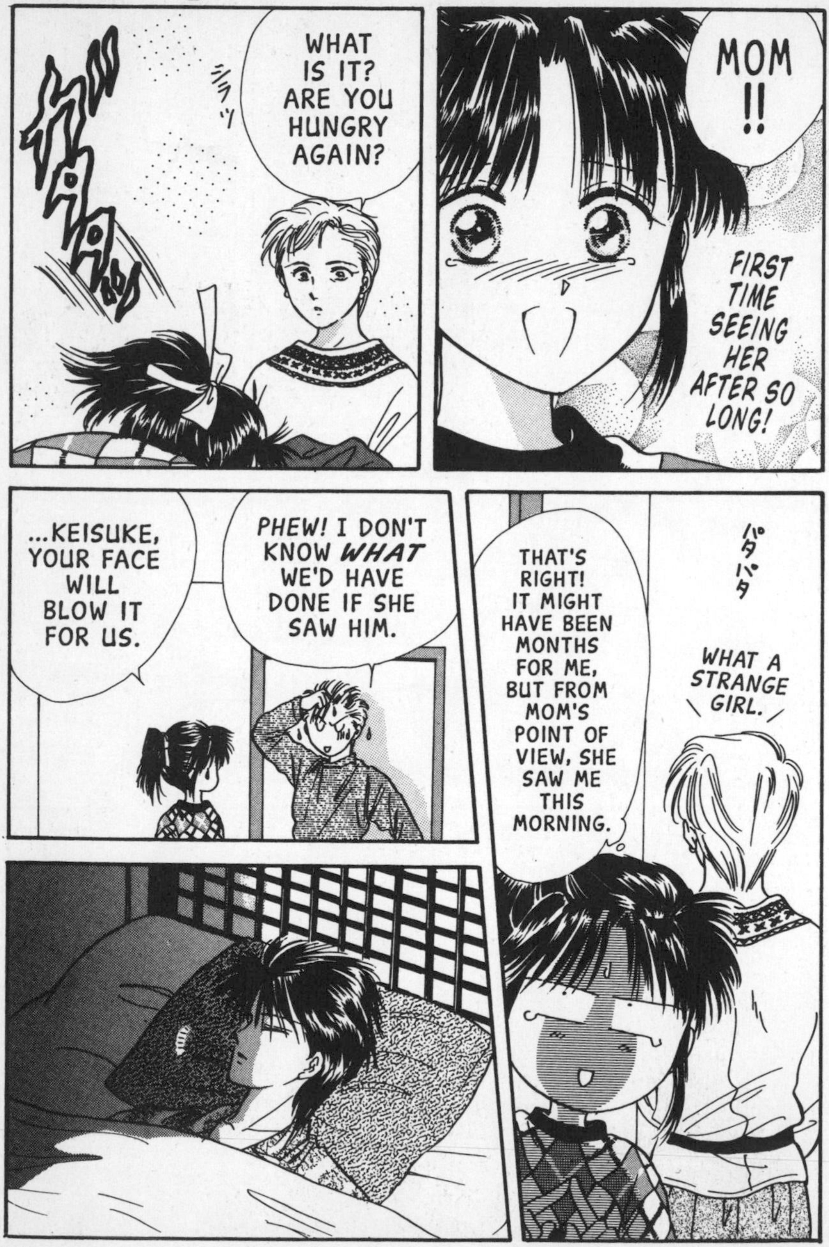
MOM !!
FIRST TIME SEEING HER AFTER SO LONG!
シラッ
WHAT IS IT? ARE YOU HUNGRY AGAIN?
パタパタ
WHAT A STRANGE GIRL.
THAT'S RIGHT! IT MIGHT HAVE BEEN MONTHS FOR ME, BUT FROM MOM'S POINT OF VIEW, SHE SAW ME THIS MORNING.
PHEW! I DON'T KNOW *WHAT* WE'D HAVE DONE IF SHE SAW HIM.
...KEISUKE, YOUR FACE WILL BLOW IT FOR US.

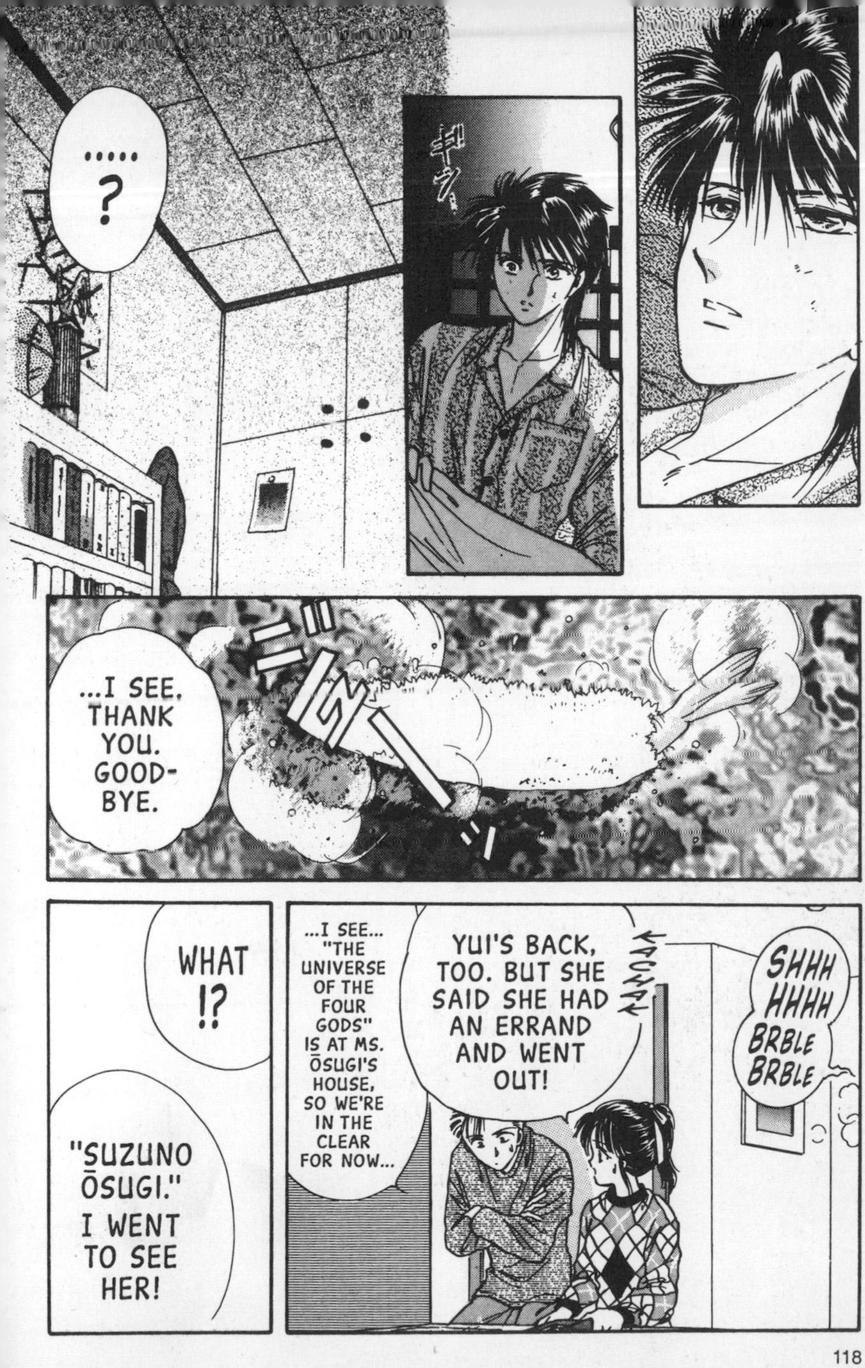
.....?
...I SEE. THANK YOU. GOOD-BYE.
SHHH HHHH BRBLE BRBLE
KACHAK
YUI'S BACK, TOO. BUT SHE SAID SHE HAD AN ERRAND AND WENT OUT!
...I SEE... "THE UNIVERSE OF THE FOUR GODS" IS AT MS. ŌSUGI'S HOUSE, SO WE'RE IN THE CLEAR FOR NOW...
WHAT!?
"SUZUNO ŌSUGI." I WENT TO SEE HER!

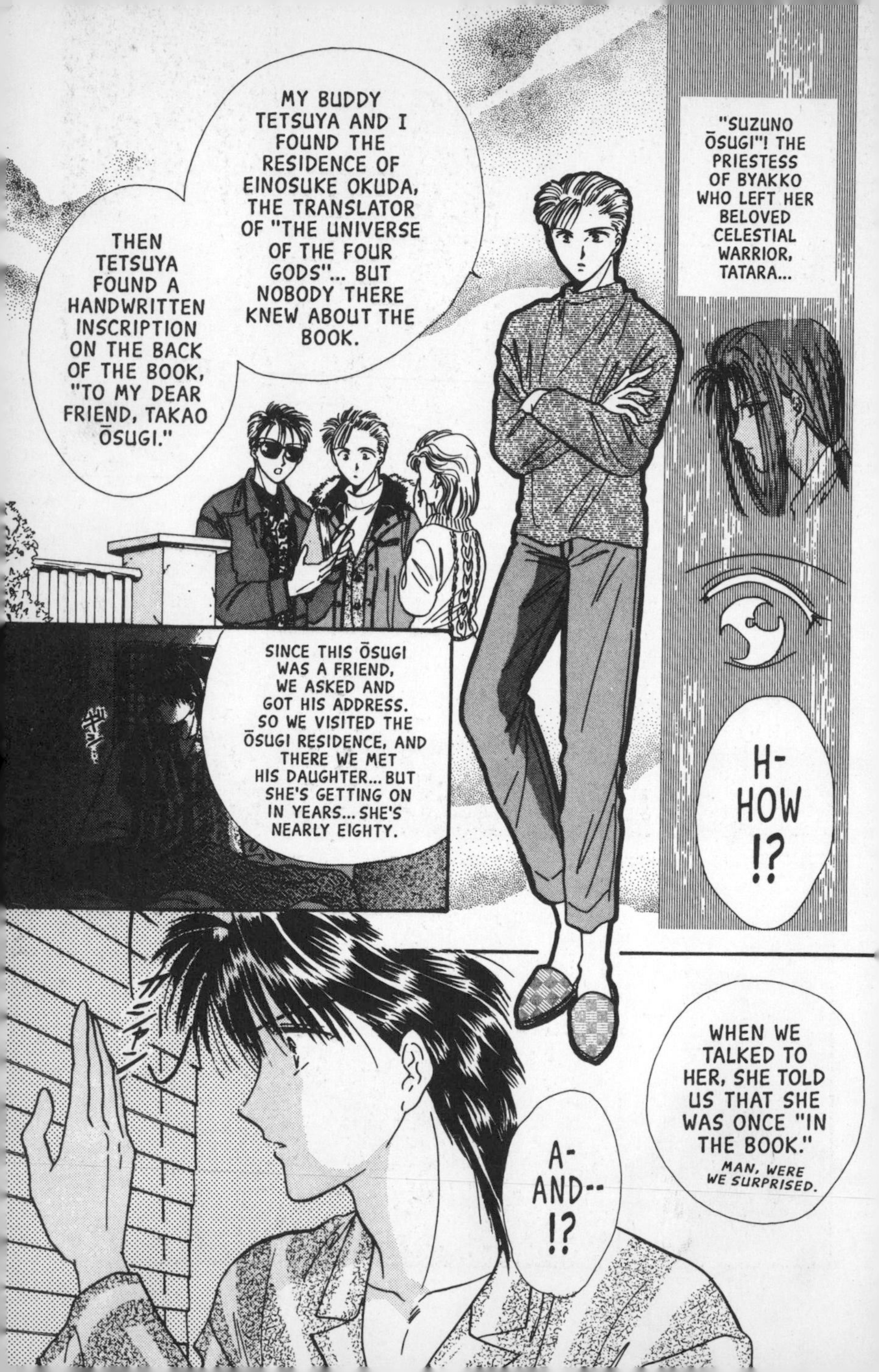
MY BUDDY TETSUYA AND I FOUND THE RESIDENCE OF EINOSUKE OKUDA, THE TRANSLATOR OF "THE UNIVERSE OF THE FOUR GODS"... BUT NOBODY THERE KNEW ABOUT THE BOOK.
THEN TETSUYA FOUND A HANDWRITTEN INSCRIPTION ON THE BACK OF THE BOOK, "TO MY DEAR FRIEND, TAKAO ŌSUGI."
SINCE THIS ŌSUGI WAS A FRIEND, WE ASKED AND GOT HIS ADDRESS. SO WE VISITED THE ŌSUGI RESIDENCE, AND THERE WE MET HIS DAUGHTER... BUT SHE'S GETTING ON IN YEARS... SHE'S NEARLY EIGHTY.
"SUZUNO ŌSUGI"! THE PRIESTESS OF BYAKKO WHO LEFT HER BELOVED CELESTIAL WARRIOR, TATARA...
H-HOW !?
WHEN WE TALKED TO HER, SHE TOLD US THAT SHE WAS ONCE "IN THE BOOK."
MAN, WERE WE SURPRISED.
A-AND-- !?

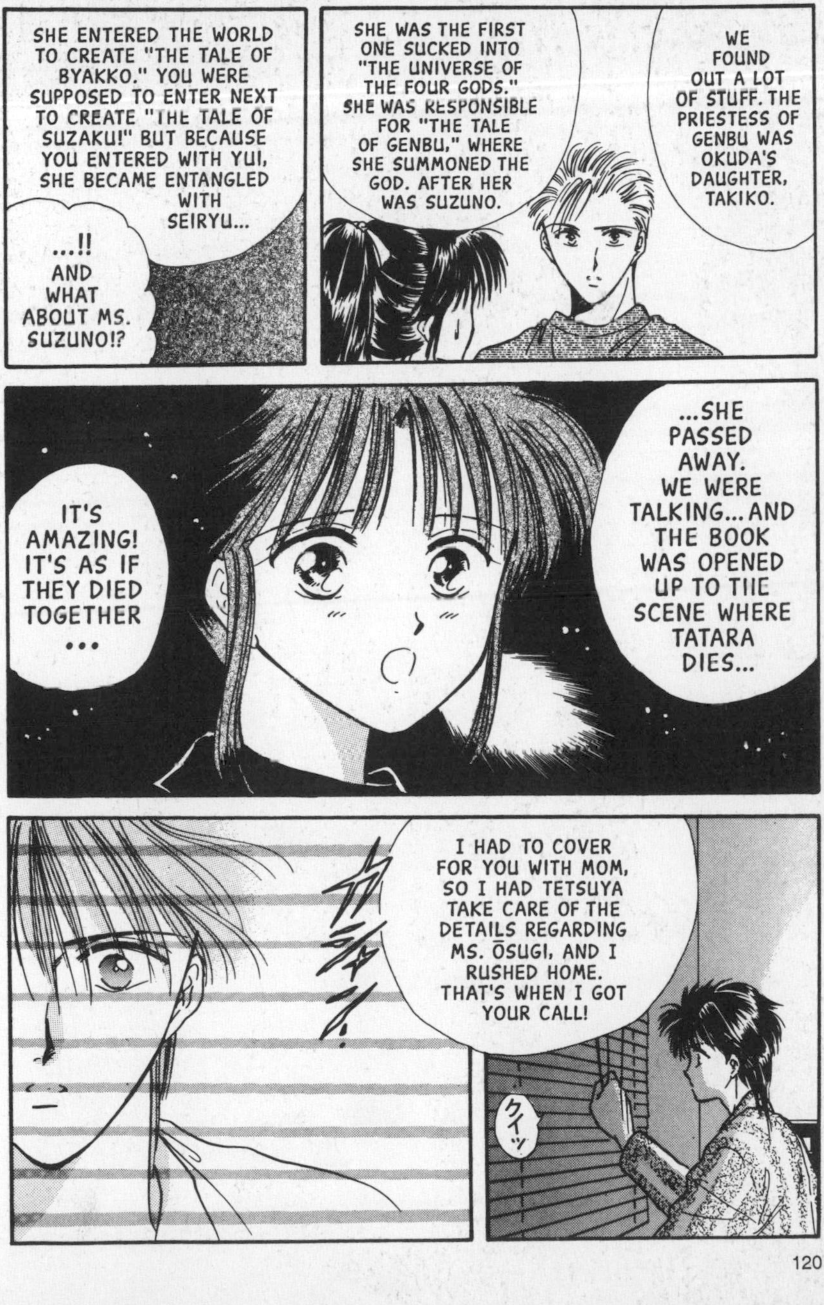
WE FOUND OUT A LOT OF STUFF. THE PRIESTESS OF GENBU WAS OKUDA'S DAUGHTER, TAKIKO.
SHE WAS THE FIRST ONE SUCKED INTO "THE UNIVERSE OF THE FOUR GODS." SHE WAS RESPONSIBLE FOR "THE TALE OF GENBU," WHERE SHE SUMMONED THE GOD. AFTER HER WAS SUZUNO.
SHE ENTERED THE WORLD TO CREATE "THE TALE OF BYAKKO." YOU WERE SUPPOSED TO ENTER NEXT TO CREATE "THE TALE OF SUZAKU!" BUT BECAUSE YOU ENTERED WITH YUI, SHE BECAME ENTANGLED WITH SEIRYU...
...!! AND WHAT ABOUT MS. SUZUNO!?
...SHE PASSED AWAY. WE WERE TALKING... AND THE BOOK WAS OPENED UP TO THE SCENE WHERE TATARA DIES...
IT'S AMAZING! IT'S AS IF THEY DIED TOGETHER...
I HAD TO COVER FOR YOU WITH MOM, SO I HAD TETSUYA TAKE CARE OF THE DETAILS REGARDING MS. ŌSUGI, AND I RUSHED HOME. THAT'S WHEN I GOT YOUR CALL!
クイッ

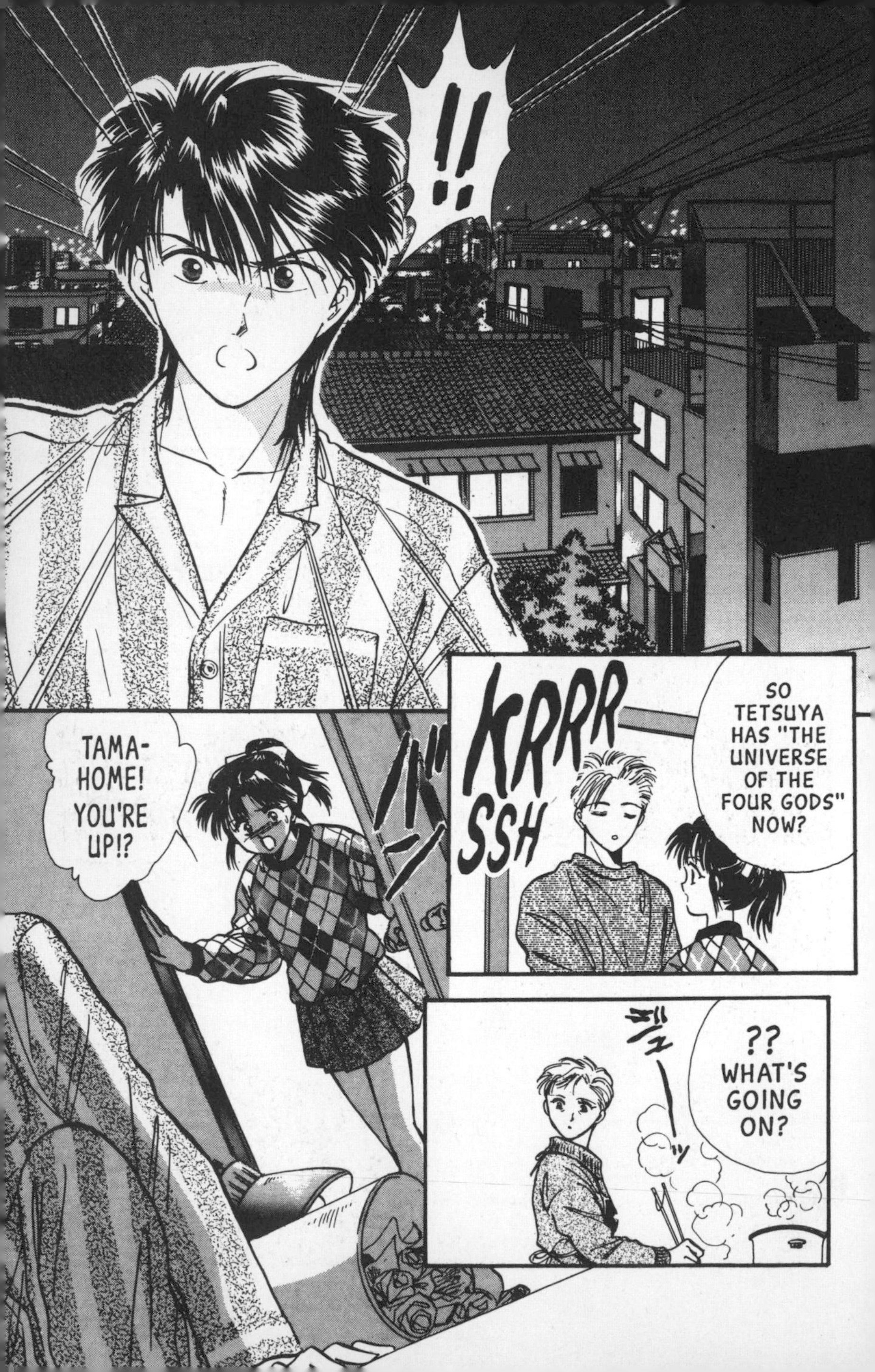
!!
KRRR SSH
SO TETSUYA HAS "THE UNIVERSE OF THE FOUR GODS" NOW?
?? WHAT'S GOING ON?
TAMA-HOME! YOU'RE UP!?

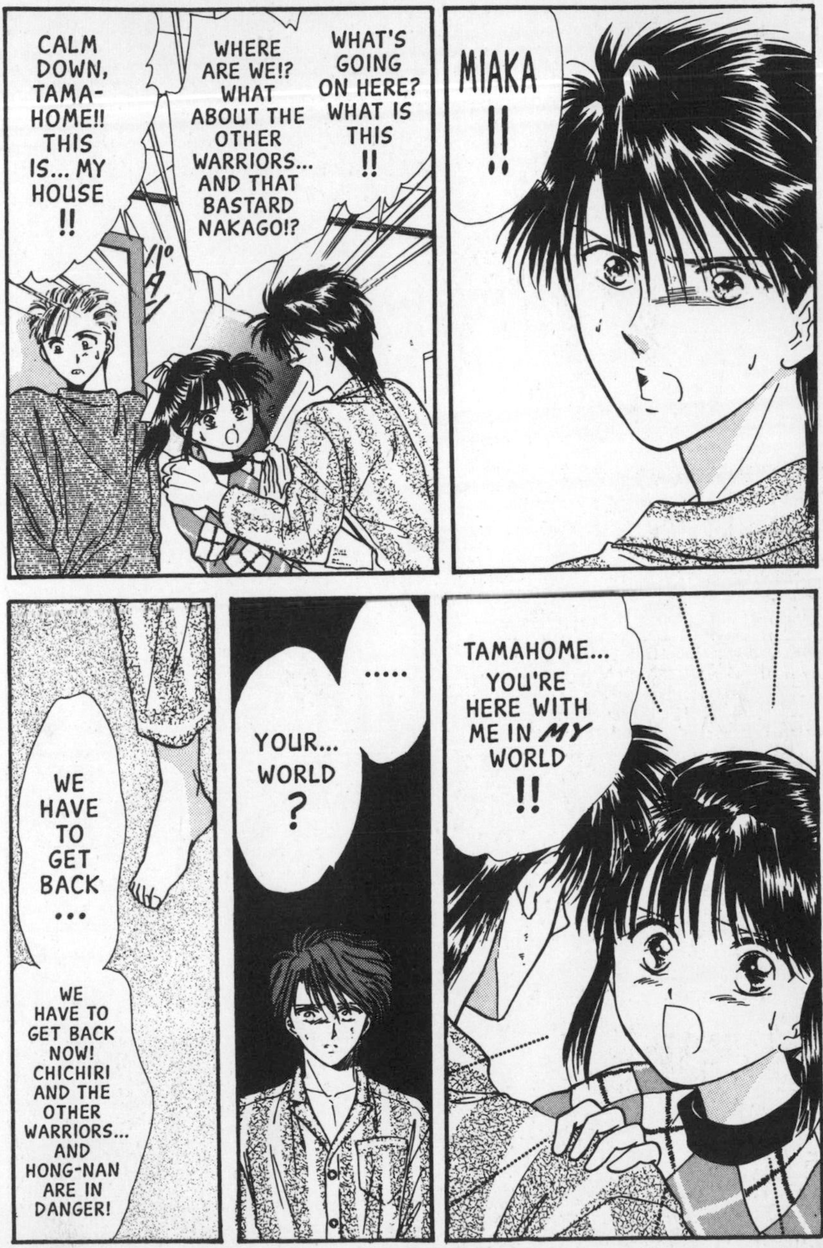
MIAKA!!
WHAT'S GOING ON HERE? WHAT IS THIS!!
WHERE ARE WE!? WHAT ABOUT THE OTHER WARRIORS... AND THAT BASTARD NAKAGO!?
CALM DOWN, TAMA-HOME!! THIS IS... MY HOUSE!!
TAMAHOME... YOU'RE HERE WITH ME IN MY WORLD!!
.....
YOUR... WORLD?
WE HAVE TO GET BACK...
WE HAVE TO GET BACK NOW! CHICHIRI AND THE OTHER WARRIORS... AND HONG-NAN ARE IN DANGER!

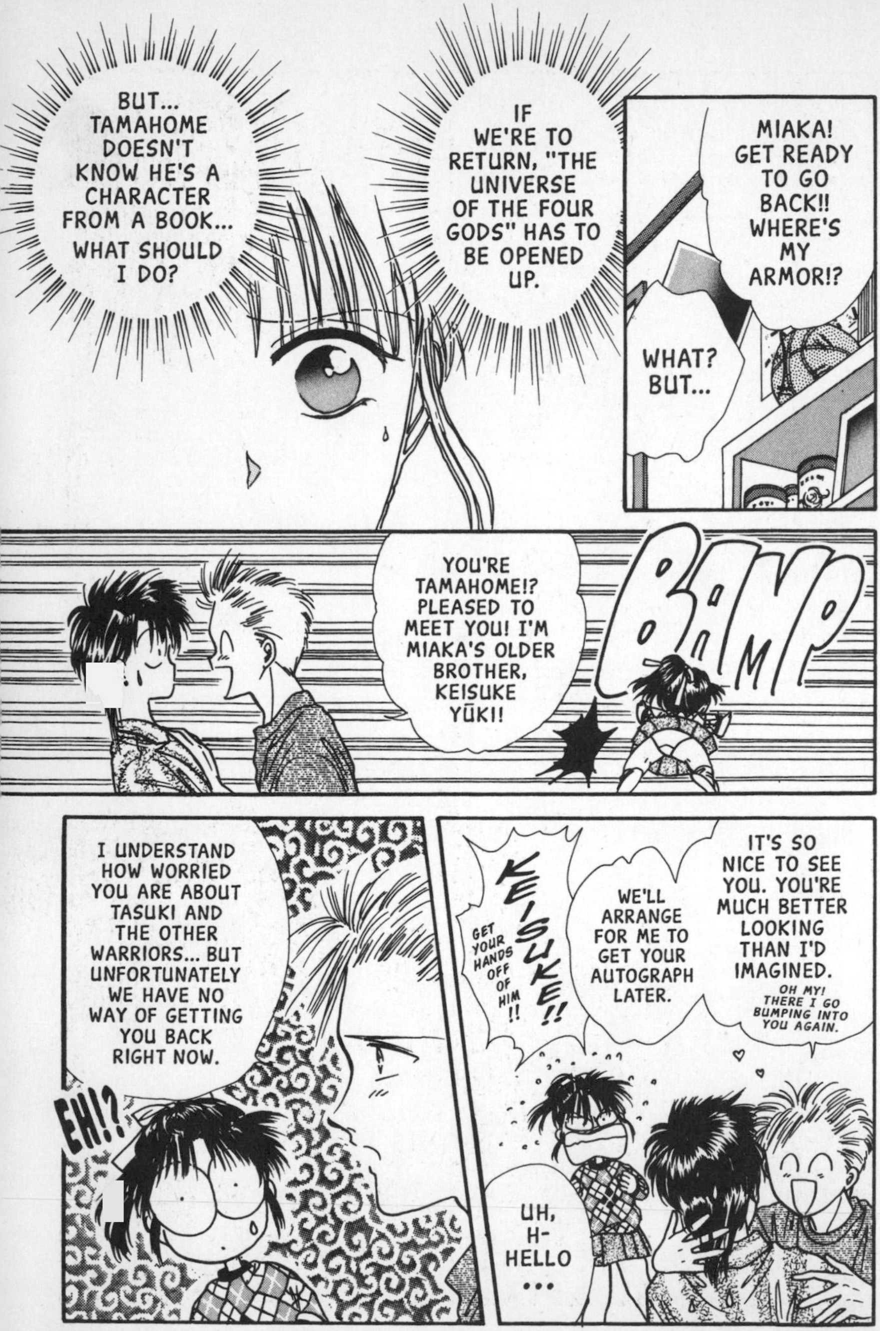
MIAKA! GET READY TO GO BACK!! WHERE'S MY ARMOR!?
WHAT? BUT...
IF WE'RE TO RETURN, "THE UNIVERSE OF THE FOUR GODS" HAS TO BE OPENED UP.
BUT... TAMAHOME DOESN'T KNOW HE'S A CHARACTER FROM A BOOK... WHAT SHOULD I DO?
BAMP
YOU'RE TAMAHOME!? PLEASED TO MEET YOU! I'M MIAKA'S OLDER BROTHER, KEISUKE YŪKI!!
IT'S SO NICE TO SEE YOU. YOU'RE MUCH BETTER LOOKING THAN I'D IMAGINED.
OH MY! THERE I GO BUMPING INTO YOU AGAIN.
WE'LL ARRANGE FOR ME TO GET YOUR AUTOGRAPH LATER.
KEISUKE!!
GET YOUR HANDS OFF OF HIM!!
UH, H-HELLO...
I UNDERSTAND HOW WORRIED YOU ARE ABOUT TASUKI AND THE OTHER WARRIORS... BUT UNFORTUNATELY WE HAVE NO WAY OF GETTING YOU BACK RIGHT NOW.
EH!?

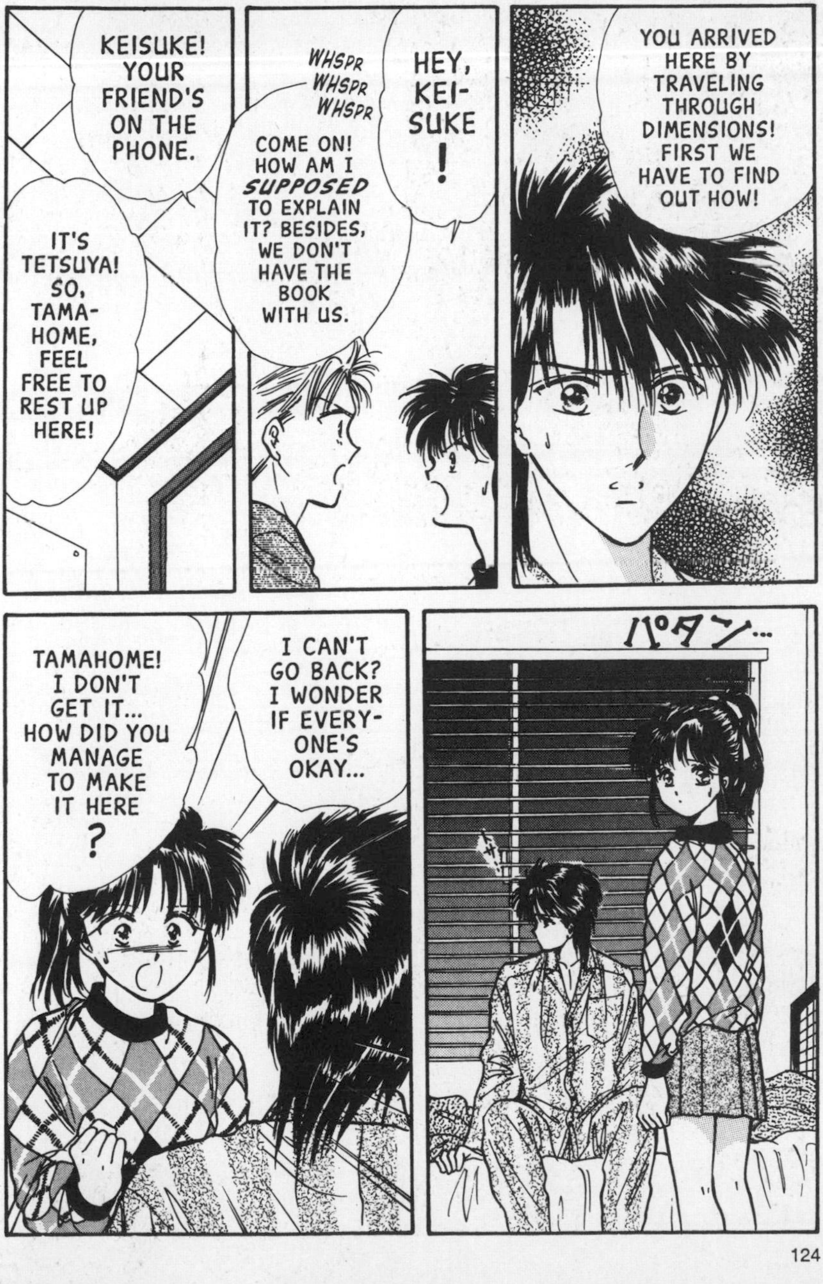
YOU ARRIVED HERE BY TRAVELING THROUGH DIMENSIONS! FIRST WE HAVE TO FIND OUT HOW!
HEY, KEI-SUKE!
WHSPR WHSPR WHSPR
COME ON! HOW AM I *SUPPOSED* TO EXPLAIN IT? BESIDES, WE DON'T HAVE THE BOOK WITH US.
KEISUKE! YOUR FRIEND'S ON THE PHONE.
IT'S TETSUYA! SO, TAMA-HOME, FEEL FREE TO REST UP HERE!
パタン…
I CAN'T GO BACK? I WONDER IF EVERY-ONE'S OKAY...
TAMAHOME! I DON'T GET IT... HOW DID YOU MANAGE TO MAKE IT HERE?

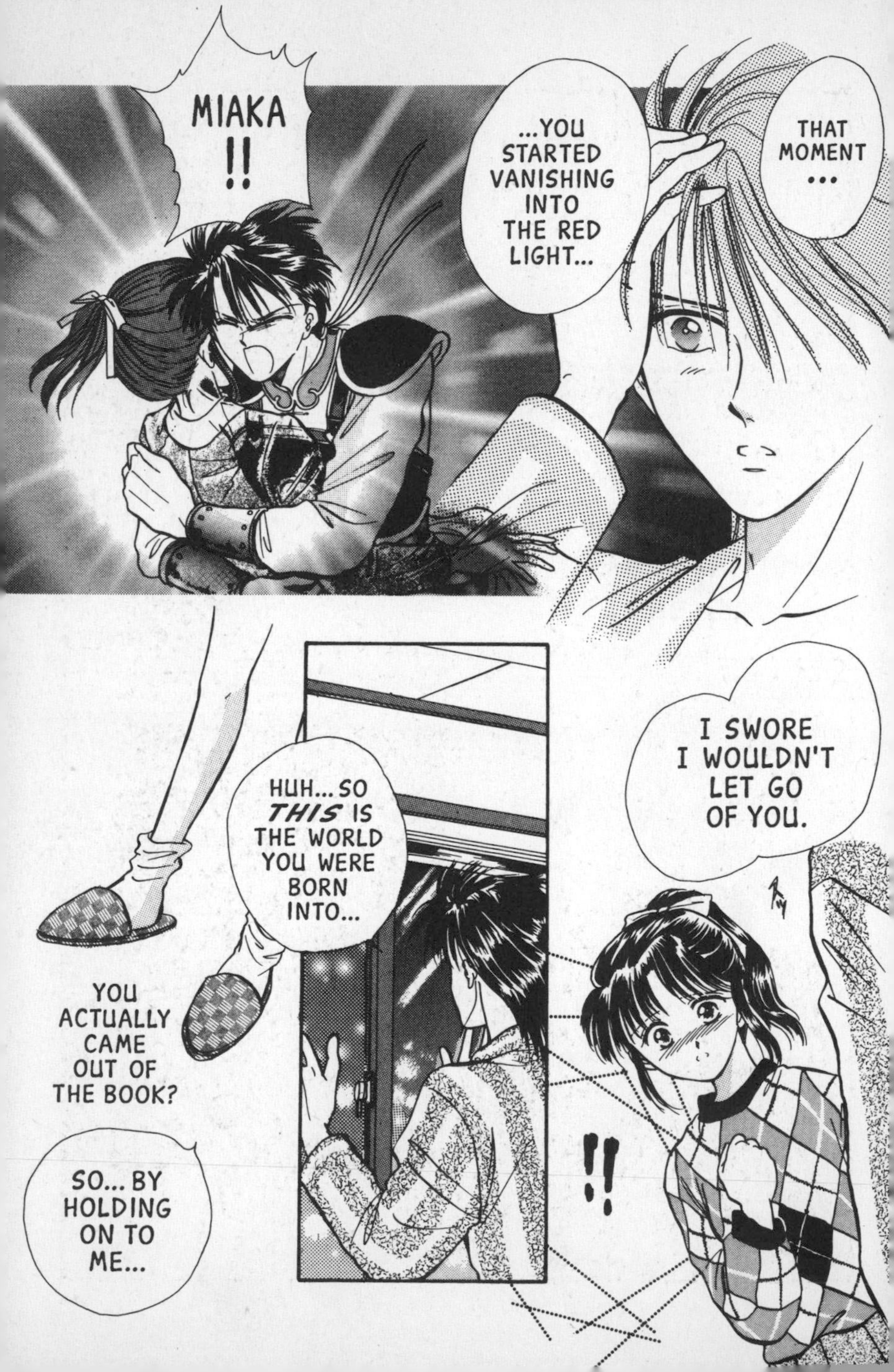
THAT MOMENT ...
...YOU STARTED VANISHING INTO THE RED LIGHT...
MIAKA !!
I SWORE I WOULDN'T LET GO OF YOU.
!!
HUH... SO *THIS* IS THE WORLD YOU WERE BORN INTO...
YOU ACTUALLY CAME OUT OF THE BOOK?
SO... BY HOLDING ON TO ME...

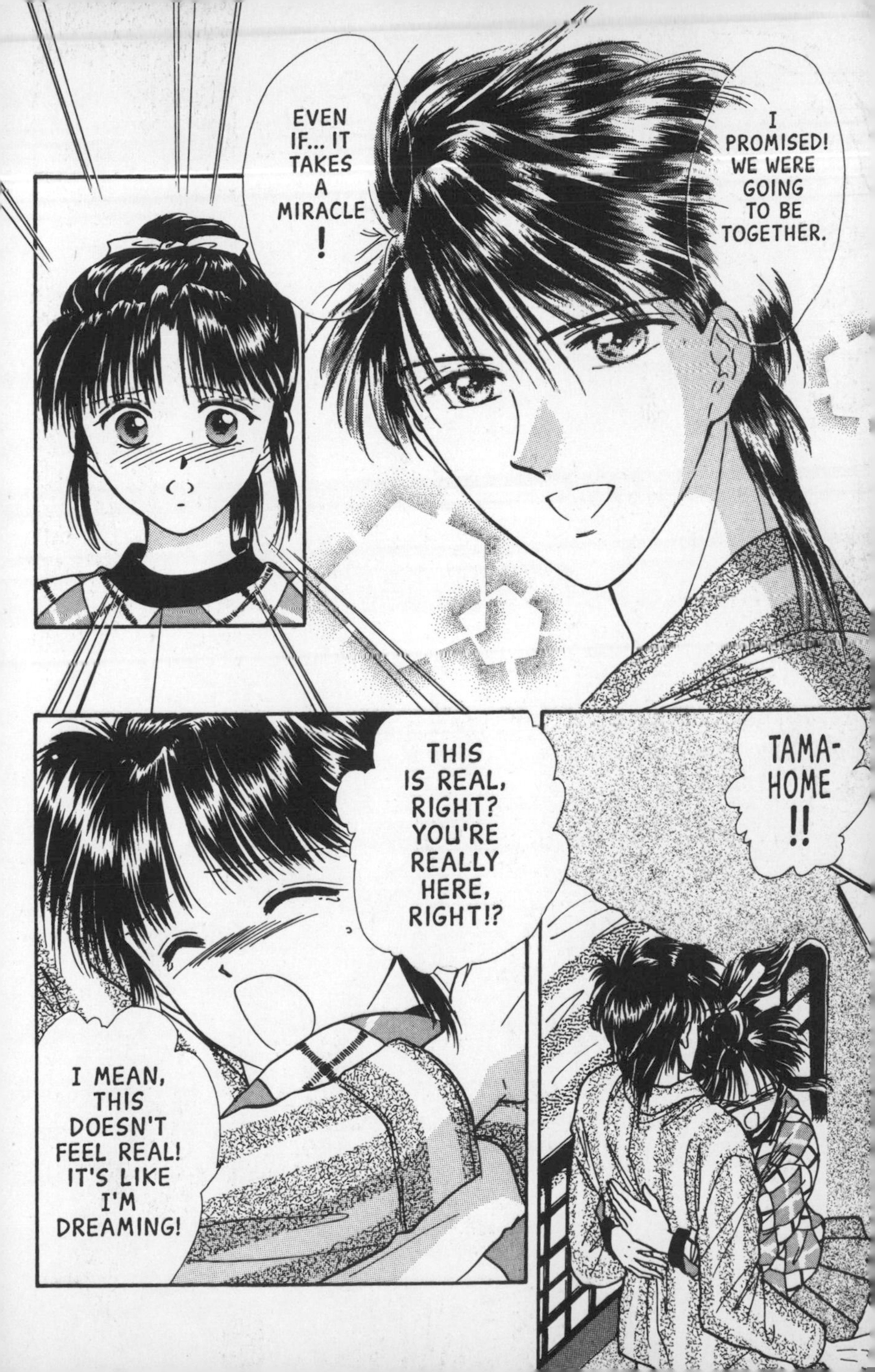
I PROMISED! WE WERE GOING TO BE TOGETHER.
EVEN IF... IT TAKES A MIRACLE!
TAMA-HOME!!
THIS IS REAL, RIGHT? YOU'RE REALLY HERE, RIGHT!?
I MEAN, THIS DOESN'T FEEL REAL! IT'S LIKE I'M DREAMING!

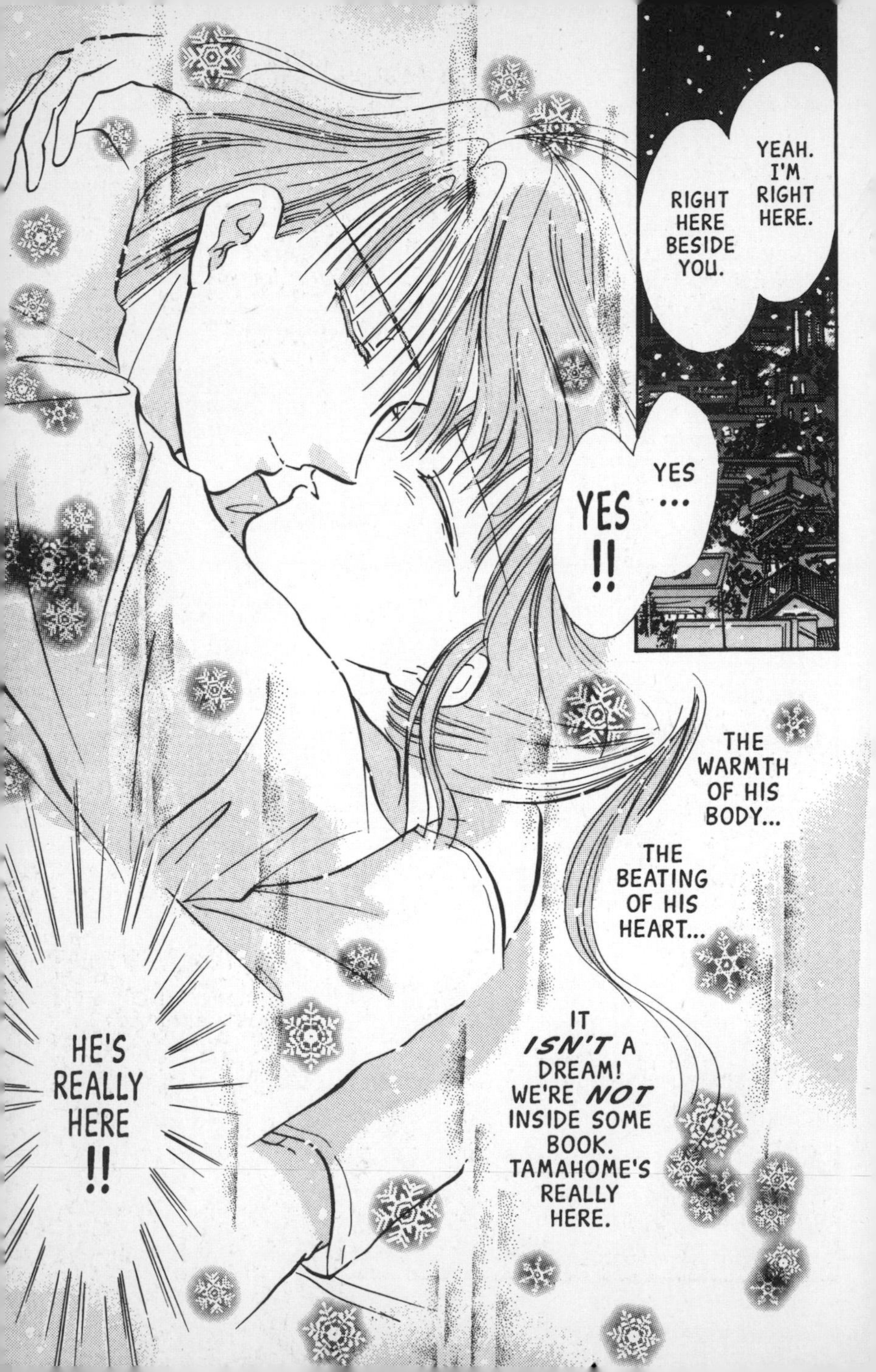
YEAH. I'M RIGHT HERE.
RIGHT HERE BESIDE YOU.
YES ...
YES !!
THE WARMTH OF HIS BODY...
THE BEATING OF HIS HEART...
IT *ISN'T* A DREAM! WE'RE *NOT* INSIDE SOME BOOK. TAMAHOME'S REALLY HERE.
HE'S REALLY HERE !!

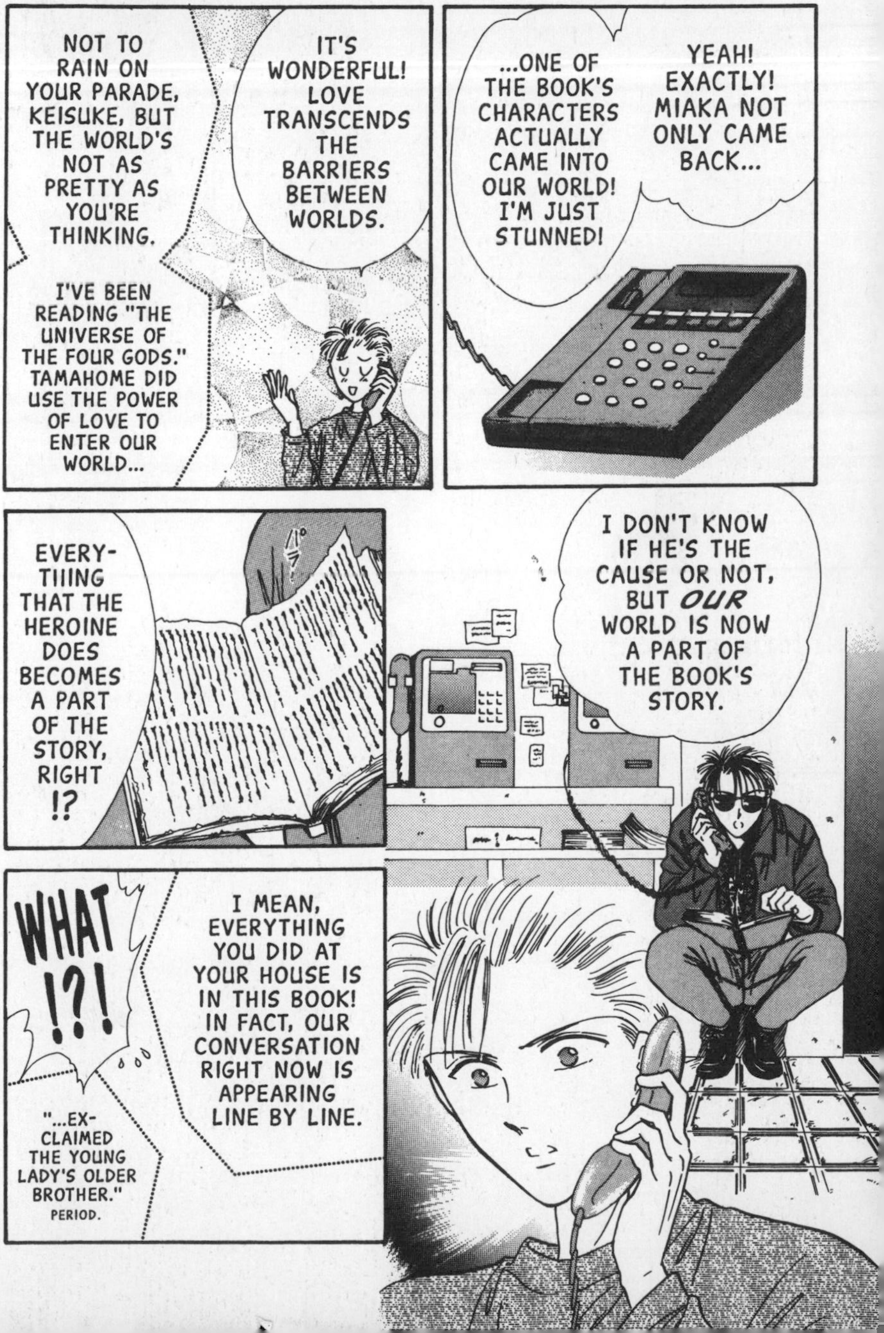
YEAH! EXACTLY! MIAKA NOT ONLY CAME BACK...
...ONE OF THE BOOK'S CHARACTERS ACTUALLY CAME INTO OUR WORLD! I'M JUST STUNNED!
IT'S WONDERFUL! LOVE TRANSCENDS THE BARRIERS BETWEEN WORLDS.
NOT TO RAIN ON YOUR PARADE, KEISUKE, BUT THE WORLD'S NOT AS PRETTY AS YOU'RE THINKING.
I'VE BEEN READING "THE UNIVERSE OF THE FOUR GODS." TAMAHOME DID USE THE POWER OF LOVE TO ENTER OUR WORLD...
I DON'T KNOW IF HE'S THE CAUSE OR NOT, BUT *OUR* WORLD IS NOW A PART OF THE BOOK'S STORY.
EVERY-TIIING THAT THE HEROINE DOES BECOMES A PART OF THE STORY, RIGHT !?
I MEAN, EVERYTHING YOU DID AT YOUR HOUSE IS IN THIS BOOK! IN FACT, OUR CONVERSATION RIGHT NOW IS APPEARING LINE BY LINE.
WHAT !?!
"...EX-CLAIMED THE YOUNG LADY'S OLDER BROTHER." PERIOD.

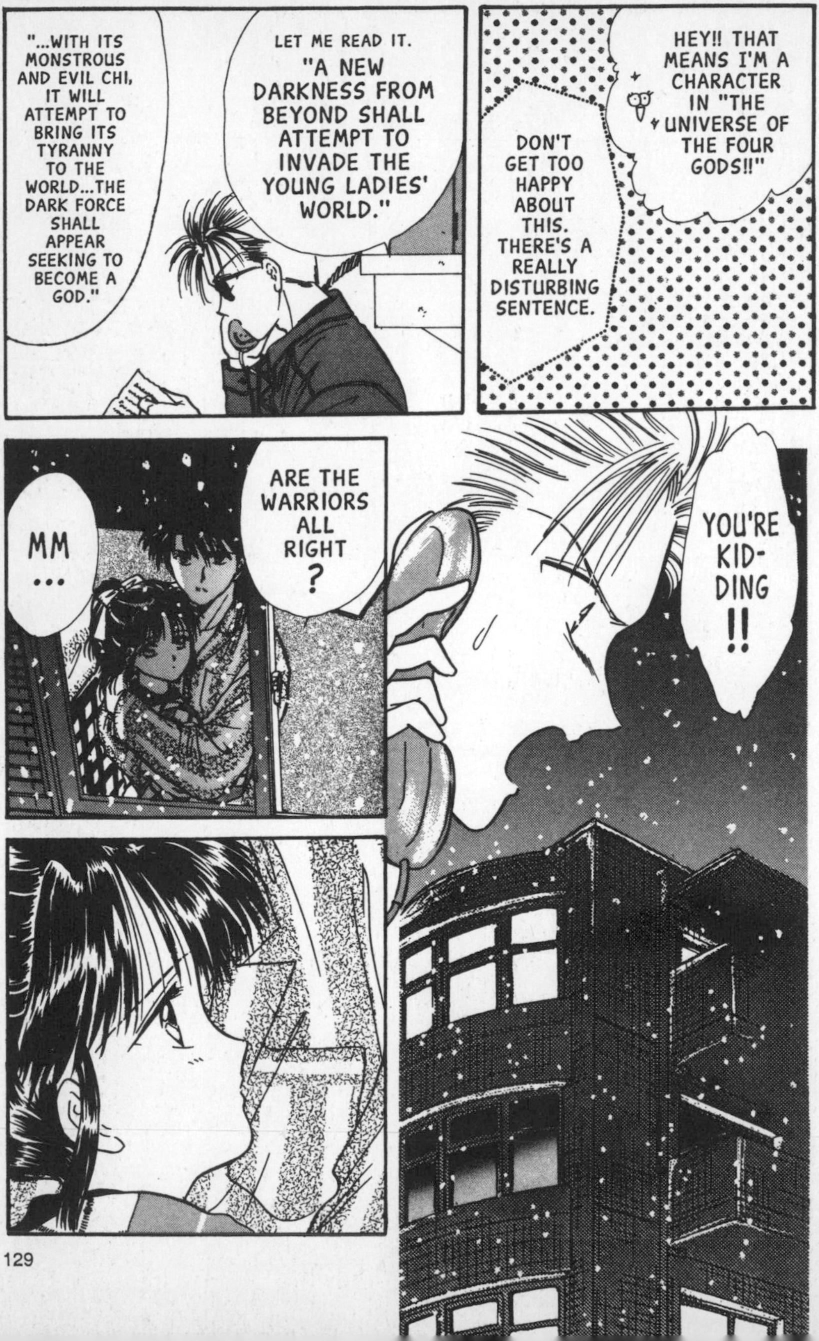
HEY!! THAT MEANS I'M A CHARACTER IN "THE UNIVERSE OF THE FOUR GODS!!"
DON'T GET TOO HAPPY ABOUT THIS. THERE'S A REALLY DISTURBING SENTENCE.
LET ME READ IT. "A NEW DARKNESS FROM BEYOND SHALL ATTEMPT TO INVADE THE YOUNG LADIES' WORLD."
"...WITH ITS MONSTROUS AND EVIL CHI, IT WILL ATTEMPT TO BRING ITS TYRANNY TO THE WORLD...THE DARK FORCE SHALL APPEAR SEEKING TO BECOME A GOD."
YOU'RE KID-DING!!
ARE THE WARRIORS ALL RIGHT?
MM...

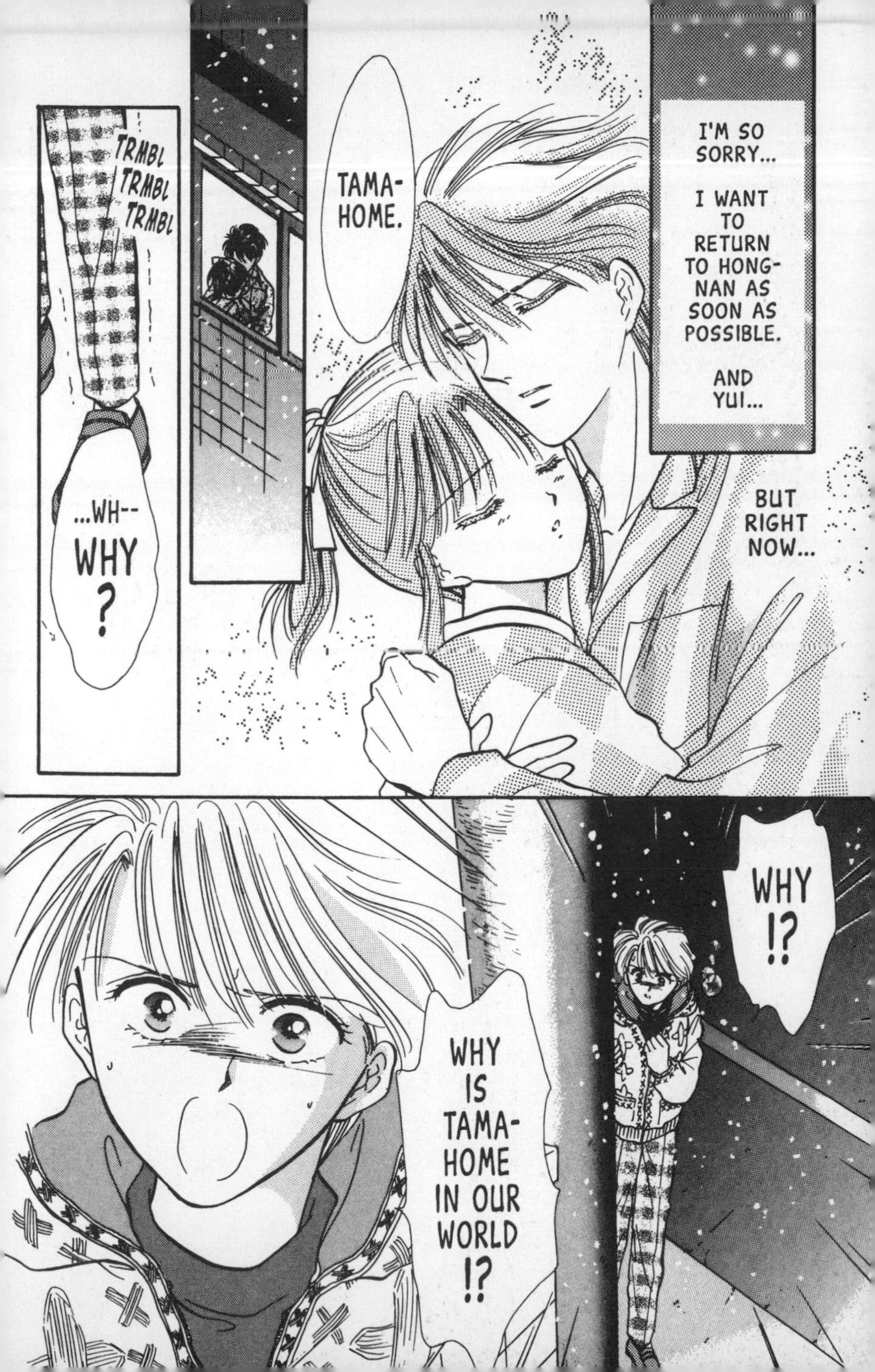
I'M SO SORRY...
I WANT TO RETURN TO HONG-NAN AS SOON AS POSSIBLE.
AND YUI...
BUT RIGHT NOW...
TAMA-HOME.
TRMBL TRMBL TRMBL
...WH-- WHY?
WHY!?
WHY IS TAMA-HOME IN OUR WORLD!?

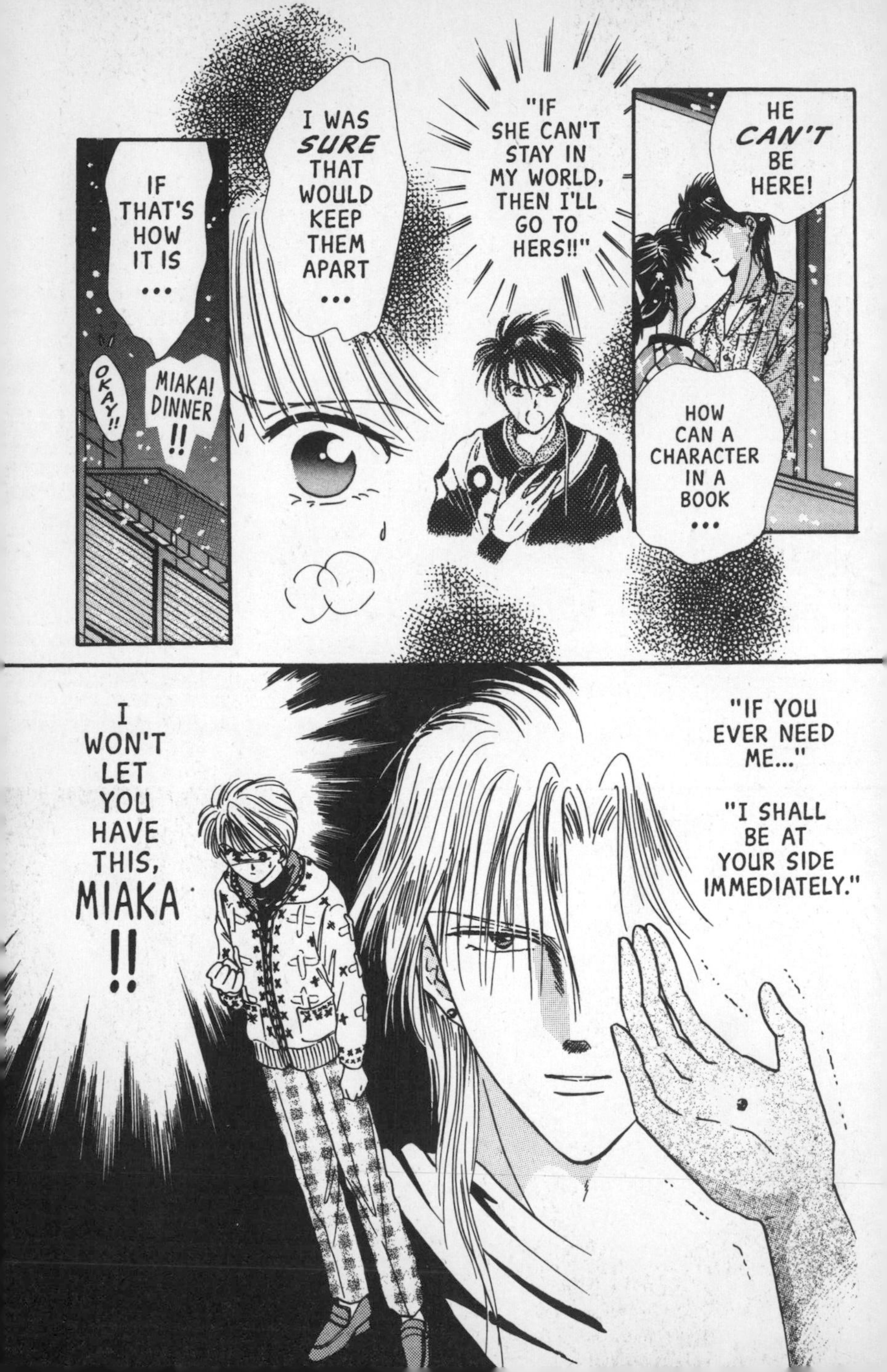
HE *CAN'T* BE HERE!
HOW CAN A CHARACTER IN A BOOK ...
"IF SHE CAN'T STAY IN MY WORLD, THEN I'LL GO TO HERS!!"
I WAS *SURE* THAT WOULD KEEP THEM APART ...
IF THAT'S HOW IT IS ...
MIAKA! DINNER !!
OKAY!!
"IF YOU EVER NEED ME..."
"I SHALL BE AT YOUR SIDE IMMEDIATELY."
I WON'T LET YOU HAVE THIS, MIAKA !!

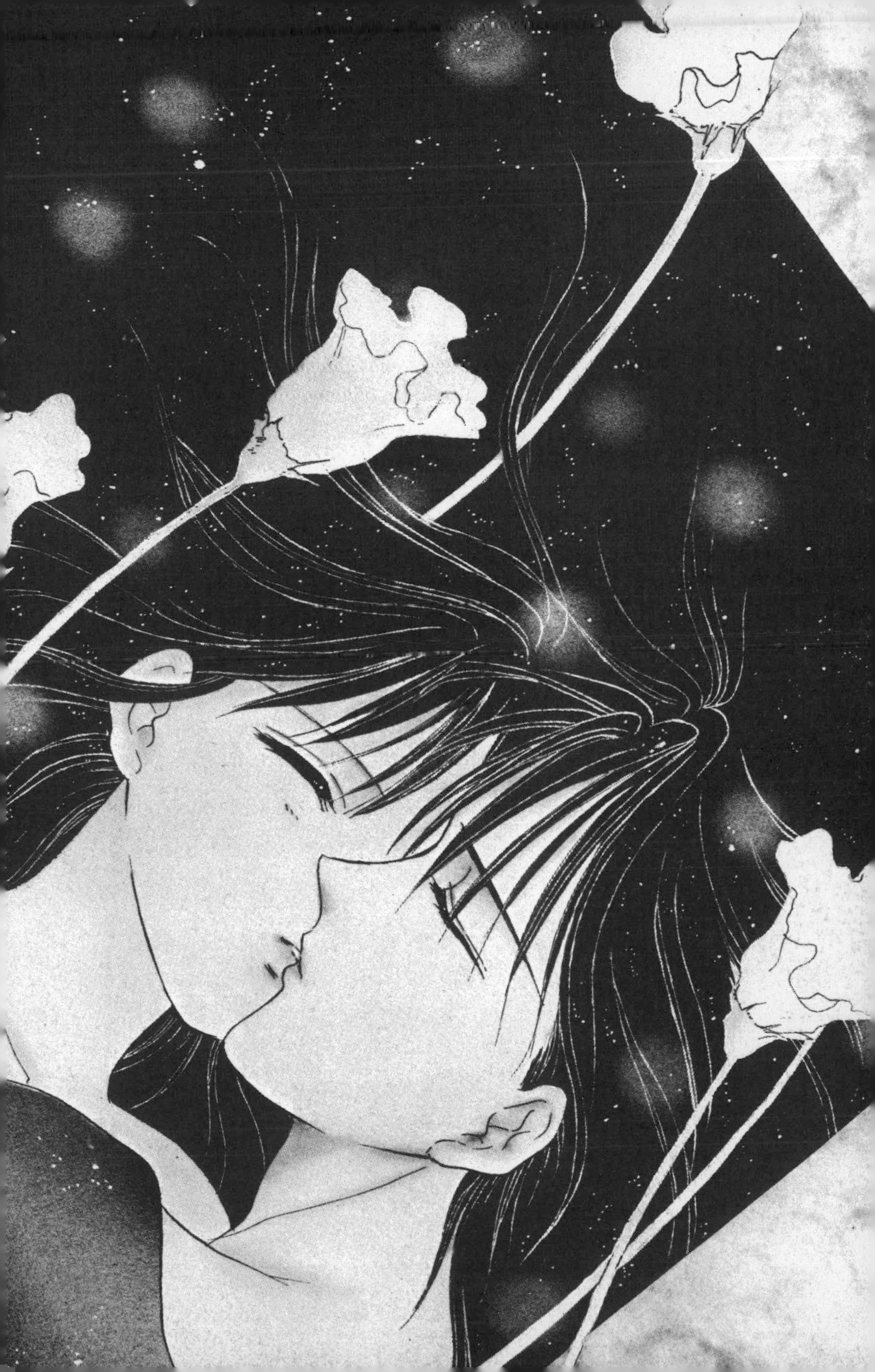

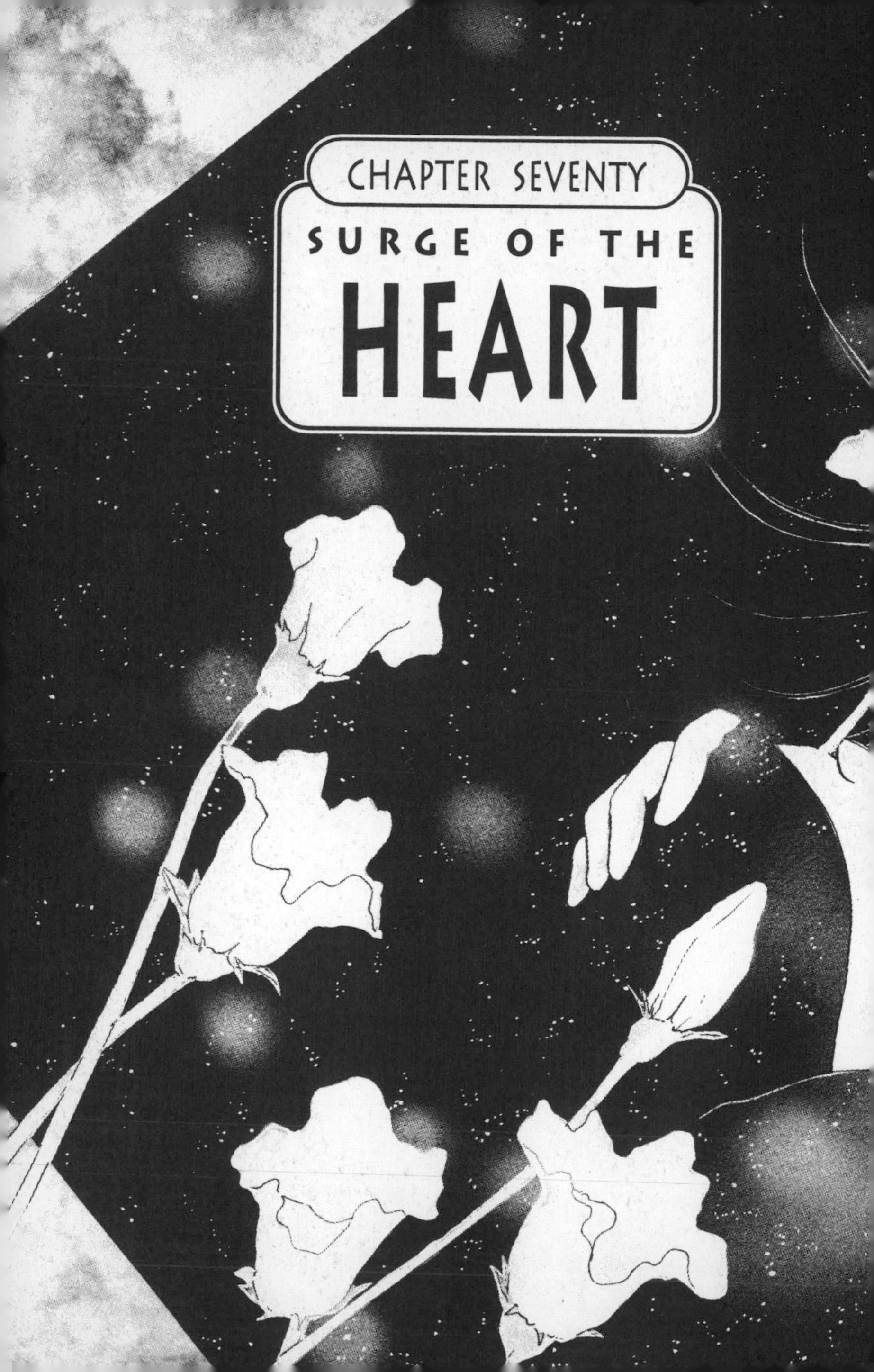
CHAPTER SEVENTY
SURGE OF THE
HEART

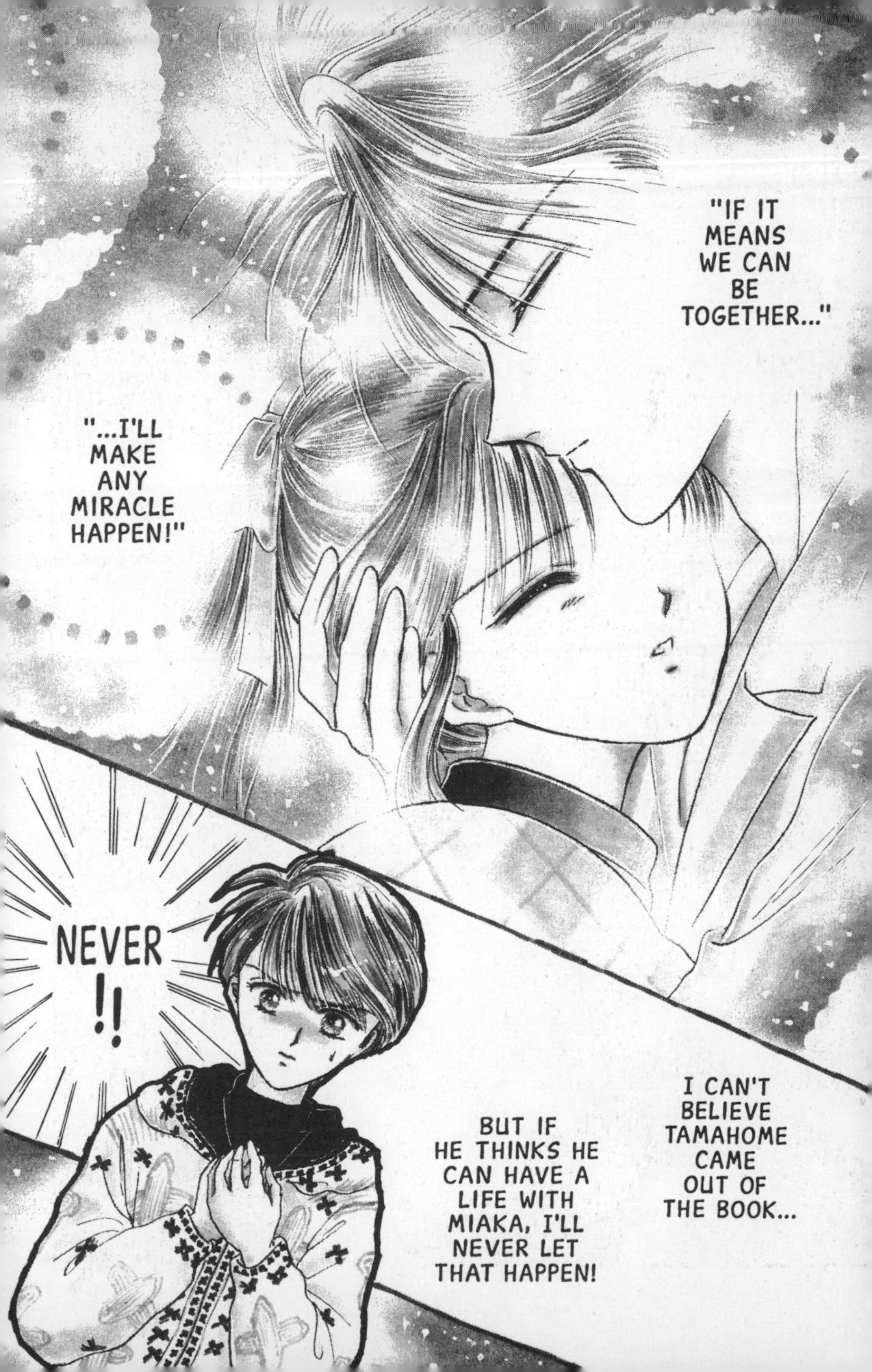
"IF IT MEANS WE CAN BE TOGETHER..."
"...I'LL MAKE ANY MIRACLE HAPPEN!"
I CAN'T BELIEVE TAMAHOME CAME OUT OF THE BOOK...
BUT IF HE THINKS HE CAN HAVE A LIFE WITH MIAKA, I'LL NEVER LET THAT HAPPEN!
NEVER !!

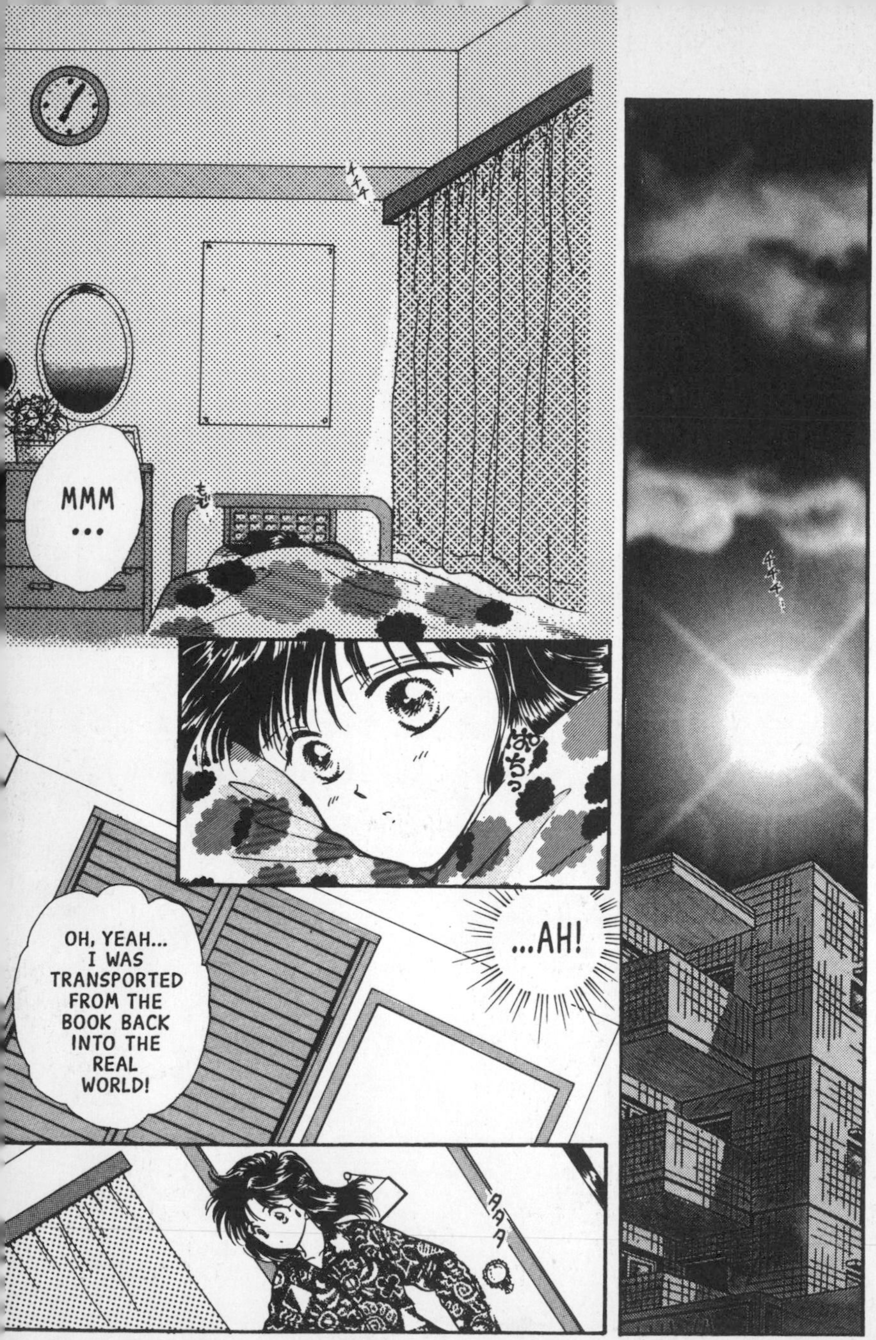

MMM ...
...AH!
OH, YEAH... I WAS TRANSPORTED FROM THE BOOK BACK INTO THE REAL WORLD!

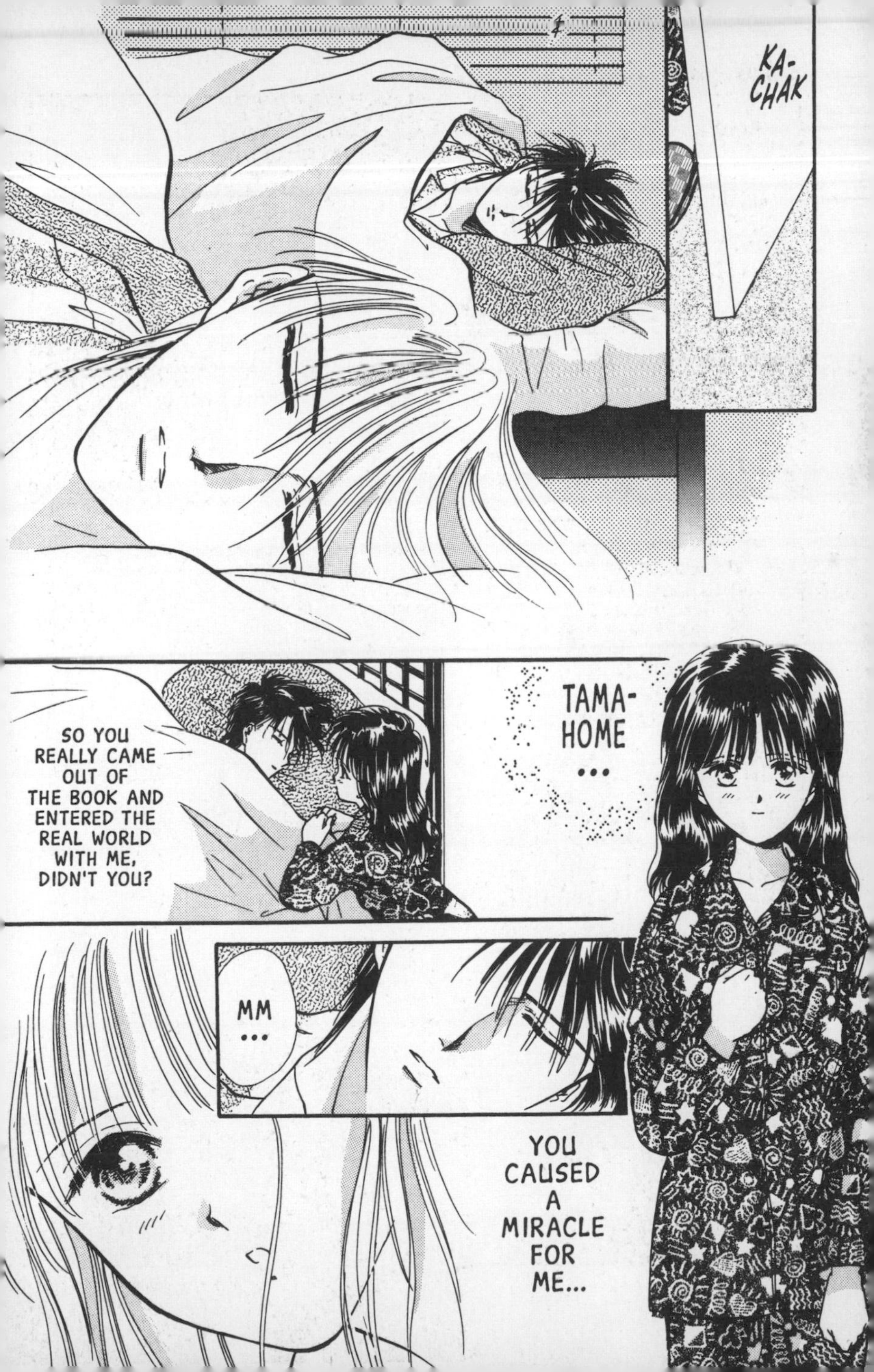
KA-CHAK
TAMA-HOME...
SO YOU REALLY CAME OUT OF THE BOOK AND ENTERED THE REAL WORLD WITH ME, DIDN'T YOU?
MM...
YOU CAUSED A MIRACLE FOR ME...

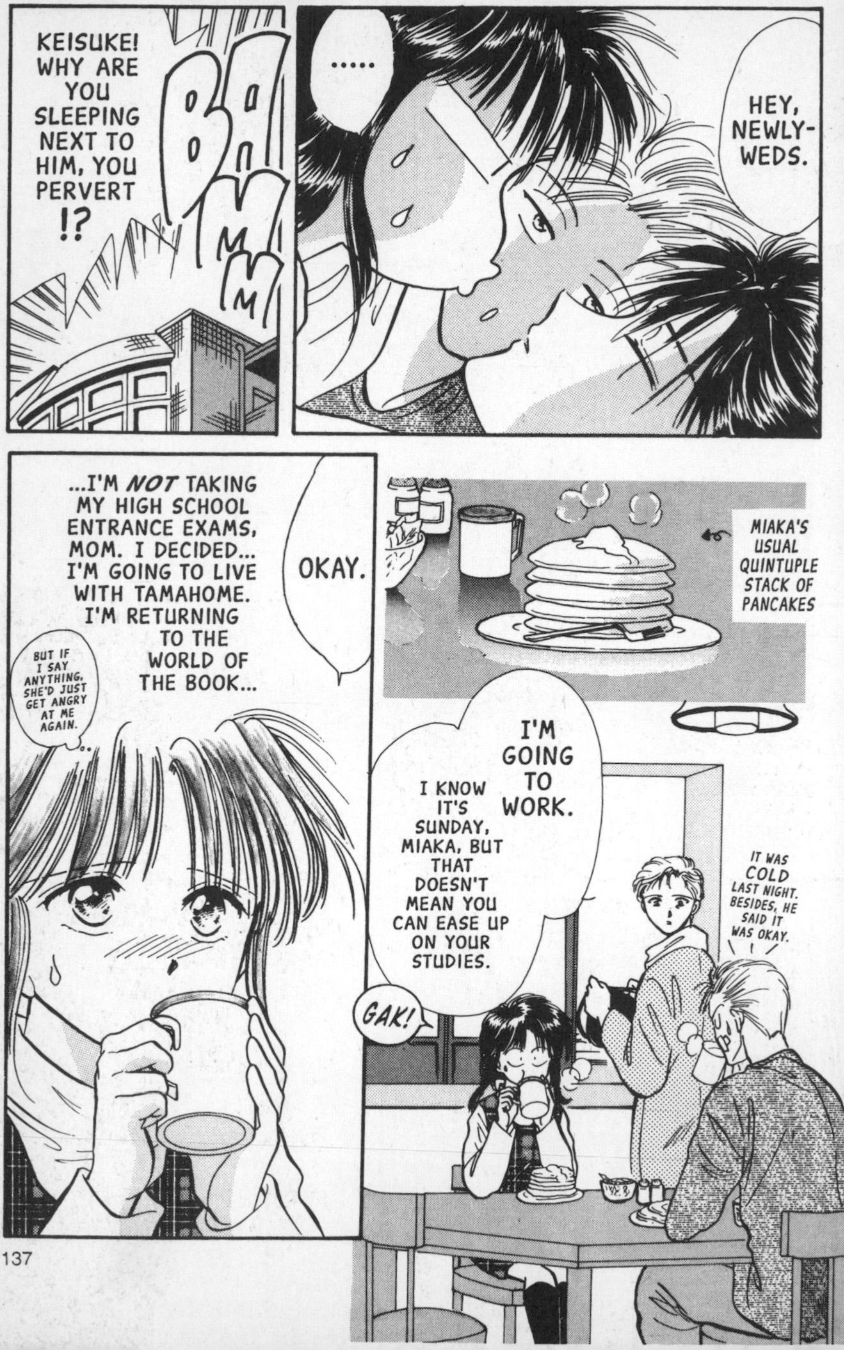
HEY, NEWLY-WEDS.
.....
BAMMMM
KEISUKE! WHY ARE YOU SLEEPING NEXT TO HIM, YOU PERVERT!?
MIAKA'S USUAL QUINTUPLE STACK OF PANCAKES
I'M GOING TO WORK.
I KNOW IT'S SUNDAY, MIAKA, BUT THAT DOESN'T MEAN YOU CAN EASE UP ON YOUR STUDIES.
GAK!
IT WAS COLD LAST NIGHT. BESIDES, HE SAID IT WAS OKAY.
OKAY.
...I'M *NOT* TAKING MY HIGH SCHOOL ENTRANCE EXAMS, MOM. I DECIDED... I'M GOING TO LIVE WITH TAMAHOME. I'M RETURNING TO THE WORLD OF THE BOOK...
BUT IF I SAY ANYTHING, SHE'D JUST GET ANGRY AT ME AGAIN.

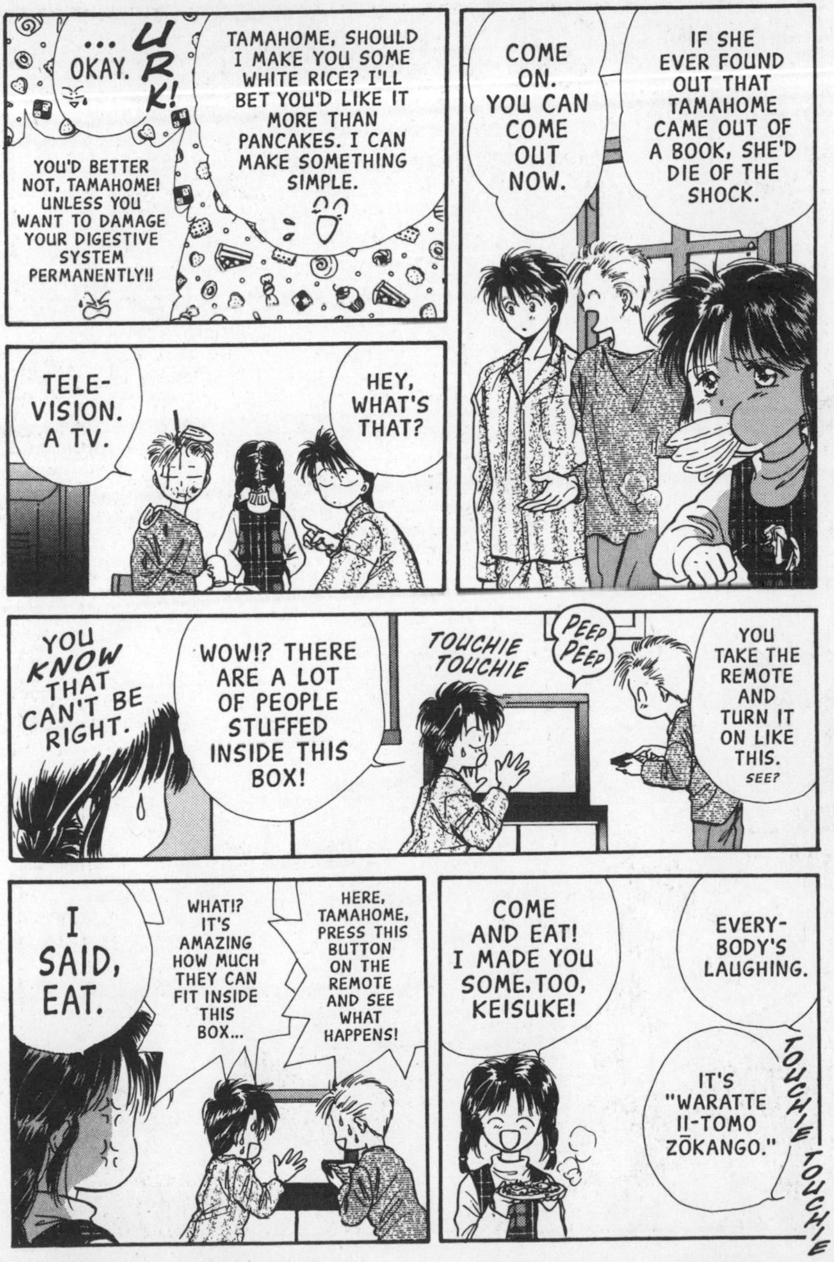
IF SHE EVER FOUND OUT THAT TAMAHOME CAME OUT OF A BOOK, SHE'D DIE OF THE SHOCK.
COME ON. YOU CAN COME OUT NOW.
TAMAHOME, SHOULD I MAKE YOU SOME WHITE RICE? I'LL BET YOU'D LIKE IT MORE THAN PANCAKES. I CAN MAKE SOMETHING SIMPLE.
URK!
... OKAY.
YOU'D BETTER NOT, TAMAHOME! UNLESS YOU WANT TO DAMAGE YOUR DIGESTIVE SYSTEM PERMANENTLY!!
HEY, WHAT'S THAT?
TELE-VISION. A TV.
YOU TAKE THE REMOTE AND TURN IT ON LIKE THIS. SEE?
PEEP PEEP
TOUCHIE TOUCHIE
WOW!? THERE ARE A LOT OF PEOPLE STUFFED INSIDE THIS BOX!
YOU KNOW THAT CAN'T BE RIGHT.
EVERY-BODY'S LAUGHING.
TOUCHIE TOUCHIE
IT'S "WARATTE II-TOMO ZŌKANGO."
COME AND EAT! I MADE YOU SOME, TOO, KEISUKE!
HERE, TAMAHOME, PRESS THIS BUTTON ON THE REMOTE AND SEE WHAT HAPPENS!
WHAT!? IT'S AMAZING HOW MUCH THEY CAN FIT INSIDE THIS BOX...
I SAID, EAT.

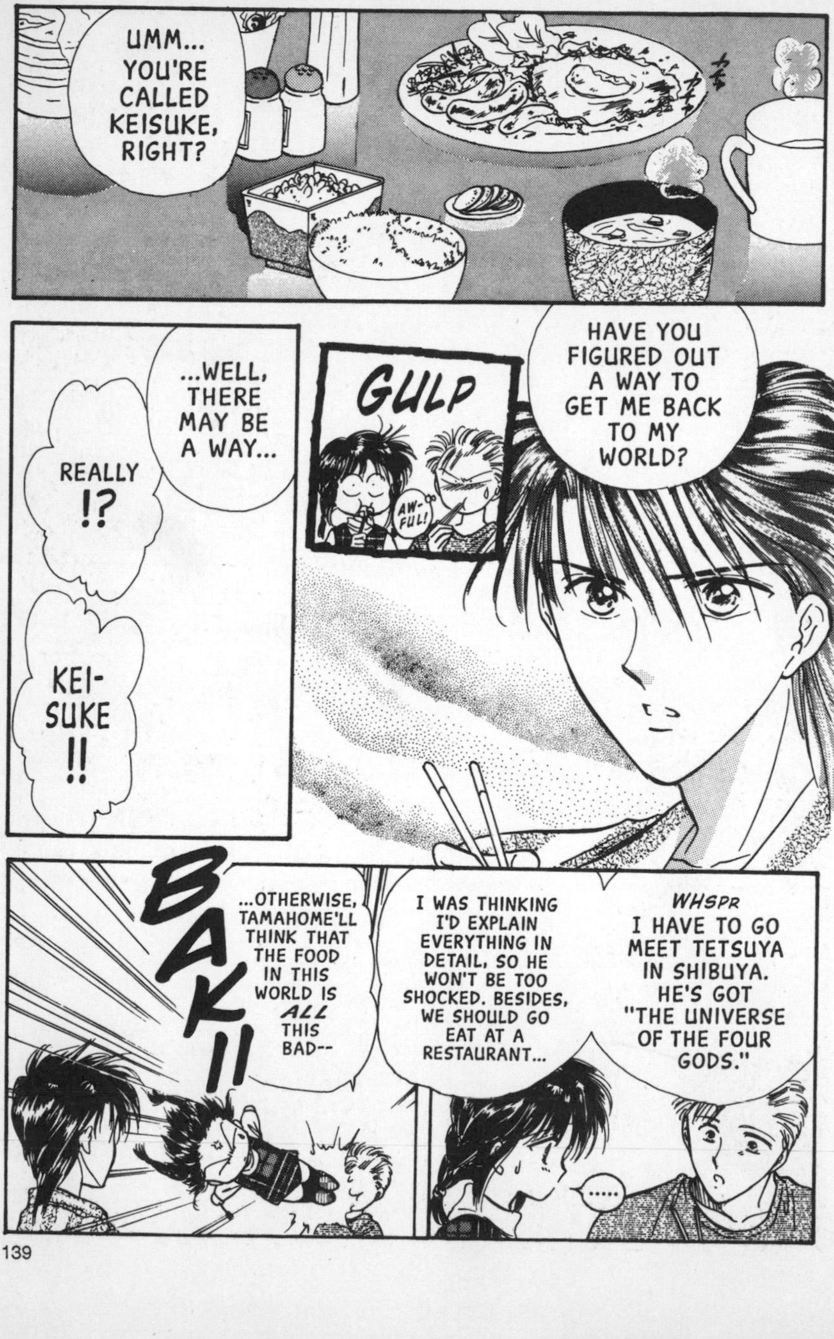
UMM... YOU'RE CALLED KEISUKE, RIGHT?
HAVE YOU FIGURED OUT A WAY TO GET ME BACK TO MY WORLD?
GULP
AW-FUL!
...WELL, THERE MAY BE A WAY...
REALLY !?
KEI-SUKE !!
WHSPR
I HAVE TO GO MEET TETSUYA IN SHIBUYA. HE'S GOT "THE UNIVERSE OF THE FOUR GODS."
I WAS THINKING I'D EXPLAIN EVERYTHING IN DETAIL, SO HE WON'T BE TOO SHOCKED. BESIDES, WE SHOULD GO EAT AT A RESTAURANT...
......
...OTHERWISE, TAMAHOME'LL THINK THAT THE FOOD IN THIS WORLD IS *ALL* THIS BAD--
BAKI!!

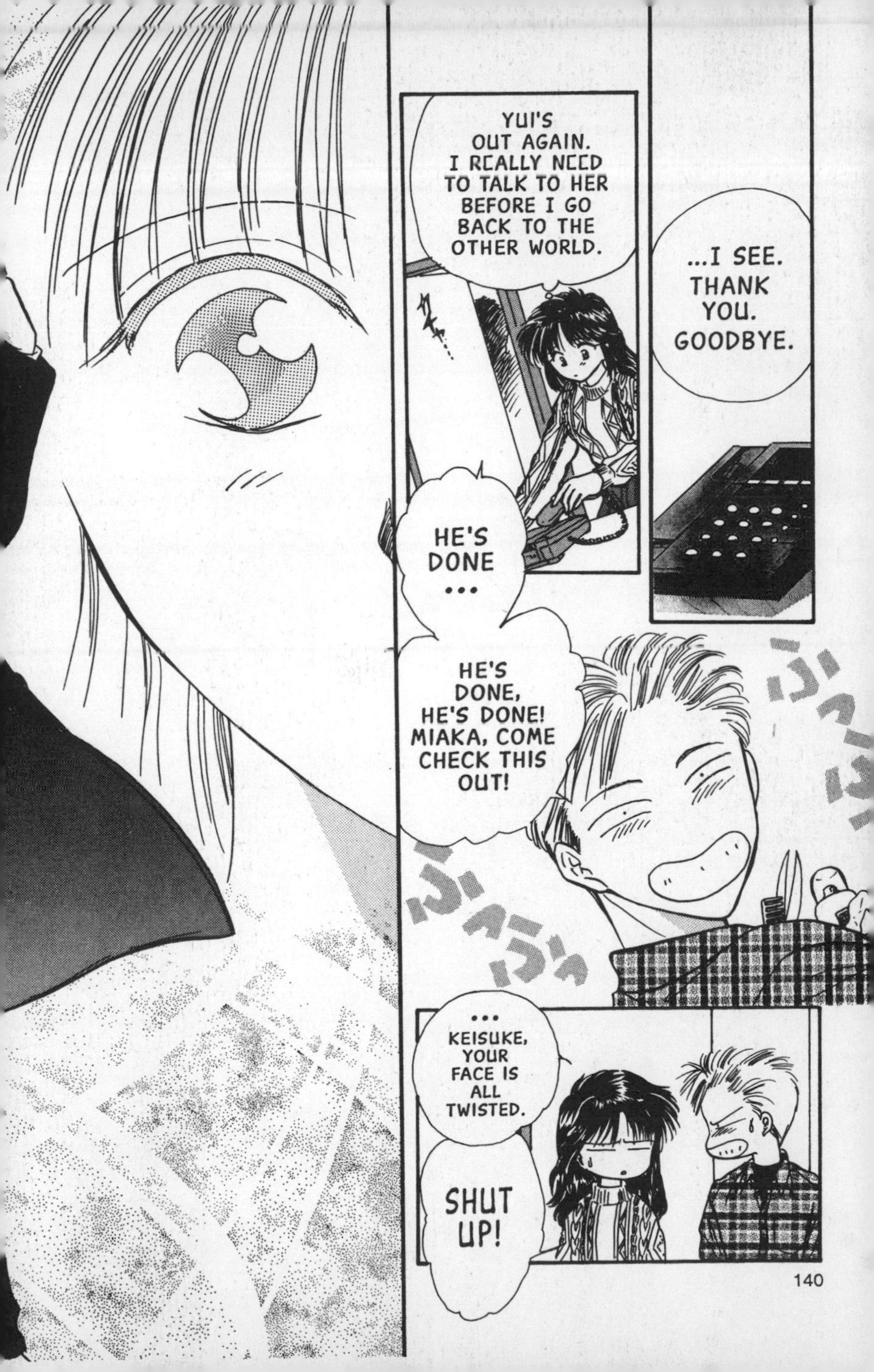
...I SEE. THANK YOU. GOODBYE.
YUI'S OUT AGAIN. I REALLY NEED TO TALK TO HER BEFORE I GO BACK TO THE OTHER WORLD.
HE'S DONE...
HE'S DONE, HE'S DONE! MIAKA, COME CHECK THIS OUT!
... KEISUKE, YOUR FACE IS ALL TWISTED.
SHUT UP!

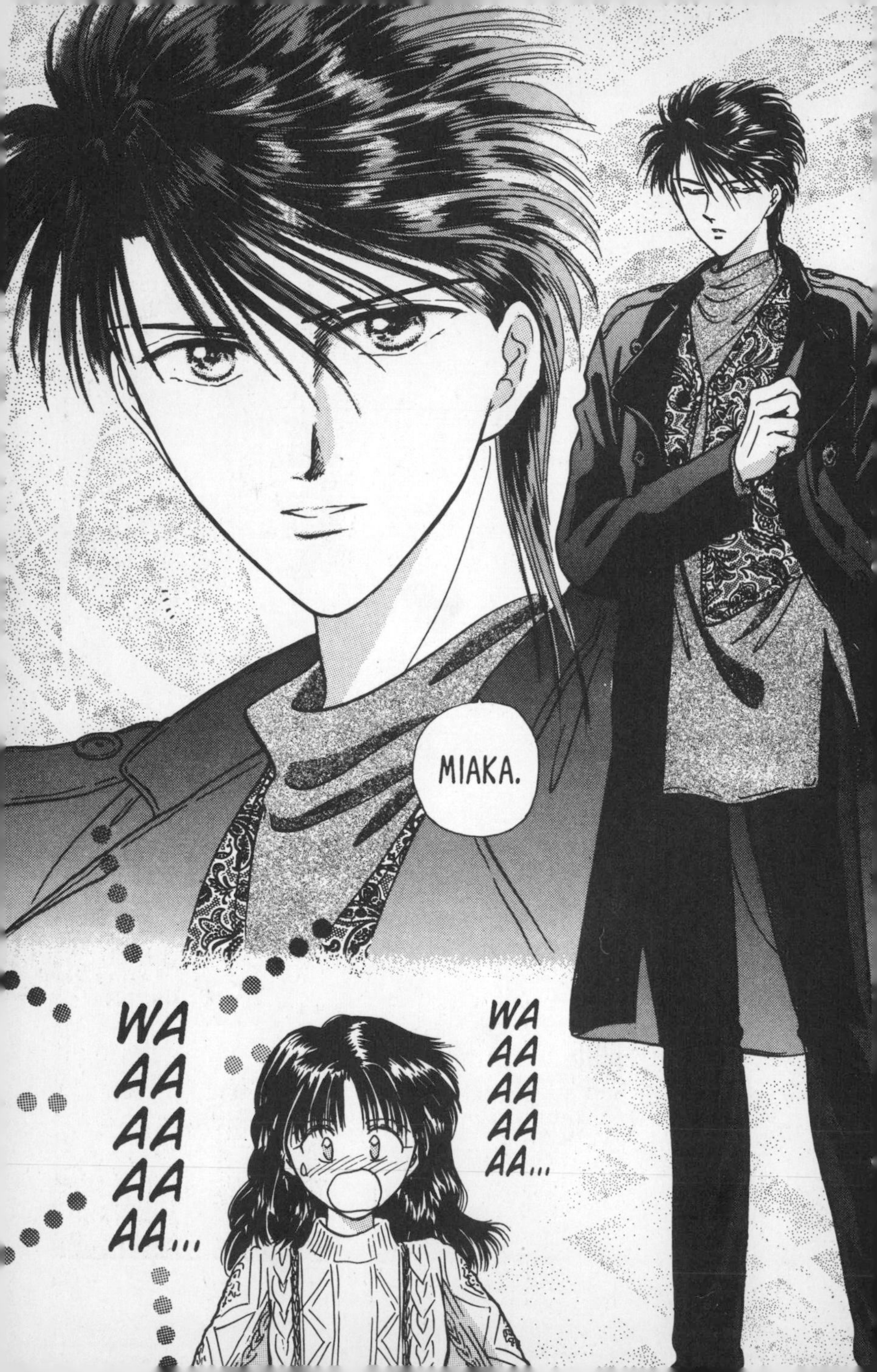
MIAKA.
WA AA AA AA AA...
WA AA AA AA AA...

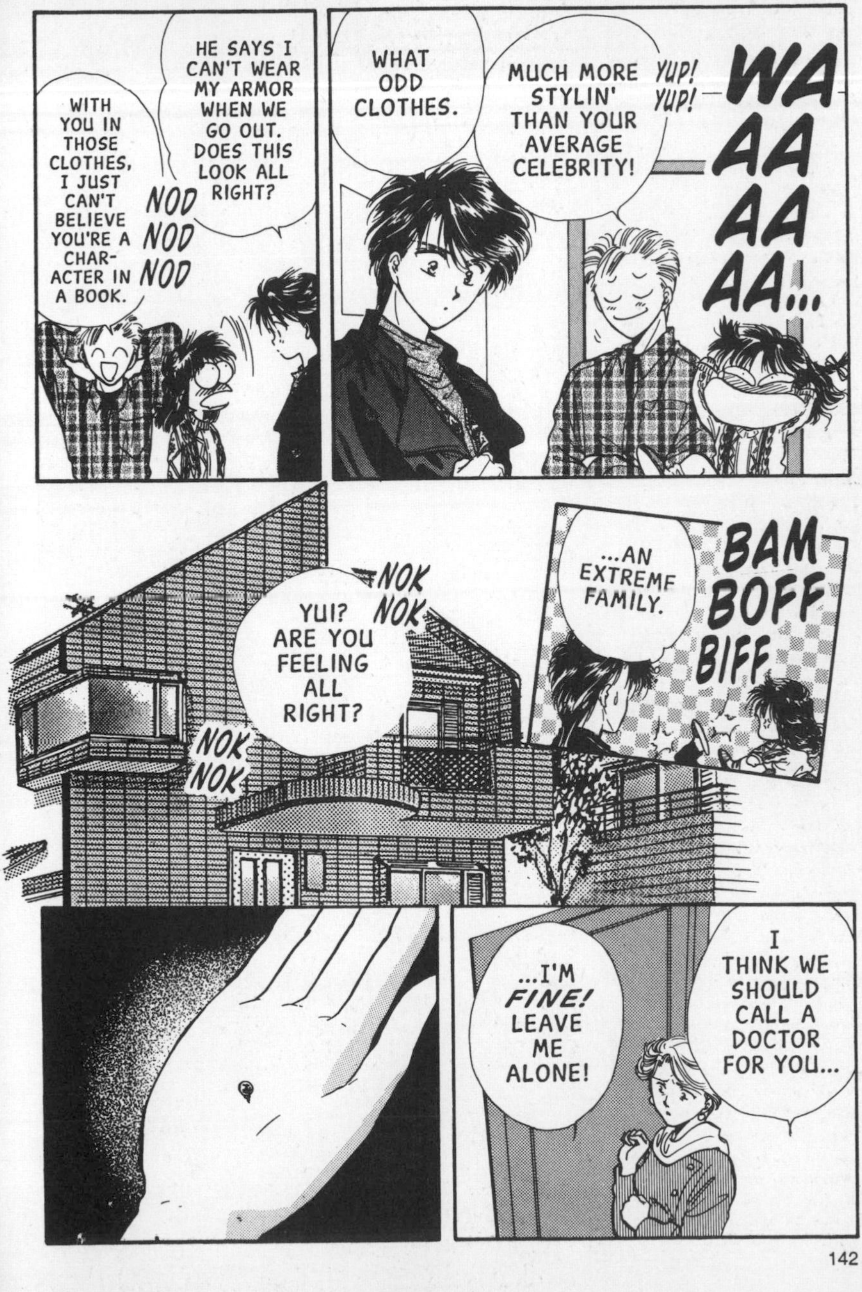
HE SAYS I CAN'T WEAR MY ARMOR WHEN WE GO OUT. DOES THIS LOOK ALL RIGHT?
NOD NOD NOD
WITH YOU IN THOSE CLOTHES, I JUST CAN'T BELIEVE YOU'RE A CHAR-ACTER IN A BOOK.
WHAT ODD CLOTHES.
MUCH MORE STYLIN' THAN YOUR AVERAGE CELEBRITY!
YUP! YUP!
WAAAAAAAA...
...AN EXTREME FAMILY.
BAM BOFF BIFF
NOK NOK
YUI? ARE YOU FEELING ALL RIGHT?
NOK NOK
I THINK WE SHOULD CALL A DOCTOR FOR YOU...
...I'M *FINE!* LEAVE ME ALONE!

Soi. With those long, elegant eyes peering out from under her cloak... at first, many readers thought that the character was a handsome boy. But in fact, she's a woman. The only female character of the Seiryu Celestial Warriors. By the way, the fact that all of the Suzaku warriors are men...there's no significance to it. *I guess Nuriko played the part of a woman.* Soi's character design was really hard! I had to design her three or four times! At first, I tried drawing her as a boyish character -- a woman in men's clothes to contrast with Nuriko -- but that didn't work. I had so many problems with her hairstyle. I was planning on having her wear armor, but...still nothing. Then one day I came up with those long, elegant eyes, and all of a sudden her hairstyle fell into place, and then her armor. She seems really tough because she talks like a man and wears armor, but her lipstick gives away her true feminine nature. She wears makeup for the man she loves. She's wearing a Chinese tribal bride's dress in the title illustration for Chapter 67. I'll bet she would have rather stood next to Nakago with that on than her armor.

Tomo. I LOVE TOMO. ♥♥ "I love him because he's so foolish, mischievous, gaudy and gay," came the strange praise from a fan, Golden boy. He didn't come to me until the very last minute. I wanted someone who was mysterious like Chichiri, but I just couldn't come up with him. We had the military man, the twins, the woman, the beast, and the child...there was nobody left! As the time crunch was getting bad, I went for a walk and caught a glimpse of a storefront sign. Yep, that was when I saw a sign in a Chinese restaurant that had a Chinese-opera mask -- the generic kind you see everywhere. And thus was born this wonderful, unique Chinese-opera gay boy. *I really liked him... Heh.*

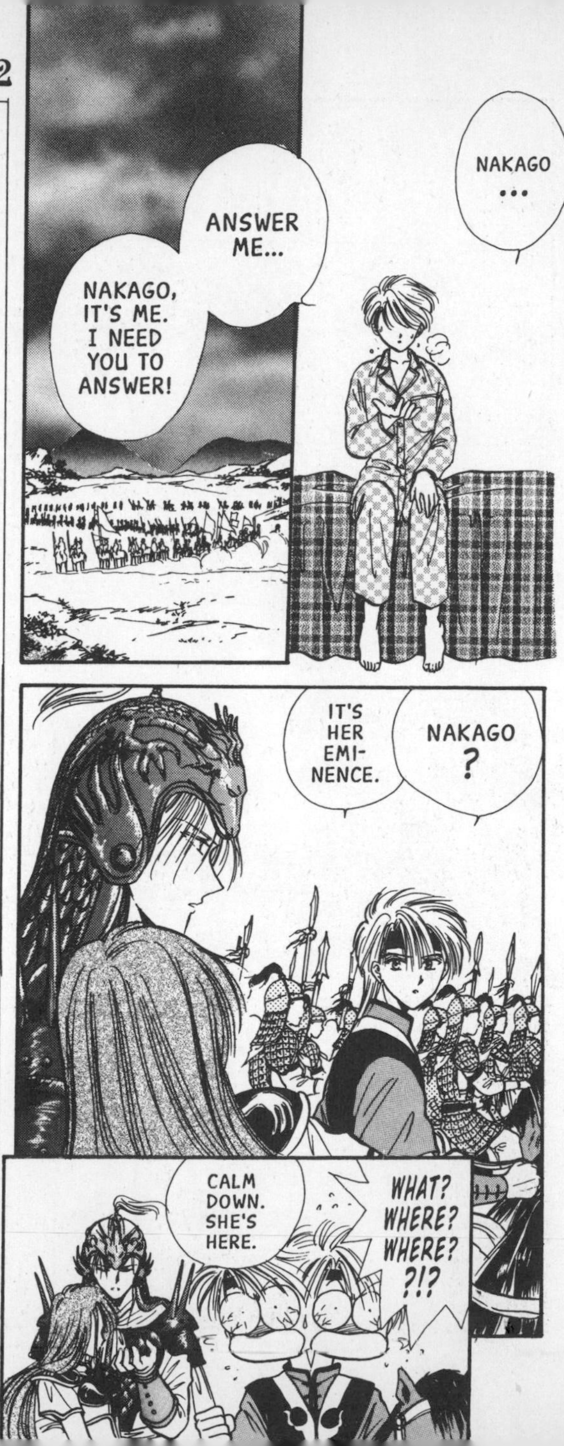
NAKAGO ...
NAKAGO, IT'S ME. I NEED YOU TO ANSWER!
ANSWER ME...
NAKAGO ?
IT'S HER EMINENCE.
WHAT? WHERE? WHERE? ?!?
CALM DOWN. SHE'S HERE.

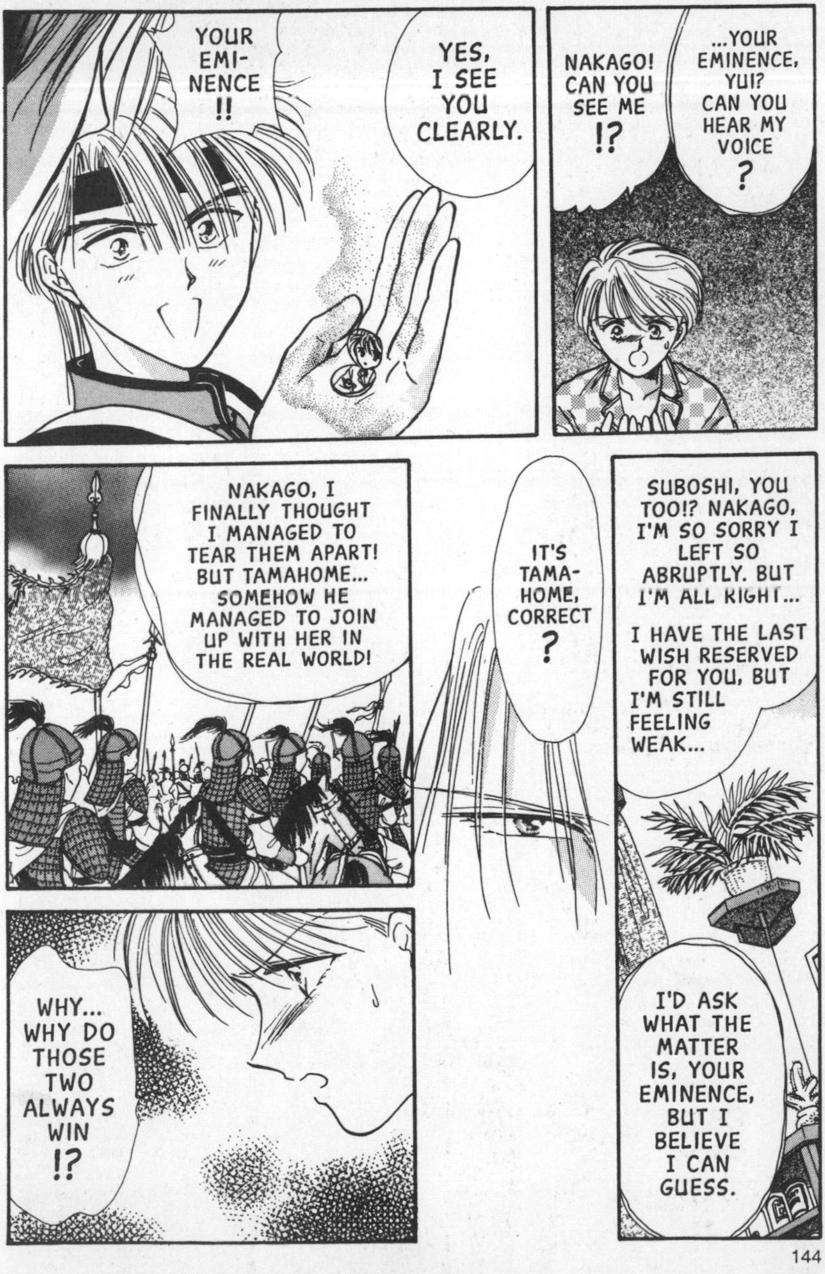

...YOUR EMINENCE, YUI? CAN YOU HEAR MY VOICE ?
NAKAGO! CAN YOU SEE ME !?
YES, I SEE YOU CLEARLY.
YOUR EMI- NENCE !!
SUBOSHI, YOU TOO!? NAKAGO, I'M SO SORRY I LEFT SO ABRUPTLY. BUT I'M ALL RIGHT...
I HAVE THE LAST WISH RESERVED FOR YOU, BUT I'M STILL FEELING WEAK...
I'D ASK WHAT THE MATTER IS, YOUR EMINENCE, BUT I BELIEVE I CAN GUESS.
IT'S TAMA- HOME, CORRECT ?
NAKAGO, I FINALLY THOUGHT I MANAGED TO TEAR THEM APART! BUT TAMAHOME... SOMEHOW HE MANAGED TO JOIN UP WITH HER IN THE REAL WORLD!
WHY... WHY DO THOSE TWO ALWAYS WIN !?

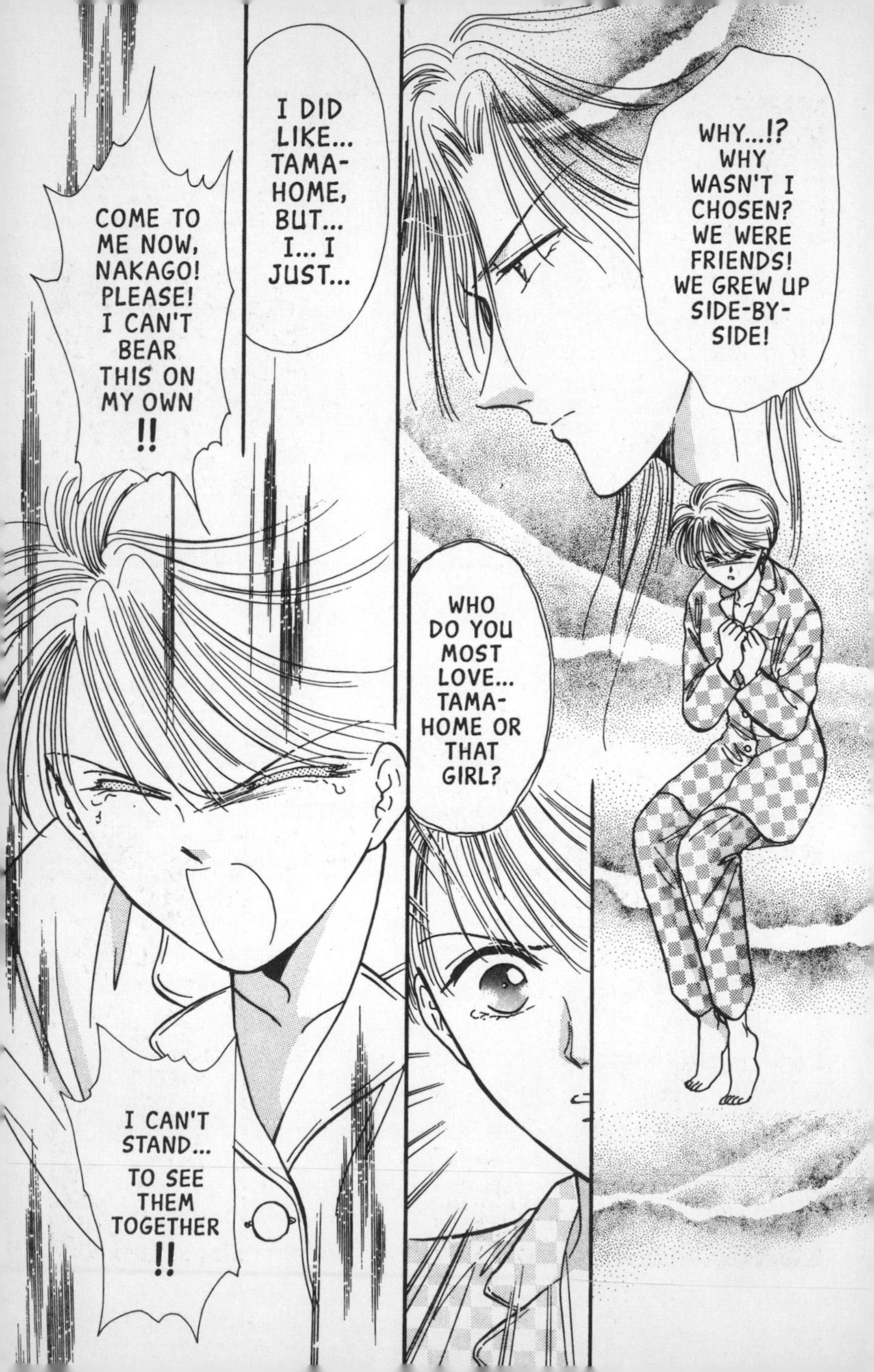
WHY...!? WHY WASN'T I CHOSEN? WE WERE FRIENDS! WE GREW UP SIDE-BY-SIDE!
WHO DO YOU MOST LOVE... TAMA-HOME OR THAT GIRL?
I DID LIKE... TAMA-HOME, BUT... I... I JUST...
COME TO ME NOW, NAKAGO! PLEASE! I CAN'T BEAR THIS ON MY OWN!!
I CAN'T STAND... TO SEE THEM TOGETHER!!

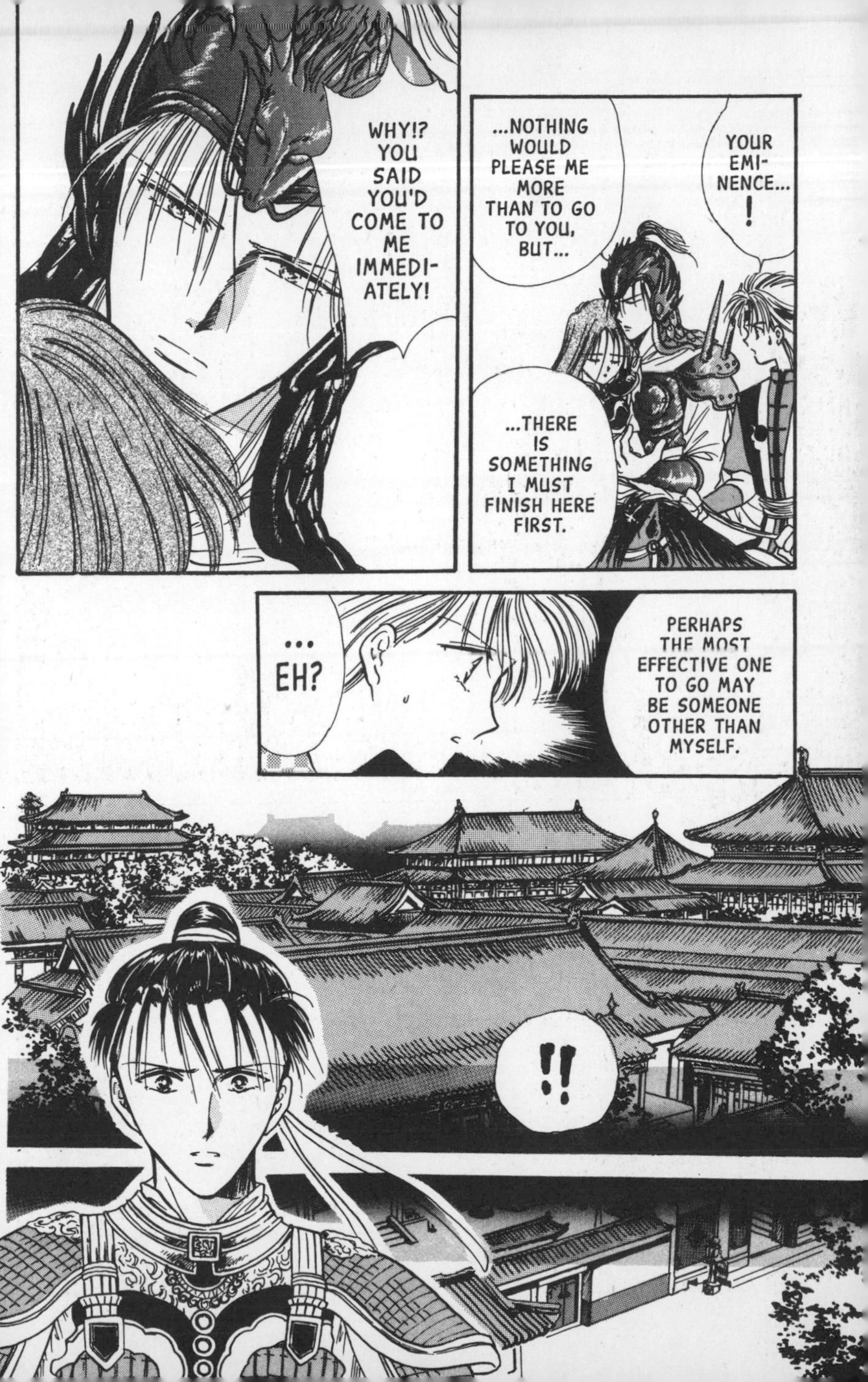
YOUR EMI-NENCE... !
...NOTHING WOULD PLEASE ME MORE THAN TO GO TO YOU, BUT...
...THERE IS SOMETHING I MUST FINISH HERE FIRST.
WHY!? YOU SAID YOU'D COME TO ME IMMEDI-ATELY!
PERHAPS THE MOST EFFECTIVE ONE TO GO MAY BE SOMEONE OTHER THAN MYSELF.
... EH?
!!

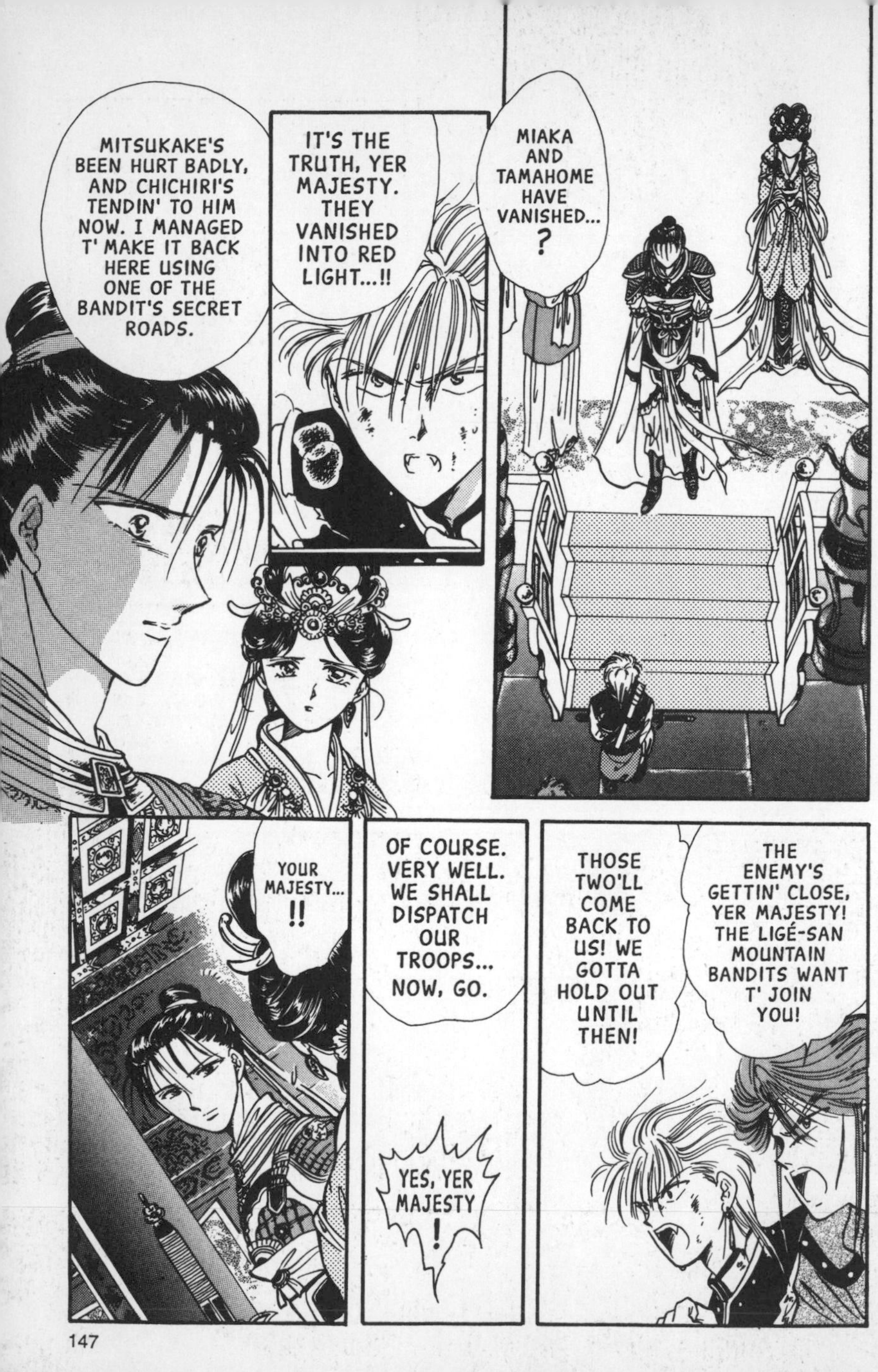
MIAKA AND TAMAHOME HAVE VANISHED... ?
IT'S THE TRUTH, YER MAJESTY. THEY VANISHED INTO RED LIGHT...!!
MITSUKAKE'S BEEN HURT BADLY, AND CHICHIRI'S TENDIN' TO HIM NOW. I MANAGED T' MAKE IT BACK HERE USING ONE OF THE BANDIT'S SECRET ROADS.
THE ENEMY'S GETTIN' CLOSE, YER MAJESTY! THE LIGÉ-SAN MOUNTAIN BANDITS WANT T' JOIN YOU!
THOSE TWO'LL COME BACK TO US! WE GOTTA HOLD OUT UNTIL THEN!
OF COURSE. VERY WELL. WE SHALL DISPATCH OUR TROOPS... NOW, GO.
YES, YER MAJESTY !
YOUR MAJESTY... !!

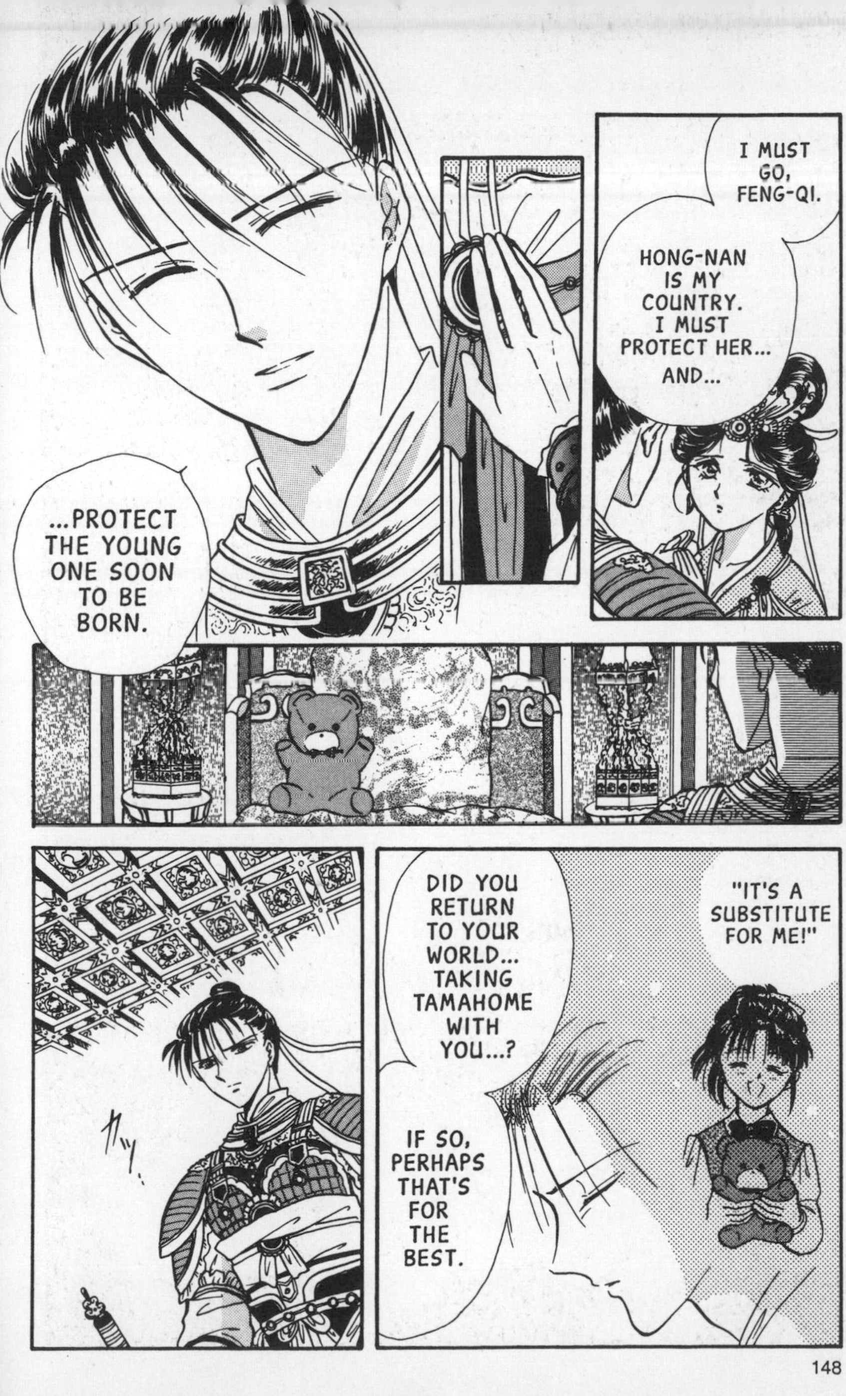

I MUST GO, FENG-QI.
HONG-NAN IS MY COUNTRY. I MUST PROTECT HER... AND...
...PROTECT THE YOUNG ONE SOON TO BE BORN.
"IT'S A SUBSTITUTE FOR ME!"
DID YOU RETURN TO YOUR WORLD... TAKING TAMAHOME WITH YOU...?
IF SO, PERHAPS THAT'S FOR THE BEST.

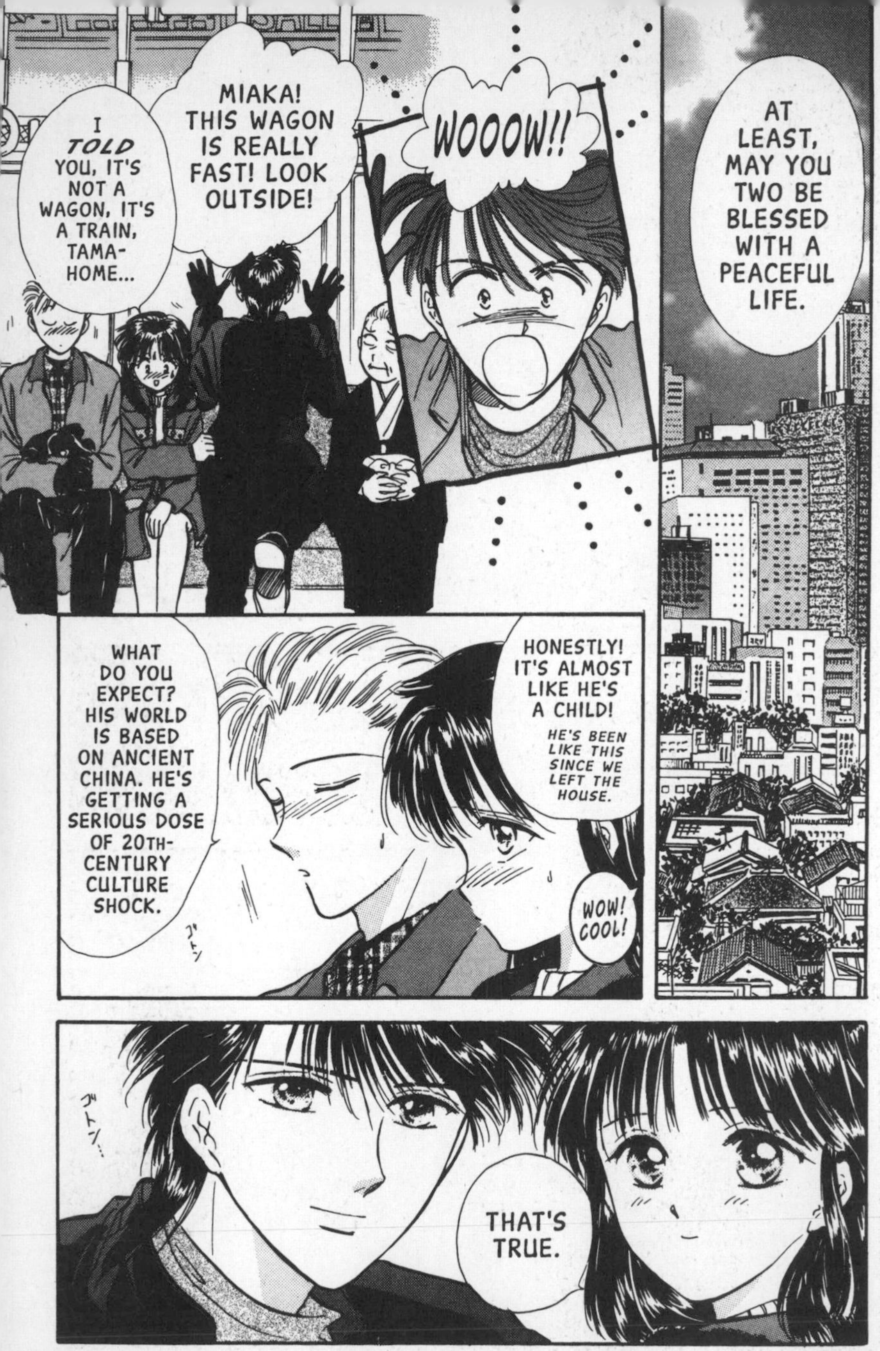
AT LEAST, MAY YOU TWO BE BLESSED WITH A PEACEFUL LIFE.
WOOOW!!
MIAKA! THIS WAGON IS REALLY FAST! LOOK OUTSIDE!
I *TOLD* YOU, IT'S NOT A WAGON, IT'S A TRAIN, TAMA-HOME...
HONESTLY! IT'S ALMOST LIKE HE'S A CHILD!
HE'S BEEN LIKE THIS SINCE WE LEFT THE HOUSE.
WOW! COOL!
WHAT DO YOU EXPECT? HIS WORLD IS BASED ON ANCIENT CHINA. HE'S GETTING A SERIOUS DOSE OF 20TH-CENTURY CULTURE SHOCK.
ゴトン
ゴトン…
THAT'S TRUE.

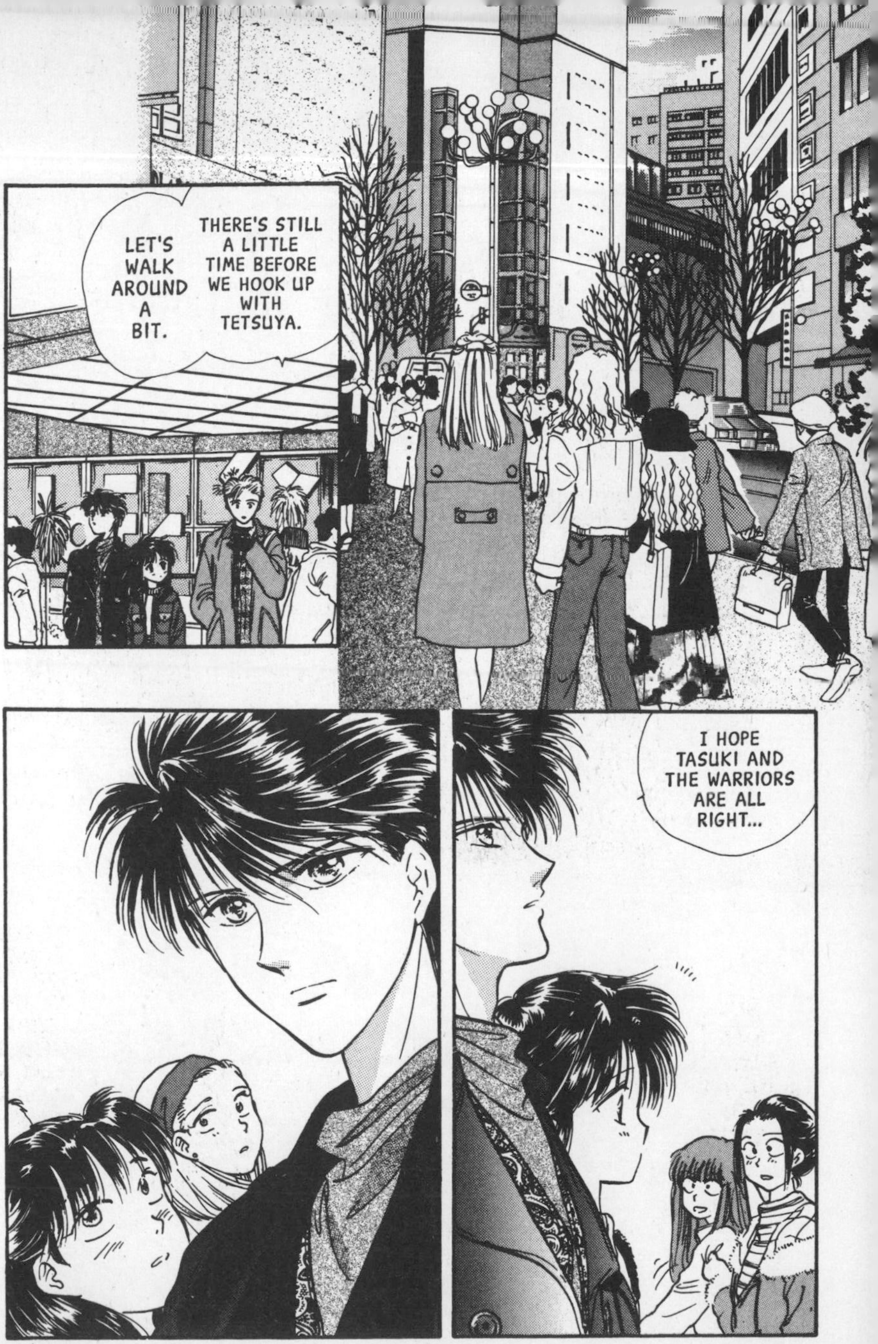
THERE'S STILL A LITTLE TIME BEFORE WE HOOK UP WITH TETSUYA.
LET'S WALK AROUND A BIT.
I HOPE TASUKI AND THE WARRIORS ARE ALL RIGHT...

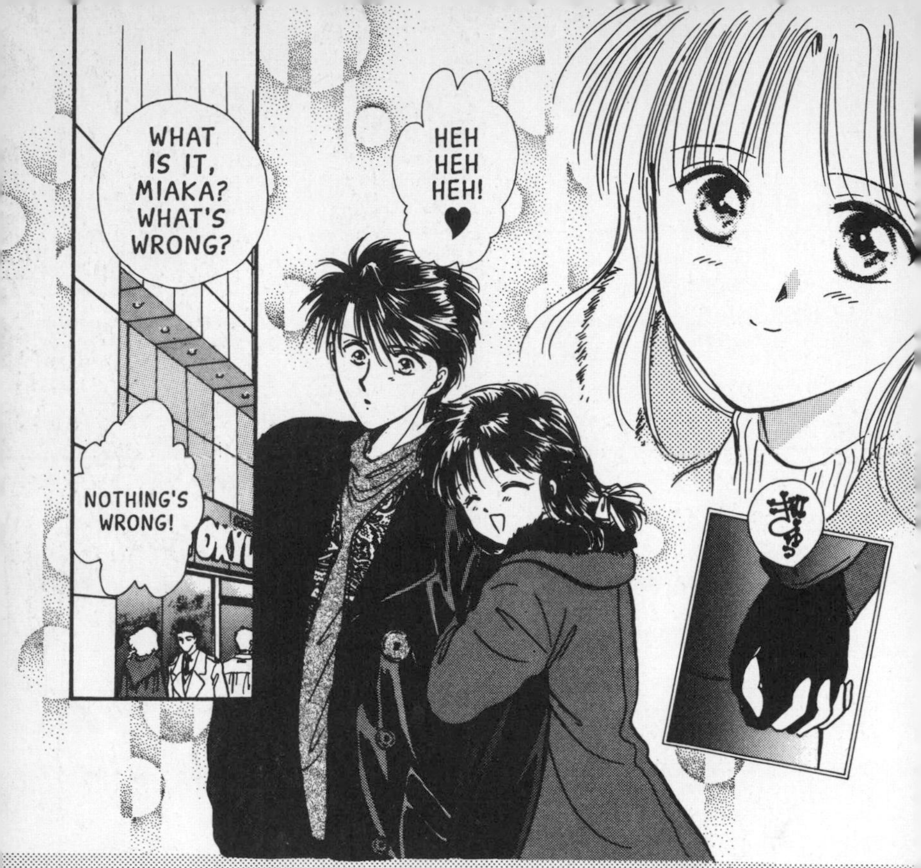
HEH HEH HEH! ♥
WHAT IS IT, MIAKA? WHAT'S WRONG?
NOTHING'S WRONG!

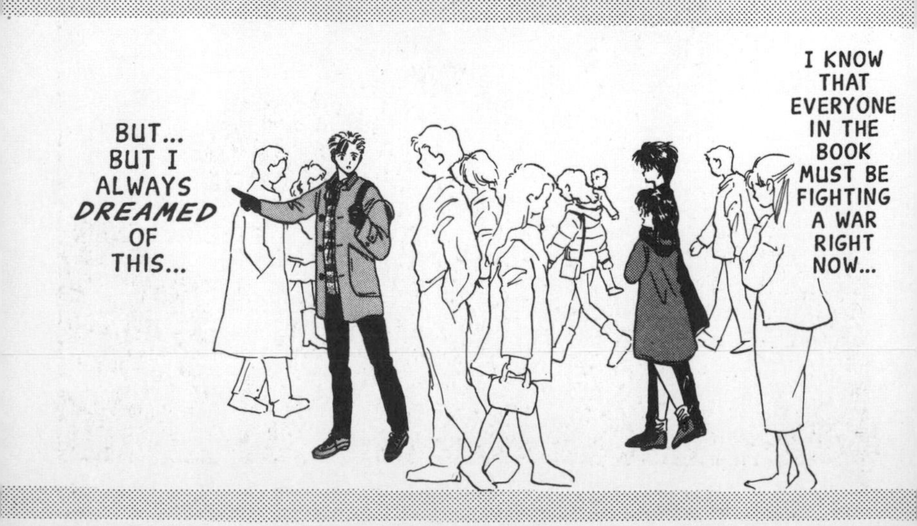
I KNOW THAT EVERYONE IN THE BOOK MUST BE FIGHTING A WAR RIGHT NOW...
BUT... BUT I ALWAYS *DREAMED* OF THIS...

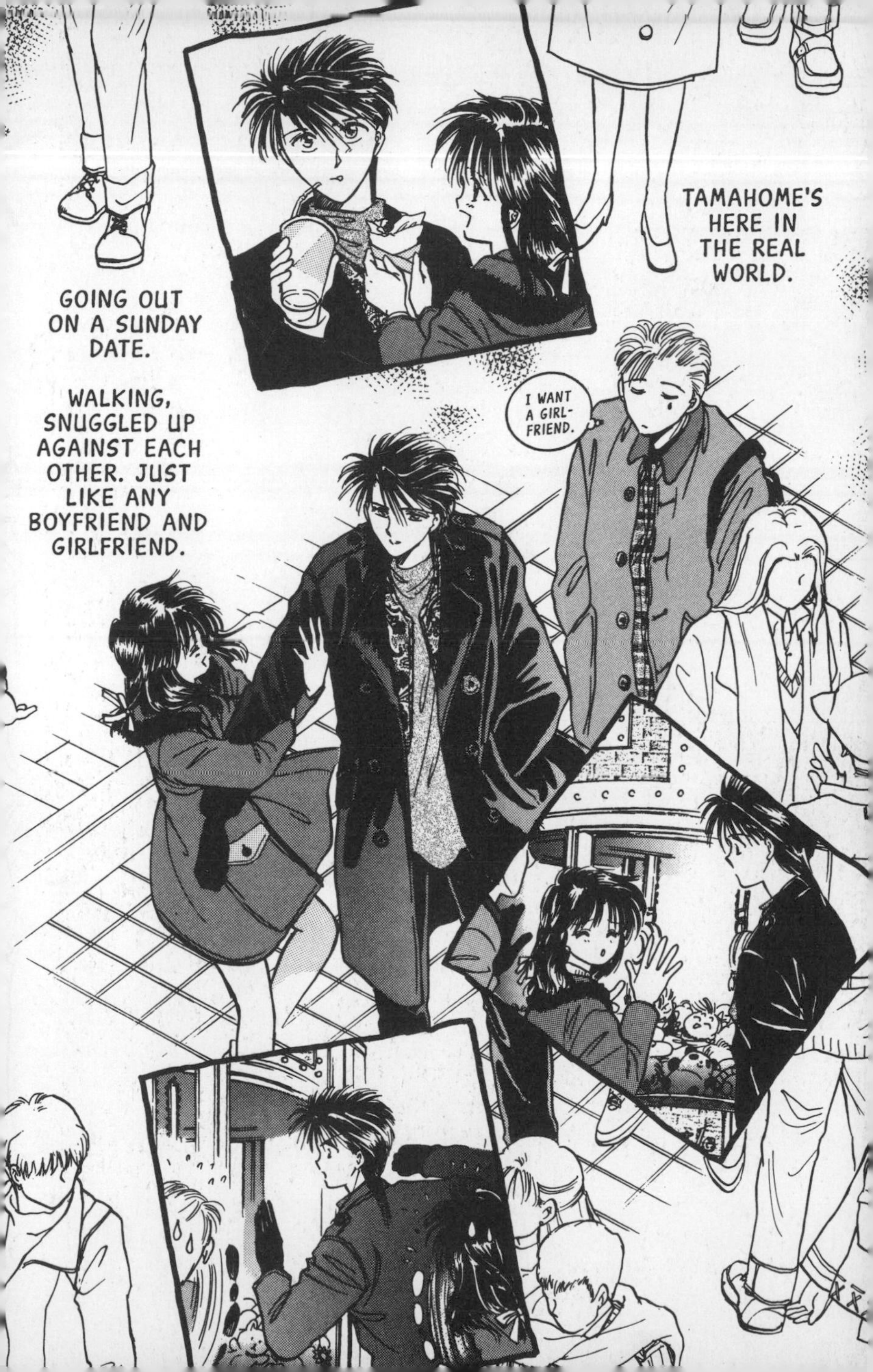
TAMAHOME'S HERE IN THE REAL WORLD.
GOING OUT ON A SUNDAY DATE.
I WANT A GIRL-FRIEND.
WALKING, SNUGGLED UP AGAINST EACH OTHER. JUST LIKE ANY BOYFRIEND AND GIRLFRIEND.

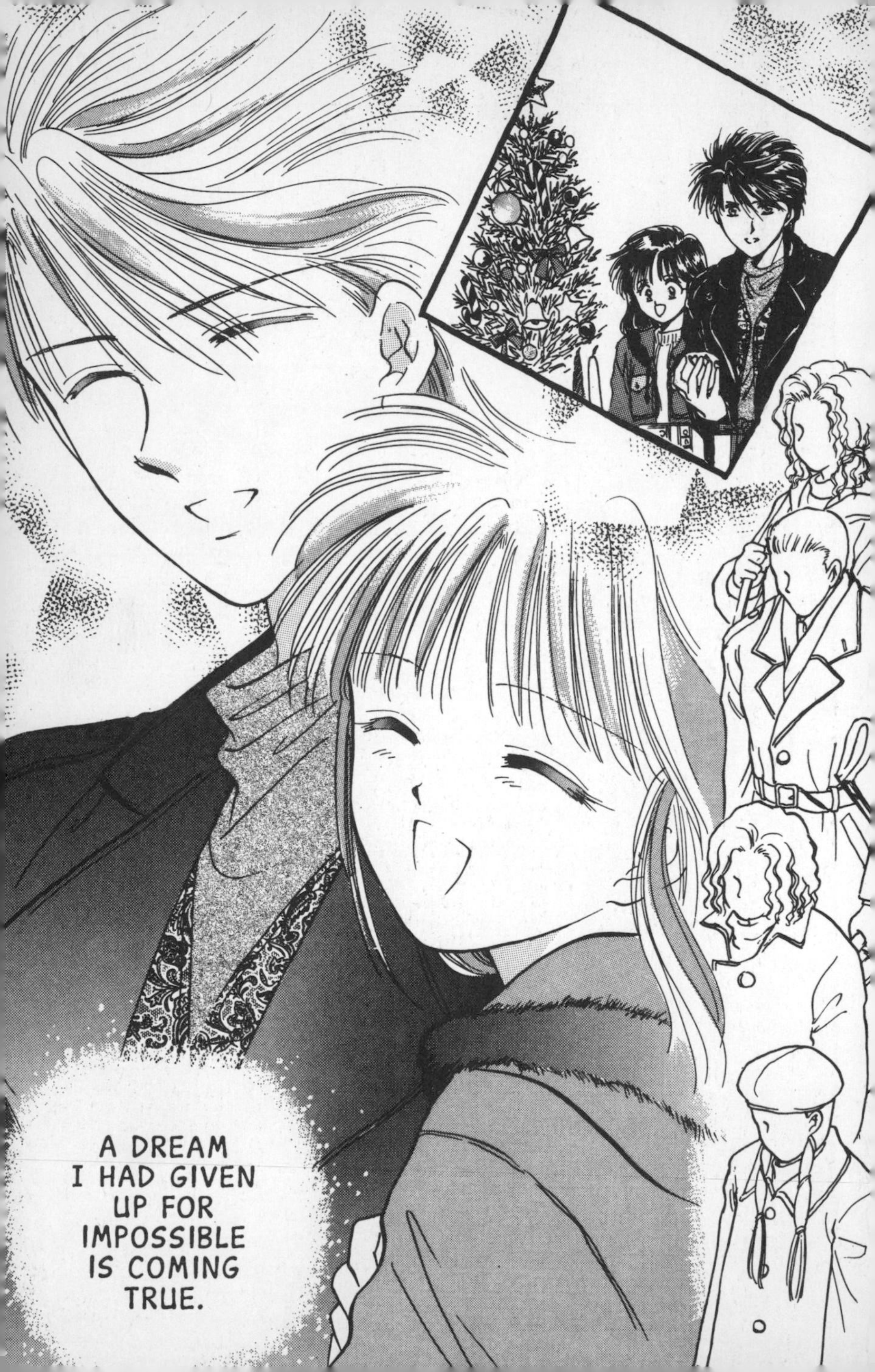
A DREAM I HAD GIVEN UP FOR IMPOSSIBLE IS COMING TRUE.

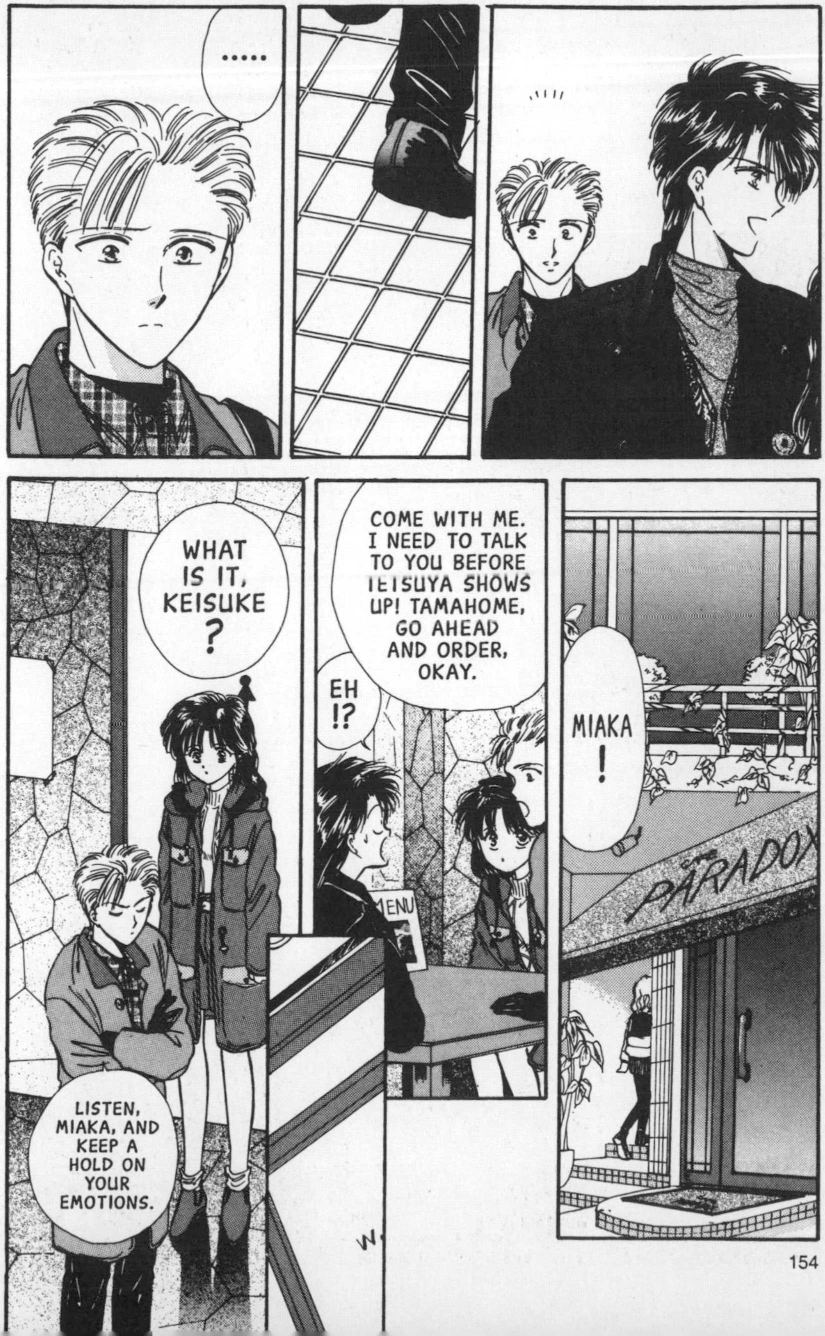
.....
MIAKA !
COME WITH ME. I NEED TO TALK TO YOU BEFORE TETSUYA SHOWS UP! TAMAHOME, GO AHEAD AND ORDER, OKAY.
EH !?
WHAT IS IT, KEISUKE ?
LISTEN, MIAKA, AND KEEP A HOLD ON YOUR EMOTIONS.
PARADOX

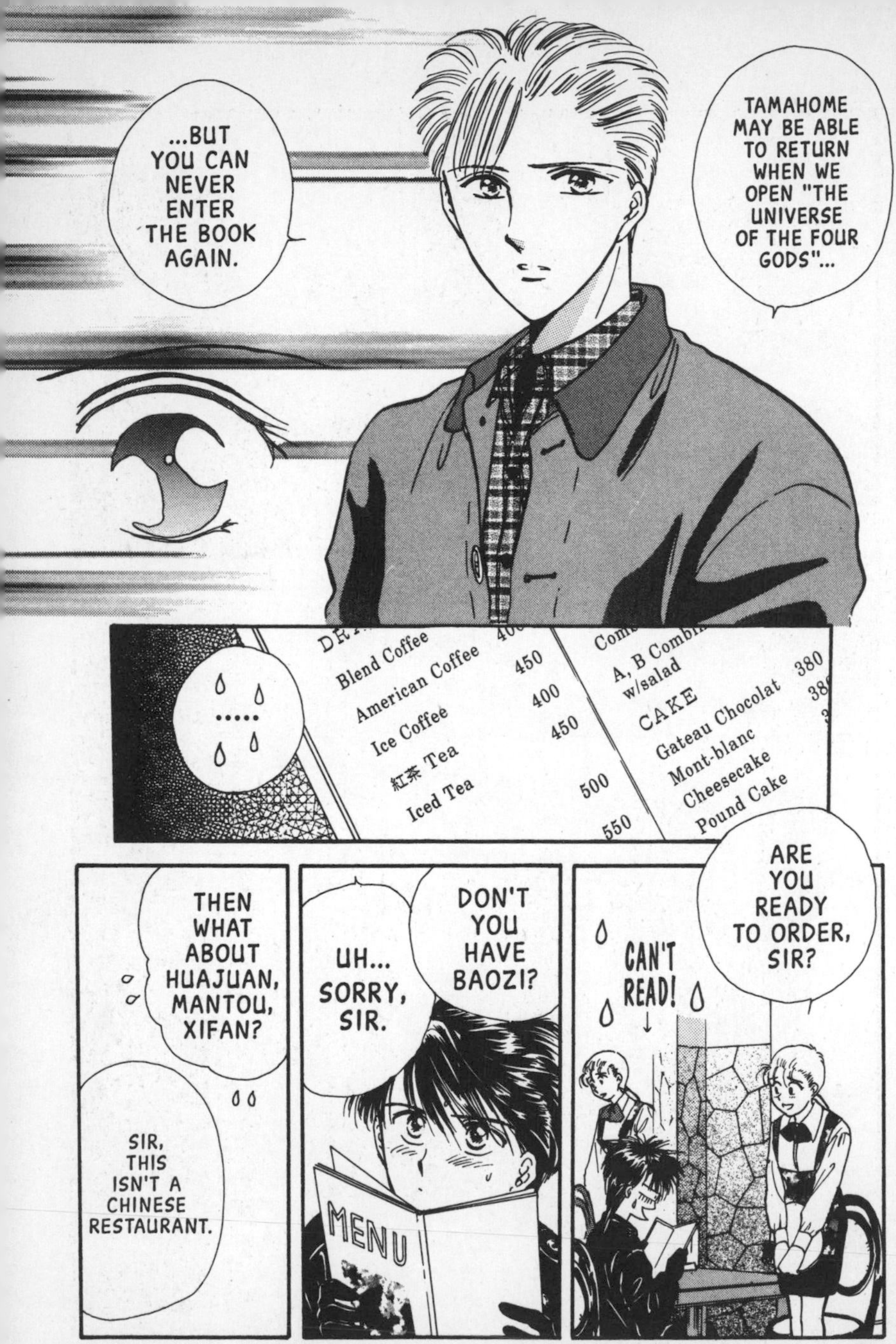
TAMAHOME MAY BE ABLE TO RETURN WHEN WE OPEN "THE UNIVERSE OF THE FOUR GODS"...
...BUT YOU CAN NEVER ENTER THE BOOK AGAIN.
.....
Blend Coffee
American Coffee 450
Ice Coffee 400
紅茶 Tea 450
Iced Tea 500
550
A, B Combi
w/salad
CAKE
Gateau Chocolat 380
Mont-blanc
Cheesecake
Pound Cake
MENU
ARE YOU READY TO ORDER, SIR?
CAN'T READ!
DON'T YOU HAVE BAOZI?
UH... SORRY, SIR.
THEN WHAT ABOUT HUAJUAN, MANTOU, XIFAN?
SIR, THIS ISN'T A CHINESE RESTAURANT.
BAOZI, HUAJUAN, AND MANTOU ARE KINDS OF CHINESE BUNS. XIFAN IS SOUP.

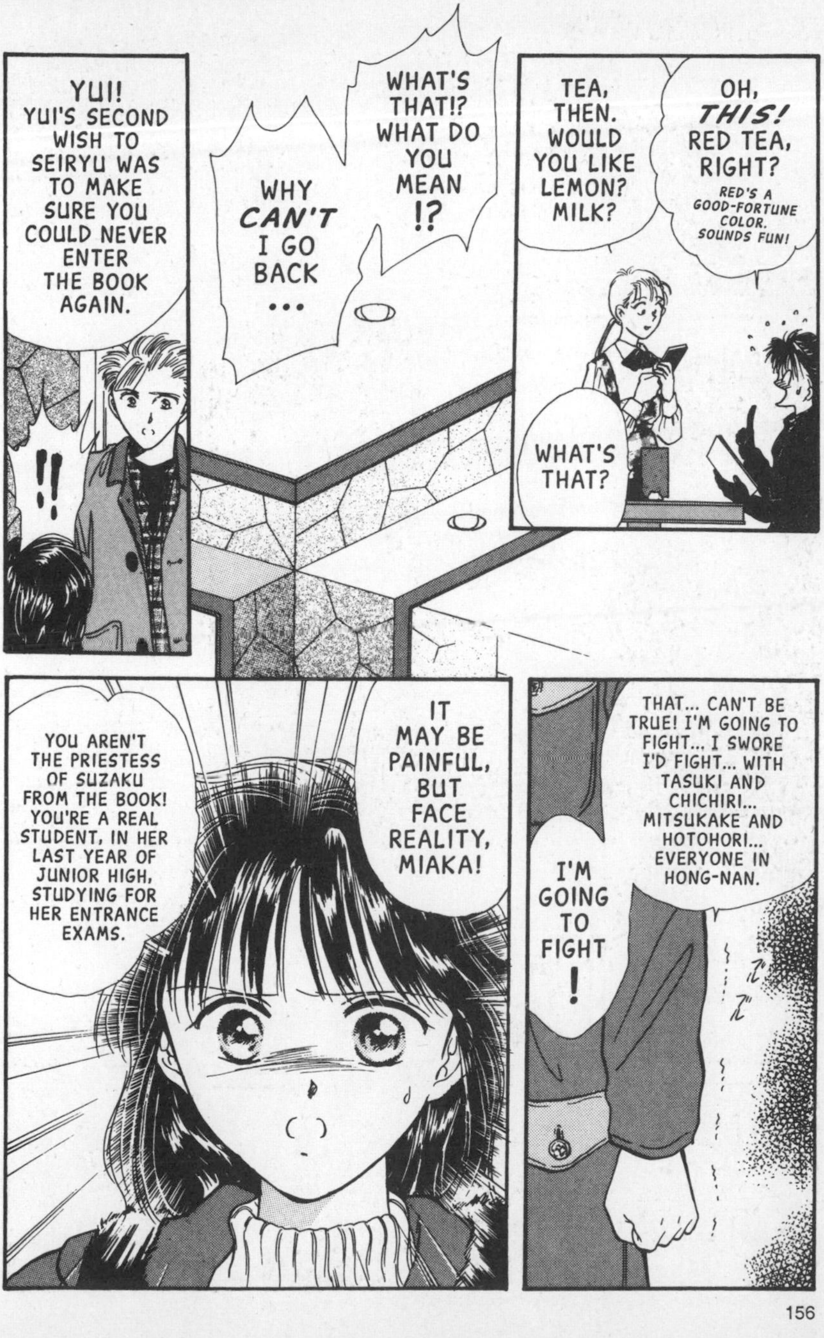
OH, *THIS!* RED TEA, RIGHT?
RED'S A GOOD-FORTUNE COLOR. SOUNDS FUN!
TEA, THEN. WOULD YOU LIKE LEMON? MILK?
WHAT'S THAT?
WHAT'S THAT!? WHAT DO YOU MEAN !?
WHY *CAN'T* I GO BACK ...
YUI! YUI'S SECOND WISH TO SEIRYU WAS TO MAKE SURE YOU COULD NEVER ENTER THE BOOK AGAIN.
!!
THAT... CAN'T BE TRUE! I'M GOING TO FIGHT... I SWORE I'D FIGHT... WITH TASUKI AND CHICHIRI... MITSUKAKE AND HOTOHORI... EVERYONE IN HONG-NAN.
I'M GOING TO FIGHT !
IT MAY BE PAINFUL, BUT FACE REALITY, MIAKA!
YOU AREN'T THE PRIESTESS OF SUZAKU FROM THE BOOK! YOU'RE A REAL STUDENT, IN HER LAST YEAR OF JUNIOR HIGH, STUDYING FOR HER ENTRANCE EXAMS.

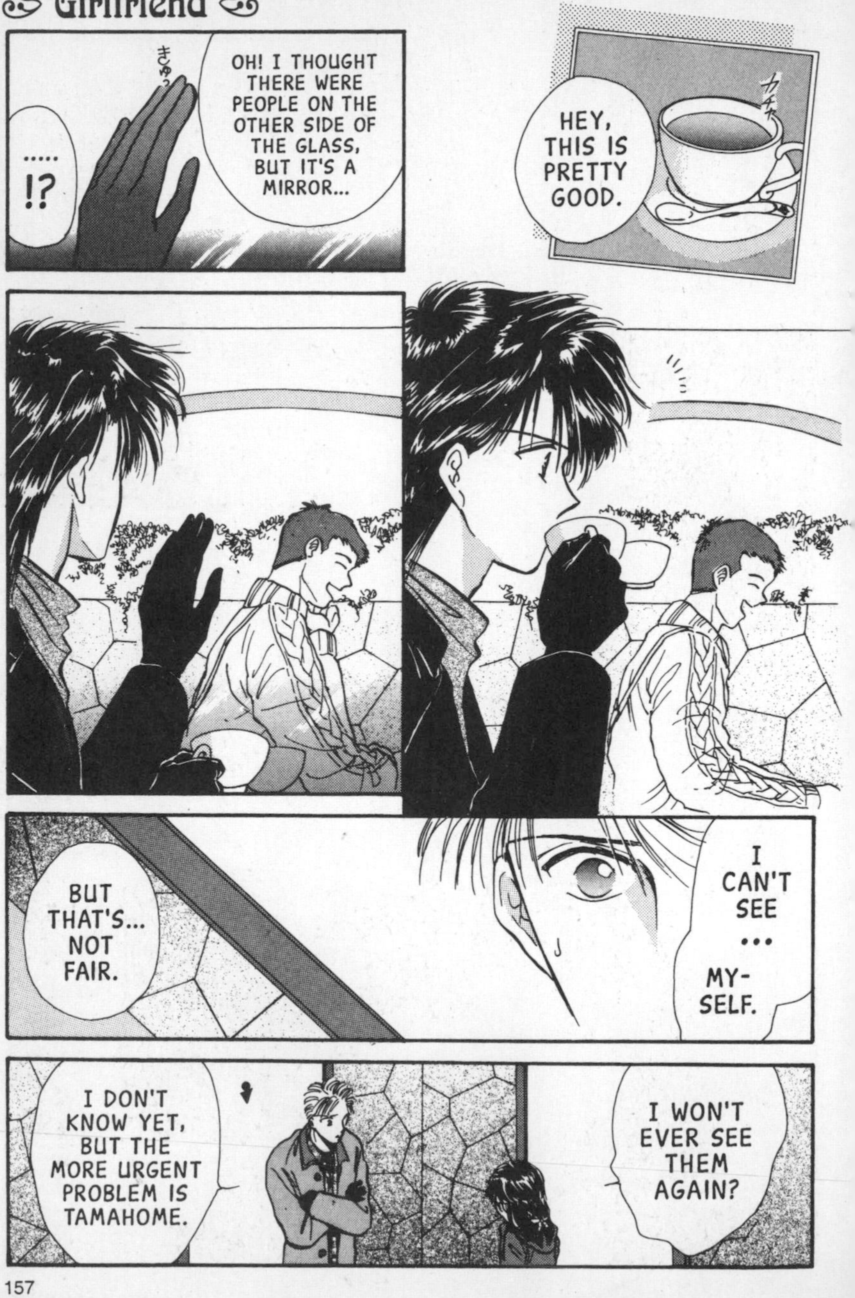
HEY, THIS IS PRETTY GOOD.
OH! I THOUGHT THERE WERE PEOPLE ON THE OTHER SIDE OF THE GLASS, BUT IT'S A MIRROR...
..... !?
I CAN'T SEE ... MY-SELF.
BUT THAT'S... NOT FAIR.
I WON'T EVER SEE THEM AGAIN?
I DON'T KNOW YET, BUT THE MORE URGENT PROBLEM IS TAMAHOME.

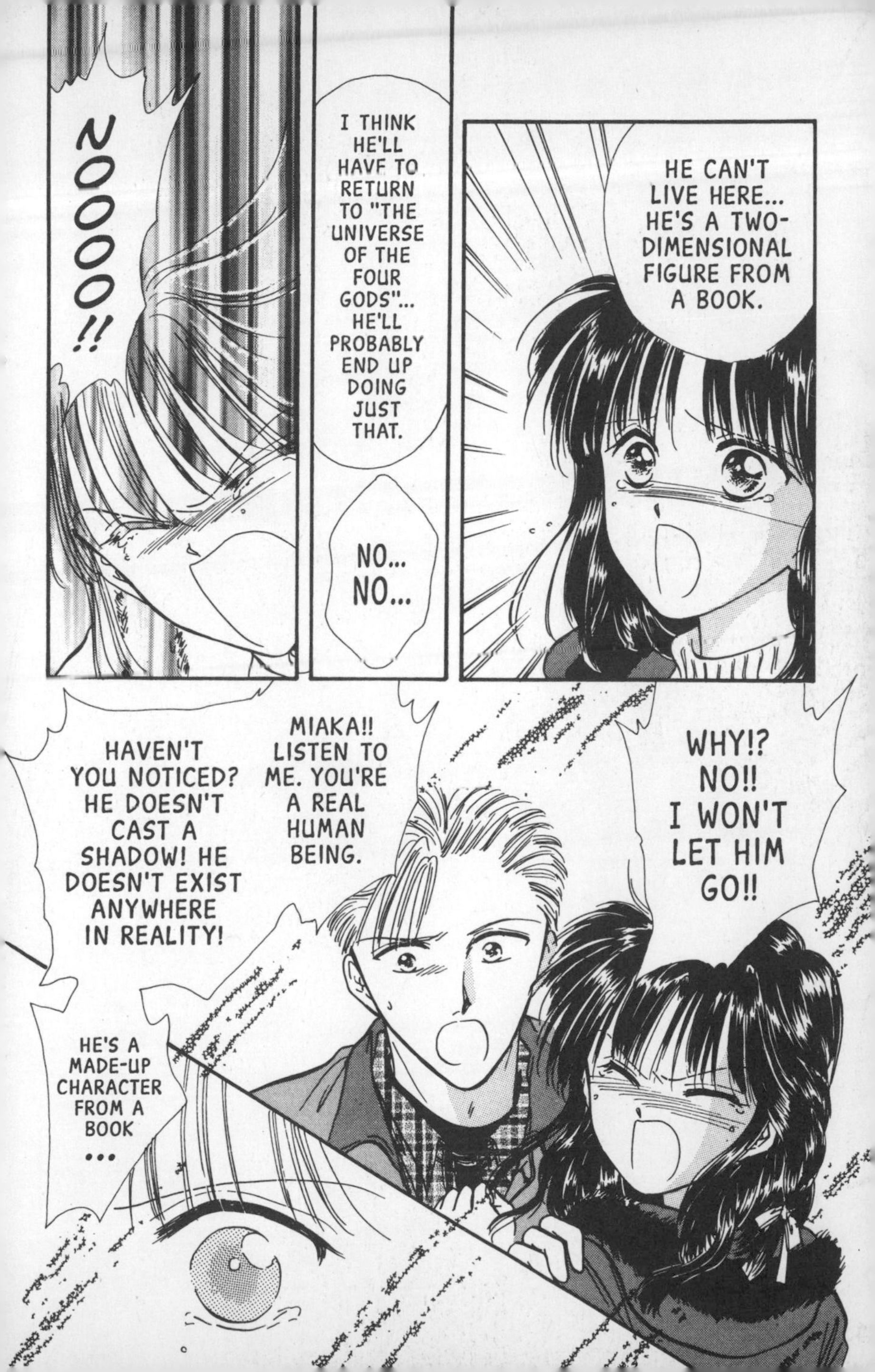
HE CAN'T LIVE HERE... HE'S A TWO-DIMENSIONAL FIGURE FROM A BOOK.
I THINK HE'LL HAVE TO RETURN TO "THE UNIVERSE OF THE FOUR GODS"... HE'LL PROBABLY END UP DOING JUST THAT.
NO... NO...
NOOOOO!!
WHY!? NO!! I WON'T LET HIM GO!!
MIAKA!! LISTEN TO ME. YOU'RE A REAL HUMAN BEING.
HAVEN'T YOU NOTICED? HE DOESN'T CAST A SHADOW! HE DOESN'T EXIST ANYWHERE IN REALITY!
HE'S A MADE-UP CHARACTER FROM A BOOK ...

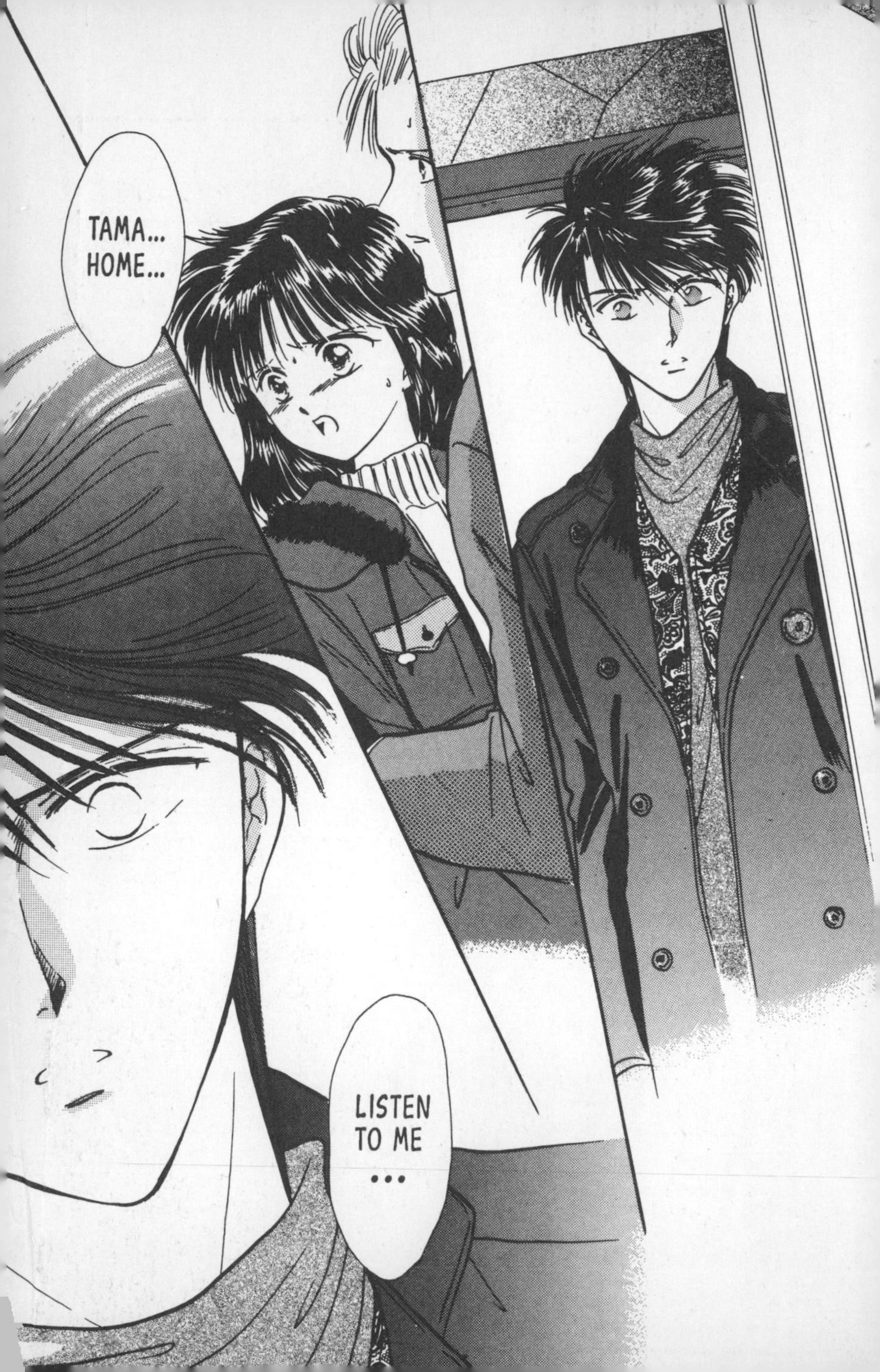
TAMA... HOME...
LISTEN TO ME ...

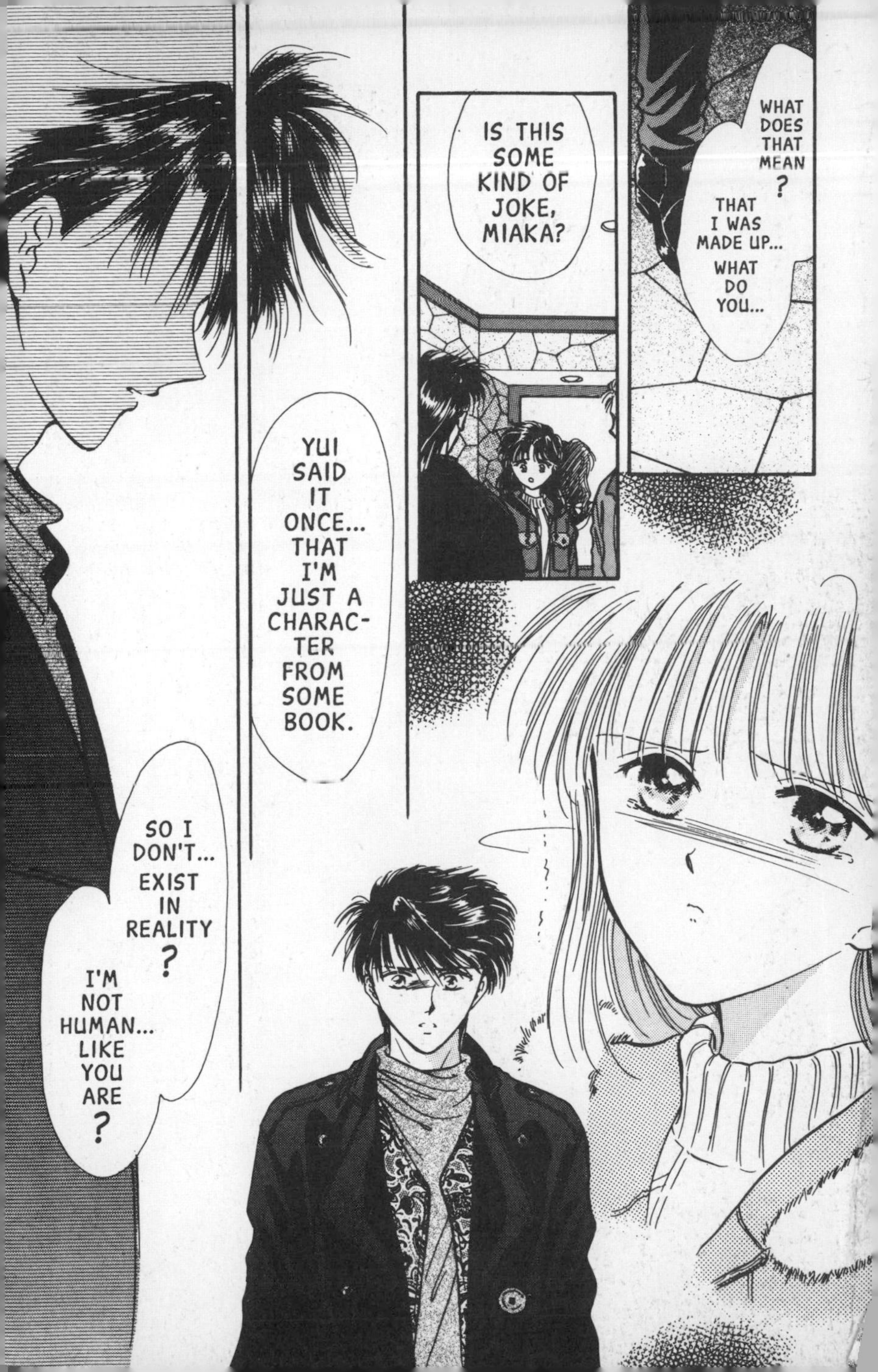
WHAT DOES THAT MEAN?
THAT I WAS MADE UP... WHAT DO YOU...
IS THIS SOME KIND OF JOKE, MIAKA?
YUI SAID IT ONCE... THAT I'M JUST A CHARAC-TER FROM SOME BOOK.
SO I DON'T... EXIST IN REALITY? I'M NOT HUMAN... LIKE YOU ARE?

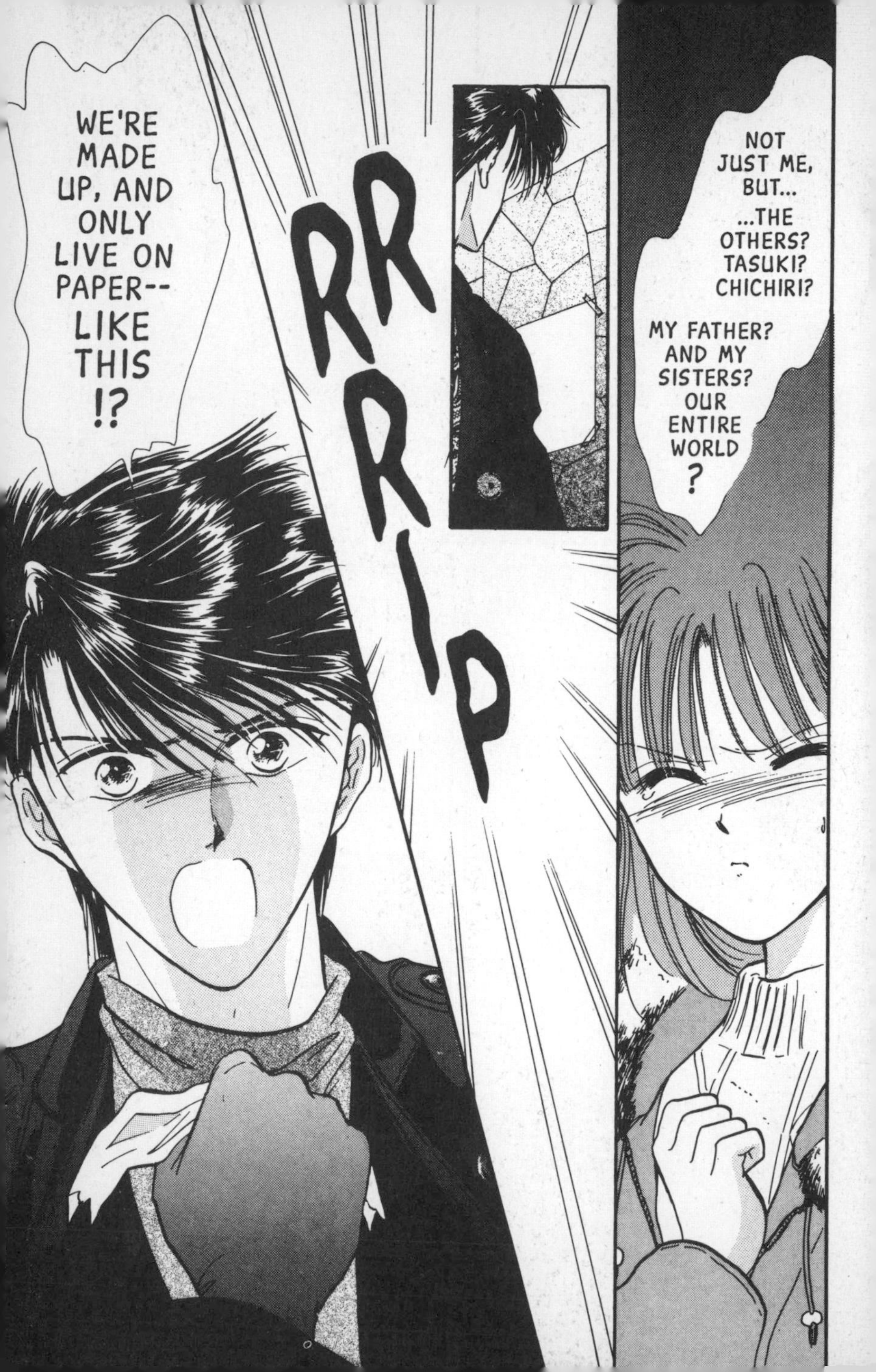
NOT JUST ME, BUT... ...THE OTHERS? TASUKI? CHICHIRI?
MY FATHER? AND MY SISTERS? OUR ENTIRE WORLD ?
RRRIP
WE'RE MADE UP, AND ONLY LIVE ON PAPER-- LIKE THIS !?

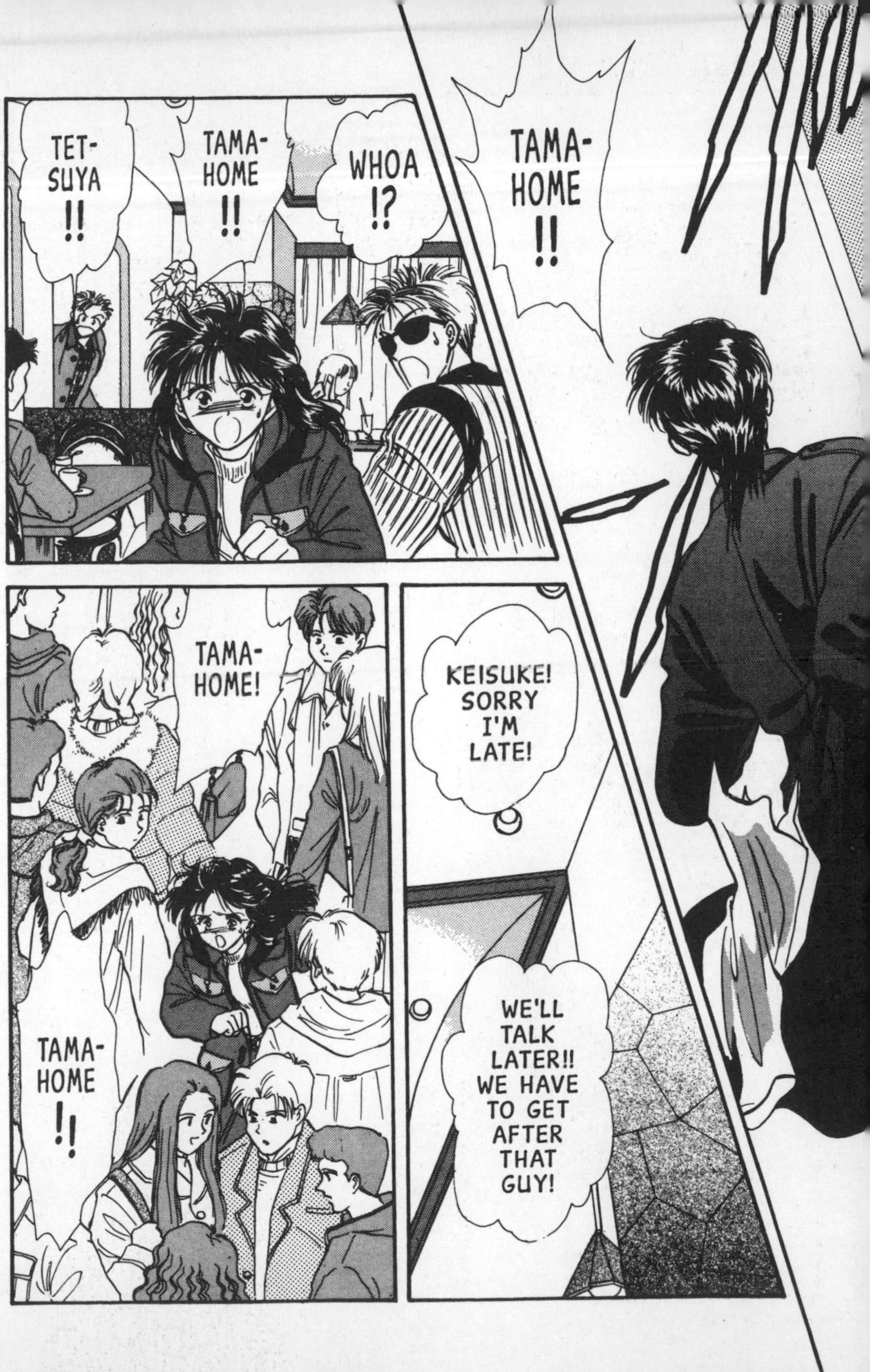
TAMA-HOME!!
WHOA!?
TAMA-HOME!!
TET-SUYA!!
KEISUKE! SORRY I'M LATE!
WE'LL TALK LATER!! WE HAVE TO GET AFTER THAT GUY!
TAMA-HOME!
TAMA-HOME!!

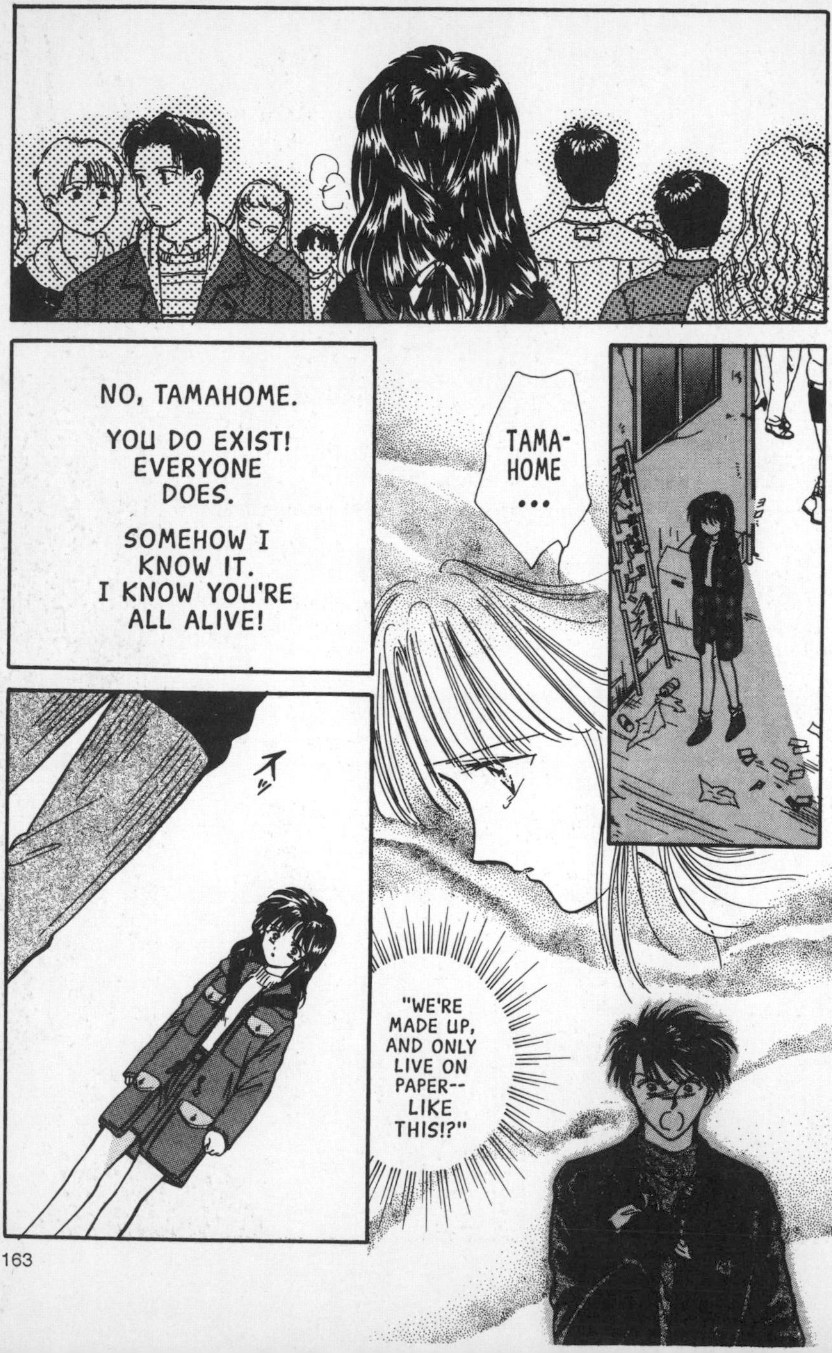
TAMA-HOME ...
"WE'RE MADE UP, AND ONLY LIVE ON PAPER-- LIKE THIS!?"
NO, TAMAHOME.
YOU DO EXIST! EVERYONE DOES.
SOMEHOW I KNOW IT. I KNOW YOU'RE ALL ALIVE!

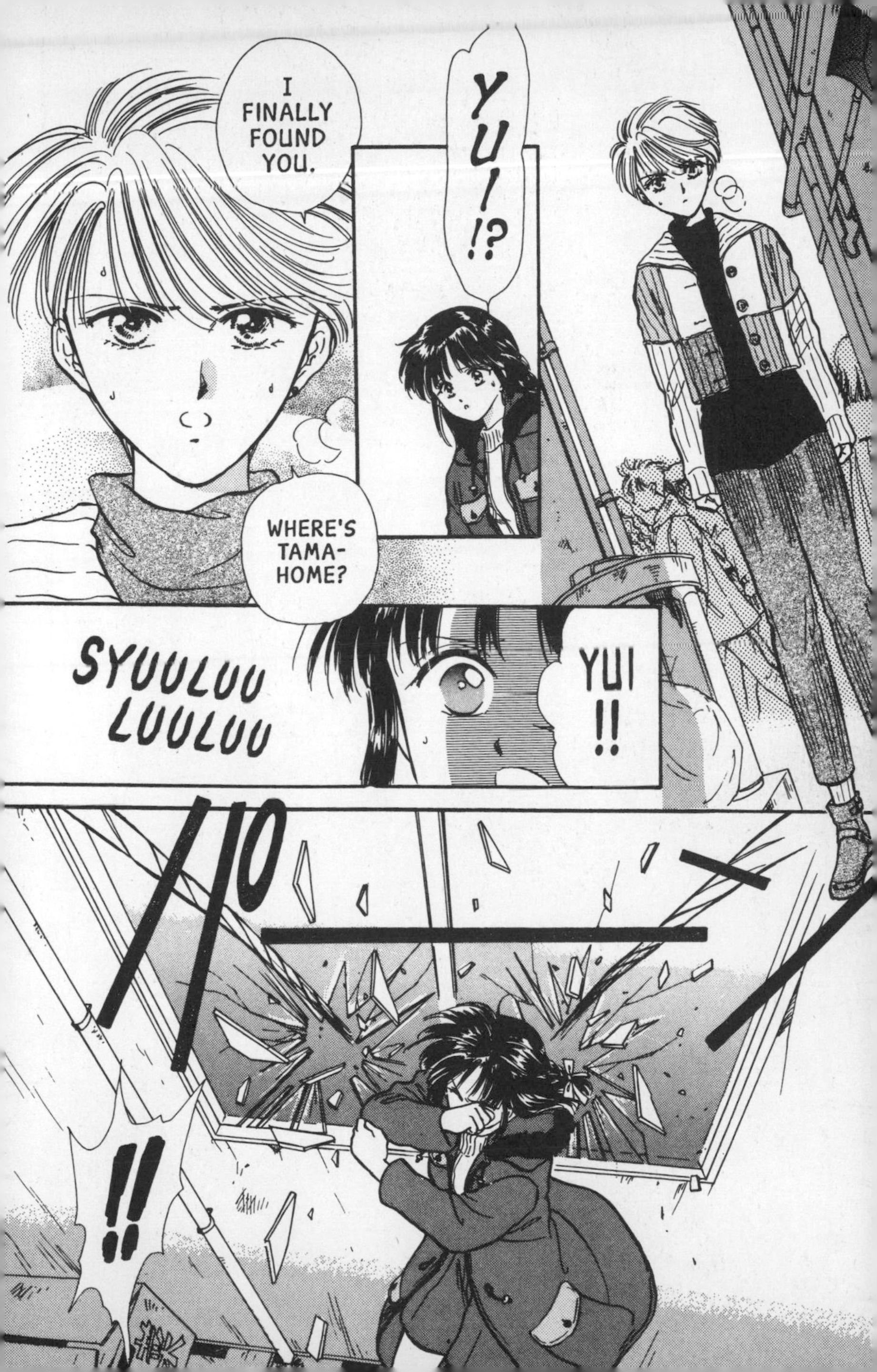

YUI!?
I FINALLY FOUND YOU.
WHERE'S TAMA-HOME?
YUI!!
SYUULUU LUULUU
!!

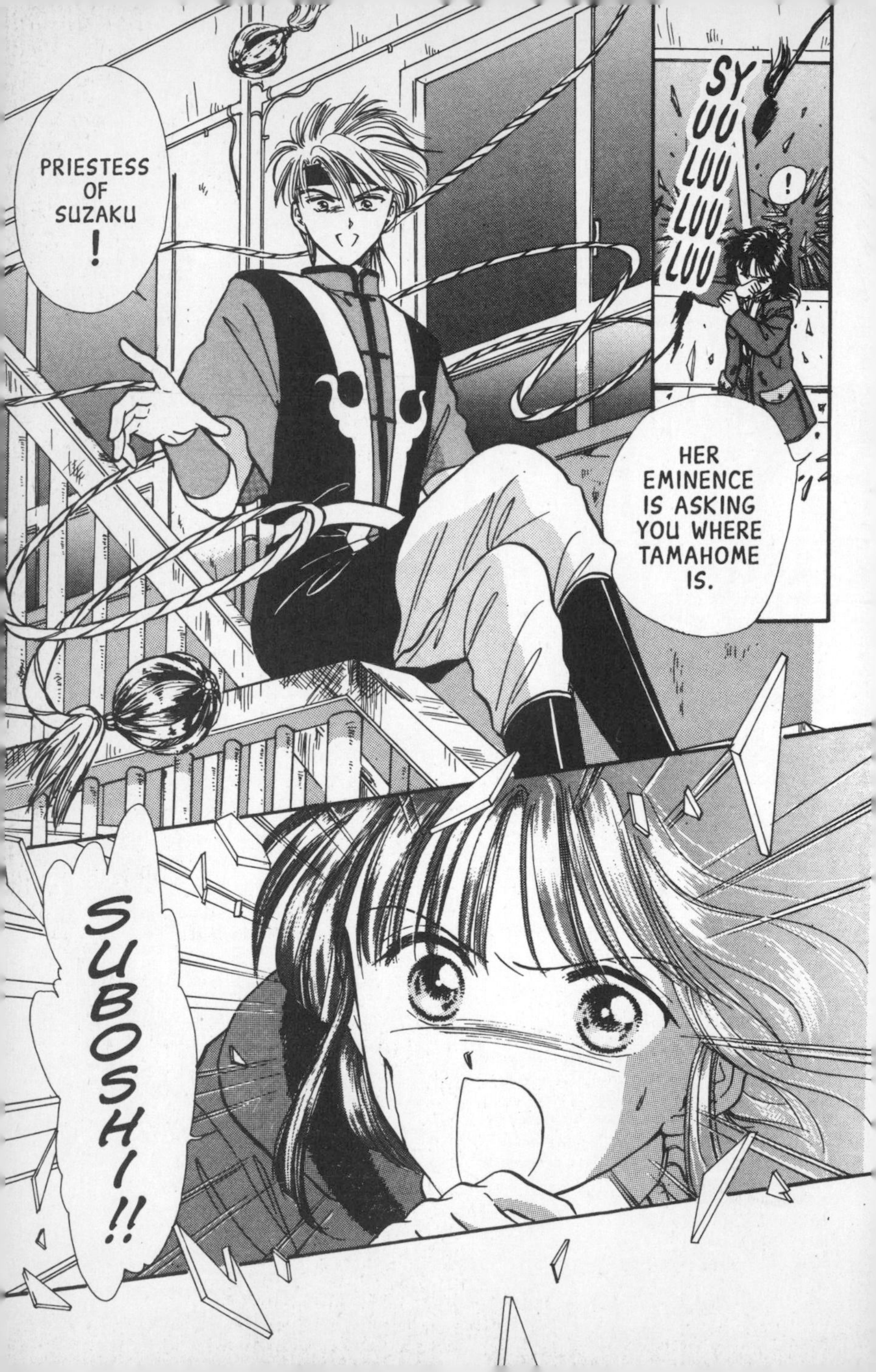
SYUULUULUULUU
!
PRIESTESS OF SUZAKU!
HER EMINENCE IS ASKING YOU WHERE TAMAHOME IS.
SUBOSHI!!

THESE TWO DIDN'T GET ALONG ON ACCOUNT OF NAKAGO.

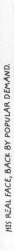

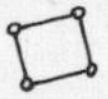
LIBRA

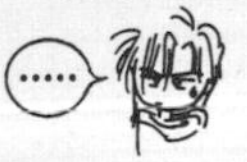
......

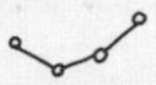
SCORPIO

LUO 羅 CHUIN 軍

BAI 白 HUA 花 WAN 婉

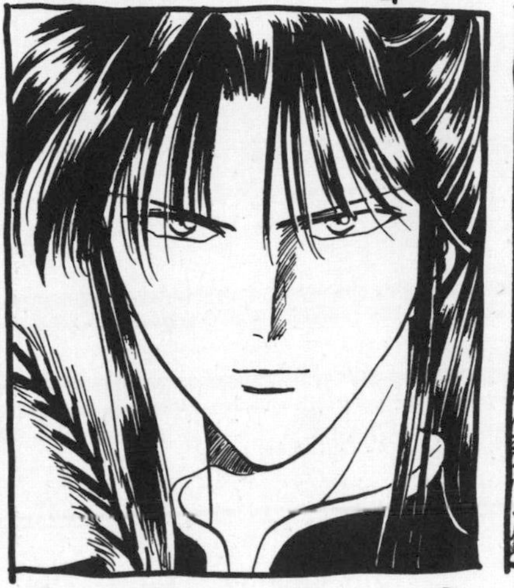

HIS REAL FACE, BACK BY POPULAR DEMAND.

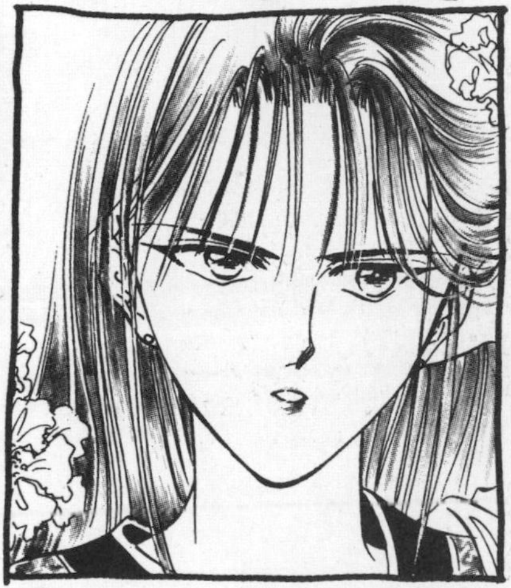

T O M O

- He was abandoned as a baby, so his birthplace remains unknown (His real name is unknown too). (His childhood caretaker gave him this name.)

- 21 years old
- Height: 184 cm (6' 0")
- Blood type: AB
- Powers: Hypnosis and illusion using a shell.
- Hobbies: Sadism (particularly with men).
  ⇧ *He rarely actually hurts anyone...*

- He has a very complicated personality. He's pretty harsh and jaded, probably due to the hardships he had to suffer as a child. But he's become a little twisted.
  Because his caretaker was a dancer, he learned the art and made a living on it (his makeup and clothes come from the stage). *A street performer really.*
  He's very nimble because of this background.
  It could be that he was surrounded only by men, or he simply could have been born that way, but he is homosexual. He's in love with Nakago, but because of his jaded personality, he can't be upfront about it. So he usually ends up saying something irritating. Although he's calm, he has a flaky side too. He doesn't like women, but he can effectively take them on (!) when he needs to.

S O I

- Born in the village of Xuan, home of the Ning tribe in the Western region (a satellite country) of Qu-Dong).*

- 19 years old
- Height: 170 cm (5' 7")
- Blood type: O
- Measurements B: 89 W: 56 H: 85 (35, 22, 33)

- Powers: Special Feng shui powers to control lightning, electro-magnetic fields, and Fangzhong (bedding) techniques.

- Because her family was so poor, as a child, she was sold to a brothel and grew up there. She fell in love with Nakago at the age of 12 when she first met him. She knew her love was unrequited, and that she was being used so he could recover and heighten his chi, but that didn't stop her from giving him everything she had.
  She is normally bound in armor, speaks like a man, and is formidable as a fighter.
  But now, everything she does is, in one way or another, to try to assist Nakago. In fact, she is very feminine and kind. Because of her jealousy toward Yui, she's sympathetic to Miaka.

* Satellite country: A country under the rule of a neighboring major power.

CHAPTER SEVENTY-ONE **TO LIVE FOR YOU**

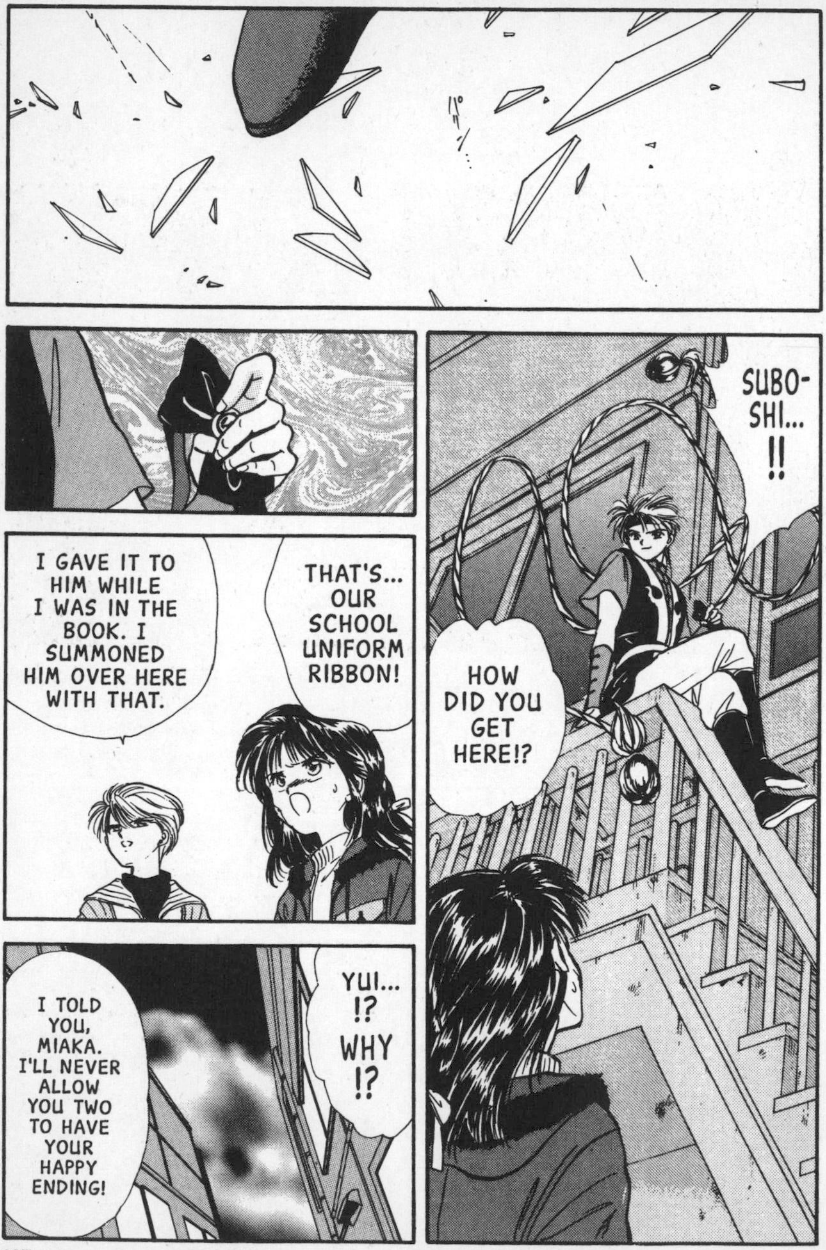
SUBO-SHI... !!
HOW DID YOU GET HERE!?
THAT'S... OUR SCHOOL UNIFORM RIBBON!
I GAVE IT TO HIM WHILE I WAS IN THE BOOK. I SUMMONED HIM OVER HERE WITH THAT.
YUI... !? WHY !?
I TOLD YOU, MIAKA. I'LL NEVER ALLOW YOU TWO TO HAVE YOUR HAPPY ENDING!

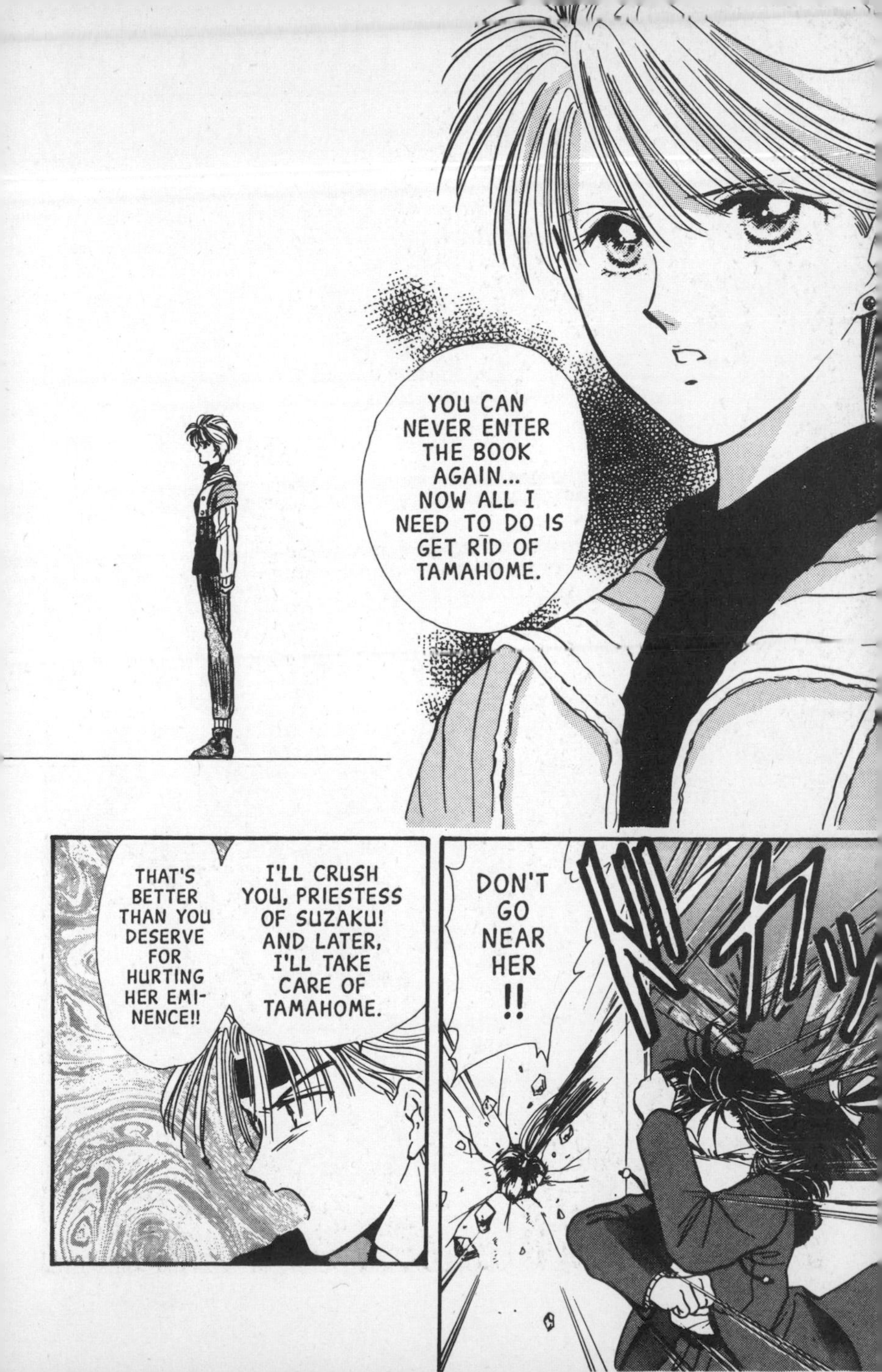
YOU CAN NEVER ENTER THE BOOK AGAIN... NOW ALL I NEED TO DO IS GET RID OF TAMAHOME.
DON'T GO NEAR HER !!
I'LL CRUSH YOU, PRIESTESS OF SUZAKU! AND LATER, I'LL TAKE CARE OF TAMAHOME.
THAT'S BETTER THAN YOU DESERVE FOR HURTING HER EMI-NENCE!!

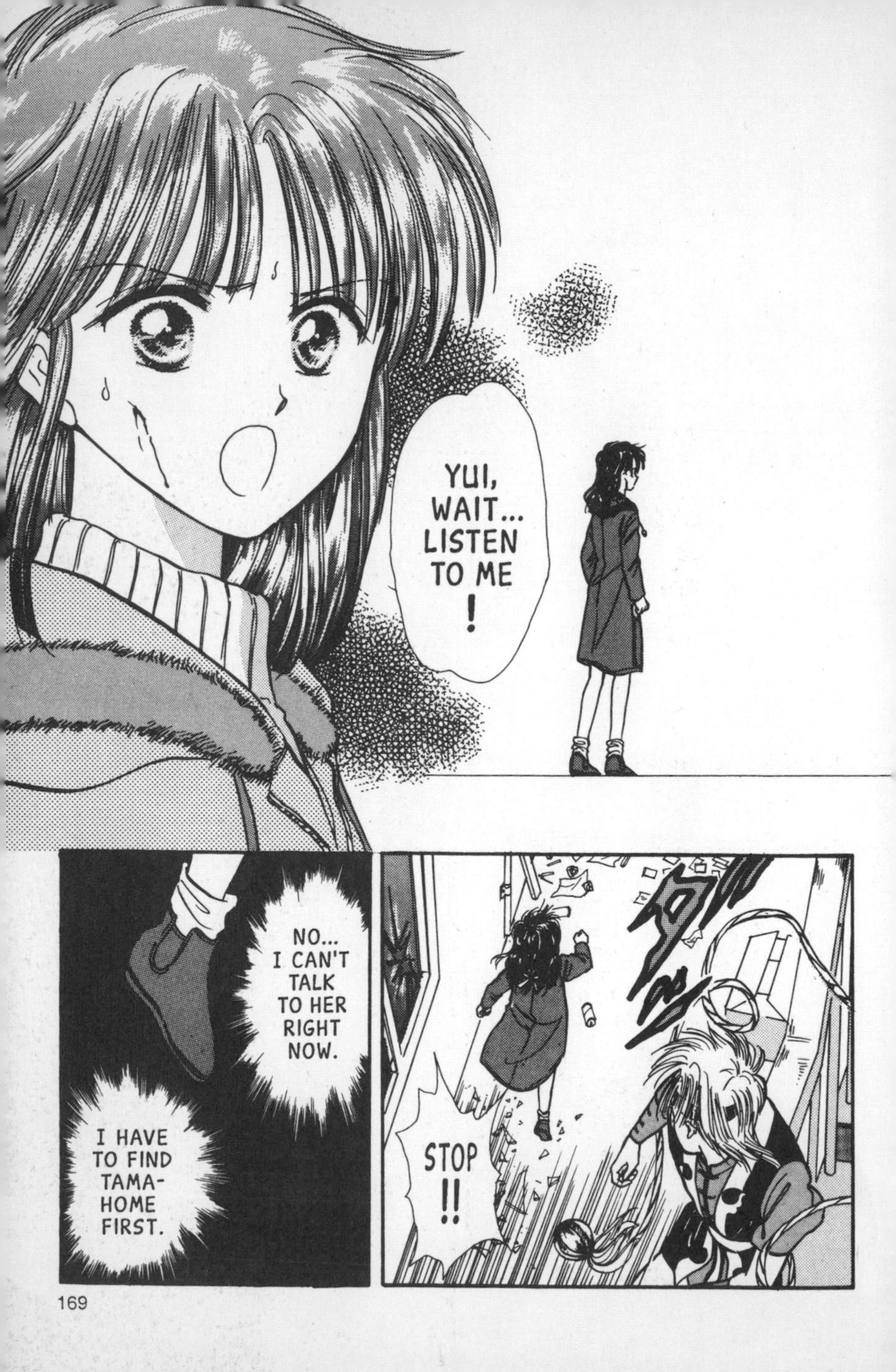
YUI, WAIT... LISTEN TO ME !
STOP !!
NO... I CAN'T TALK TO HER RIGHT NOW.
I HAVE TO FIND TAMA-HOME FIRST.

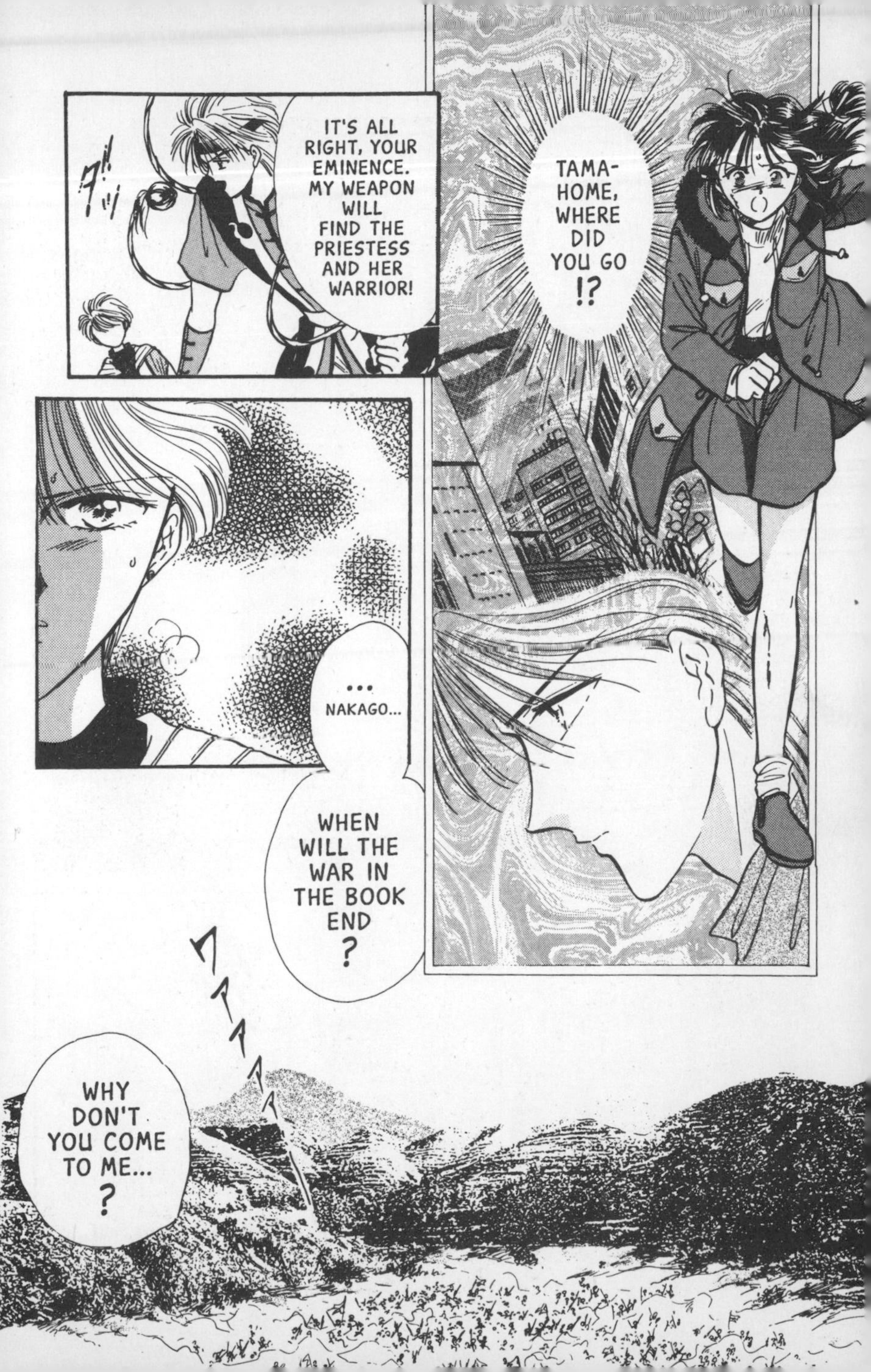
TAMA-HOME, WHERE DID YOU GO !?
IT'S ALL RIGHT, YOUR EMINENCE. MY WEAPON WILL FIND THE PRIESTESS AND HER WARRIOR!
... NAKAGO...
WHEN WILL THE WAR IN THE BOOK END ?
WHY DON'T YOU COME TO ME... ?

By the way, I came up with the idea of having Tomo use a shell to help with his illusions because in ancient times, it was said the "Shinkirō" ("mirage") was created by the "Shin," a giant shell which had dreams in the ocean and exhaled its chi which floated upwards and rose into the air as an illusion. (Of course, I have to wonder how a mirage can still occur in the middle of a desert!)

Ashitare. No comment, really. I think it's all right to have a character who's pretty mindless... But I did enjoy drawing him.

Miboshi. A sorcerer who controlled monsters. The villain who concocted the potion that controlled Tamahome's mind. The temple was based on the famous Pokhara Temple, but the interior resembles an ancient Indian temple. Miboshi isn't holding a rattle, it's a prayer wheel (Tibetans always use them, don't they (?)). His is inscribed with Buddhist sutras to summon demons. (Of course, that's not what they're really for.) If I could afford the pages, I wanted Chichiri to summon a good spirit and have it fight Miboshi's demons! But *this is a shōjo manga here...maybe if it were a video game...* He's actually an old man. I don't think we need the background on these two. Sorry! I doubt they have any fans though.

Oh, no! I'm running out of space already... Hm? What about Yui? Hold on, we still have more coming. That's right... the next volume will be the last for Fushigi Yūgi (Waaaah! How sad!) After this book is published, the serial will come to an end with issue 5 of Shōjo Comic which is published on February 5th (1995). But the CD book 3 will come out in February too. The book of illustrations (sorry, it will only contain material from Fushigi Yūgi, nothing from Prepubescence) will be packed with plenty of material! No definite publication date yet though... See you then in volume 13! *I want to tell the tale of Genbu and Byakko too. Someone give me the chance!*

'94 11/30

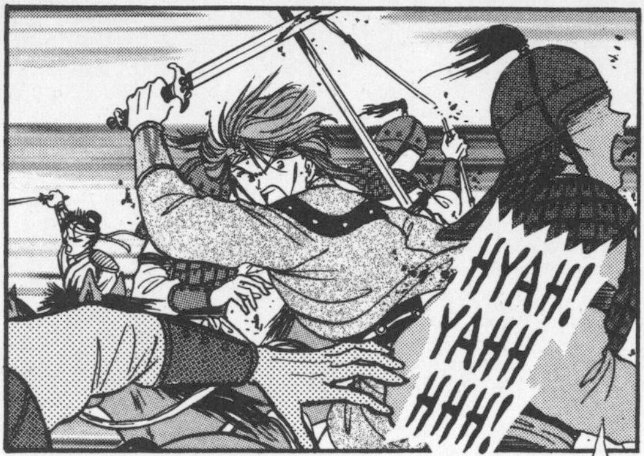
HYAH! YAHHHHH!

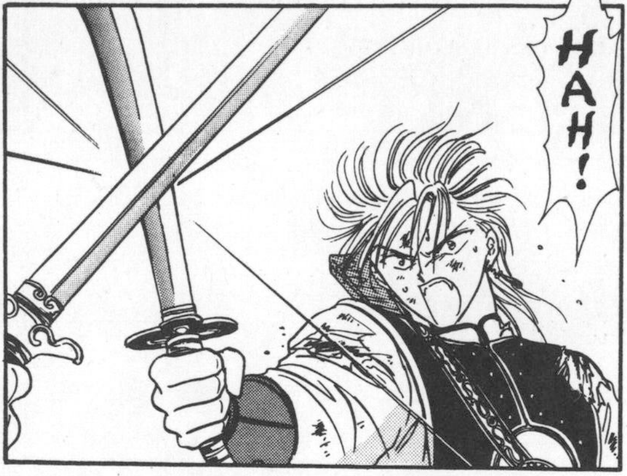
HAH!

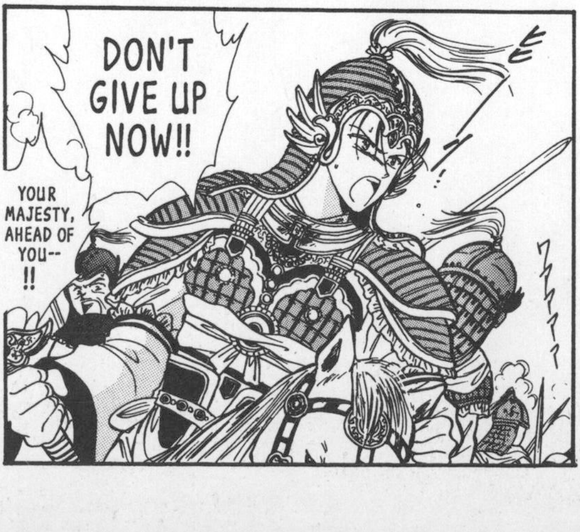
DON'T GIVE UP NOW!!
YOUR MAJESTY, AHEAD OF YOU-- !!

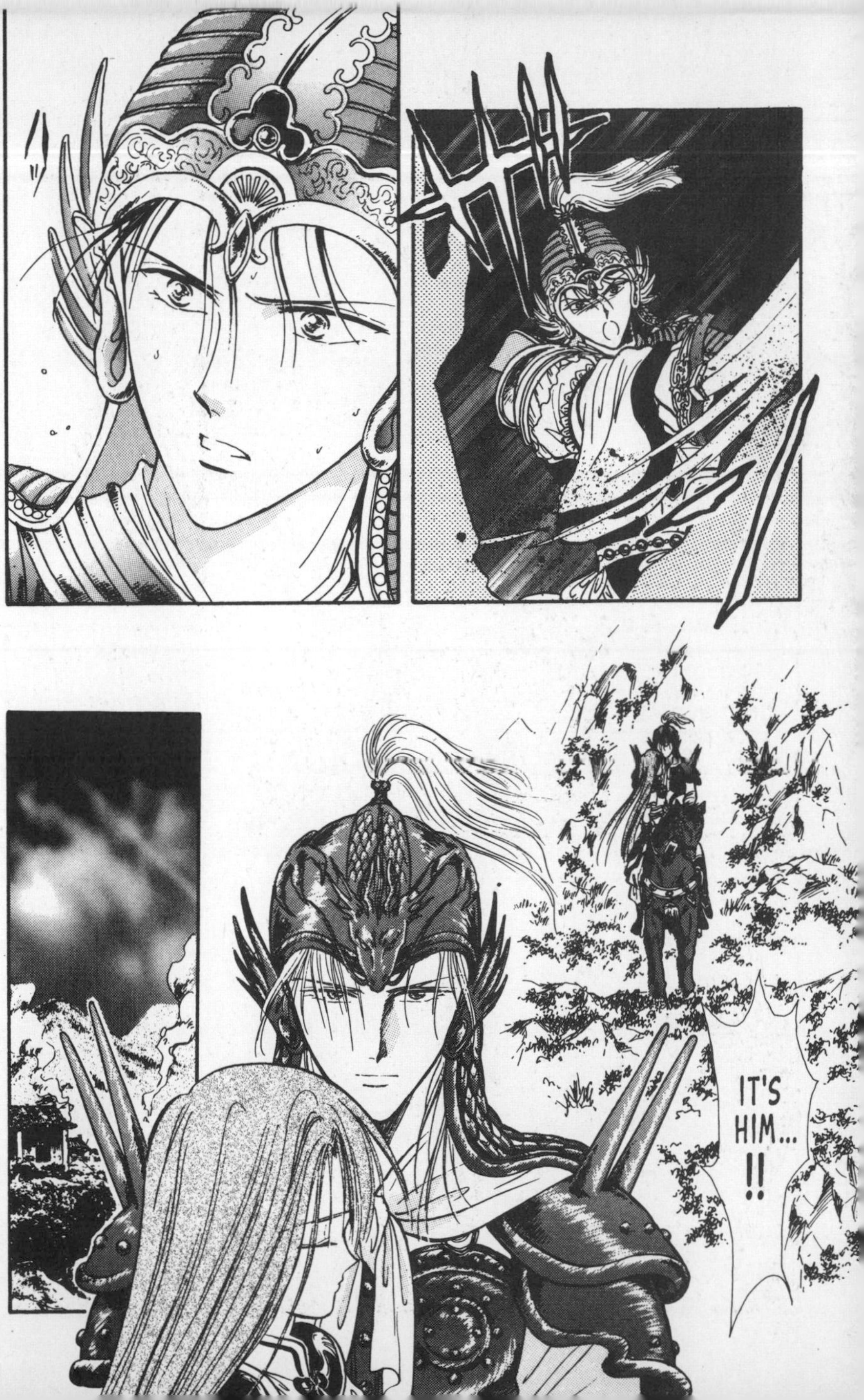
IT'S HIM... !!

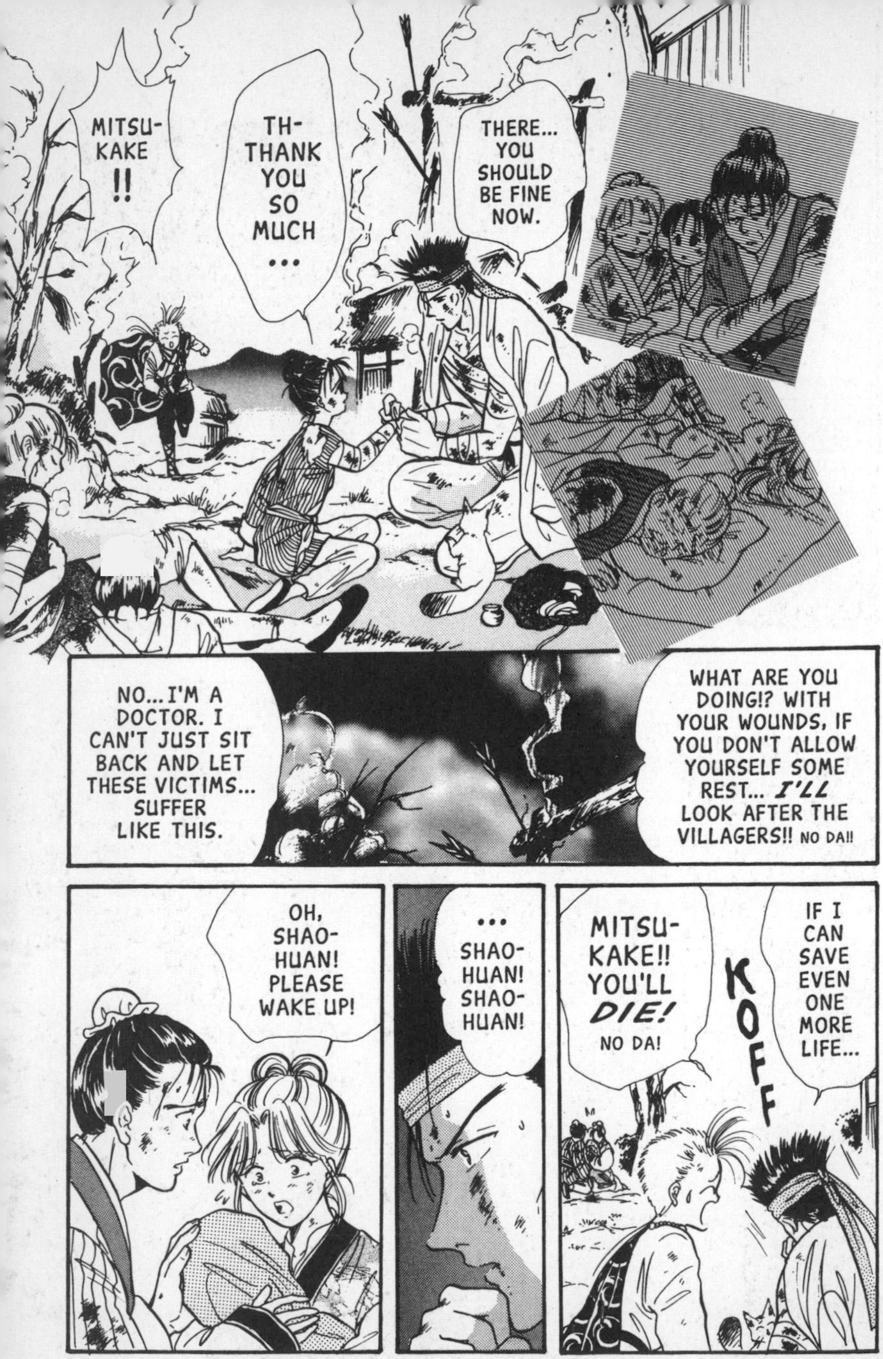
THERE... YOU SHOULD BE FINE NOW.
TH-THANK YOU SO MUCH...
MITSU-KAKE !!
WHAT ARE YOU DOING!? WITH YOUR WOUNDS, IF YOU DON'T ALLOW YOURSELF SOME REST... I'LL LOOK AFTER THE VILLAGERS!! NO DA!!
NO...I'M A DOCTOR. I CAN'T JUST SIT BACK AND LET THESE VICTIMS... SUFFER LIKE THIS.
IF I CAN SAVE EVEN ONE MORE LIFE...
KOFF
MITSU-KAKE!! YOU'LL DIE! NO DA!
... SHAO-HUAN! SHAO-HUAN!
OH, SHAO-HUAN! PLEASE WAKE UP!

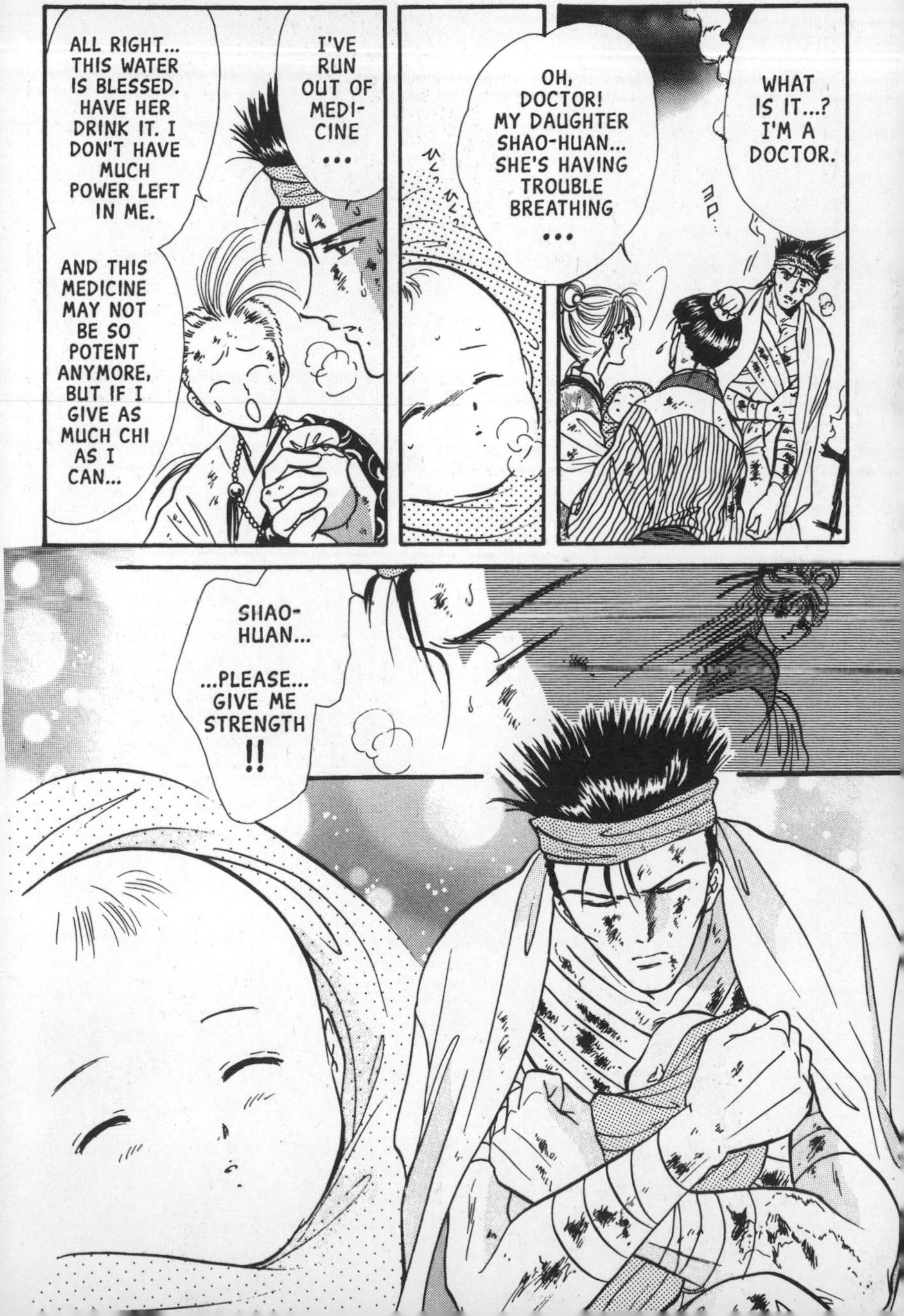
WHAT IS IT...? I'M A DOCTOR.
OH, DOCTOR! MY DAUGHTER SHAO-HUAN... SHE'S HAVING TROUBLE BREATHING ...
I'VE RUN OUT OF MEDI-CINE ...
ALL RIGHT... THIS WATER IS BLESSED. HAVE HER DRINK IT. I DON'T HAVE MUCH POWER LEFT IN ME.
AND THIS MEDICINE MAY NOT BE SO POTENT ANYMORE, BUT IF I GIVE AS MUCH CHI AS I CAN...
SHAO-HUAN...
...PLEASE... GIVE ME STRENGTH !!

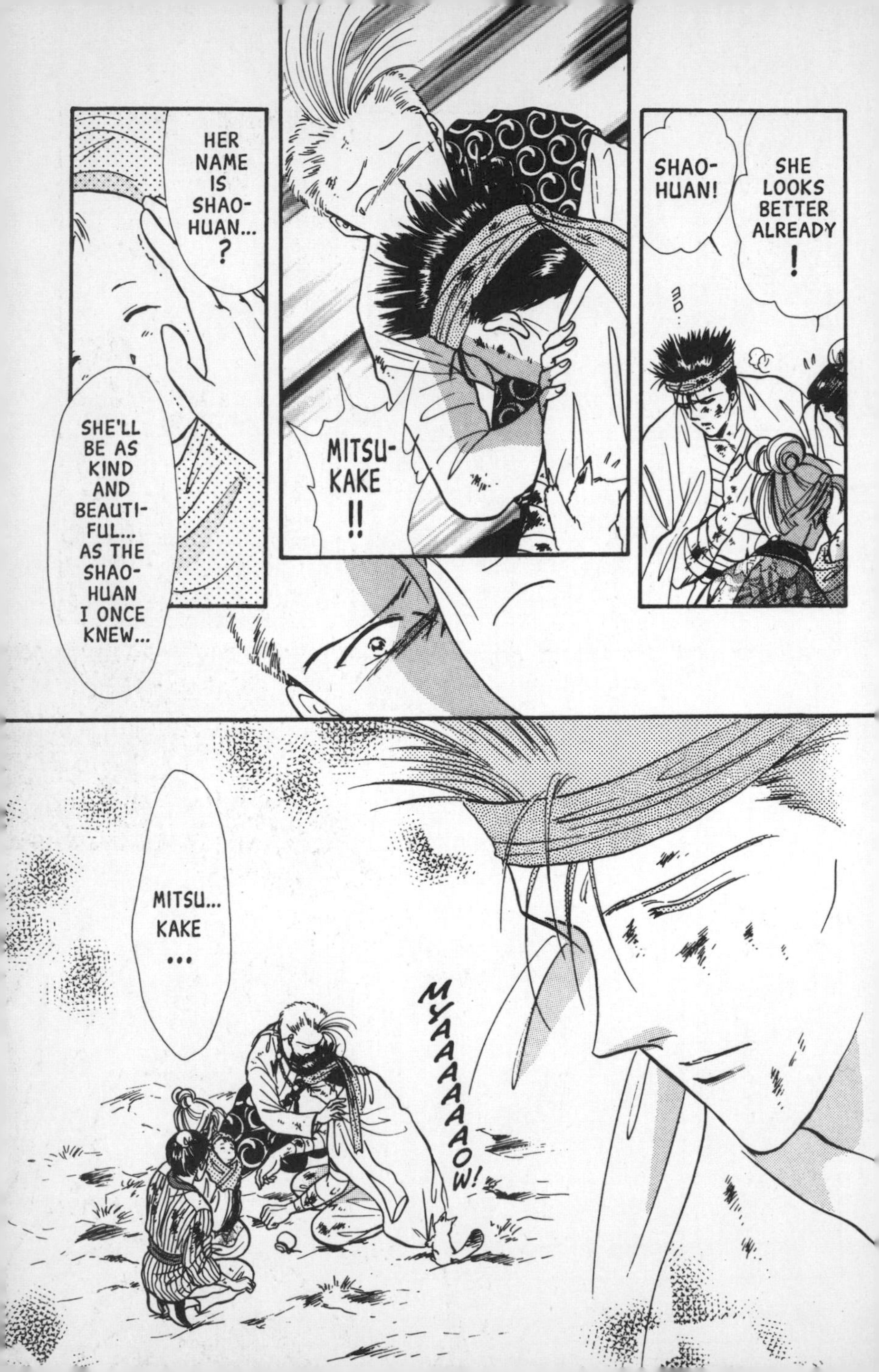
SHE LOOKS BETTER ALREADY!
SHAO-HUAN!
MITSU-KAKE!!
HER NAME IS SHAO-HUAN...?
SHE'LL BE AS KIND AND BEAUTIFUL... AS THE SHAO-HUAN I ONCE KNEW...
MYAAAAAAAOW!
MITSU...KAKE...

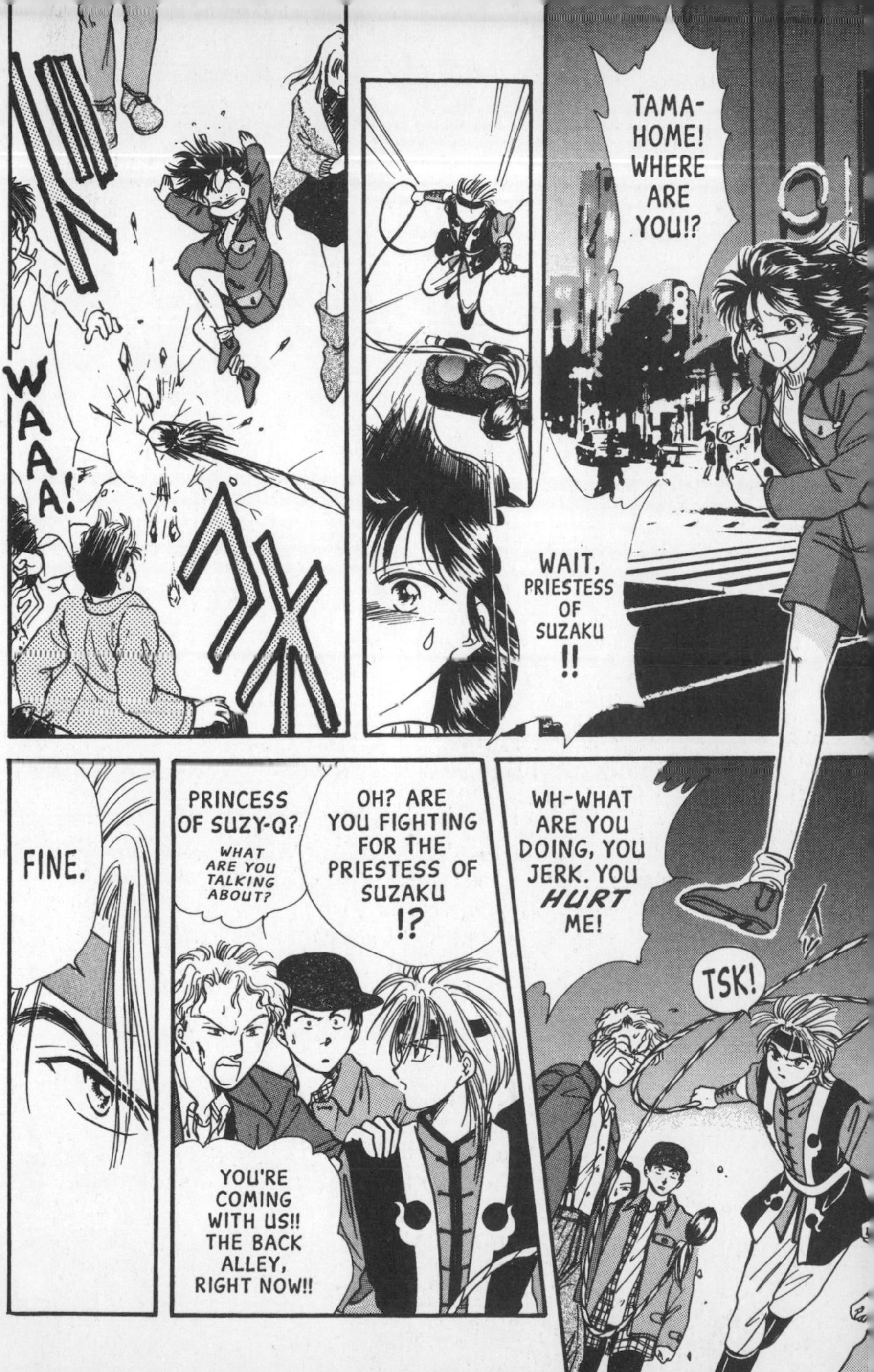
TAMA-HOME! WHERE ARE YOU!?
WAIT, PRIESTESS OF SUZAKU !!
WAAA!
WH-WHAT ARE YOU DOING, YOU JERK. YOU *HURT* ME!
TSK!
OH? ARE YOU FIGHTING FOR THE PRIESTESS OF SUZAKU !?
PRINCESS OF SUZY-Q?
WHAT ARE YOU TALKING ABOUT?
YOU'RE COMING WITH US!! THE BACK ALLEY, RIGHT NOW!!
FINE.

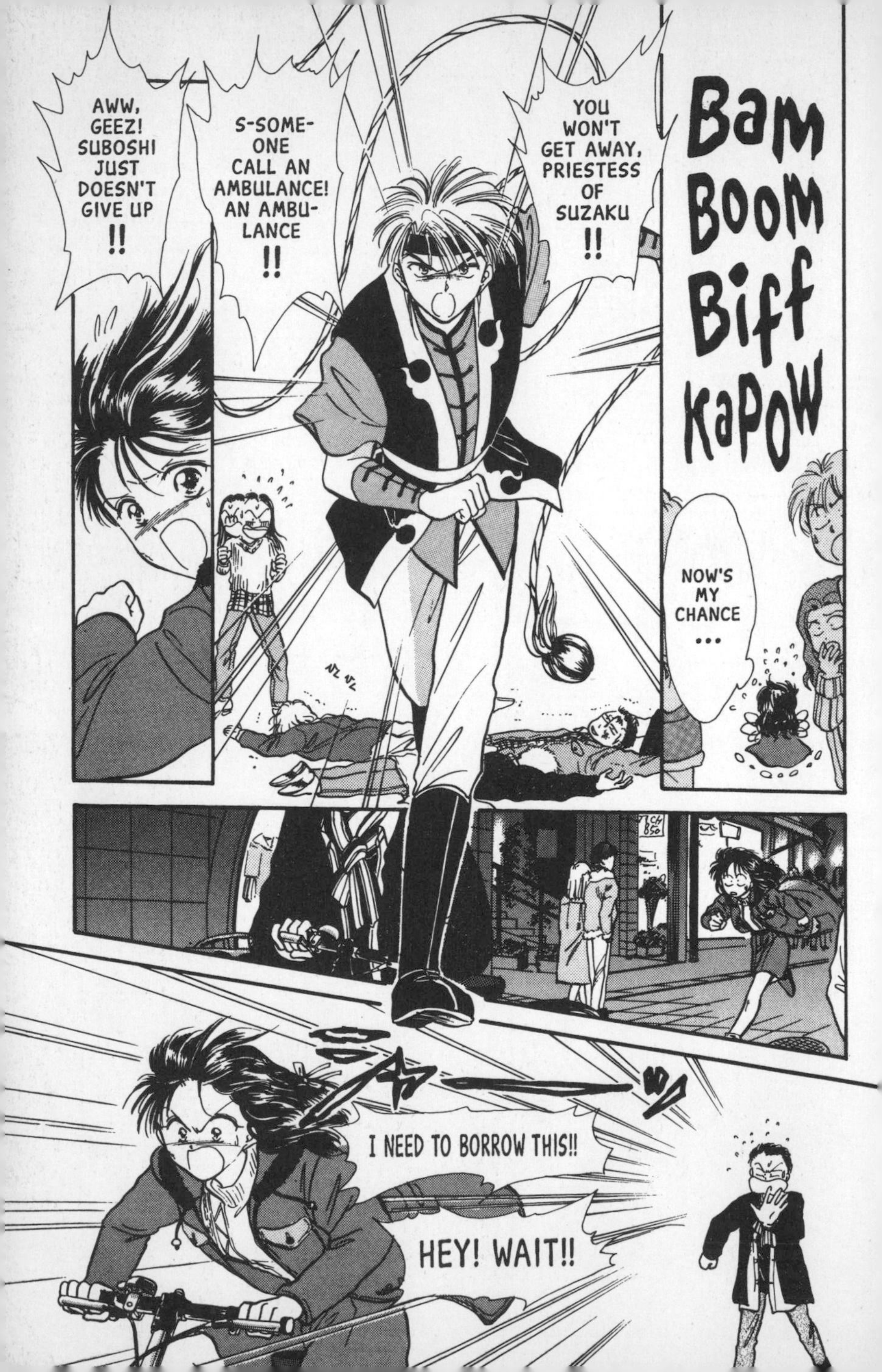
Bam Boom Biff Kapow
NOW'S MY CHANCE ...
YOU WON'T GET AWAY, PRIESTESS OF SUZAKU !!
S-SOME-ONE CALL AN AMBULANCE! AN AMBU-LANCE !!
AWW, GEEZ! SUBOSHI JUST DOESN'T GIVE UP !!
I NEED TO BORROW THIS!!
HEY! WAIT!!

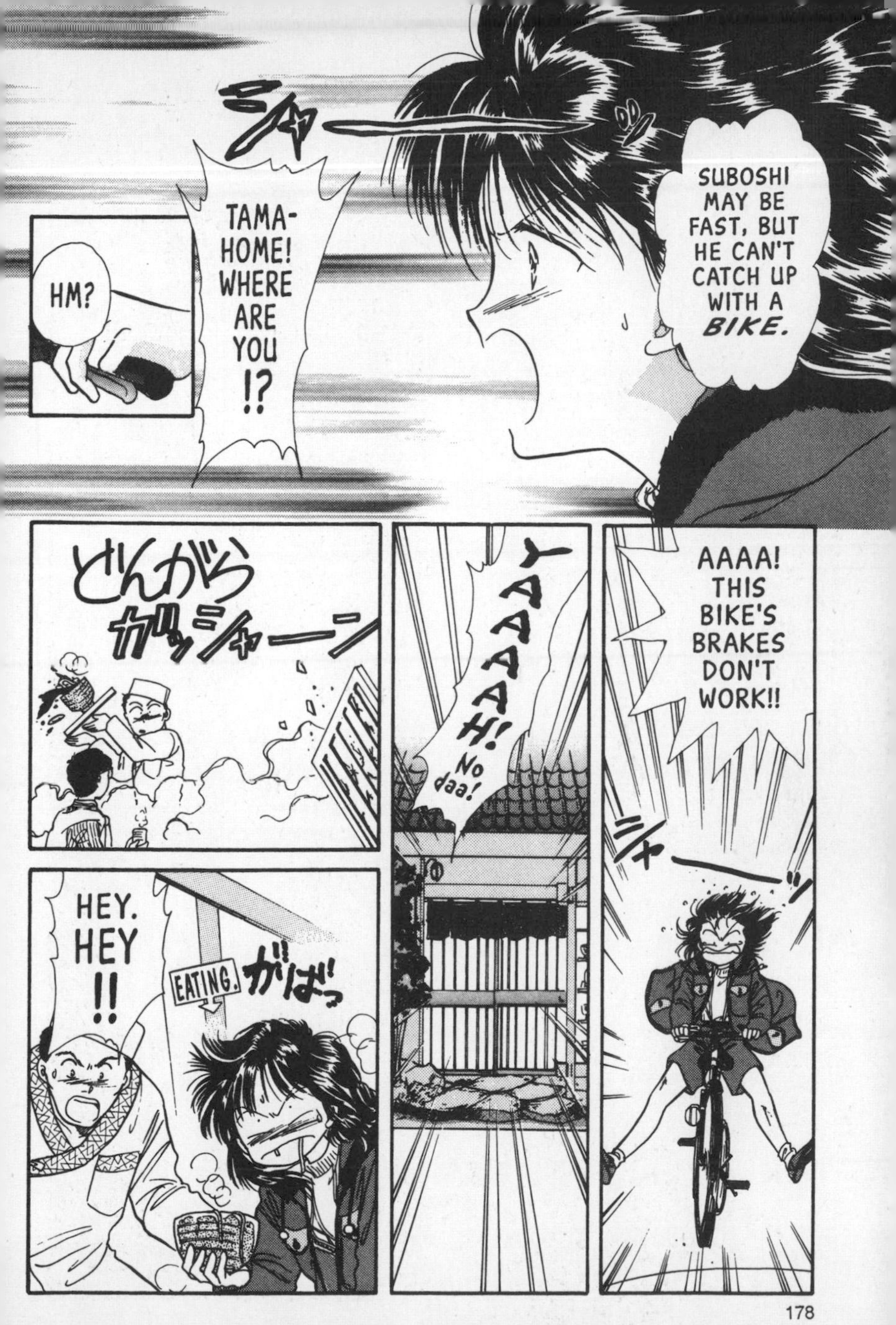
SUBOSHI MAY BE FAST, BUT HE CAN'T CATCH UP WITH A *BIKE.*
TAMA-HOME! WHERE ARE YOU !?
HM?
AAAA! THIS BIKE'S BRAKES DON'T WORK!!
YAAAAAH! No daa!
どんがら
HEY. HEY !!
EATING.
がばっ

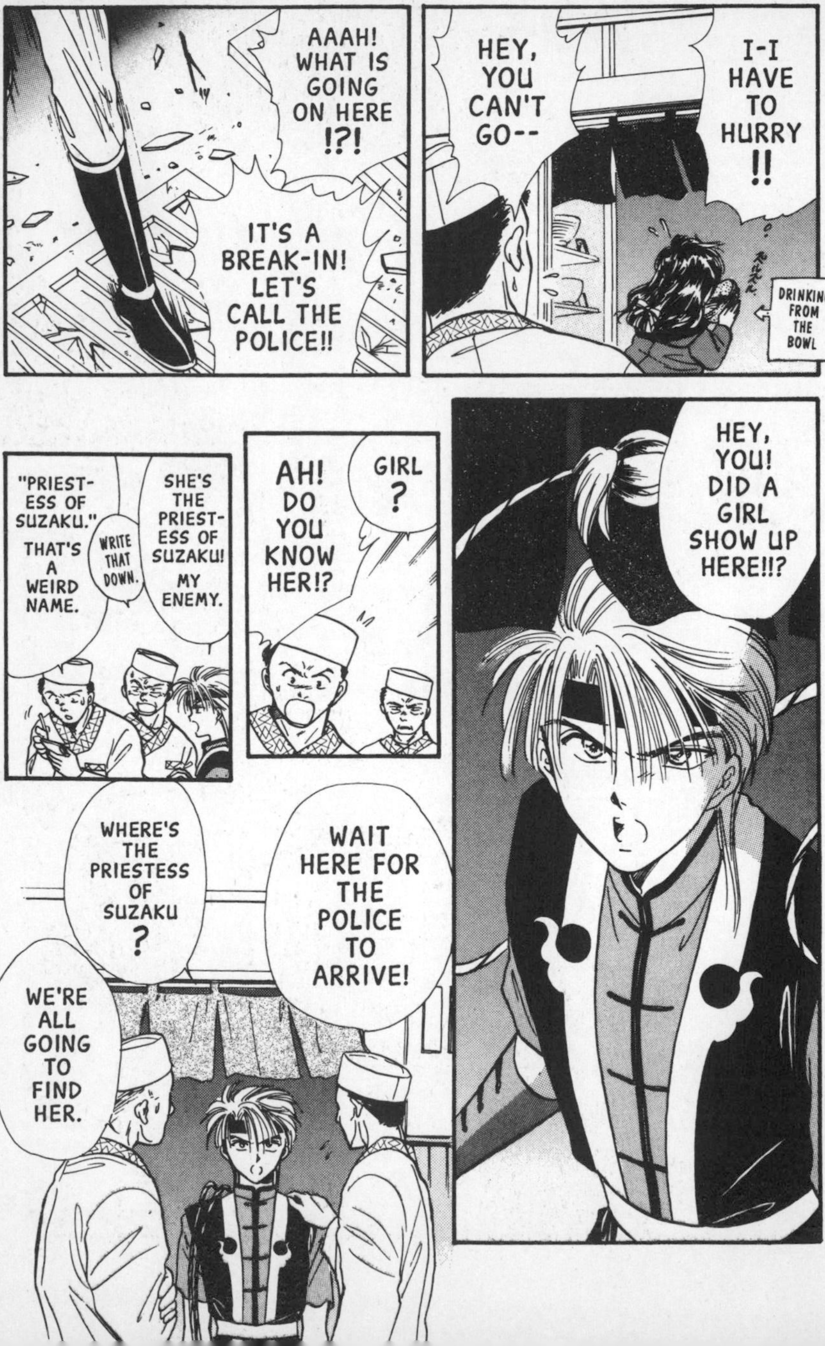
I-I HAVE TO HURRY!!
HEY, YOU CAN'T GO--
DRINKING FROM THE BOWL
AAAH! WHAT IS GOING ON HERE!?!
IT'S A BREAK-IN! LET'S CALL THE POLICE!!
HEY, YOU! DID A GIRL SHOW UP HERE!!?
GIRL?
AH! DO YOU KNOW HER!?
SHE'S THE PRIESTESS OF SUZAKU! MY ENEMY.
WRITE THAT DOWN.
"PRIESTESS OF SUZAKU." THAT'S A WEIRD NAME.
WAIT HERE FOR THE POLICE TO ARRIVE!
WHERE'S THE PRIESTESS OF SUZAKU?
WE'RE ALL GOING TO FIND HER.

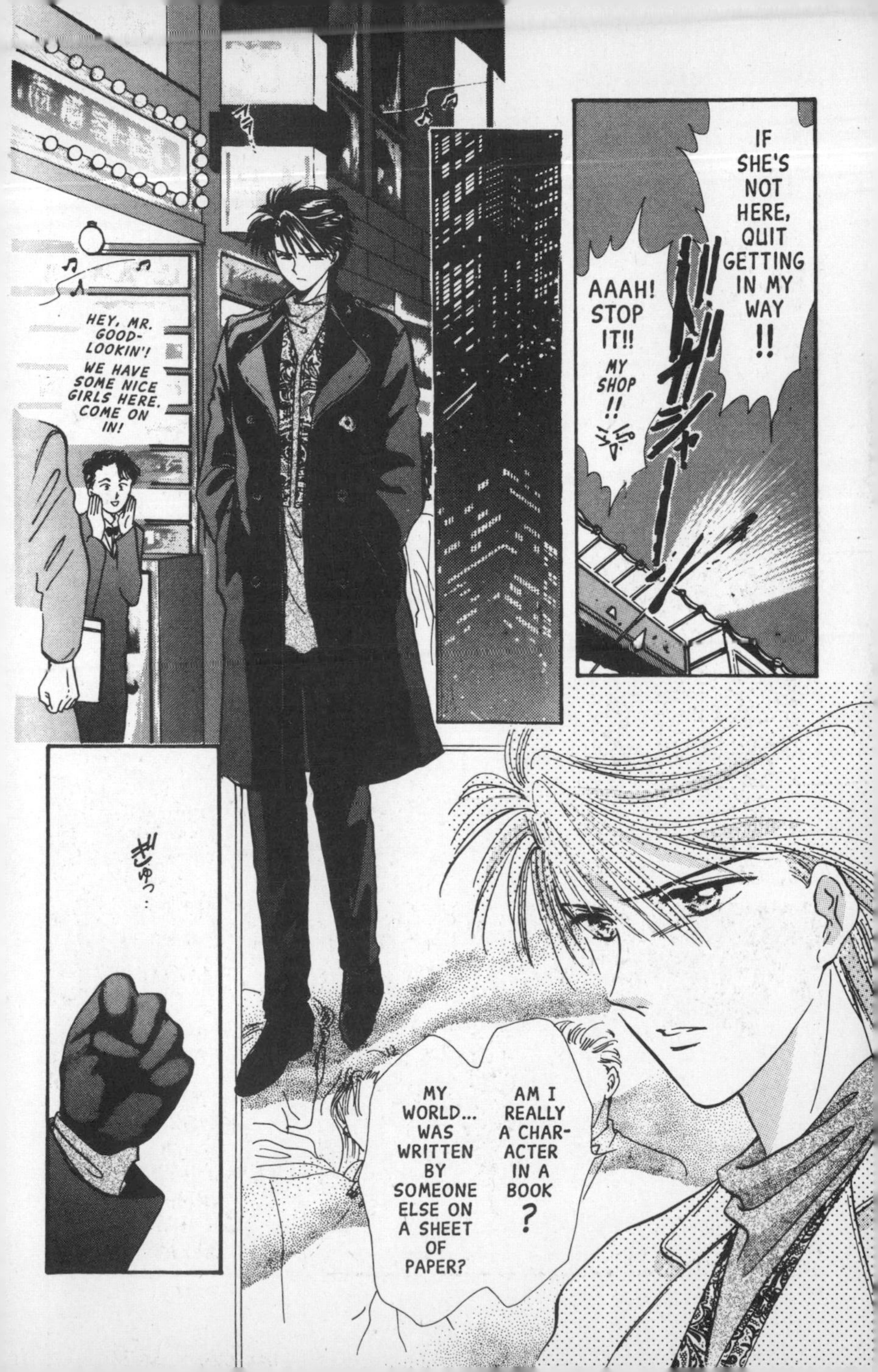
IF SHE'S NOT HERE, QUIT GETTING IN MY WAY !!
AAAH! STOP IT!!
MY SHOP !!
HEY, MR. GOOD-LOOKIN'! WE HAVE SOME NICE GIRLS HERE. COME ON IN!
AM I REALLY A CHARACTER IN A BOOK ?
MY WORLD... WAS WRITTEN BY SOMEONE ELSE ON A SHEET OF PAPER?
ぎゅっ

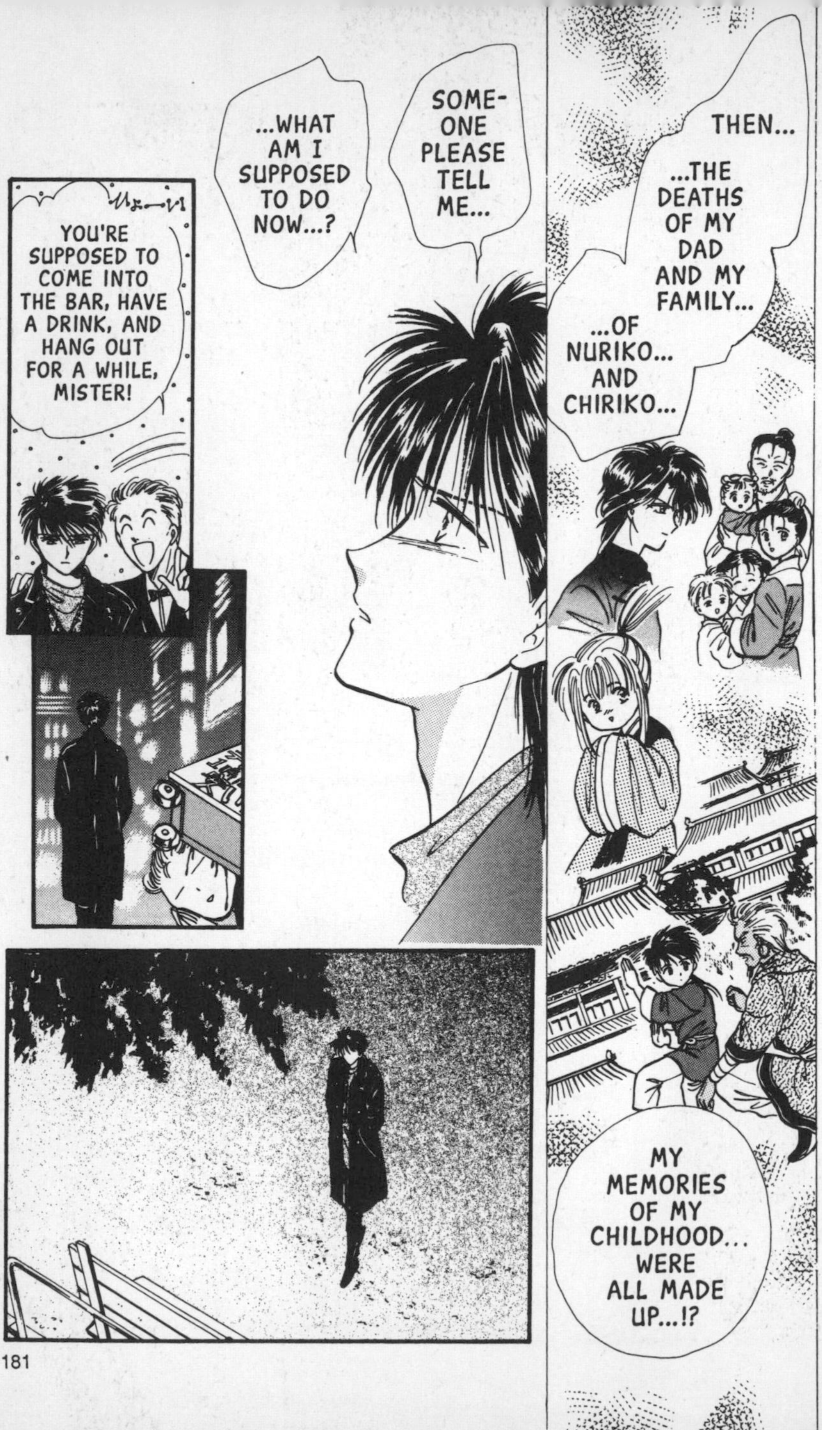
THEN...
...THE DEATHS OF MY DAD AND MY FAMILY...
...OF NURIKO... AND CHIRIKO...
MY MEMORIES OF MY CHILDHOOD... WERE ALL MADE UP...!?
SOME-ONE PLEASE TELL ME...
...WHAT AM I SUPPOSED TO DO NOW...?
YOU'RE SUPPOSED TO COME INTO THE BAR, HAVE A DRINK, AND HANG OUT FOR A WHILE, MISTER!

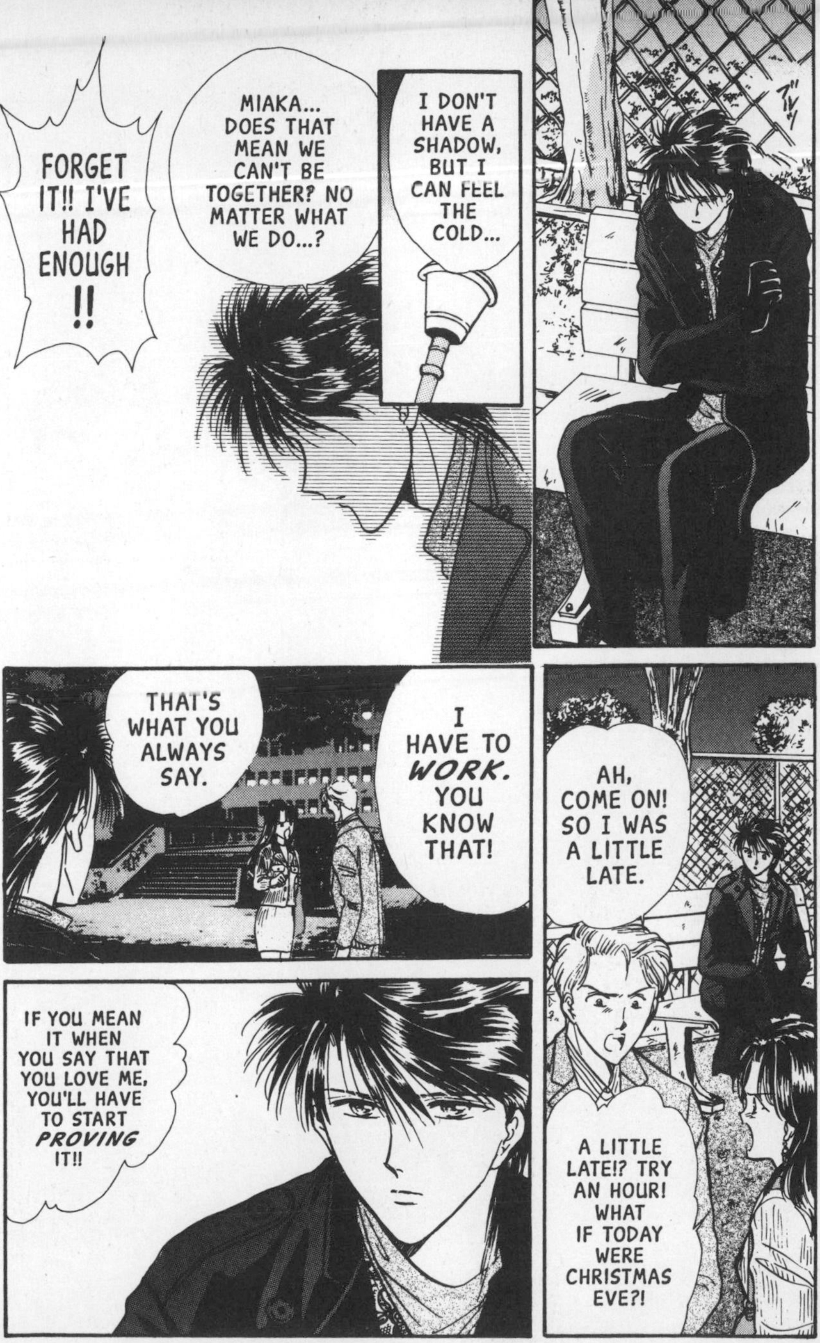
I DON'T HAVE A SHADOW, BUT I CAN FEEL THE COLD...
MIAKA... DOES THAT MEAN WE CAN'T BE TOGETHER? NO MATTER WHAT WE DO...?
FORGET IT!! I'VE HAD ENOUGH !!
AH, COME ON! SO I WAS A LITTLE LATE.
A LITTLE LATE!? TRY AN HOUR! WHAT IF TODAY WERE CHRISTMAS EVE?!
I HAVE TO *WORK.* YOU KNOW THAT!
THAT'S WHAT YOU ALWAYS SAY.
IF YOU MEAN IT WHEN YOU SAY THAT YOU LOVE ME, YOU'LL HAVE TO START *PROVING* IT!!

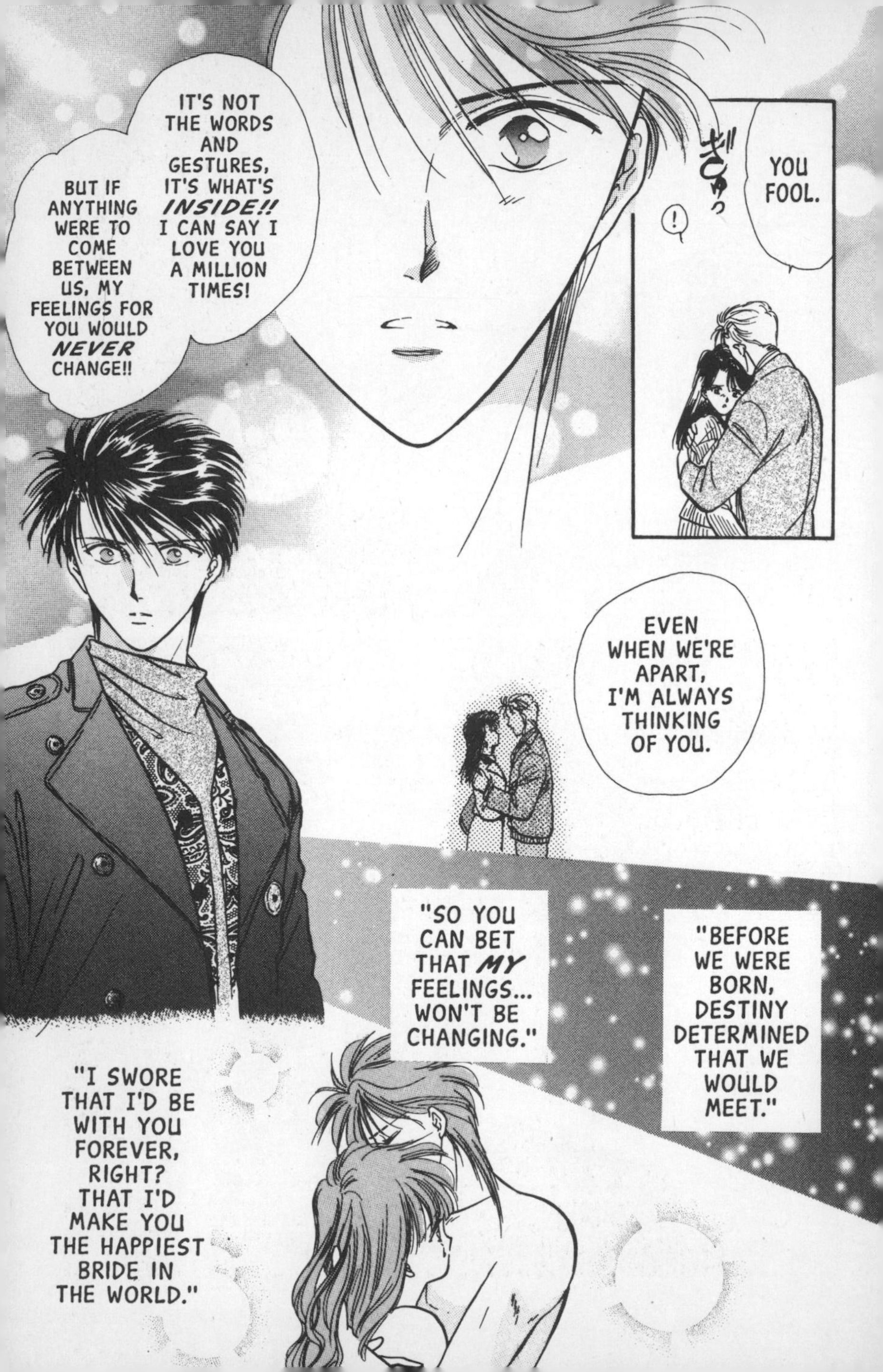
ぎゅっ
!
YOU FOOL.
IT'S NOT THE WORDS AND GESTURES, IT'S WHAT'S *INSIDE!!* I CAN SAY I LOVE YOU A MILLION TIMES!
BUT IF ANYTHING WERE TO COME BETWEEN US, MY FEELINGS FOR YOU WOULD *NEVER* CHANGE!!
EVEN WHEN WE'RE APART, I'M ALWAYS THINKING OF YOU.
"BEFORE WE WERE BORN, DESTINY DETERMINED THAT WE WOULD MEET."
"SO YOU CAN BET THAT *MY* FEELINGS... WON'T BE CHANGING."
"I SWORE THAT I'D BE WITH YOU FOREVER, RIGHT? THAT I'D MAKE YOU THE HAPPIEST BRIDE IN THE WORLD."

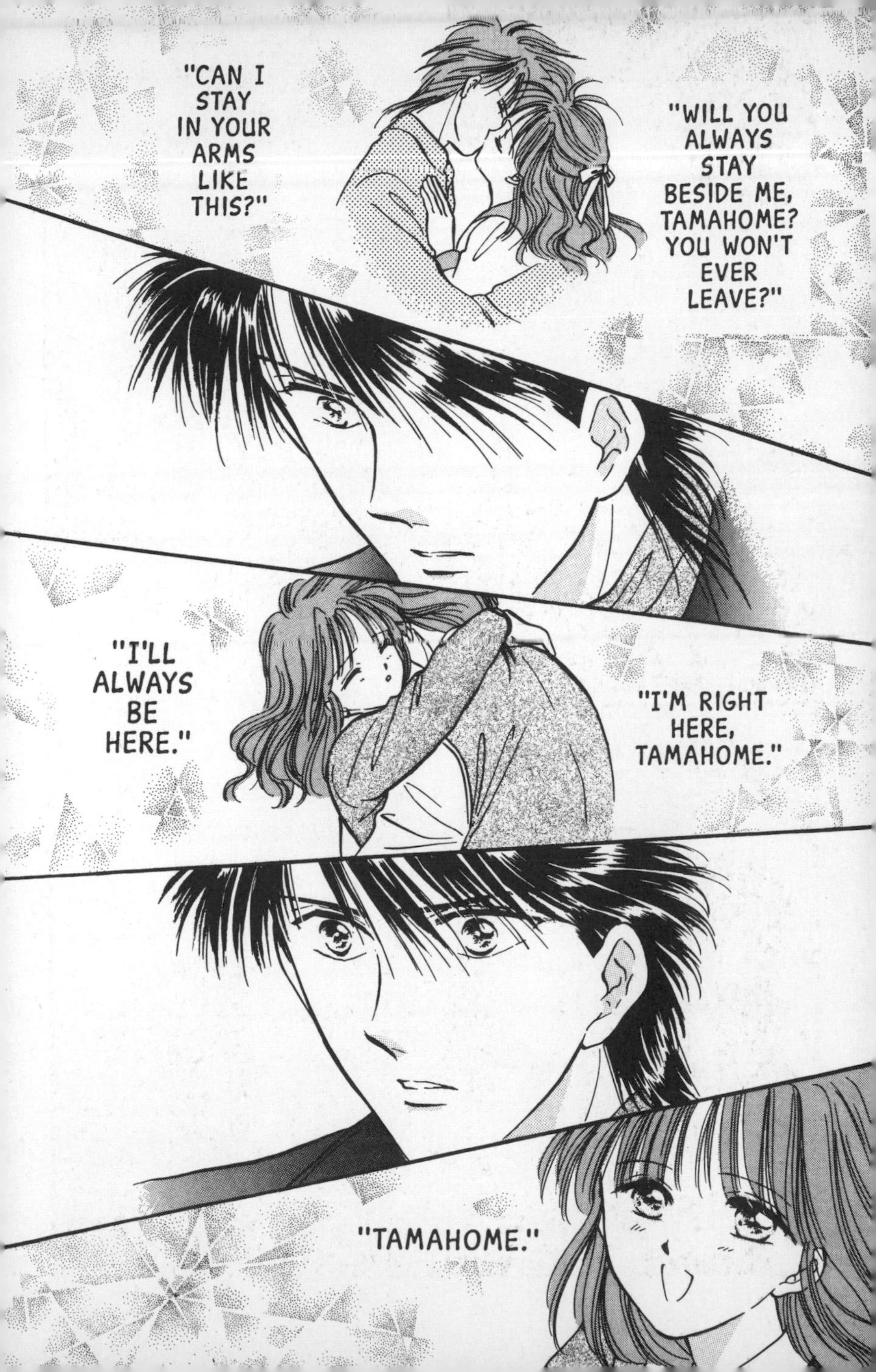
"WILL YOU ALWAYS STAY BESIDE ME, TAMAHOME? YOU WON'T EVER LEAVE?"
"CAN I STAY IN YOUR ARMS LIKE THIS?"
"I'M RIGHT HERE, TAMAHOME."
"I'LL ALWAYS BE HERE."
"TAMAHOME."

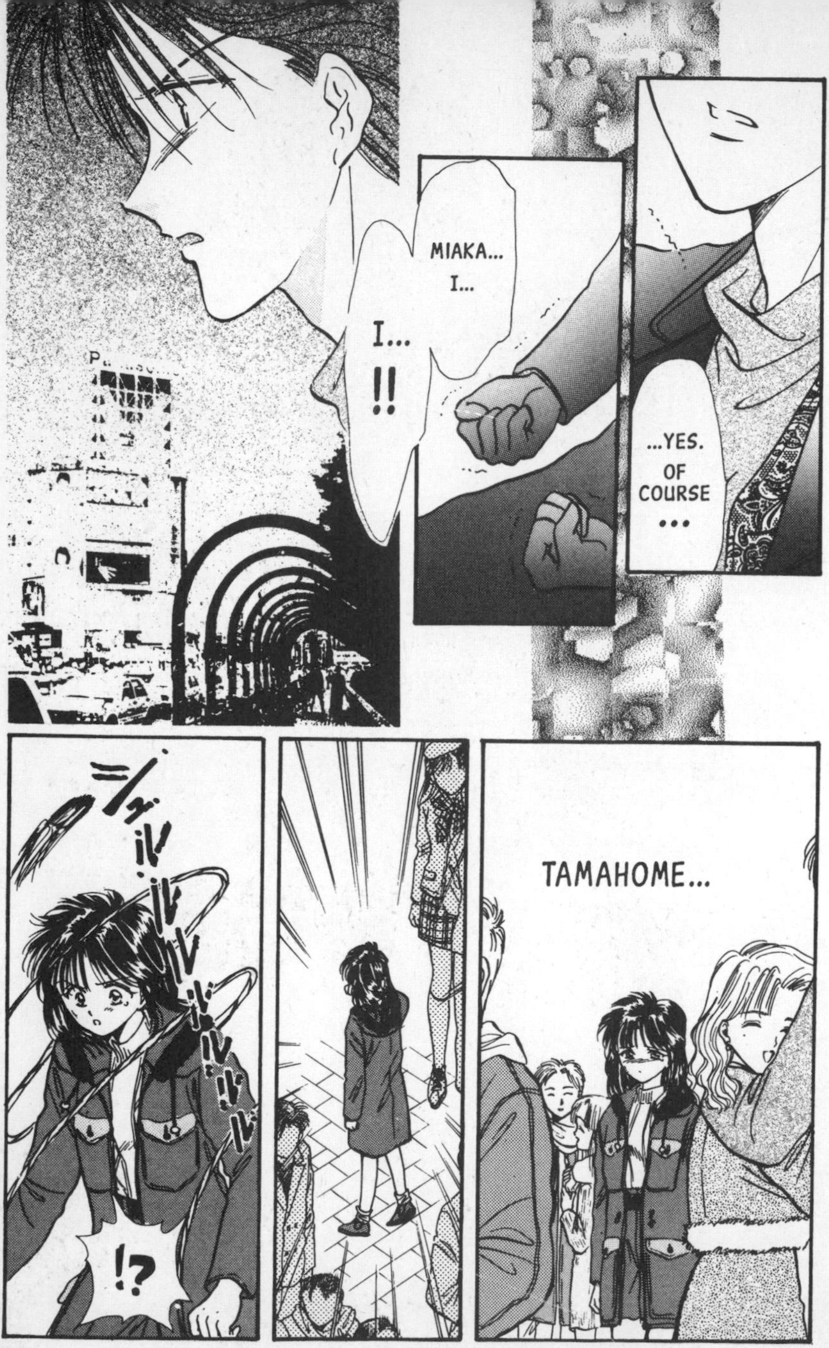
...YES. OF COURSE ...
MIAKA... I...
I... !!
TAMAHOME...
!?

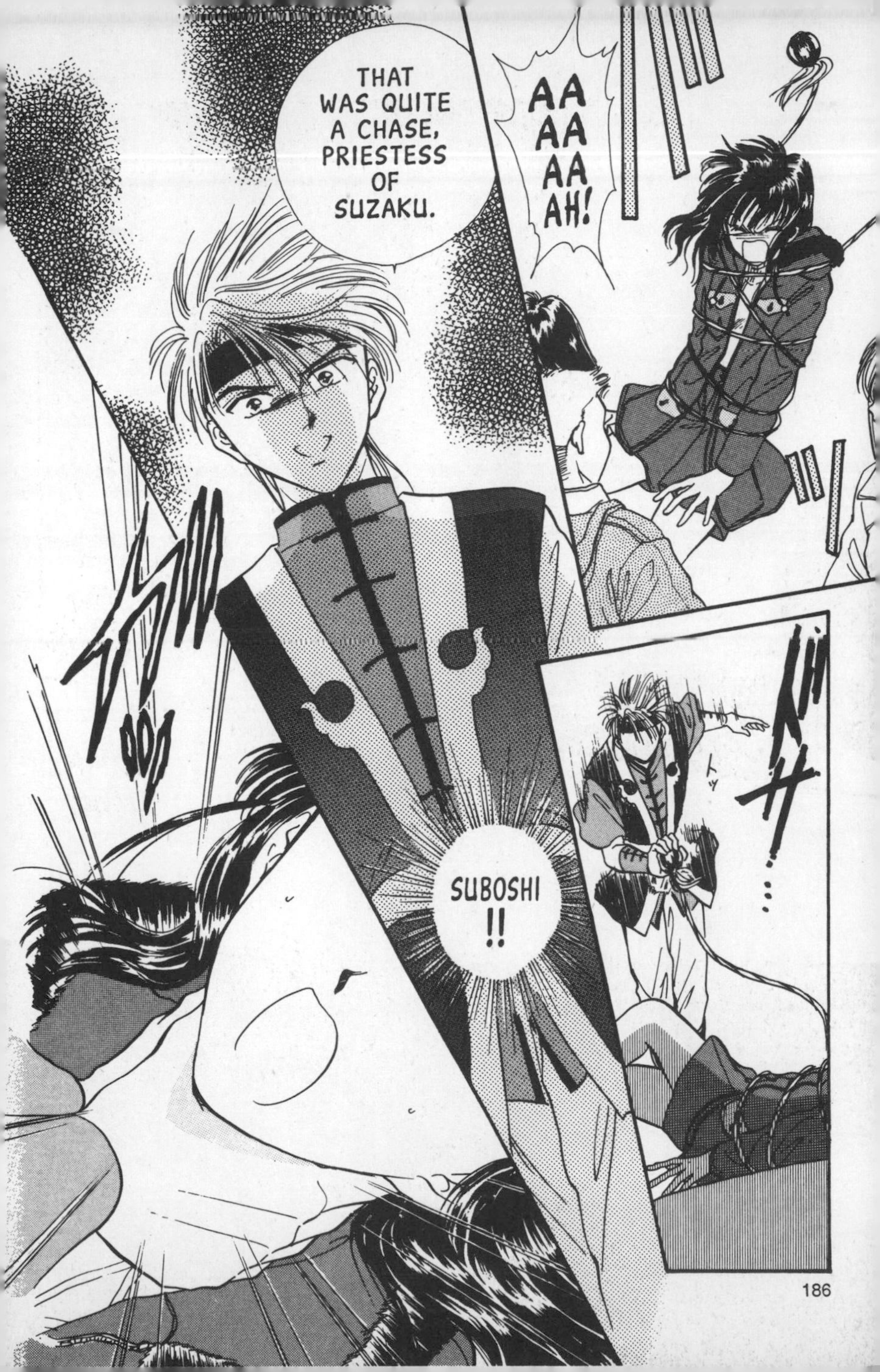
AAAAAAAH!
THAT WAS QUITE A CHASE, PRIESTESS OF SUZAKU.
SUBOSHI !!

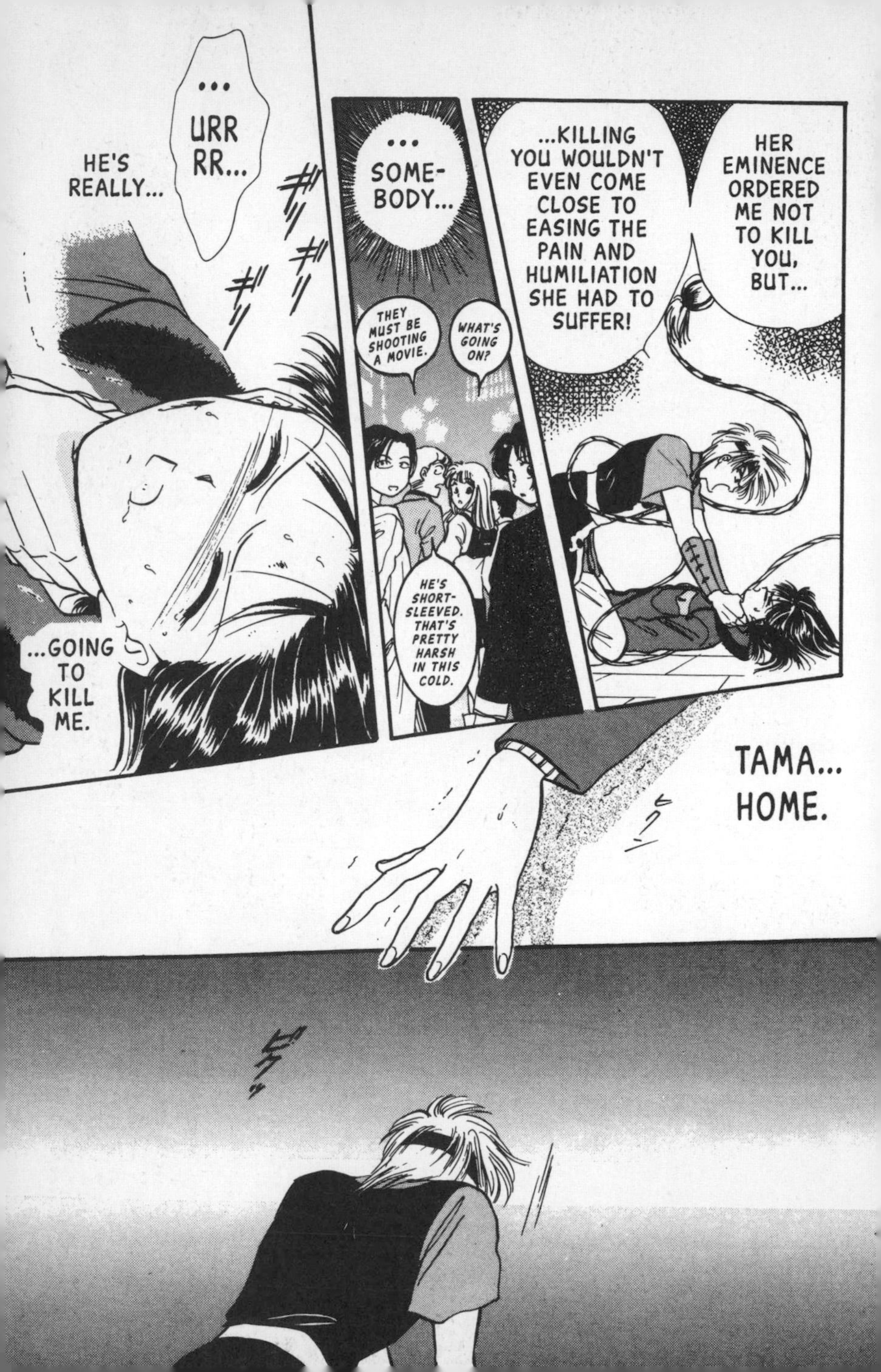
HER EMINENCE ORDERED ME NOT TO KILL YOU, BUT...
...KILLING YOU WOULDN'T EVEN COME CLOSE TO EASING THE PAIN AND HUMILIATION SHE HAD TO SUFFER!
... SOME-BODY...
WHAT'S GOING ON?
THEY MUST BE SHOOTING A MOVIE.
HE'S SHORT-SLEEVED. THAT'S PRETTY HARSH IN THIS COLD.
... URRR RR...
HE'S REALLY...
...GOING TO KILL ME.
TAMA... HOME.

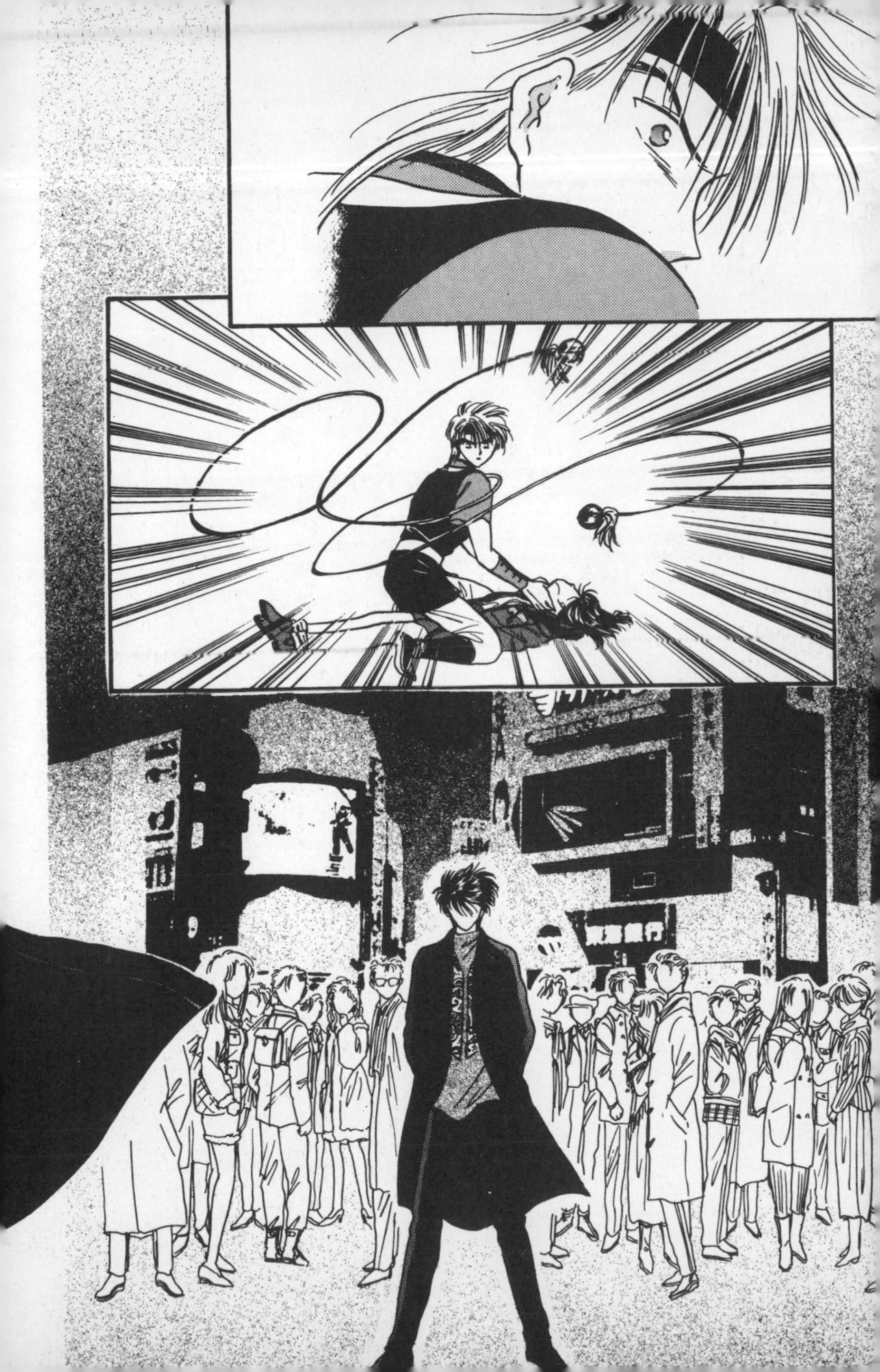

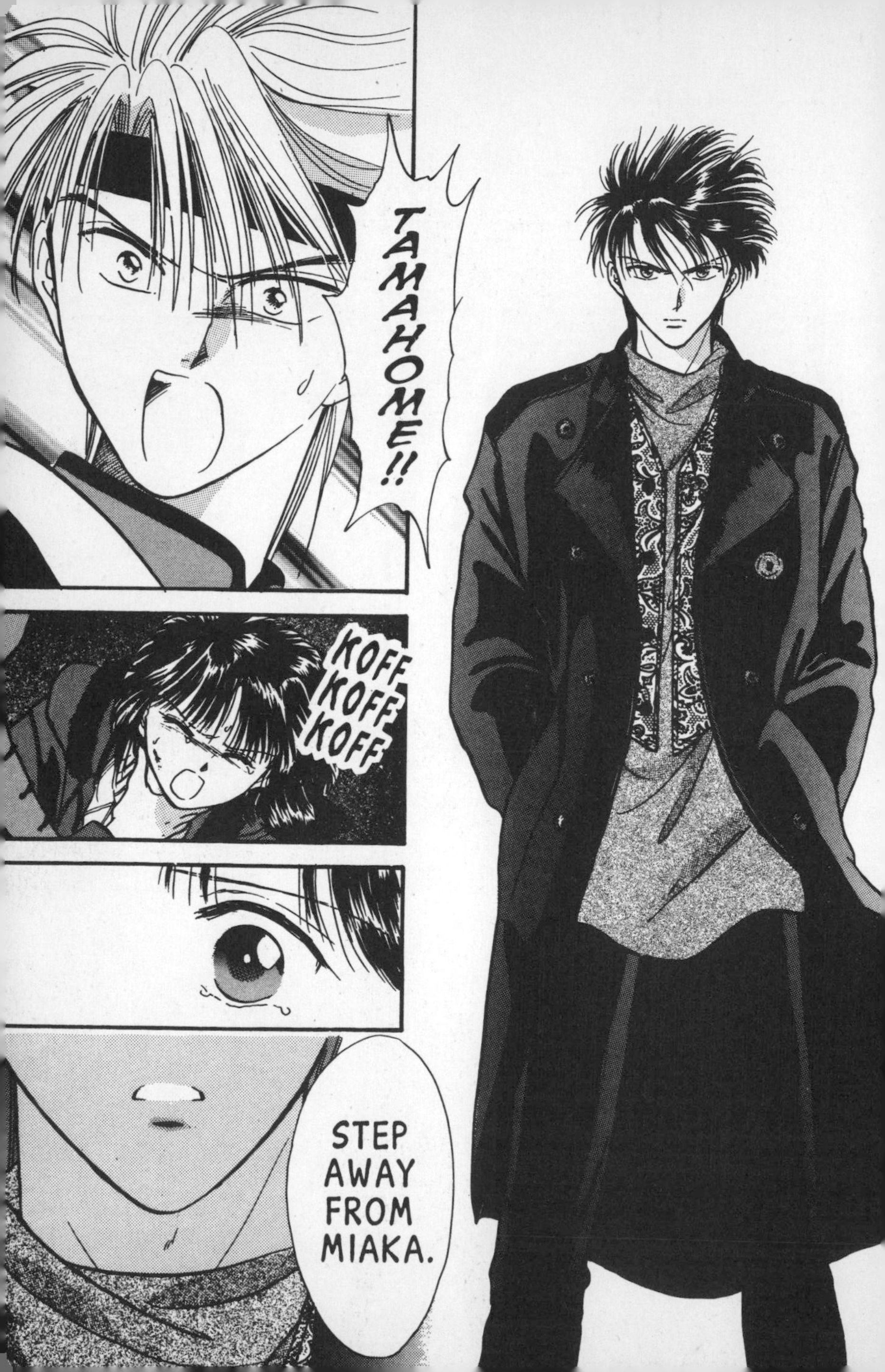
TAMAHOME!!
KOFF KOFF KOFF
STEP AWAY FROM MIAKA.

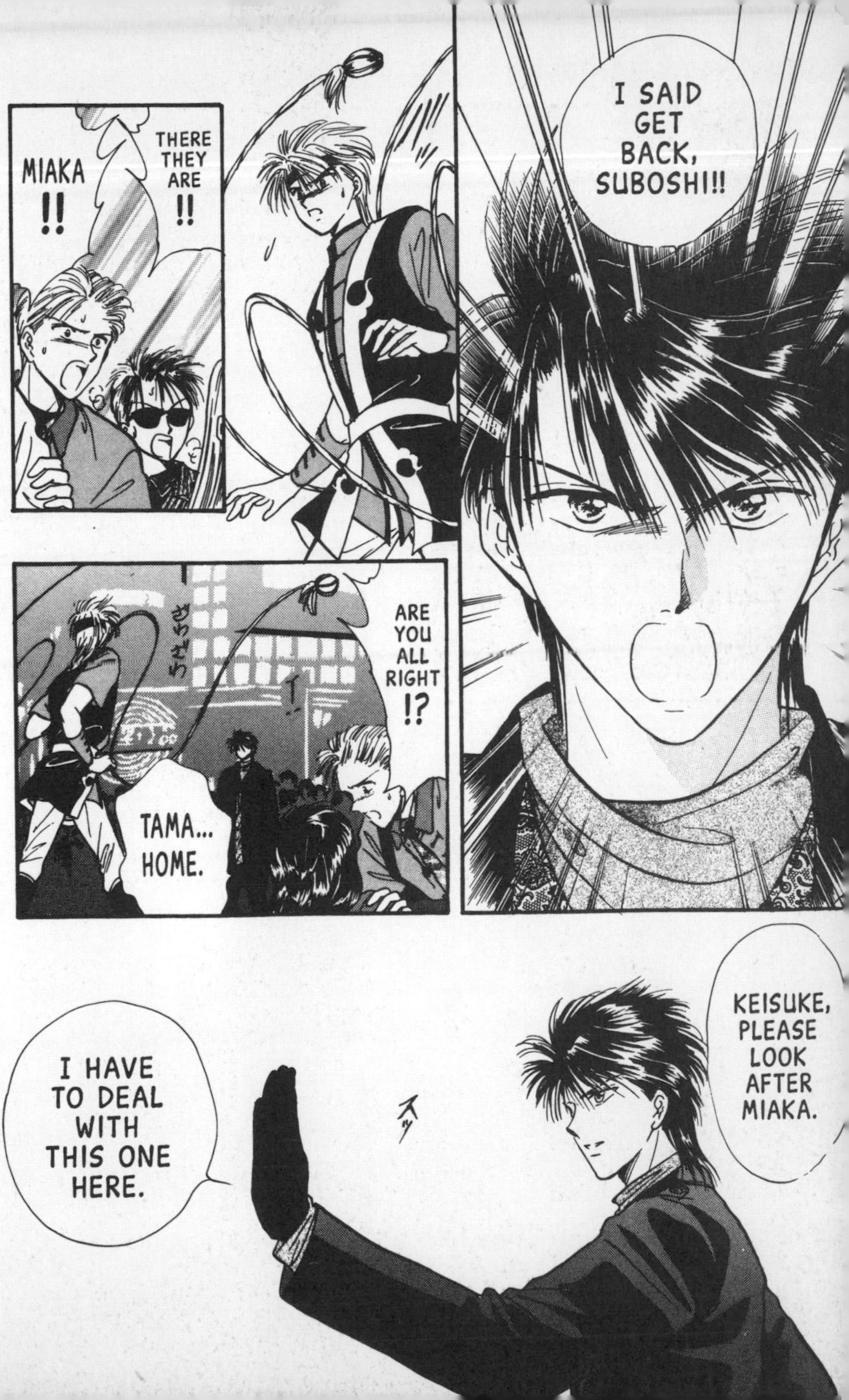
I SAID GET BACK, SUBOSHI!!!
THERE THEY ARE!!
MIAKA!!
ARE YOU ALL RIGHT!?
TAMA... HOME.
KEISUKE, PLEASE LOOK AFTER MIAKA.
I HAVE TO DEAL WITH THIS ONE HERE.

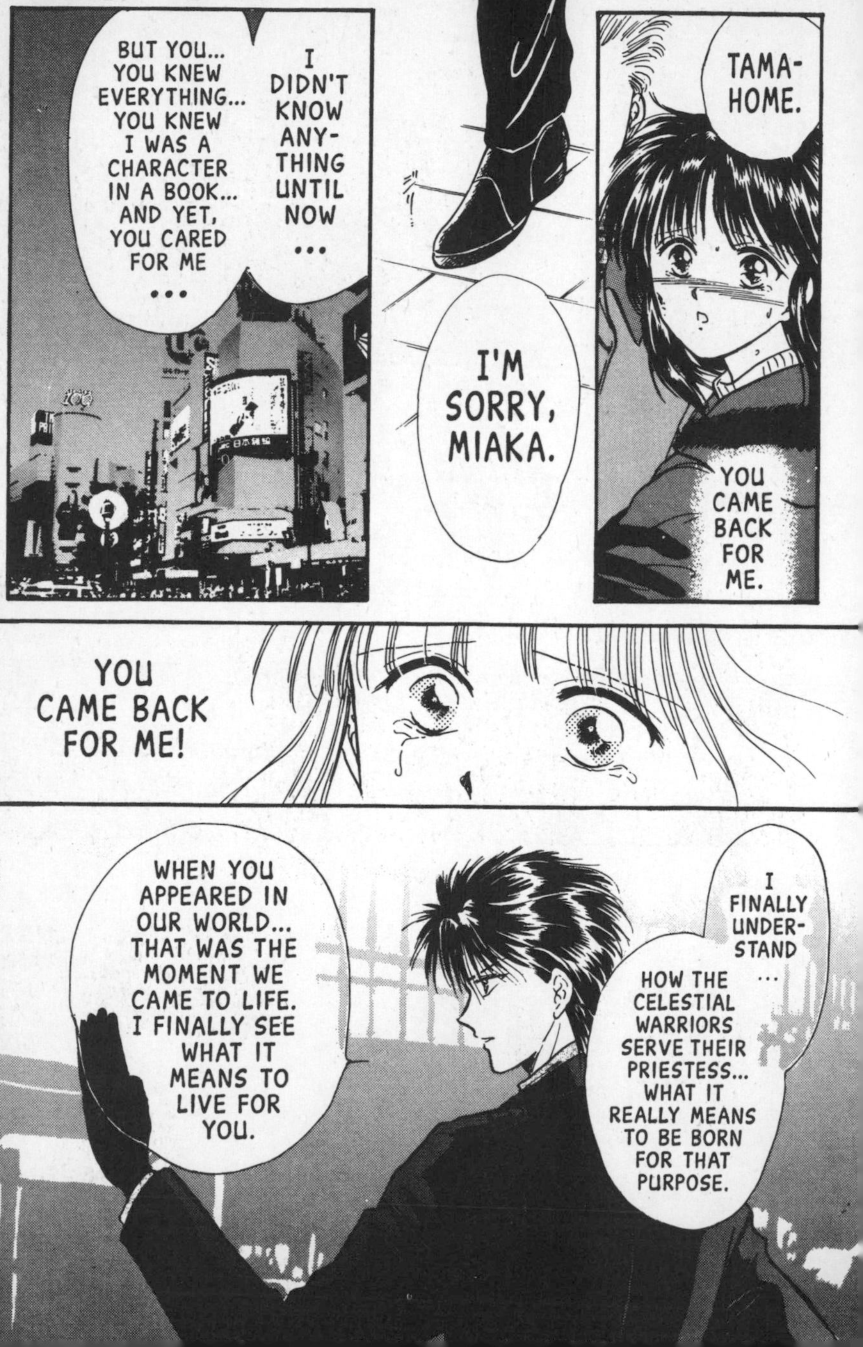
TAMA-HOME.
YOU CAME BACK FOR ME.
I'M SORRY, MIAKA.
I DIDN'T KNOW ANYTHING UNTIL NOW...
BUT YOU... YOU KNEW EVERYTHING... YOU KNEW I WAS A CHARACTER IN A BOOK... AND YET, YOU CARED FOR ME...
YOU CAME BACK FOR ME!
I FINALLY UNDERSTAND...
HOW THE CELESTIAL WARRIORS SERVE THEIR PRIESTESS... WHAT IT REALLY MEANS TO BE BORN FOR THAT PURPOSE.
WHEN YOU APPEARED IN OUR WORLD... THAT WAS THE MOMENT WE CAME TO LIFE. I FINALLY SEE WHAT IT MEANS TO LIVE FOR YOU.

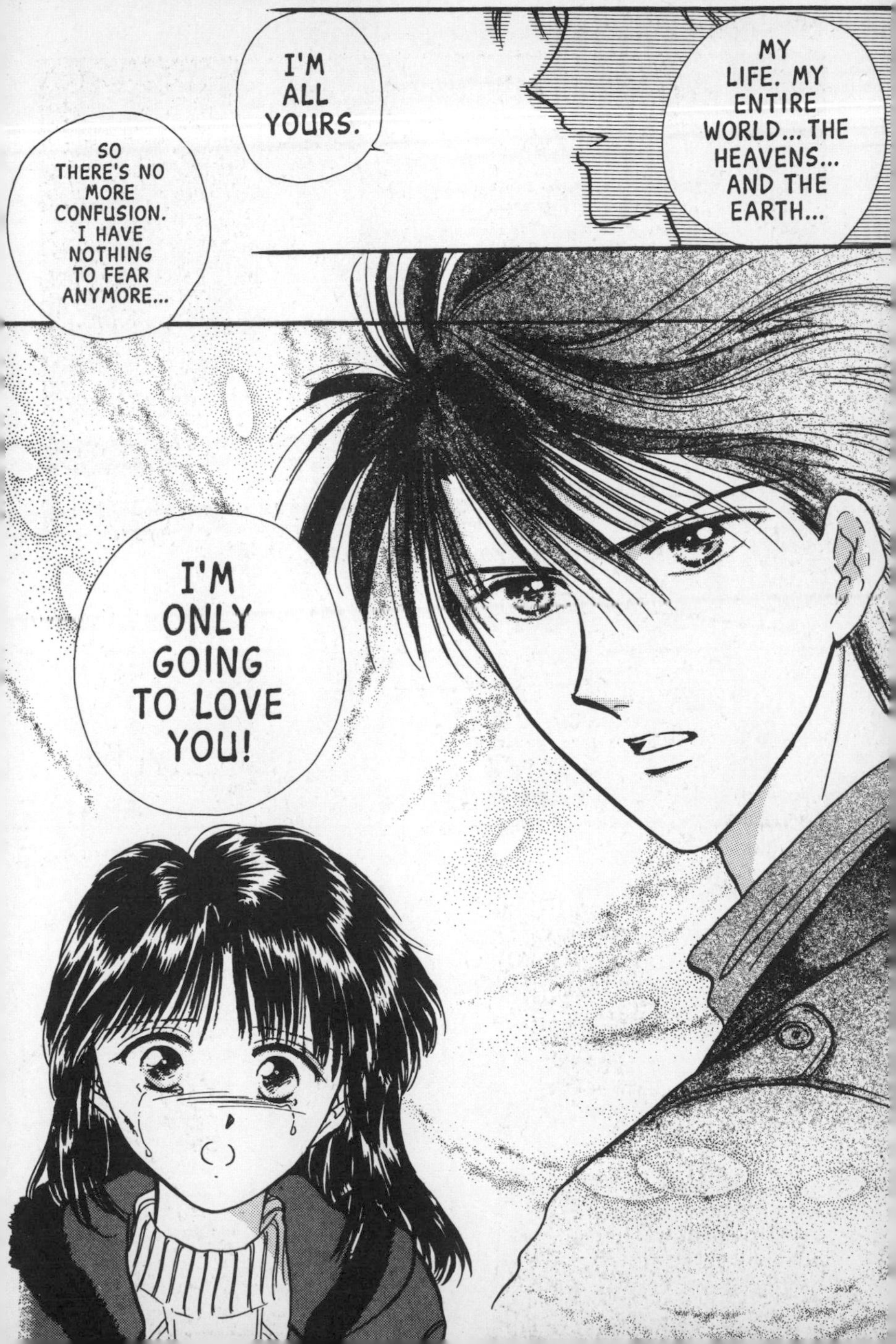
MY LIFE. MY ENTIRE WORLD... THE HEAVENS... AND THE EARTH...
I'M ALL YOURS.
SO THERE'S NO MORE CONFUSION. I HAVE NOTHING TO FEAR ANYMORE...
I'M ONLY GOING TO LOVE YOU!

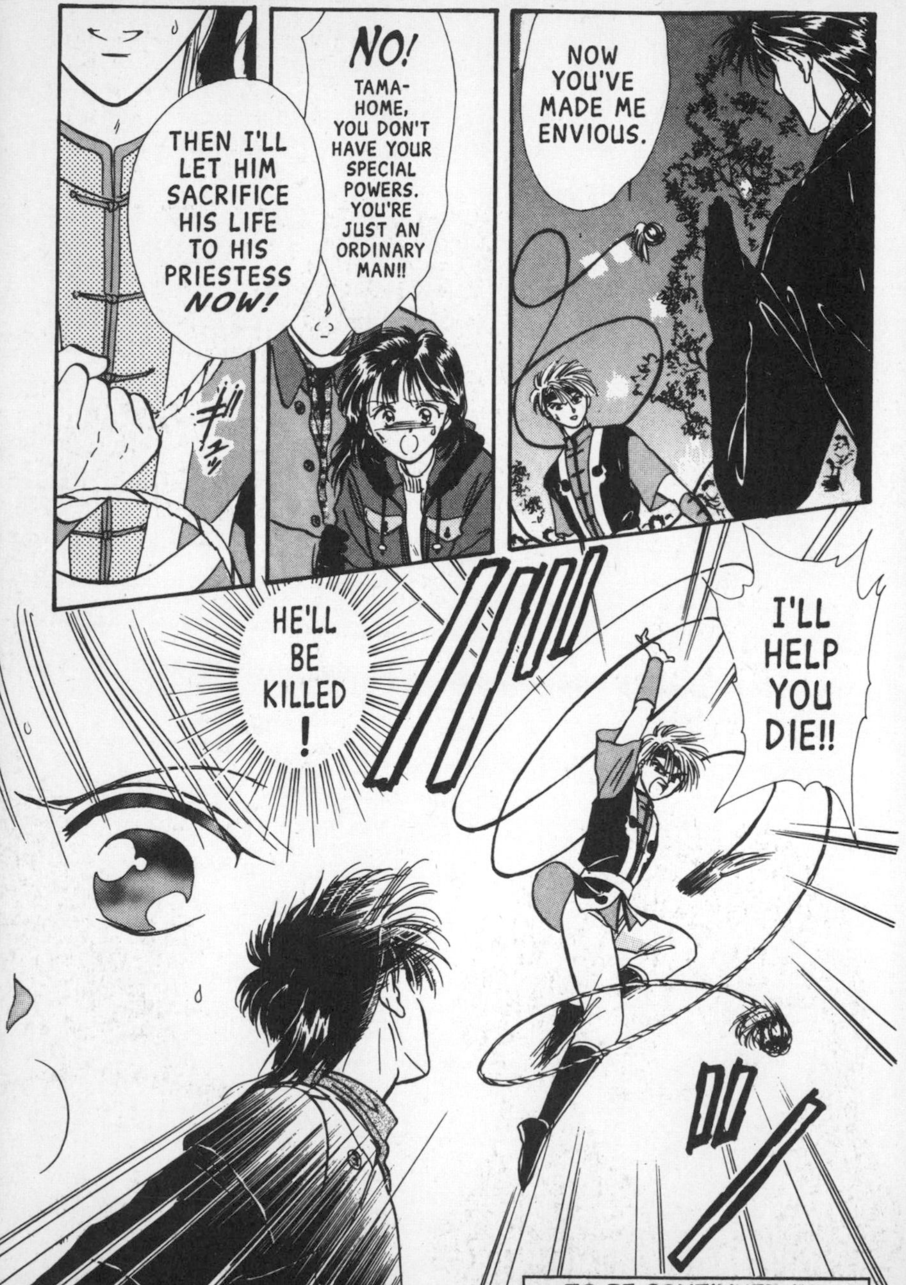
NOW YOU'VE MADE ME ENVIOUS.
NO! TAMA-HOME, YOU DON'T HAVE YOUR SPECIAL POWERS. YOU'RE JUST AN ORDINARY MAN!!
THEN I'LL LET HIM SACRIFICE HIS LIFE TO HIS PRIESTESS NOW!
I'LL HELP YOU DIE!!
HE'LL BE KILLED!
TO BE CONTINUED IN VOLUME 13: GODDESS

The Fushigi Yûgi Guide to Sound Effects

Most of the sound effects in FUSHIGI YÛGI are the way Yû Watase created them, in their original Japanese.

We created this glossary for a page-by-page, panel-by-panel explanation of the action and background noises. By using this guide, you may even learn some Japanese.

The glossary lists page and panel number. For example, page 1, panel 3, would be listed as 1.3.

26-27.1	FX: Oooooo (rumbling)
28.2	FX: Go go go (tremor)
28.3	FX: Go go go (tremor)
29.4	FX: Zawa (commotion)
31.1	FX: Heta (kneeling down)
31.4	FX: Fu (looking down)
31.5	FX: Ka (ray)
33.2	FX: Ba (sudden movement)
33.4	FX: Suu (removal)
34.1	FX: Don (blow)
35.2	FX: Fu (vanishing)
35.5	FX: Zu zu… (tremor)
35.5	FX: Pishi pishi (cracking)
36.1	FX: Zu zu zu (tremor)
36.5	FX: Shan (clanking)
37.1	FX: Ka (beam)
37.1	FX: Su…(opening)

**CHAPTER SIXTY-SIX:
EMBRACING EVIL**

7.3	FX: Ka (flash)
7.4	FX: Doohn (explosion)
11.1	FX: Suto (landing)
13.4	FX: Ha (realization)
13.5	FX: Doo (wham)
14.1	FX: Gutaa (collapse)
15.6	FX: Kaaah (flash)
17.2	FX: Suu (appearing kanji characters)
17.5	FX: Da (dash forward)
18.1	FX: Bashi (smack)
18.2	FX: Ga (grabbing)
18.3	FX: Ka (blush)
19.2	FX: Doka (kick)
19.3	FX: Ka (footstep)
21.2	FX: Su (slipping through)
21.3	FX: Da (step)
21.4	FX: Ban (shut)
23.2	FX: Kaaah (flashing)
24.2	FX: Dohhh (burst)
25.1	FX: Ka (flash)
25.1	FX: Ka (flash)
25.2	FX: Gohh (swirling)
25.3	FX: Ka… (footstep)

76.4 FX: Dokun (heart beating)
76.4 FX: Dokun dokun dokun (heart beating)

77.2 FX: Dokun dokun dokun dokun (heart beating)

83.1 FX: Pa (appearing)
83.2 FX: Pa (appearing)
83.4 FX: Su (open)

87.1 FX: Gyu (squeeze)
87.3 FX: Ba (slam open)
87.5 FX: Sukaa (snoozing)

88.1 FX: Dogashaaan (crashing)
88.2 FX: Doooh (galloping)
88.3 FX: Ohhh (clamor)

89.2 FX: Wahhh (shouting)
89.5 FX: Pori pori (scratching)

90.2 FX: Ka (flash)
90.3 FX: Dooohn (explosion)

91.1 FX: Doka doka doka (galloping)
91.3 FX: Ha (realization)
91.4 FX: Ka (footfall)

92.2 FX: Su (hand movement)
92.3 FX: Ha (sudden realization)
92.4 FX: Dohhh (crashing)

93.1 FX: Dosa (fall)
93.1 FX: Zaku (fall against ground)
93.2 FX: Pishaaan (crackling)
93.2 FX: Heheeen! (neighing)
93.3 FX: Pari pari pari (crackling)

94.4 FX: Ton (step)

95.3 FX: Dosu (stab)
95.5 FX: Yoro (sway)

96.1 FX: Bashi (slap)
96.2 FX: Gui (tug)
96.4 FX: Zuru… (slip)

97.4 FX: Para (ribbon undone)

38.1 FX: Su (vanishing)
38.3 FX: Su (vanishing)
38.3 FX: Dohn (explosion)

40.1 FX: Gyu (hug)
40.3 FX: Ba (getting up)

CHAPTER SIXTY-SEVEN: MATRIMONY

44.2 FX: Kaaah (flashing)
44.5 FX: Gakun (jolt)

47.4 FX: Dosa (fall)

53.1 FX: Ki (anger)
53.3 FX: Doka (kick)

54.2 FX: Ban (slam open)

55.1 FX: Gaba (hug)
55.2 FX: Gunya (squish)

58.4 FX: Bata bata bata (running)

61.1 FX: Za (marching)
61.3 FX: Kappo kappo (clopping)

62.5 FX: Gyu (squeeze)

63.3 FX: Bun bun (shaking head)

64.2 FX: Doki doki doki (heart thumping)
64.2 FX: Doki doki doki (heart thumping)

69.4 FX: Gyu (squeeze)

71.2 FX: Shuru (slipping off)
71.5 FX: Pasa (falling lightly)

72.4 FX: Bururu (horse whinny)

CHAPTER SIXTY-EIGHT: THE DIVIDING LIGHT

76.3 FX: Dokun (heart beating)
76.3 FX: Dokun dokun dokun dokun (heart beating)

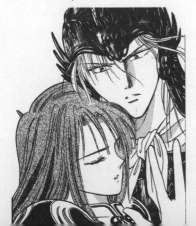

98.3 FX: Kaaaa (flash)

99.3 FX: Kaaaa (flash)

100.1 FX: Suuu (vanishing)
100.2 FX: Suuu (vanishing)

102.3 FX: Gaba (getting up)

CHAPTER SIXTY-NINE: REAL/UNREAL BOY

105.1 FX: Dokun dokun dokun (heart thumping)
105.2 FX: Dokun dokun (heart thumping)
105.2 FX: Dokun dokun (heart thumping)

106.5 FX: Gaba (cowering)
106.6 FX: Doki doki doki doki doki doki (heart thumping)

108.3 FX: Pori pori (crackle crackle)

110.2 FX: Su (held up)

111.1 FX: Uoooo (shout)
111.3 FX: Doooh (roar)

113.1 FX: Ha (alarm)
113.2 FX: Ba (impact)
113.4 FX: Za (footstep)

116.3 FX: Batan (door shutting)
116.5 FX: Sa sa (swift retreat)

117.2 FX: Shira (unemotional)
117.2 FX: Gatata (falling)
117.3 FX: Pata pata (walking away)

118.2 FX: Gishi (creak)
118.4 FX: Juu (frying)

119.3 FX: Gishi (creak)
119.4 FX: Kashan (shutter moving)

120.4 FX: Kui (twist)
120.5 FX: Kashan (shutter opening)

121.3 FX: Juuu (frying)
121.4 FX: Ban (opening door)

122.2 FX: Patan (door shutting)

124.4 FX: Patan (door shutting)
124.4 FX: Tosa (sitting down)

125.3 FX: Su (rising)

128.4 FX: Para (flip)

CHAPTER SEVENTY: SURGE OF THE HEART

135.1 FX: Chi chi chi… (chirping)
135.2 FX: Chi chi chi… (chirping)
135.2 FX: Mozo… (stir)
135.3 FX: Pachi (opening eyes)
135.5 FX: Ta ta ta (scurry)

136.2 FX: Chi chi (chirping)

138.5 NOTE: Waratte Ii-tomo Zokango ("Sure, It's Okay to Laugh -- Bonus Program") is an ensemble comedy program much like Saturday Night Live.

139.1 FX: Kacha kacha (dishes)

140.2 FX: Kacha (click)
140.3 FX: Fu fu fu fu (laughing)

148.5 FX: Ka (step)

177.2 FX: Hiku hiku (twitching)
177.5 FX: Shaaa (coasting)

178.1 FX: Shaaa (riding away)
178.3 FX: Shaaa (coasting)
178.5 FX: Dongara (crash)
178.5 FX: Gasshaan (crash)
178.6 FX: Gaba (getting up)

179.1 FX: Zuru zuru (slurping)
179.2 FX: To (step)

180.1 FX: Dogashaan (crash)
180.3 FX: Fura (slump)
180.5 FX: Gyu (squeeze)

181.3 FX: Hyoooi (boing)

182.1 FX: Buru (shiver)

183.1 FX: Gyu (hug)

185.6 FX: Shururururururururu (swirling)

186.1 FX: Ba (tug)
186.2 FX: Dosa (falling)
186.2 FX: To (land)
186.4 FX: Ga (grab)

187.3 FX: Giri giri giri (choking)
187.4 FX: Hikun (jerk)
187.5 FX: Biku (alarm)

190.2 FX: Ba (retreat)
190.2 FX: Zawa zawa (crowd noise)
190.5 FX: Su (lifting hand)

191.2 FX: Jiri (step)

193.3 FX: Gyu (squeeze)
193.4 FX: Ba (dramatic move)

149.4 FX: Goton (train rumbling)
149.5 FX: Goton (train rumbling)

150.1 FX: Gyu (squeeze)

156.4 FX: Buru buru (trembling)

157.1 FX: Kacha (click)
157.3 FX: Kyu (rub)

162.1 FX: Ban (slam open)

163.2 FX: Yoro (wobbling)
163.5 FX: Su (appearance)

164.5 FX: Paan (crashing)

CHAPTER SEVENTY-ONE:
TO LIVE FOR YOU

167.1 FX: Parin (cracking)
167.1 FX: Shirin (breaking)

168.2 FX: Doka (smash)

169.2 FX: Da (dash)

170.2 FX: Da (whip)
170.4 FX: Waaaa (battle cry)

171.3 FX: Hiheen (neighing)
171.3 FX: Wahhh (shouting)

172.1 FX: Zan (slash)
172.2 FX: Ha (alarm)

174.1 FX: Yoro (swaying)
174.2 FX: Hiku hiku (panting)

175.1 FX: Yoro (sway)

176.3 FX: Dokoo (smash)
176.4 FX: To (land)
176.5 NOTE: In Japanese, he said, "the beautiful girl of vinegared octopus" ("Sudako no Miko"), which sounds like "Priestess of Suzaku" ("Suzaku no Miko").

EDITOR'S RECOMMENDATIONS

Did you like *FUSHIGI YÛGI*? Here's what VIZ recommends you try next:

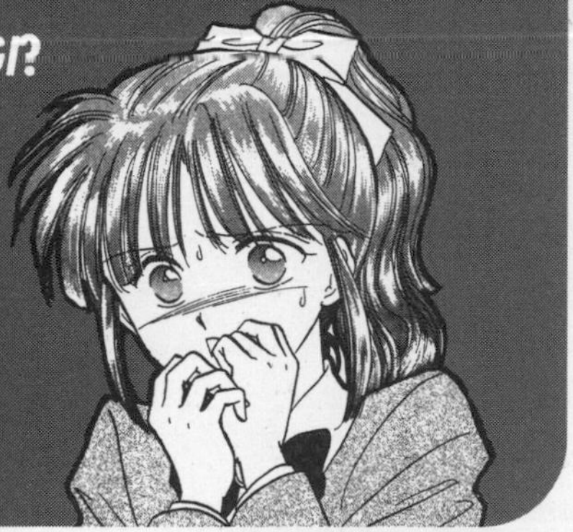

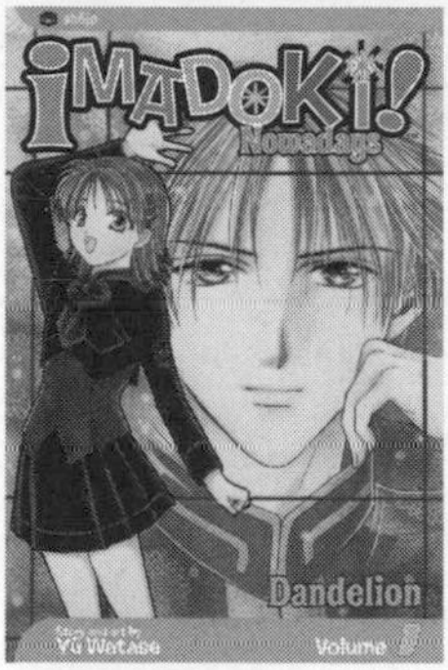

shôjo
IMADOKI!
Nowadays
Dandelion
Yû Watase
Volume

IMADOKI! (NOWADAYS)

The newest series from Yû Watase available in America, *Imadoki!* follows the trials and tribulations of Tanpopo Yamazaki, a budding young horticulturist, as she makes her way down the winding road to friendship. Snubbed by the rich kids at her new school, the elite Meio Academy, Tanpopo starts up a gardening club. But will this help her survive in an environment where superficiality and nepotism reign supreme?

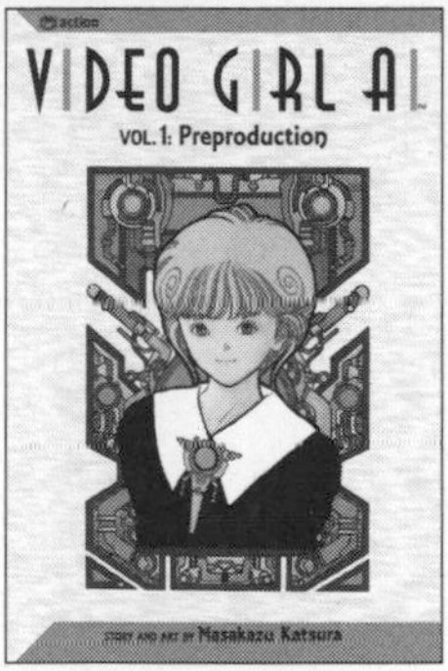

action
VIDEO GIRL AI
VOL. 1: Preproduction
STORY AND ART BY Masakazu Katsura

VIDEO GIRL AI

When Moemi, the object of Yota's incurable crush, turns out to be in love with the dashing and popular Takashi, poor Yota is devastated. He rents a video to distract himself, but Ai, the cute idol featured on the tape, magically bursts out of the TV and into Yota's world. Ai's mission is to fix Yota's hopeless love life, but when Ai develops romantic feelings towards Yota, things get complicated. A true manga classic—sweet and hilarious!

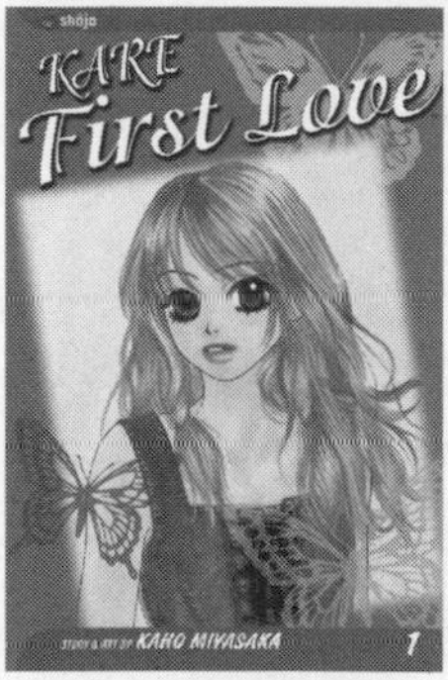

shôjo
KARE
First Love
STORY & ART BY KAHO MIYASAKA
1

KARE FIRST LOVE

Sixteen-year-old plain-Jane Karin finds herself torn between keeping the friendship of her classmate Yuka and entertaining the advances of a boy named Kiriya, who also happens to be the object of Yuka's affections. Living happily ever after in high school isn't on the curriculum, as Karin soon finds herself the center of Kiriya's attention, as well as the bull's-eye in embittered pal Yuka's dartboard of hate. Experience the spine-tingling roller coaster ride of Karin's first experiences in love!

COMPLETE OUR SURVEY AND LET US KNOW WHAT YOU THINK!

☐ Please do NOT send me information about VIZ products, news and events, special offers, or other information.

☐ Please do NOT send me information from VIZ's trusted business partners.

Name: ______________________________

Address: ______________________________

City: ________________ **State:** ________ **Zip:** ____________

E-mail: ______________________________

☐ **Male** ☐ **Female** **Date of Birth (mm/dd/yyyy):** ___/___/______ (**Under 13? Parental consent required**)

What race/ethnicity do you consider yourself? (please check one)

☐ Asian/Pacific Islander ☐ Black/African American ☐ Hispanic/Latino

☐ Native American/Alaskan Native ☐ White/Caucasian ☐ Other: ____________

What VIZ product did you purchase? (check all that apply and indicate title purchased)

☐ DVD/VHS ______________________________

☐ Graphic Novel ______________________________

☐ Magazines ______________________________

☐ Merchandise ______________________________

Reason for purchase: (check all that apply)

☐ Special offer ☐ Favorite title ☐ Gift

☐ Recommendation ☐ Other ____________________

Where did you make your purchase? (please check one)

☐ Comic store ☐ Bookstore ☐ Mass/Grocery Store

☐ Newsstand ☐ Video/Video Game Store ☐ Other: ____________

☐ Online (site: ______________________________)

What other VIZ properties have you purchased/own? ______________________________

____

How many anime and/or manga titles have you purchased in the last year? How many were VIZ titles? **(please check one from each column)**

ANIME	MANGA
☐ None	☐ None
☐ 1-4	☐ 1-4
☐ 5-10	☐ 5-10
☐ 11+	☐ 11+

I find the pricing of VIZ products to be: **(please check one)**

☐ Cheap ☐ Reasonable ☐ Expensive

What genre of manga and anime would you like to see from VIZ? **(please check two)**

☐ Adventure ☐ Comic Strip ☐ Science Fiction ☐ Fighting

☐ Horror ☐ Romance ☐ Fantasy ☐ Sports

What do you think of VIZ's new look?

☐ Love It ☐ It's OK ☐ Hate It ☐ Didn't Notice ☐ No Opinion

Which do you prefer? **(please check one)**

☐ Reading right-to-left

☐ Reading left-to-right

Which do you prefer? **(please check one)**

☐ Sound effects in English

☐ Sound effects in Japanese with English captions

☐ Sound effects in Japanese only with a glossary at the back

THANK YOU! Please send the completed form to:

NJW Research
42 Catharine St.
Poughkeepsie, NY 12601

All information provided will be used for internal purposes only. We promise not to sell or otherwise divulge your information.